S. A. Frost

Our new cook book and household receipts

S. A. Frost

Our new cook book and household receipts

ISBN/EAN: 9783744785907

Printed in Europe, USA, Canada, Australia, Japan

Cover: Foto ©Lupo / pixelio.de

More available books at **www.hansebooks.com**

OUR
NEW COOK BOOK

AND

HOUSEHOLD RECEIPTS.

CAREFULLY SELECTED AND INDEXED.

BY

S. ANNIE FROST.

SOLD ONLY BY SUBSCRIPTION.

PHILADELPHIA:
THE PRESBYTERIAN JOURNAL COMPANY,
No. 15 NORTH SEVENTH STREET.
1883.

PREFACE.

In offering to the public the present volume of valuable receipts, we feel that we are supplying a long-felt and urgent want. Although the market is over-stocked with so-called *Cook Books*, yet none of them contain the receipts here presented, nor do they contain those that will supply their places in a satisfactory manner.

It has been in answer to frequent urgent inquiries from those who have tested these receipts as to where to find certain directions, that this book has been most carefully compiled and published.

It is almost needless to remind all housekeepers, that the best way to make a husband happy and contented is to feed him well. Nothing is of more importance in a household than good cooking; and when so much comfort and happiness can be gained at such a small expense, we wonder that more attention is not paid by housekeepers to this all-important subject.

No trouble has been spared in the endeavor to render it complete and useful, by the addition of a complete alphabetical index, that will aid those in search of any subject treated, to turn at once to the page wanted, without hunting through the whole book.

TABLE OF CONTENTS

CHAPTER.	PAGE
I.—Soups	17
II.—Fish	35
III.—Sauces and Pickles	47
IV.—Meats	79
V.—Vegetables and Salads	145
VI.—Puddings and Pastry	188
VII.—Creams and Desserts	245
VIII.—Preserves and Jellies	273
IX.—Butter, Cheese, and Eggs	296
X.—Bread, Biscuit, Cakes, and Yeast	309
XI.—Beverages	379
XII.—Invalid Cookery	406
XIII.—Miscellaneous	414
XIV.—Weights and Measures	429
Alphabetical Index	431

SOUPS.

	PAGE		PAGE
How to make soups	17	Nursery soup	23
Stocks for soups	18	Economical veal soup	23
Good stock for ordinary purposes	19	Imitation of mock turtle soup	23
White stock	19	Veal gravy soup	24
Economical stock	20	White soup	24
Rich, strong stock	20	Calf's-head soup	25
Plain beef soup	21	Vermicelli soup	25
Beef soup	21	Salt meat soup	26
Mutton soup	22	Chicken broth	26
Mutton broth	22	Brown chicken soup	26
		Partridge soup	27

TABLE OF CONTENTS.

	PAGE
Rabbit soup	27
Carrot soup	27
Vegetable soup	28
Clear gravy soup	28
Gumbo	29
Okra or gumbo soup	30
Southern gumbo soup	30
Soup for the million	30
Lobster soup	31
New England chowder	31
Oyster soup	32
Clam soup	32
Bisque of lobster	32
Coloring for soups	33
Roast veal and chicken soup	34

FISH.

To bake a large fish whole	35
Rock fish	35
Stuffed fish	35
To fry trout	36
Sturgeon	36
Fried codfish and halibut	36
Fried eels	37
Potted salmon	37
To pickle fish	37
To pickle herring	38
Salt fish	38
Salt fish with parsnips	39
Picked up codfish	39
Codfish balls	40
Cod sounds	40
Fish cakes	40
Kedjeree	41
Lobster patties	41
Lobster rissoles	42
To fry oysters	42
Pickled oysters	42
Oyster stew	43
German receipt for oyster powder	43
Crumbed oysters	43
Scalloped oysters	44
Oyster forcemeat	44
Oyster patties and batter	45
Oyster omelette	45
Oyster sauce	45
Clam fritters	45
Boiled crabs	45
Terrapins	46

SAUCES AND PICKLES.

	PAGE
Sauces	47
Fish sauces	48
Mushroom catsup	49
Tomato catsup	50
Tomato marmalade	50
Belsize tomato sauce	50
Tomato vinegar	51
Lemon pickle	51
Chutney	52
Browning	53
Mushroom powder	53
Fish sauce	54
Tomato sauce	54
Mushroom sauce	54
Bread sauce	55
Sauce for fowls	55
Sauce for boiled poultry	55
Savory sauce for a roast goose	56
Giblet sauce	56
Sauce for wild duck	56
Venison ravigote sauce	56
Green mint sauce	57
Sauce Robert	57
Celery sauce	57
Horseradish sauce	58
Potato sauce	58
Rice sauce	58
Wine sauce	59
Madeira sauce	59
Pudding sauce, No. 1	59
Pudding sauce, No. 2	59
Lemon sauce	59
Orange sauce	59
Sweet egg sauce	60
Sweet pudding sauce	60
Pickles	60
To pickle string beans	61
To pickle red cabbage	62
Pickled nasturtiums	63
To pickle cabbage a good color	63
To pickle mushrooms	63
Small onion pickle	63
Spiced onions	64
Pickled onions	64
To pickle beet-root	64
Carolina chow-chow	65
Pickle chow-chow	66
Chow-chow	66

TABLE OF CONTENTS.

	PAGE		PAGE
Old Virginia chow-chow	66	Pickling beef	86
India pickle	67	Potted ox tongue	86
Yellow pickle	67	Tongue toast	87
Pickled red cabbage	68	Tongue	87
Artichokes, pickled	68	Spiced tripe	87
Gherkins	69	Potted beef	88
To make lemon pickle	69	Bubble and squeak	88
Tomato catsup, No. 1	70	Beef cakes, No. 1	89
Tomato catsup, No. 2	70	Beef cakes, No. 2	89
Tomato soy	70	Beef croquettes	89
Ripe cucumber pickle	70	To roll loin of mutton	90
Green cucumber pickle	71	Panned mutton	90
Pickled eggs, No. 1	71	Mutton cutlets	90
Pickled eggs, No. 2	72	Mutton cutlets à la bene	92
Piccalillie	72	Shoulder of mutton	92
Pickled walnuts, No. 1	73	Mutton prepared like venison	93
Pickled walnuts, No. 2	74	Saddle of mutton à la Portuguese	93
Sweet peach pickle	74		
Sweet pickle	75	Cold mutton	94
Sweet tomato pickle	75	Minced mutton	97
Green tomato pickle	75	Baked minced mutton	79
Tomatoes	76	Browned minced mutton	98
Spiced tomatoes	76	To roast lamb	98
Mixed pickle	77	Fore quarter of lamb	98
Cold catsup	78	Leg of lamb	99
Pepper catsup	78	Ribs of lamb	99
		Garnish and vegetables for roast lamb	99
MEATS.			
Stewed beef	79	To stew a breast of lamb	99
Rump of beef	79	To boil a neck or breast of lamb	100
Spanish steak	79		
Beef stewed with onions	80	Lamb chops	100
Brisket of beef stuffed	80	Lamb cutlets and spinach	101
A la mode beef	80	Loin, neck, and breast of lamb	101
Beef cutlets	81		
Fillet of beef with mushrooms	81	Broiled lamb steak	101
		Leg of lamb to boil	102
Fillet of beef	82	Leg of lamb to roast	102
English beef pie	82	Boned quarter of lamb	102
Beefsteak pie	83	Fricassee of lamb	102
Beefsteak pudding	83	Savory lamb pie	103
Beefsteak smothered with onions	83	Stewed breast of lamb with peas or cucumbers	103
Minced beef	83	Stewed leg of lamb	104
Beef balls	84	Lamb sweetbreads	104
Mock venison of corned beef	84	Larded lamb	105
Hash balls of corned beef	84	Chops with cucumbers	105
Yorkshire pudding with roast beef	85	To dress kidneys	105
		Fried sheep kidneys	106
Corned beef, boiled	85	Mutton kidneys, broiled	106
Corned beef hash	85	Kidney omelette	106

TABLE OF CONTENTS.

	PAGE		PAGE
Kidney à la brochette	107	Scrapple	125
Roast veal	107	To prepare fowls for cooking	126
Spiced veal	107	Fowl stewed with onions	127
Curry of veal	108	Steamed fowls	127
Fricassee of veal	108	Fowl cutlets	127
Veal cutlets with sweet herbs	108	Choice fowl pudding	128
Calf's head	109	To bone fowls for fricassee	128
Veal chops, breaded	109	To roast a fowl	128
Veal cutlets with ragout	110	To bake a fowl	129
Fillet of veal, boiled	110	To roast a turkey	129
Breast of veal with oyster sauce	110	To bake a turkey	129
Shoulder of veal	111	Stuffing for a turkey	130
Hashed calf's head	111	Baked turkey	130
Collared calf's head	112	Giblet pie	130
Tea pie of veal	112	To fricassee small chickens	131
Veal pot-pie	112	To broil chicken without burning	131
Veal, minced	113	Chicken pot-pie	132
Minced veal with poached eggs	113	White fricassee	132
		To fry cold chicken	132
Minced veal	114	Chicken baked in rice	133
Fried patties	114	Chicken puffs	133
Veal forcemeat	115	To boil a goose	133
Veal croquettes	115	To cook partridges	134
Veal sausages	116	To roast partridges	134
Veal rolls	116	To broil partridges	134
Superior veal rolls	116	Partridge pie	135
Veal sweetbreads	116	To boil partridges	135
Sweetbreads	117	To stew partridges	135
Fried sweetbread	117	To fry partridges	136
Veal olives	117	Quails cured in oil	136
Roast leg of pork	118	Woodcock	136
Fresh pork pot-pie	119	Snipes	137
Pork chops	119	Wild ducks	137
Pork steak, broiled	120	To keep game	137
Pork cutlets	120	Venison steak	138
Pork and apple fritters	120	Rabbit pie	138
English raised pork pie	121	Roman pie	138
Fresh pork pie	121	Potted fish and meats	139
Scrambled pork	121	Potted salmon	141
To cure hams	122	Potted lobster	141
Baked ham	122	Potted rabbit	142
Ham pie	122	Potted pigeons	142
Ham omelette	123	Potted birds	142
Ham Toast	123	To pot veal	142
Omelette of ham, tongue, or sausage	123	Potted calves' feet	143
		Potted veal and bacon	143
Sausages, No. 1	124		
Sausages, No. 2	124	**VEGETABLES AND SALADS.**	
Sausage dumplings	125	Vegetables	145
Sausage cakes	125	To boil potatoes	145

TABLE OF CONTENTS. 7

	PAGE		PAGE
To broil potatoes	146	String beans for winter use	166
Potato chips	146	To cook beans in a French style	167
Steamed potatoes	146		
Baked potatoes	147	String beans	167
Pommes de terre, à la Danoise	147	Boiled beans	168
		Parsnips	168
Potato surprise	148	Broiled parsnips	168
Mironton of potatoes	148	Parsnip cutlet	168
Potatoes, mashed and fried	149	Parsnip fritters, No. 1	168
Potato rolls	151	Parsnip fritters, No. 2	169
Stewed potatoes	152	Fricassee of parsnips	169
Browned potatoes	152	Fried plantains or bananas	169
Potato fritters	152	Vegetables and sauces	169
New potatoes	153	Carrots	170
Potato salad	153	Carrot fritters	170
Potato patties	153	Parsley and butter	171
Potato sconces	153	Fried artichokes	171
Potatoes in meat, puddings, and pies	154	Summer squashes	171
		Stewed spinach	172
Roasted potatoes	154	Spinach to boil	172
Jury pie	154	Boiled onions	173
Potato croquettes	155	Buttered onions	173
Potato pone	155	Roasted onions	173
Stuffed potatoes	155	Flaked onions	173
Pommes de terre en pyramids	156	Onions and caper sauce	174
Potatoes fried with batter	156	Stewed celery	174
Potatoes à la crême	156	Fried celery	174
French mashed potatoes	157	Essence of celery	174
Savory potato cakes	157	Vegetable oyster cakes	175
Cauliflower	157	Egg plant	175
Boiled cauliflower	159	Boiled beets	175
Cauliflower omelette	160	Asparagus	175
Cauliflower in milk	160	Stewed asparagus	176
Fried cauliflower	160	Asparagus soup	177
Corn balls	161	Asparagus toast	177
Corn oysters	161	Asparagus omelette	177
Corn in cans	161	Turnips à la poulette	177
Corn porridge	161	Turnips	177
Succotash	162	Turnip tops	178
Green corn dumplings	163	To boil peas	178
Corn fritters	163	Green peas	178
Broiled tomatoes	163	Lettuce peas	178
Tomato fritters	164	To stew peas	179
Browned tomatoes	164	Peas au sucre	179
Tomato soup	164	Cabbage boiled with meat	179
Tomato toast	164	To stew cabbage	180
To bake tomatoes	165	Cold cabbage	180
Breakfast tomatoes	165	Dressing for cold slaw	180
Chinese rice	165	Red cabbage, stewed	180
Carolina rice	166	Stewed cabbage	181
Rice and milk	166	Cabbage jelly	181

TABLE OF CONTENTS.

	PAGE		PAGE
Hot slaw	181	Cocoanut custard pudding	202
Broiled mushrooms	181	Cocoanut cup puddings	202
Stewed mushrooms	182	Lemon pudding	202
To dry mushrooms	182	Excellent lemon pudding	203
Preserving mushrooms for winter use	182	Iced lemon pudding	203
		Baked lemon pudding	203
To stew okra	183	Sponge pudding	204
To fry okra	183	Baked sponge pudding	204
To dry okra for winter use	184	Clara's sponge pudding	204
Cucumber salad	184	Boiled fig pudding	204
Salad dressing without oil	184	Fig pudding	204
Salad dressing	184	Raisin pudding	205
Italian salad dressing	185	Boiled raisin pudding	205
Salad	185	Plain raisin pudding	205
Potato salad	185	Fruit raised pudding	206
Chicken salad	186	Tomato pudding	206
Lobster salad	186	Caromel pudding	206
English salad sauce	186	Cassandra pudding	207
Sweet salad sauce	187	Brighton pudding	207
Swiss salad dressing	187	Golden pudding	207
Piquante sauce for salads	187	Luncheon pudding	208
Mayonnaise for salad	187	Moulded pudding	208
		Stale loaf pudding	208
PUDDINGS AND PASTRY.		Farmer's pudding	209
Puddings	188	Steamboat pudding	209
St. Claire pudding	191	Treacle pudding	209
Ice pudding	192	Rich pudding	210
Half pay pudding	192	Economical pudding	210
Minute pudding	193	Family pudding	210
Queen pudding	193	Flour pudding	211
Gray pudding	193	Simple pudding	211
Cottage pudding	193	Suet pudding	211
Soyer's new Christmas pudding	194	Boiled suet pudding	211
		Tapioca pudding	211
Christmas pudding	195	Arrowroot pudding	212
Plum pudding	196	Potato suet pudding	212
Suet plum pudding	196	Boiled Indian pudding	212
Barbara's plum pudding	196	Corn meal pudding	212
Rich plum pudding without flour	196	Indian meal pudding	213
		Pound pudding	213
Cottage plum pudding	197	Potato pudding	213
Unrivalled plum pudding	198	Biscuit pudding	213
Christmas plum pudding	198	Macaroni pudding	214
Apple pudding	199	Cake pudding	214
Boiled apple pudding	199	Sago pudding	214
Baked apple pudding	200	Crumb pudding	214
Rich sweet apple pudding	200	Custard pudding	214
Pippin pudding	200	Cup pudding	215
Apple roll	201	Cold cup pudding	215
Cocoanut pudding	201	Green corn pudding	215
Fine cocoanut pudding	201	Carrot pudding	215

TABLE OF CONTENTS.

	PAGE		PAGE
Chocolate pudding	216	Cracker pies	234
Rice pudding	216	Soda cracker pie	234
Boiled batter pudding	216	Orange pie	234
Quaking pudding	217	Aunt Harriet's pie	235
Pennsylvania pudding	217	Washington pie	235
Variety puddings	217	German puffs	235
Blackberry pudding	218	Lemon puffs	236
Ripe gooseberry pudding	218	Spiced puffs	236
Green currant pudding	218	Preserve puffs	236
Orange pudding	218	Apple puffs	237
Almond pudding	219	Egg puffs	237
Citron pudding	219	Lemon custard tart	237
Supper pudding	219	Lemon pie, No. 1	237
Peripatetic pudding	220	Lemon pie, No. 2	238
Fortunatus pudding	220	Custard cream pie	238
Transparent pudding	220	Cream pie	238
Cream pudding	220	Cornstarch pie	238
Chocolate cream custard pudding	221	Frosted pie	238
		Macaroni pie	239
Cream tapioca pudding	221	Superior peach pies	239
Railway pudding	222	Cranberry tart	239
Simple bread pudding	222	Sand tart	239
Bread pudding	222	Black Currant tart	240
Brown bread pudding	222	Cherry currant tart	240
Steamed bread and butter pudding	223	Raspberry cream tart	240
		Orange tart	241
Soufflé pudding	223	Lemon tart	241
Prince Albert pudding	223	Almond tart	241
German pudding	223	Rhubarb tart	241
Syllabub pudding	224	Greengage tart	242
Bird's nest pudding	224	Rich mince pie	242
Omnibus pudding	224	Mock mince pie	242
Biddle pudding	225	Mincemeat	242
Birthday pudding	225	Pastry sandwiches	243
Orris pudding	225	Florentines	244
Grandmamma's pudding	226	Rhubarb pie	244
West Point pudding	226		
Union pudding	226	**CREAMS AND DESSERTS.**	
Snow pudding	226	Chocolate creams	245
Persian pudding	227	Scotch creams	245
Various kinds of pastry	227	Caledonian cream	245
Flaky and short crusts	229	Orange cream	245
Raised crust	230	Snow cream	246
Puff-paste	231	French cream	246
Superior puff-paste	231	Velvet cream	246
Sweet paste	232	Apple cream	247
Crust for savory pies	232	Italian cream	247
Icing pastry	232	Madeira cream	247
French crust for raised pies	233	Spanish cream	248
Pie crust for meat pies	233	Lemon cream	248
Farmer's pie	234	Lemon rice	248

TABLE OF CONTENTS.

	PAGE		PAGE
Lemon flummery	249	Buttered orange juice	266
Meringues	249	Cakes for dessert	266
Trifle	250	Apple charlotte	266
Sweet soufflé	251	Pommes au riz	267
Sweet dish of macaroni	251	Delicious dish of apples	267
Lemon honeycomb	251	Gateau de pommes	268
Bibavoe	252	Apple Soufflé	268
Delicate dessert	252	Apple in jelly	268
German fluttkrengel	252	Apple float	268
Custard and whey	253	Apple snow	269
Fine floating island	253	Floating island of apples	269
Floating island	253	Apple island	269
French island	254	Apple cheesecakes	270
Floats	254	Apple pique	270
Tapioca blanc mange	254	Sponge cake for dessert	270
Blanc mange	254	A dish of snow	271
Chocolate blanc mange	255	Sugar drops	271
Cornstarch blanc mange	255	Ice creams	271
Peach rolls	255	Water ices	272
Spiced sugar for fritters	256		
Snowballs	256	PRESERVES AND JELLIES.	
Suet dumplings with currants	256	Directions for preserving fruits, etc.	273
Oxford dumplings	257	To preserve peaches	273
Suet dumplings	257	Peach marmalade	274
Apple custard	257	Peach jam	275
Solid custard	257	Raspberry fool	275
Orange custard	258	Raspberry jam	275
French custard	258	Celery preserve	275
Milk pancakes	258	Preserved lettuce stalks	276
Cream pancakes	258	To preserve watermelon rind	276
Orange nuts	259	Preserved citron	276
Compote aux confitures	259	Apricot jam	277
Washington or cream pie	259	To preserve hedge pears	278
Custard fritters	260	Pears for the tea table	278
Bun fritters	260	Preserving pears	278
Apple fritters	260	Blackberry jelly	278
Cherry fritters	261	Blackberries	279
Elegant fritters	261	Greengage jam	279
Snitz and knep	261	Greengages	280
Stewed pears	262	Bottled green gooseberries	280
Chocolate caromel	262	Gooseberry jelly	281
Caromels	262	Gooseberry and raspberry jelly	281
Burnt sugar	263	Red gooseberry jam	281
Friar's omelette	263	Green gooseberry jam	282
Angel's food	263	White gooseberry jam	282
Chocolate butter	263	Dried strawberries	282
Chocolate charlotte russe	264	To preserve strawberries	283
Charlotte russe	264	Strawberry jelly	283
Charlotte de russe	265	Strawberry jam	283
Jam or marmalade charlotte	265		

TABLE OF CONTENTS.

	PAGE		PAGE
Preserved pineapple	284	Eggs, plain boiled	302
Pineapples without cooking	285	Lait de poule	303
Pineapple jelly	285	Egg balls	303
Pineapple marmalade	285	Eggs à l'ardennaise	303
Pineapple preserve	285	Eggs à l'aurore	303
Rhubarb jam	286	Broiled eggs	304
Rhubarb preserve	286	Minced eggs	304
Plums, to preserve	286	Brown eggs	304
To preserve purple plums	287	Egg dumplings	305
Preserved cherries	287	Rumbled eggs	305
Cherry marmalade or jam	288	Omelette soufflé	305
Spiced cherries	288	Omelette à la creppe	306
Bottling cherries	288	Egg cheesecakes	306
Cherry or strawberry fool	288	Egg sandwiches	306
Cherry jam	289	Preserving eggs	306
Currant jelly	289	Egg omelette	307
Black currant jelly	290	Buttered eggs	307
Black currant jam	290	Bacon omelette	307
To can fruit and vegetables	291	Kidney omelette	307
To can peaches	291	Omelette aux crouton	308
To can raspberries, etc.	291		
To can vegetables	291	**BREAD, BISCUIT, CAKES, AND YEAST.**	
Brandy peaches	291		
Quinces preserved whole	292	Bread	309
Quince marmalade	292	Rolls and bread	309
Quince jelly	292	Bread receipt	310
Quinces for the tea table	293	Wheaten bread	310
Quince and apple jelly	293	Potato bread	311
Apple jelly	293	Homemade bread	311
Apple jam	294	Premium rye bread	312
Apple marmalade	295	Rice bread	312
Apple preserve	295	Corn bread	312
Crab apple jam	295	Brown bread	312
		Light corn bread	312
BUTTER, CHEESE, AND EGGS.		Cornmeal bread	313
Butter that threatens to turn rancid	296	Graham loaf	313
Butter making	296	Graham biscuit	313
To preserve butter	297	Graham crackers	313
Curled butter	297	Graham bread	314
Rancid butter, to restore	297	Italian bread	314
Manufacture of pineapple and potato cheeses	298	Potato bread	315
Cheese biscuit	299	Indian corn bread	315
Cheesecakes	299	Scotch short bread	315
Buttermilk cheese	300	Common corn bread	315
Potted cheese	300	Genuine scottish short bread	316
Cheese straws	300	Short bread	316
Cream cheese	301	Dinner rolls	317
How to cook and serve eggs	302	French rolls	317
Eggs, sour le plat	302	Pennsylvania rusk	317
		Tea rusks	318
		Rusk	318

TABLE OF CONTENTS.

	PAGE		PAGE
Light biscuits	318	Plum, pound, and bride cakes	332
Biscuits	318	Rock cakes	334
Butter biscuits	319	Love cakes	334
Biscuit cakes	319	Buns	334
Cream biscuits	319	Bath buns	335
German cream biscuits	319	Rich buns	335
Sour cream biscuits	320	Ground rice buns	335
Milk biscuit	320	Spanish buns	335
Potato biscuits	320	Excellent spanish bun	335
Soda biscuit	320	Children's cake	336
Judge's biscuit	321	Molasses drop cakes	336
Abernethy biscuits	321	Molasses cup cakes	336
Sally Lunn	321	Cornstarch cake	337
Superior Sally Lunn	322	Soda cake	337
Light Sally Lunn	322	Rye drop cakes	337
Johnny cakes	322	Good plain cake	337
Indian cakes	322	Children's loaf cake	338
Short cake	322	Cheap cake	338
Corn cake	323	French cake	338
Green corn cakes	323	Thick gingerbread	338
Soda cake	323	Soft gingerbread	338
Rice cakes	323	Ginger biscuits	339
Muffins	323	Gingersnaps	339
German waffles	324	Gingerbread	339
Waffles	324	Almond peppernuts	339
Raised waffles	324	Peppernuts	340
Crumpets	324	Lemon drop cakes	340
Cornmeal muffins	325	Superior lemon cake	340
Buttermilk breakfast cakes	325	Lemon cake	341
Breakfast short cakes	325	Lemon cheesecakes	341
Hominy breakfast cakes	326	Orange cheesecakes	341
Breakfast waffles	326	Sweet macaroon	341
Breakfast Johnny cake	326	Bitter macaroon	342
Fried breakfast cakes	326	Pop overs	342
Breakfast puffs	327	Ginger sponge cake	342
Coffee cake	327	Ginger loaf cake	342
Virginia breakfast cake	327	Ginger jumbles	343
Breakfast soda cake	327	Connecticut loaf cake	343
French breakfast rolls	328	New England loaf cake	343
Breakfast Sally Lunn	328	Clay cake	343
Light breakfast rolls	328	Old fashioned doughnuts	343
French tea cakes	328	Doughnuts	344
Tea cakes	328	Crullers	344
German tea cakes	329	Bordeaux cakes	344
Pennsylvania tea cake	329	Christmas cake	345
Plain tea cakes	329	Yule tide cake	345
Superior tea cakes	329	Jelly cake	346
Simple tea cakes	330	Rose water cake	346
Lemon tea cakes	330	Almond jelly cake	346
Hints for making and baking sweet cakes	330	Army cake	346
		Navy cake	346

TABLE OF CONTENTS.

	PAGE		PAGE
Fruit cake	347	Lady fingers	360
Fruit cake without eggs	347	German ladies' fingers	360
Good fruit cake	347	Ladies' fingers	360
Soda fruit cake	347	Cake sandwiches	361
Molasses fruit cake	347	Cocoanut cake	361
Pound cake	348	Grated cocoanut cake	361
Rice pound cake	348	White cocoanut cake	362
Almond cake	348	Cocoanut loaf cake	362
Almond cup cake	349	Chocolate cake	362
Sweet almond cake	349	Chocolate drop cake	363
Seed cake	349	Chocolate paste cake	363
Caraway cake	350	Currant loaf cake	363
Frosted loaf cake	350	Bachelor buttons	363
Maximilian cake	350	Princess cakes	363
Bitter almond cake	351	Queen's biscuit	364
Stevens cake	351	Lincoln cake	364
Good boy's cake	351	Boston cake	364
Cup cake	351	Gold cake	364
Traveller's cake	351	Silver cake	365
Apple cake	352	White cake	365
Pippin cake	352	Mrs. W's. snow cake	365
Gateau de pommes	352	Snow cake	365
School cake	352	Scotch cake	366
Sugar cake	352	Dutch cake	366
Black cake	353	Derby short cake	366
Arrowroot biscuits	353	Queen cake	366
Marble cake	353	Medley cake	367
Railroad cake	354	Congress cake	367
Josephine cake	354	German sponge cake	367
Jenny Lind cake	354	Sponge cake	368
Jefferson cake	354	Sponge biscuits	368
Apple cheesecakes	354	Berwick sponge cake	369
Cocoanut cheesecakes	355	Superior sponge cake	369
Citron cheesecakes	355	Fine sponge cake	369
Blackberry cake	355	French cream cake	369
Prune cake	356	Cream cake	370
French jumbles	356	Cream biscuits	370
Soft jumbles	356	Washington cake	371
Jumbles	356	Washington pie cake	371
Cocoanut jumbles	356	German cornucopia cakes	371
Cookies	357	Swiss cake	372
Butter cookies	357	Molly's cake	372
Good cookies	357	Luncheon cake	372
Ground rice cake	357	Lady cake	372
Bride cake	358	Bun loaf	373
Wine biscuits	358	French cake	373
Rock biscuits	358	Honey cake	373
Rough biscuits	359	Almond custard cake	373
Almond biscuits	359	Jumbles	374
Biscuits	359	Wine cakes	374
Sweet biscuits	360	Trafalgar cake	374

TABLE OF CONTENTS.

	PAGE
Raisin cake	374
Mountain cake	375
White mountain cake	375
Ash cake	375
Fine icing for cakes	375
Hot icing	376
Yeast	376
Potato yeast	376
Homemade yeast	377
Sweetened yeast	377
Hops and potato yeast	378

BEVERAGES.

	PAGE
To make good tea	379
To make good chocolate	379
Chocolate à la francaise	379
Cocoa shells	380
Broma	380
Coffee and its preparation	380
Café au lait	382
Café noire	382
Good coffee	384
Concentrated coffee	385
Fruit syrups	386
Currant syrup	388
Morello cherry syrup	388
Mulberry syrup	388
Gooseberry syrup	388
Lemon syrup	388
Raspberry vinegar syrup	389
Sour orange syrup	389
Syrup of cloves	389
Orange syrup	390
Lemonades	390
Excellent portable lemonade	391
Mock lemonade	391
Superior lemonade à la soyer	392
Lemonade à la soyer	392
Orangeade à la soyer	392
Barley lemonade	393
Barley orangeade	393
Another mock lemonade	393
Plain orangeade	393
Orange lemonade	394
Orangeade	394
Fruit vinegars	394
Strawberry vinegar	394
Raspberry vinegar	396
Gooseberry vinegar	396
Norwegian raspberry vinegar	397
Mixed fruit vinegars	397

	PAGE
Strawberry drink	397
Lemon water	398
Tomato wine	398
Muscadine wine	398
Rhubarb wine	399
Ginger wine	399
Lemon wine	399
Imperial	400
Imperial pop	400
Capilliare	400
Pleasant drink in summer	400
Decoction of sarsaparilla	401
Soda water	401
Cooling summer beverage	401
Ginger beer	402
Common ginger beer	402
Ginger pop	402
Ginger beer powders	403
Lemonade powders	403
Eau sucré	403
Agras	403
Sherbet	403
Watermelon sherbet	404
Nectar	404
Lemon water ice	404
Blackberry cordial	404
Tamarinds	405

INVALID COOKERY.

	PAGE
Beef tea	406
Liebig's soup	406
Beef tea and baked flour	407
Flaxseed jelly for a cough	407
Sago	407
Tapioca	407
Oatmeal porridge	408
Milk and oatmeal gruel	408
Panada of fine flour	409
Chicken panada	409
Baked crumbs of bread	409
Bread panada	410
Bouillie of baked flour	410
Bouillie of boiled flour	410
Glycerine and yolk of egg	411
Wine whey	411
Arrowroot pap with milk	411
Port wine jelly	412
Orange jelly	412
Porter jelly	412
Sago jelly	412
Gelatine	413
Jelly from gelatine	413

TABLE OF CONTENTS.

MISCELLANEOUS.

	PAGE
A bill of fare	414
Coloring for gravies and ragouts	414
Rich gravy	415
Meat or fish omelettes, generally	415
Milk toast	415
Breakfast dish	416
Small egg balls to serve with calf's head	417
Good meat cake	417
Superior meat pies	417
To use the meat and gristle of a soup bone	417
Rissoles	418
Rissoles of cold meat	418
Rissables	419
Lard	419
Forcemeat	419
Forcemeat for veal, turkeys, fowls, &c.	420
Ramakins	421
Eggs to keep	421
Farmhouse syllabub	421
Lait sucré	421
Nutmegs	421
Essence of nutmegs	422
Essence of rose	422
How to mix mustard	422
To make good vinegar	422
Excellent vinegar	422
Mint vinegar	423
Cayenne vinegar	423
Quajada	423
Toad in the hole	424
A relish	424
Pickelets	424
Cheesikins	425
German Entremet	425
Gravy for fowls	425
To keep sausage fresh	426
Rolled patties	426
Culinary couplets	426
Weights and measures	429
Alphabetical index	431

2

CHAPTER I.

SOUPS.

How to Make Soups.—The word soup, to many minds, conveys the idea of something that is extravagantly rich in composition and elaborately difficult in manner of preparation. Consequently, we more frequently meet with soups as costly and cloying as real turtle, instead of finding them to be light, exhilarating and appetizing. Unfortunately, many cooks do not appear to be alive to the fact that the less pretentious they make a soup the more certain it is to give satisfaction, and of all cooking, nothing is easier to do well, and nothing more difficult to do badly, than soup-making—too much pains being productive of the same results as too many cooks. Simply employ ingredients that are quite fresh, utensils that are thoroughly clean, and skim carefully.

If meat is used that is very fat, a cook is often obliged to let the soup grow cold, so as to remove all the fat from the top, re-warming the soup before serving it; but if we only make use of meat which is sufficiently lean, and do not neglect skimming the liquor while it is simmering, we shall be spared the necessity of sacrificing the flavor of the soup for the sake of avoiding greasiness. A small quantity of fat, however, softens soup, half an ounce of butter to a quart of pottage being enough. Housekeepers should be aware that, though bones and bony joints are economical for soups, yet, when it can be had, the flesh of butchers' meat is preferable. Of course, this does not apply to poultry and game. A small slice of ham or sausage, an anchovy, or a spoonful of sugar, improves the flavor of soups generally.

Any of the things from the following list will, with the proper addition of herbs, roots, and seasoning, make a tureen of good soup for a small family:

One pound of lean meat.
A wild pigeon.
A small rabbit.
A sheep's or lamb's head.
A chicken or old fowl.
Two pounds of raw bones.
A tame pigeon.
A set of giblets.

The reduced liquor in which has been boiled a calf's head, fowl, turkey, rabbit, joint of meat, etc., etc.

STOCKS FOR SOUPS AND HOW TO MAKE THEM.

The word "stock" for soup frequently occurs in receipts. We now give some receipts for making them:

GOOD STOCK FOR ORDINARY PURPOSES.—Four pounds of shin-bone, and one pound of lean neck of beef, four carrots, one turnip, one stick of celery, two parsnips, two leeks, one onion, six cloves, six peppers, a bunch of sweet herbs, one gallon of water. Cut the meat into slices, crack the bone, and put it into an earthen pipkin that will stand the fire, as this makes far better soup than a metal saucepan; add the water, and let it stew slowly till the scum rises, and skim it clear; stick the cloves into the onion and then add the vegetables, and let the whole stew slowly till the meat is in rags, which will be in about eight hours. It must simmer very slowly, for if it boils, the meat will not yield the gravy so well, and the stock will be thick in place of being clear. When cold, it should be strained through a cullender and kept in a covered pan or jar for use.

WHITE STOCK.—Four pounds of knuckle of veal, any poultry trimmings, four slices of lean ham, three carrots, two onions, one head of celery, twelve white pepper-corns, two ounces of salt, one blade of mace, a bunch of herbs, one ounce of butter, four quarts of water. Cut up the veal, and put it with the bones and trimmings of poultry, and the ham, into the stewpan, which has been rubbed with the butter. Moisten with half a pint of water, and simmer till the gravy begins to flow. Then add the four quarts of water and the remainder of the ingredients; simmer for five hours.

After skimming and straining it carefully through a very fine hair sieve, it will be ready for use. When stronger stock is desired, double the quantity of veal, and put in an old fowl. The liquor in which a young turkey has been boiled is an excellent addition to all white stock or soup.

ECONOMICAL STOCK—The liquor in which a joint of meat has been boiled, say four quarts; trimmings of fresh meat or poultry, shank-bones, etc., roast-beef bones, any pieces the larder may furnish; vegetables, spices, and the same seasoning as in the foregoing receipt. Let all the ingredients simmer gently for six hours, taking care to skim carefully at first. Strain it off, and put by for use.

RICH STRONG STOCK.—Four pounds shin of beef, four pounds knuckle of veal, quarter pound of good lean ham, any poultry trimmings, two ounces of butter, three onions, three carrots, two turnips, (the latter should be omitted in summer, lest they ferment,) one head of celery, a few chopped mushrooms, when obtainable; one tomato, a bunch of savory herbs, not forgetting parsley; one and a half ounce of salt, three lumps of sugar, twelve white pepper-corns, six cloves, three small blades of mace, four quarts of water. Line a perfectly clean stewpan with the ham cut in thin, broad slices, carefully trimming off all its rusty fat; cut up the beef and veal in pieces about three inches square, and lay them on the ham; set it on the stove, and draw it down, and stir frequently. When the meat is equally browned, put in the beef and veal bones, the poultry trimmings, and pour in the cold water. Skim well, and occasionally add a little cold water to stop its boiling, until it becomes quite clear; then put in all the other ingredients, and simmer very slowly for five hours. Do not let it come to a brisk boil, that the stock be not wasted, and that its color may be preserved. Strain through a very fine hair sieve, or cloth, and the stock will be fit for use.

PLAIN BEEF SOUP.—One gallon of cold water, one pound of beef and two tablespoonfuls of rice. Let this boil, then add an onion or two or three leeks; boil an hour. Peel and slice eight potatoes; wash them in warm water; add them to the soup, with a seasoning of salt and pepper; stir it frequently; boil another hour, and then serve.

BEEF SOUP.—Get what is called a good beef soup bone, boil two hours, leaving about two quarts of broth; break two eggs into some flour, and knead it very stiff; roll out in three sheets to the thickness of wrapping paper; spread them on a table to dry for half an hour; then place them on one another and roll them up as you would jelly cake; with a sharp knife cut very fine strips from the end, not wider than the thickness of a case knife; shake them up to separate them; drop into your broth slowly, stirring your soup all the while. Boil ten minutes; season with pepper, salt, celery, or a little parsley.

MUTTON SOUP.—A neck of mutton, weighing five or six pounds, three large carrots, three large turnips, two large onions, a bunch of sweet herbs; salt and pepper to taste; a sprig of parsley, three quarts of water.

Lay the ingredients in a covered pan before the fire, and let them remain there one day, stirring occasionally. The next day put the whole into a stewpan, and place it on a brisk fire. As soon as it boils, take the pan off the fire, and put it on one side to simmer until the meat is done. When ready for use, take out the meat, dish it with the carrots and turnips; strain the soup, let it cool, skim off the fat, season it, and thicken it with a tablespoonful of arrowroot dissolved in cold water. Simmer for five minutes before serving.

MUTTON BROTH.—Take two pounds of scrag mutton; to take the blood out, put it into a stewpan, and cover it with cold water; when the water becomes milk warm, pour it off; then put it in four or five pints of water, with a teaspoonful of salt, a tablespoonful of best grits, and an onion; set it on a slow fire, and when you have taken all the scum off, put in two or three turnips; let it simmer very slowly for two hours, and strain it through a clean sieve.

NURSERY SOUP.—To be prepared the day before it is wanted for use. Two pounds of scrag mutton or the knuckle of a leg; put it into two quarts of cold water; add two large turnips, sliced, and a tablespoonful of rice or barley. Let this simmer for one hour; take out the meat from the soup into a dish, and put away the liquor until the next day, when all the fat must be removed from the top.

Turn the soup into a pot and add the meat cut into small pieces, a finely minced onion, a little parsley, a small head of celery, an ounce of butter, a tablespoonful of flour, mixed in cold water to the consistency of cream, burn a little brown sugar in an iron spoon, and pour a little boiling water over it into the flour; strain the browned flour into the soup, add the other ingredients; let all boil for an hour, when serve with small square dice of toasted bread.

ECONOMICAL VEAL SOUP.—Boil a piece of veal, suitable for a fricassee, pie, or hash. When tender, take the meat up and slip out all the bones; put these back into the kettle and boil for two hours. Then strain the liquor, and stand away until the next day. When wanted, take off the fat, put the soup into a clean pot, add pepper, salt, an onion, a half teacupful of rice, a tablespoonful of flour mixed in cold water, and slices of potato. Boil thirty minutes and serve hot.

IMITATION OF MOCK-TURTLE SOUP.—Put into

a pan a knuckle of veal, two calf's feet, two onions, a few cloves, peppers, allspice, mace, and sweet herbs; cover them with water, then tie a thick paper over the pan, and set it in an oven for three hours. When cold, take off the fat very nicely, cut the meat and feet into bits an inch and a half square, remove the bones and coarse parts, and then put the rest on to warm, with a large spoonful of walnut and one of mushroom ketchup, half a pint of sherry, or Madeira wine, a little mushroom powder, and the jelly of the meat. When hot, if it requires any further seasoning, add some, and serve with hard eggs, forcemeat balls and a squeeze of lemon soy.

VEAL GRAVY SOUP.—Garnish the bottom of a stewpan with thin pieces of lard, add a few slices of ham, slices of veal cutlet, slices of onion, carrot, parsnips, celery, a few cloves upon the meat, and a spoonful of broth. Soak it on the fire in this way until the veal throws out its juice. Then put it on a stronger fire until the meat catches to the bottom of the pan, and is well browned. Then add about two quarts of light broth, and simmer all on a slow fire until the meat is thoroughly done; add a little thyme and mushrooms. Skim and strain all clear for use.

WHITE SOUP.—Boil a knuckle of veal and four calf's feet in five quarts of water, with three sliced onions, a bunch of sweet herbs, four heads of white celery, cut small, a tablespoonful of whole pepper, a small teaspoonful of salt, and six large blades of mace. Let all boil very slowly till the meat is in rags, and has dropped from the bone, and the gristle has quite dissolved. Skim well while boiling. When done strain through a sieve into a deep white ware pan. Next day take off all the fat, and put the jelly into a clean soup pot, with two ounces of vermicelli; set over a clear fire. When the vermicelli is dissolved stir in, gradually, a pint of thick cream while the soup is hot. Do not let it come to a boil after the cream is in, lest it should curdle. Cut up a few rolls in the bottom of a tureen, pour on the soup, and serve.

CALF'S HEAD SOUP.—Procure a calf's head, wash it well, and let it stand in salt and water two or three hours. Then soak it in fresh water. Put it on to boil, and when the meat will separate from the bone take it off. Strain the broth, cut the meat in small pieces, and add it to the broth. Then season with sweet marjoram, sage, thyme, sweet basil, pepper, salt, mace, and cloves. Take one pound of suet, and two pounds of veal, chopped fine, and, with sufficient bread crumbs and seasoning as above, make some forcemeat balls, and fry them in butter. Make also some small dumplings with a little flour, butter, and water. Add the dumplings, the forcemeat balls, two or three eggs, chopped fine, a spoonful of browned flour, and as much wine as you think fit to the soup.

VERMICELLI SOUP.—Put a shin of veal, one onion, two carrots, two turnips, and a little salt into four quarts of water. Boil this three hours. Add two cups of vermicelli, and boil it an hour and a half longer. Before serving take out the bone and vegetables.

SALT MEAT SOUP.—Two pounds of salt beef or salt pork, four carrots, four parsnips, four turnips, four potatoes, one cabbage, two ounces of ground rice, seasoning of salt and pepper, two quarts of water. Cut the meat in small pieces, add the water, and let it simmer for three quarters of an hour. Cut the vegetables in thin slices, add them to the meat, and boil all together for one hour. Thicken with the rice flour dissolved in cold water. Simmer for five minutes, and serve.

CHICKEN BROTH.—Cut up a chicken (an old one is best), and put it into an iron pot with two quarts of water, one onion, two tablespoonfuls of rice, and a little salt. Boil for two hours, and strain through a sieve.

BROWN CHICKEN SOUP.—Cut up a nicely dressed chicken. Put it in the pot with water to cover it, which must be measured, and half as much more added to it before the soup is dished. Keep it covered tight, boiling slowly, and take off the fat as fast as it rises. When the chicken is tender take it from the pot and mince it very fine. Season it to the taste, and brown it with butter in a dripping pan. When brown put it back in the pot. Brown together butter and flour, and make rich gravy by adding a pint of the soup. Stir this in the soup, and season it with a little pepper, salt, and butter. Be careful the chopped chicken does not settle and burn on the pot. It will be well to turn a small plate on the bottom of the kettle to prevent this. Toast bread quite brown and dry, but do not burn it, and lay the toast in the tureen, and serve it with the soup. Stir the chicken through it, and pour it in the tureen.

PARTRIDGE SOUP.—A brace of old partridges make a capital soup. Cut them up, and together with some celery, a slice of ham, and an onion, sliced; toss them in a little butter and set over the fire until they are somewhat browned. Stew them, closely covered, in five pints of water, for two hours; strain the soup, heat it again, and add to it some small dice of toasted bread, and a little stewed celery. Season with salt and pepper and serve hot.

RABBIT SOUP.—Cut one or two rabbits into joints; lay them for an hour in cold water; dry and fry them in butter till about half done, with four or five onions and a middling-sized head of celery cut small; add to this three quarts of cold water, one pound of split peas, some pepper and salt; let it stew gently for four or five hours, then strain and serve it.

CARROT SOUP.—Four quarts of liquor in which a leg of mutton or a piece of beef has been boiled a beef or mutton bone, six large carrots, two large onions, one large turnip; seasoning of salt and pepper to taste. Put the liquor, bones, onions, turnips, pepper and salt into a stewpan, and simmer for three hours. Scrape the carrots and cut them in thin slices, strain the soup over them, and stew till soft enough to pulp through a hair sieve or coarse cloth; boil the pulp in the soup until about the consistency of pea soup; add Cayenne. Pulp only the red part of the carrot, and make the soup the day before it is served.

VEGETABLE SOUP.—Peel and slice six large onions, six potatoes, six carrots, and four turnips; fry them in half a pound of butter, and pour on them four quarts of boiling water. Toast a crust of bread as brown and hard as possible, but do not burn it, and put it in, with some celery, sweet herbs, white pepper and salt. Stew it all gently for four hours, and then strain it through a coarse cloth. Have ready thinly sliced carrot, celery and a little turnip. Add them to your liking, and stew them tender in the soup. If approved of, a spoonful of tomato catsup may be added.

CLEAR GRAVY SOUP.—Lay at the bottom of the stewpan half a pound of lean ham sliced, then three pounds of lean beef, and over it three pounds of veal, all in slices. If any bones be left, break them and lay them on the meat; peel four onions, slice two carrots, two turnips, and a head of celery, and with a bunch of sweet herbs, four cloves, and a blade of mace, add all to the meat, over which pour one quart only of water, and place the stewpan, covered, over a slow fire till the meat is brown; then turn it, but be careful it does not scorch. Then add three quarts of boiling water, and let it stew gently for an hour till you have carefully removed all the scum that rises; after which, place the stewpan at the side of the fire, now adding two teaspoonfuls of salt. Let it simmer for four hours, strain it through a tamis into an earthenware vessel, and set it by to cool. Then carefully remove the fat; and when poured off to heat, do not disturb the sediment. The soup should be perfectly clear, and of an amber color; and will look better without any addition of vegetables.

GUMBO.—Take one chicken, two slices of cold cooked ham, three large onions; cut the chicken into pieces after it has laid in salt and water a half hour; slice the onions, and put all into a skillet with the ham, and fry together, until a nice brown, add a large tablespoonful of butter. Take half a gallon of young okra sliced very thin. After peeling one quart of ripe tomatoes, add to the okra with three quarts of water; let it boil well, then add the fried meat and onions; season with Cayenne and black pepper, salt to taste. Boil about four hours until the okra is perfectly dissolved, over a slow fire. Then strain, according to taste. Some prefer it not strained, and not too thick; in that case do not let it boil quite so long. It is then ready for table.

OKRA OR GUMBO SOUP.—Boil a chicken and a slice of ham in sufficient water to make a tureen of soup. When the fowl is thoroughly done, take it with the ham from the broth. Flavor the soup with onions, pepper, salt, and sweet herbs; make a paste with eggs and flour, roll it as thin as wafers, dry a little, then roll it as tightly as possible, and slice in thin shreds; put in the soup a teacupful of this, a teacupful of chopped okra, and a pint of oysters.

SOUTHERN GUMBO SOUP.—Fry one chicken, when cut up, to a light brown; also two slices of bacon, pour on them three quarts of boiling water, add one onion and some sweet herbs tied in a rag; simmer them gently three hours and a half; strain off the liquor, take off the fat, and then put the ham and chickens cut into small pieces into the liquor; add half a teacup of okra, also half a teacup of rice. Boil all half an hour, and just before serving add a glass of wine and a dozen oysters with their juice.

SOUP FOR THE MILLION.—Put the bones, skin, and all the rough residue of any joint, into a sauce-pan, with a quart and half a pint of cold water, one large carrot, scraped and cut up, two large onions, sliced and fried brown in one ounce of butter; and one *very small* head of celery washed and cut up. Let it stew for two hours; then add three medium-sized potatoes, peeled; a saltspoonful of salt; half a saltspoonful of pepper, and half a saltspoonful of mustard. Let it simmer three quarters of an hour longer. Take out the bones and then rub the whole through a sieve.

LOBSTER SOUP.—A shin of veal, two carrots, two onions, pepper, salt, mace, and four quarts of water; boil together four hours. Break up a large boiled lobster, take the meat out of the shell, break up the shell into a stewpan, with water enough to cover it. Let this simmer while the soup is boiling. Strain the vegetables, meat, and lobster shell, and put the liquor into the soup pot. Cut the meat of the lobster fine, and boil in the soup two hours. If you have the roe or coral of the lobster, grate it into the soup, as it adds to its tempting appearance. Add a quarter of a pound of butter, braided into two tablespoonfuls of flour, a cup of wine, the juice of a lemon, or a tablespoonful of vinegar.

NEW ENGLAND CHOWDER.—A good haddock, cod, or any other solid fish. Cut in pieces three inches square. Put a pound of fat salt pork cut in strips into a stewpan, set it on hot coals, and fry out the oil. Take out the pork, put in a layer of fish, over that a layer of onions in slices, another layer of fish with strips of fat salt pork, another layer of onions. Alternate in this way until your fish is consumed. Mix some flour with as much water as will fill the pot, season with black pepper and salt to taste, and boil for half an hour. Have ready some crackers (Philadelphia pilot bread is the best) soaked in water until they are a little softened; throw them into the chowder five minutes before taking it off the fire. Serve in a tureen.

Oyster Soup.—To one hundred oysters take one quart of milk, half a pint of water, four spoonfuls of flour, half a cup of butter, and one teaspoonful of salt, with a very little Cayenne pepper. Boil and skim the liquor of the oysters. Steam the flour and butter over the teakettle until soft enough to beat to a froth; then stir it in the liquor while boiling; after which add the other ingredients, and throw in the oysters, allowing them merely to scald.

Clam Soup.—Separate fifty small clams from the juice, which put into a stewpan, and let simmer five minutes, put it on to cook and slowly add two tablespoonfuls of butter and one of flour rubbed together, stirring it well; after this add half a teaspoonful of salt, half a nutmeg, and one pint of cream or milk, stir all well; let it simmer ten minutes; chop up parsley and add the clams. One boil up is sufficient, as clams require little cooking. If large clams are used, it is necessary to chop them up.

Bisque of Lobster.—A soup made with fish is always called a bisque. It is made either with crabs or lobsters. Remove a portion from either side of the head and use the rest. To boil a lobster, put it in a fish-kettle, and cover it with cold water, cooking it on a quick fire. Two lobsters will make soup for six or eight persons, and also salad. All the under shell and small claws are pounded in a mortar to make the bisque. When it is pounded, put it in a pan and set it on the fire with broth or water. The meat is cut in small pieces to be added afterwards. The bisque is left on the fire to boil gently for half an hour. Then pour it into a sieve and press it with a masher to extract the juice. To make it thicker a small piece of parsnip can be added and mashed with the rest into a pan, so that all the essence is extracted in that way from the lobster. When you have strained it, put a little butter with it, and add as much broth as is required. Put some of the meat in the soup tureen, and pour the soup over it.

Coloring for Soups.—As soups often require coloring, it is well to prepare browning for that purpose. Two baked onions, well browned in the oven and then chopped fine, make an excellent coloring and flavoring. The shells of green peas dried in the oven brown, but not black, will also answer to brown soup, and will keep all winter if hung in a perfectly dry place.

It will be found much better to use either of the above for coloring soup than the caramel or brown sugar used by many cooks, as the sweet taste is apt to be perceptible.

Roast Veal and Chicken Bones make a very nice soup, boiled with vegetables; but add a handful of macaroni, break it up fine, and boil the soup half an hour after it is put in. Color the soup with a little soy or ketchup.

CHAPTER II.

FISH.

To BAKE A LARGE FISH WHOLE.—Cut off the head, and split the fish down nearly to the tail; prepare a nice dressing of bread, butter, pepper and salt, moistened with a little water. Fill the fish with this dressing, and bind it together with fine cotton cord or tape, so as to confine it; the bindings may be three inches apart; lay the fish on a grate on a bake pan or a dripping-pan, and pour round it a little water and melted butter. Baste frequently. A good sized fish will bake in an hour. Serve with the gravy of the fish, drawn butter or oyster sauce.

ROCK FISH.—Rock fish or bass are best boiled plain, leaving on the head and tail. Boil steadily for half an hour. Serve with drawn butter with hard boiled eggs in it, chopped fine.

STUFFED FISH.—Soak some bread in water, and squeeze it out, add a small onion, chopped fine, fried with butter till nearly done; add to the onion the bread, salt, pepper, a little nutmeg, a little broth, the yelk of one egg. Stir rapidly, cooking over a clear fire; when done, add a little parsley, chopped fine. Cut the back-bone out of a two pound fish, put the stuffing in its place, and sew it up with a trussing needle and twine; put a little salt and pepper on the fish, inside and outside, a few pieces of butter under it in the pan, cover with a gill of broth, and bake in the oven.

To Fry Trout.—Dry them thoroughly, and fry in hot oiled butter without scorching, or in pork fat. If the latter rub salt on the fish. Lay on the fish, before serving, lumps of sweet butter.

Sturgeon.—The meat of this tenant of the deep waters partakes very much of the properties of veal, both in flavor and appearance, and is of an insipid character unless it is treated with condiments so as to render it commendable to the palate of the gastronomist. When purchased at the fishmonger's it should be cut into small fillets about one inch in thickness, and these should be covered over on both sides with a liberal supply of crumbs of bread, chopped parsley, lemon rind, and an egg to cause the above to adhere to the meat. Wrap the fillets in clean white writing paper, which has been buttered on the inside, and place on a gridiron over a clear fire until they are well done. Serve them with a sauce of melted butter, caviare and catsup, with salt and pepper to taste.

Fried Cod-Fish.—Take the middle or tail part of a fresh cod-fish, and cut it into slices not quite an inch thick, first removing the skin. Season them with a little salt and Cayenne pepper. Have ready in one dish some beaten yelk of egg, and in another some grated bread crumbs. Dip each slice of fish twice into the egg, and then twice into the crumbs. Fry them in fresh butter, and serve them up with the gravy about them.

Halibut may be fried as above.

FRIED EELS.—Clean and skin the eels. If large cut them into pieces, if small skewer them round and fry them whole. First dust them over with flour, then rub them with yelk of egg and sprinkle them with bread crumbs. Put them into boiling lard and fry until nicely browned.

POTTED SALMON. — Salmon, pounded mace, cloves, and pepper to taste, three bay leaves, a quarter of a pound of butter. Skin the salmon, and clean it thoroughly by wiping with a cloth (water would spoil it). Cut it into square pieces, which rub with salt, let them remain till thoroughly drained, then lay them in a dish with the other ingredients, and bake. When quite done drain them from the gravy, press into pots for use, and when cold pour over it clarified butter.

To PICKLE FISH.—Take any freshly caught fish, clean and scale them, wash and wipe them dry. Cut them into slices a few inches thick, put them in a jar with some salt, some allspice, and a little horseradish. When filled cover them with good strong vinegar. Cover it well with a good cover. Let it stand in your oven a few hours. Don't let the oven be too hot. This will keep six months. Put it immediately in the cellar, and in a few months they will be fit for use. No bones will be found.

To Pickle Herrings.—Wash fifty herrings well, and cut off their heads, tails, and fins. Put the fish into a stewpan, with three ounces of ground allspice, one tablespoonful of coarse salt, and a little Cayenne. Lay the fish in layers, and strew the spice equally over it, with a few bay leaves and anchovies interspersed. Pour over the whole a pint of vinegar mixed with a little water. Tie a bladder over the stewpan and bake in a slow oven. Skim off the oil, and with a little of the liquor boil about half a pint of claret or port wine. The fish should be baked so slowly and so thoroughly that when cooked the bones should not be perceptible.

Salt Fish.—Lay the fish to soak over night in cold water with a little vinegar in it. Wash it thoroughly, put it into a fish-kettle, with sufficient cold water to cover it. Let it heat gradually, but not boil quickly, or the fish will become hard. A large fish will require to be kept boiling half an hour. Before taking the fish from the kettle remove all the scum from the top of the water. Drain well. Parsnips may be laid around the fish on the edge of the dish, and hard boiled eggs, cut in slices, between the parsnips. Parsnip and egg sauce, in separate dishes, should also be served with salt fish.

SALT FISH WITH PARSNIPS.—Salt fish must always be well soaked in plenty of cold water the whole of the night before it is required for the following day's dinner. The salt fish must be put on to boil in plenty of cold water, without any salt, and when thoroughly done should be well drained free from any water, and placed on a dish with plenty of well-boiled parsnips. Some sauce may be poured over the fish, which is to be made as follows, viz.: Mix two ounces of butter with three ounces of flour, pepper, and salt, a small glassful of vinegar, and a good half pint of water. Stir this on the fire till it boils. A few hard-boiled eggs chopped up and mixed in this sauce would render the dish more acceptable.

PICKED-UP CODFISH.—This is an old-fashioned dish and name, but none the less to be admired on that account, being with most persons, when properly prepared, a great favorite. Pick up the fish in small particles, separating the fibres as near as possible, the finer the better. Freshen by leaving it in water one hour. Pour off the water and fill up with fresh. Bring it to a scald, pour it off, and put on the fish just enough water to cover it. Add to a quart of the soaked fish a bit of butter the size of half an egg, a very little flour, and a dust of pepper. Beat up two eggs, and after taking off the fish thicken it by stirring in the egg. Some let it boil after the egg is added, but if this is done the egg will be curdled. Another way is to boil eggs, chop and mix them in the gravy.

CODFISH BALLS.—Pick up as fine as possible a teacup of nice white codfish. Freshen all night, or if wanted for any other meal than breakfast, from the morning. Scald it once, and drain off the water. Chop and work it until entirely fine. Put it in a basin with water, a bit of butter the size of an egg, and two eggs. Beat it thoroughly, and heat it until it thickens without boiling. It should, when all is mixed, be about a quart. Have some potatoes ready prepared and nicely mashed. Work the fish and potatoes thoroughly together as above, make it in flat cakes, and brown both sides.

COD SOUNDS (AN ENTRÉE).—Boil the sounds gently, and not too much. Take them out of the water and let them remain until quite cold. Make a forcemeat out of chopped oysters, crumbs of bread, a lump of butter, spice, pepper and salt, and the yelks of two eggs. Fill the sounds and skewer them up in the shape of chickens, and lard them down each side in the same manner as though they were the breasts of fowls. Dredge them with flour, put them before the fire to bake, basting them well with butter. When they are sufficiently cooked, pour upon them some oyster sauce. They make an excellent *entrée*.

FISH CAKE.—Carefully remove the bones and skin from any fish, previously cooked, and let it soak for a short time in warm water. After taking it out, press it dry, add to it an equal quantity of mashed potatoes, and beat together in a mortar to a fine paste; season to taste. Then make up the mass into round flat cakes, sift a little flour over each one, and fry in butter or lard till they are brown. Codfish recooked in this way is an excellent breakfast dish.

KEDJEREE.—Take some fish that has been dressed, bone it carefully, and pull it into very small bits. Add hard-boiled eggs chopped, and as much rice well boiled as you require to fill your dish. Mix all these well together, with sufficient butter or cream to moisten them, adding a little Cayenne, mustard, and salt. Put all into a saucepan and stir with a *fork* (not a spoon) until quite hot. The fire must not be too fierce, and the dish must be served up very hot.

LOBSTER PATTIES.—Make some puff paste, and spread it on very deep patty pans. Bake it empty. Having boiled well two fine lobsters, extract all the meat and mince it very small, mixing with it the coral smoothly mashed, and some yelks of hard boiled eggs, grated. Season it with a little salt, some Cayenne, some powdered mace or nutmeg, adding a little yellow lemon rind, grated. Moisten the mixture well with cream, fresh butter, or salad oil. Put it into a stewpan, add a very little water, and let it stew till it just comes to a boil. Take it off the fire, and the patties being baked, remove hem from the tin pans, place them on a large dish, and fill them to the top with the mixtures. Similar patties may be made of crabs.

LOBSTER RISSOLES.—Extract the meat of a boiled lobster, mince it as fine as possible, mix with it the coral, pounded smooth, and some yelks of hard-boiled eggs, pounded also. Season it with Cayenne pepper, powdered mace, and a very little salt. Make a batter of beaten egg, milk, and flour. To each egg allow two large tablespoonfuls of milk, and a large teaspoonful of flour. Beat the batter well, and then mix the lobster with it gradually, till it is stiff enough to make into oval balls about the size of a large plum. Fry them in the best salad oil, and serve them either warm or cold. Similar rissoles may be made of raw oysters, minced fine, or of boiled clams. These should be fried in lard.

TO FRY OYSTERS.—Beat up an egg in one vessel and grate one or two crackers in another. Dip the oysters singly, first into the egg, then into the cracker. Fry the oysters so prepared in equal parts of butter and lard. It is also recommended to dry the oysters with a towel, beforehand. Clams may be fried in the same way.

PICKLED OYSTERS.—Lay the oysters on a sieve to drain the liquor from them; leave it to settle, then pour off the clear portion, and boil it up well with pepper, salt, mace, and ginger to the taste, then wash the oysters well in several waters to remove all the slime, and give them one boil up in the liquor.

OYSTER STEW.—To one hundred oysters, take one quart of milk, a half pint of water, four tablespoonfuls of flour, one teaspoonful of salt, a half cup of butter and a little Cayenne pepper. Put the liquor of the oysters on to boil. Mix butter and flour and steam it in a bowl over the teakettle till soft enough to beat to a froth, then stir it into the liquor, after which add the other ingredients.

GERMAN RECEIPT FOR OYSTER POWDER.— Take fresh oysters, beard them, and place them in a vessel over the fire for a few moments in order to extract the juice, then put them to cool, and chop them very fine with pounded biscuit, mace, and finely-minced lemon-peel; pound them until they become a paste; make them up into thin cakes, place them on a sheet of paper in a slow oven, and let them bake until they become quite hard, pound them directly into powder, and place the powder in a nice, dry tin box. Keep in a dry place, and when oysters are out of season you will find this powder very serviceable in imparting the flavor of the fish to various sauces and dishes.

CRUMBED OYSTERS.—Eight square soda-crackers rolled fine, seven ounces of butter, one quart of oysters; drain the oysters; put the crackers and oysters in alternate layers; divide the butter equally, putting it on the oysters at each layer, with a dust of pepper; be careful not to salt too much, leaving the bottom and top layer crackers. A moment before baking add a coffee cup of the liquor from the oysters; bake a light brown.

SCALLOPED OYSTERS.—Wash out of the liquor two quarts of oysters, pound very fine eight soft crackers, or grate a stale loaf of bread; butter a deep dish, sprinkle in a layer of crumbs, then a layer of oysters, a little mace, pepper, and bits of butter; another layer of crumbs, another of oysters, then seasoning as before, and so on until the dish is filled; cover the dish over with bread-crumbs, seasoning as before; turn over it a cup of the oyster liquor. Set it into the oven for thirty or forty minutes to brown.

OYSTER FORCEMEAT.—Open carefully a dozen fine plump natives, take off the beards, strain the liquor, and rinse the oysters in it. Grate four ounces crumb of a stale loaf into fine light crumbs, mince the oysters, but not too small, and mix them with the bread; add one and a half ounce of good butter, broken into minute bits, the grated rind of half a small lemon, a small saltspoonful of pounded mace, some Cayenne, a little salt, and a large teaspoonful of parsley; mix these ingredients well, and work them together with the unbeaten yelk of one egg, and a little oyster liquor, the remainder of which can be added to the sauce which usually accompanies this forcemeat.

OYSTER PATTIES IN BATTER.—Make a batter with the yelk of one egg (or more, according to the quantity of oysters you intend to prepare), a little nutmeg, some beaten mace, a little flour, and a little salt; dip in the oysters, and fry them in lard to a nice light brown. If preferred, a little parsley may be shred very fine, and mixed with the batter. The batter may also be made thicker, and formed into the shape of a patty, or put into a small tin mould, the oyster being dropped in and covered over, and the whole baked as a pudding would be.

OYSTER OMELETTE.—Three eggs well beaten, a little parsley, and an onion well minced, a little pepper and salt, one dozen good oysters; fry in butter with a little cream. The omelette must not be turned, but when done on the one side must be browned, or held close to the fire when it rises and browns; serve hot with good gravy.

OYSTER SAUCE.—Boil the oysters in their own liquor until they look plump, then take them out and strain the liquor; add to it wine, vinegar, and pepper to your taste, and pour it over the oysters.

CLAM FRITTERS.—Strain the clams thoroughly from the juice, chop them fine, season with pepper and salt, and add an egg or two, with a little cream or milk; sift in flour enough to make them stick together—and fry.

TO BOIL CRABS.—Boil for twenty minutes, wipe and crack the claws, rub the shells with oil, and dish as with lobster. To cook soft-shell crabs, remove the claws, cut open and take away the sandbag and spongy part; then put some butter in a pan and fry brown on both sides.

TERRAPINS.—Boil three terrapins till the bones can be easily removed, after which chop the meat very fine; add two tablespoonfuls of butter, one pint of tomato catsup, half a pint of sherry or Madeira wine, one tablespoonful of mixed mustard, two onions, boiled and chopped fine, salt, black and red pepper to taste; stir the mixture well; scrape and clean two of the backs.

CHAPTER III.

SAUCES AND PICKLES

SAUCES.—Melted butter, a sauce, is, in its simplest form, a mixture of butter, flour, salt and water; and the talent consists in bringing those ingredients together, and in the quantities employed of each. It ought not to be a mixture of flour and water with a little butter added to it—this is the common form—but, as its name implies, it ought to be butter and water, with a little flour added to it to thicken the mixture. If you like your sauce thick, put more flour; and if thin, put less. To be well made, the sauce should be smooth and velvety in appearance, and, above all, devoid of what are called knobs. To obtain this result proceed in this way: Melt the butter in a saucepan, and then add the flour, which will amalgamate very easily with it; salt and stir in enough of hot water, keep stirring the mixture on the fire until it thickens then serve.

The above is the simplest form, but like all simple things, it is the foundation of an imposing array of sauces, to be eaten with fish, flesh, fowl, and vegetables without end.

1. Beat up the yelk of an egg and the juice of a lemon, and stir in just before serving, *off the fire.*

2. Use milk, or milk and water, instead of water.

3. Throw in, just before serving, some chopped parsley, capers, or pickles chopped small. These additions are not incompatible with the arrangements Nos. 1 and 2.

4. Let the butter and flour get a good brown color, then add water, and when the sauce is made, Worcester Sauce, ketchup, pepper and other spices and condiments to taste.

5. Use a mixture of half water and half tomato sauce instead of water, and add condiments to taste, if the tomato sauce is not sufficiently flavored.

N. B.—This is *not* to be used in dressing macaroni, but only for cutlets, boiled fowls, with rice, various vegetables, etc.

6. Cut up some onions, a very small piece of garlic, and boil in milk, with whole pepper, mace, a clove or two, etc., tied up in a piece of muslin, and some parsley. When the mixture is well flavored, strain and use the milk instead of water to make your sauce; egg and lemon may be added if wished. Without these last two it is not a bad substitute for onion sauce. Shad or rock fish boiled in the flavored milk, and served with the sauce over them, are not bad eating. The great rock to be avoided is excess of any one thing in flavoring the milk, chiefly in the spice line.

7. For puddings and sweet dishes the sauce is made in the same way, excepting that the salt is replaced by sugar, in larger quantities, of course. This should be made with milk, or milk and water, and an egg or two used, with or without lemon, according to taste; or the egg should be beaten up with brandy or wine.

MUSHROOM CATSUP.— Get fine-grown, fresh-gathered mushrooms, break them up, and sprinkle a good handful of salt over every layer. Let them lie for all the juice to run out, stirring them up often, but put no water. When the juice has run out, strain it off, and boil it well, with very little ginger, and a sufficient quantity of pepper. It is a mistake to give mushroom catsup all kinds of flavorings, as it is the full flavor of the mushroom which it is all-important to preserve, and in using it the cook can add the spices her dish requires. All that is necessary or good to make the catsup keep is to put salt and pepper enough. A matter of yet greater importance is to use the pure juice without water, as any mixture of water spoils the flavor and the keeping, too. There is no better sauce for fried or broiled fish than a really good mushroom catsup, and nothing else; and mixed with equal parts of soy and lemon pickle, it makes a delicious flavoring for any sauce or gravy. Make it a *quartette* with a fourth equal part of red wine, and "it's no ill," as the Scot says.

Tomato Catsup.—Take six pounds of tomatoes, sprinkle them with salt, let them remain for a day or two, then boil them until the skins will separate easily; press them through a colander or coarse sieve, leaving the skins behind. Put into the liquor a handful of shalots, a pint of Chili vinegar, a pint of wine, salt, pepper, cloves, ginger, and allspice. Boil all together until a third is wasted, bottle it, and when it is cold cork the bottles very well. Shake it before using it. Good either for sauce or for flavoring.

Tomato Marmalade.—Take fine ripe tomatoes, cut them in halves, and squeeze out the juice. Put them in a preserving-pan, with a few peach-leaves, a clove of garlic, some slices of onion or shalot, and a bundle of parsley. Stew them until they are sufficiently done, pulp them through a sieve, and boil them down like other marmalade, adding salt. Put them into small jars, pepper the tops, and pour clarified butter over. Eat it with fish, etc., or stir the contents of a small pot into the gravy of stews or fricassees.

Belsize Tomato Sauce.—Slice tomatoes in a jar, and sprinkle salt over every layer of slices. Place the jar in a warm place by the fire, stir the contents pretty often for three days, and let it remain untouched for twelve days. Press out the juice, and boil it with mace, pepper, allspice, ginger, and cloves. There should be two ounces of spice to a quart of juice, the pepper and allspice greatly predominating. At the end of three months it should be boiled up with fresh spice.

TOMATO VINEGAR.—Quarter three dozen fine tomatoes, leave the bottoms undivided; rub half a pound of salt over them, place them in a wide-mouthed jar in a cool oven, or by the side of the fire, for a day or two; add a little mace, cloves, and grated nutmeg; slice in a clove of garlic, sprinkle in half a pint of mustard seed, and pour over all two quarts of boiling vinegar; tie a bladder over the jar, and let it remain five or six days more by the fire, shaking it well every day. Put it by in the same jar as long as convenient, and when you wish to bottle it press out all the liquor; let it stand several hours to clear, and then bottle the clear, and keep that which is not quite clear for present use.

Tomato vinegar and tomato sauce should both be kept in store, as the sub-acid flavor is sometimes an improvement in the dishes in which it is used, whereas at other times we require the flavor of the tomato unmingled with acid.

LEMON PICKLE.—Grate off the rind of twenty lemons, or pare it off so thin as to cut through the little globules, grating or cutting it into a small quantity of vinegar, to be added to the lemon pickle with the vinegar. Cut the lemons in quarters, leaving the bottoms whole. Rub over them equally half a pound of bay salt, and put them into a stone jar in a cool oven, or on the hob by the fire, until the juice is dried into the peels. Then put in amongst them a blade of mace, a few cloves beaten fine, some grated nutmeg, a clove of garlic peeled and sliced, and half a pint of mustard seed bruised, and pour over all two quarts of boiling vinegar. Close the jar well, let it stand in its warm place five or six days, shaking it up every day. Tie it down tight with a bladder, and put it by for three months to take off the bitter. After this it may be bottled when convenient. Put all into a hair sieve, and squeeze out the liquor. Let the liquor stand until the next day, and bottle the fine. Let the remainder stand two days, bottle the fine part, and repeat the same until all is bottled. A little will not hurt the color of white sauce, and it is capital for flavoring stews and ragouts, and also makes a very nice fish sauce. In using it for flavoring put it in before the gravy is thickened, especially if cream be used, lest the sharpness should make it curdle.

CHUTNEY.—Pare and core a quarter of a pound of sharp apples, weigh the same quantity of tomatoes, raisins, figs, brown sugar, and salt. Pound them in a mortar, and pound and mix with them a quarter of an ounce of chilis or Cayenne pepper, the same of powdered ginger, half an ounce each of garlic and shalots. Mix all well together in a large jar, put in three pints of vinegar and one of lemon juice, and stand the jar where it will be in heat amounting to 130° Fahrenheit for a month, stirring it twice a day. If sour apples are not to be had, gooseberries will do, but not so well. The top liquor or quihi may be poured off and bottled. It is an excellent fish sauce. The thick part is the chutney, and should be put into wide-mouthed bottles. Both are excellent for flavoring sauces or gravies, or to eat as sauce.

BROWNING.—Beat fine four ounces of refined sugar, and put it into a very clean frying-pan, with one ounce of butter. Mix them together over a clear fire, and when the sugar froths in dissolving, hold the pan a little off the fire, and when the sugar is of a deep brown pour in by degrees, little by little, and stirring the mixture all the time, a pint of red wine. Stir in half an ounce of allspice, six cloves, four shalots, peeled, a blade of mace, a wineglass of catsup, and the rind of a lemon. Simmer it for ten minutes or a quarter of an hour, pour it into a basin to get cold, then skim it very clean, and bottle it for use. It is good for any brown gravy. Browning is often made for present use by burning a good teaspoonful of brown sugar in a large iron spoon. Stirred into brown gravy it gives both richness and color. Another browning is made by allowing flour to bake until it is of one uniform dark-brown color. It takes many days, and must be stirred about from time to time while doing.

MUSHROOM POWDER.—Peel the thickest large

buttons you can get, and just pare off the root end, but do not wash them. Place them on pewter dishes, so that their liquor will dry into them, and put them into a slow oven until they will powder. Beat them up in a mortar, sift the powder through a sieve with a little Cayenne pepper and pounded mace, bottle it, and keep it in a dry place.

Fish Sauce.—Take half a pint of milk and cream together, two eggs well beaten, salt, a little pepper, and the juice of half a lemon. Put it over the fire and stir it constantly until it begins to thicken.

Tomato Sauce.—Take seven pounds of ripe tomatoes. Skin them, put them in a preserving kettle, with four pounds of sugar, and boil until the sugar penetrates the tomatoes; add one pint of vinegar, one ounce of cloves, and one ounce of ground cinnamon; boil thirty minutes, and then seal up close in stone jars. This will keep for years.

Mushroom Sauce.—Half a pint of button mushrooms, half a pint of good beef gravy, one tablespoonful of mushroom catsup, thickening of butter and flour. Put the gravy into a saucepan, thicken it, and stir it over the fire until it boils. Prepare the mushrooms by cutting off the stalks, and wiping them free from grit and dirt; the large, flat mushrooms cut into small pieces will answer for a sauce, when the buttons are not obtainable. Put them into the gravy, and let them simmer very gently for ten minutes, then add the catsup, and serve. When fresh mushrooms are not in season, the mushroom powder makes a good sauce for roast meats.

BREAD SAUCE.—Cut some bread into slices, adding to it some pepper, an onion, a little salt and butter, and enough boiling milk to cover it. Let it simmer gently before the fire, until the whole of the milk is soaked up by the bread, then add a little thick cream, remove the onion and rub through a hair sieve. Serve very hot in a sauce tureen.

SAUCE FOR FOWLS.—An excellent white sauce for fowls may be made of two ounces of butter, two small onions, one carrot, half a teacupful of flour, one pint of new milk, salt and pepper to taste. Cut up the onions and carrots very small and put them into a stewpan with the butter; simmer them until the butter is nearly dried up; then stir in the flour, and add the milk. Boil the whole gently until it thickens, strain it, season with salt and Cayenne, and serve.

SAUCE FOR BOILED POULTRY.—Chop a stick of blanched celery very fine, in a quart of new milk; let it boil gently in a stewpan, with a few black pepper-corns till reduced to one pint. Stir till the whole is a smooth pulp. Thicken with the yelk of a fresh egg well beaten with half a teacupful of fresh cream.

Savory Sauce for a Roast Goose.—A tablespoonful of made mustard, half a teaspoonful of Cayenne pepper, and three spoonfuls of port wine. When mixed, pour this (hot) into the body of the goose before sending it up. It wonderfully improves with sage and onions.

Giblet Sauce.—Take the livers, lights, gizzards, and hearts from fowls. Boil very tender, and chop them fine. Make a nice thin drawn-butter, and stir them in; or boil and chop them, and use the water in which they were boiled; season with butter, pepper and salt; beat up the yelks of two eggs, add them, and keep the sauce stirring until it thickens. This sauce is best for roast fowls.

Sauce for Wild Duck.—A tablespoonful of made mustard, a teaspoonful of essence of anchovies, a pinch of Cayenne pepper, a tablespoonful of mushroom ketchup, and a wineglass of claret. Mix the mustard and anchovy essence thoroughly in a saucepan, add the Cayenne, then the ketchup, a few drops at a time; the claret last; heat over a clear fire. Slice the breast of the duck, and pour the sauce over it very hot.

Venison Ravigote Sauce.—Put three pounds of venison in a vessel; set on the fire in a pan one pint of vinegar, two bay leaves, two cloves, two leaves of garlic, one onion sliced, two stalks of thyme, four of parsley, and one dozen pepper-corns. Let it boil, and turn it over the venison. Leave it for a day, turning the venison occasionally. Then put the venison in a pan with some spices, and pour the juice and vinegar back over it, adding salt and a few pieces of butter, and bake it. If you roast the venison, put the vinegar and spices in the dripping pan, and baste with it. For the sauce take an onion chopped fine and set on the fire with one ounce of butter; when nearly done, add a dessertspoonful of flour, one gill and a half of broth, and stir. Then add the drippings from the venison, and boil gently over a slow fire. The ravigote sauce can be used with beef, mutton or pork. Keep it on the fire five minutes, add chopped parsley, and serve.

GREEN MINT SAUCE.—The French use this for boiled lamb. It is made by putting green mint, chopped fine, and parsley, in vinegar.

SAUCE ROBERT.—Cut a few onions into dice, which put into a frying-pan with a bit of butter, and fry them lightly; when nicely browned, add a dessertspoonful of flour, a ladleful of stock, the same of vinegar, some salt and pepper; reduce it to a proper thickness, and when ready for table stir in two dessertspoonfuls of mustard.

CELERY SAUCE.—Make half a pint of melted butter, of course, using only milk or cream, or both mixed. Have ready three heads of celery, the white parts well washed and cut up into small bits, and boiled for a few minutes in water, which strain off; put the celery to the melted butter, and keep it stirred over the fire for ten or twelve minutes. It is better to put the celery in before the melted butter boils up—as soon as it is hot will do. This is a very nice sauce for boiled fowl or turkey.

HORSERADISH SAUCE.—One tablespoonful of grated horseradish, one saltspoonful of mustard, a pinch of salt, four tablespoonfuls of cream, and two tablespoonfuls of white vinegar. Mix well together, adding the vinegar last, and stirring very rapidly when pouring that on the mixture.

POTATO SAUCE.—Smoothly mash one large steamed potato when it is hot, and add a little salt, shred-lemon peel and white pepper; mix with it some dissolved butter, the beaten yelk of a new-laid egg, and pour over it enough boiling milk to render it sufficiently thin in consistency. Gravy instead of milk may be added when a white sauce is not wanted, and potato flour, instead of mashed potato used when easily procured. Any particular flavor may be imparted to this sauce according to taste, such as chopped herbs, olives or pickles.

RICE SAUCE.—This is a delicate white sauce for eating with game or chicken, as a change from the usual bread sauce, and is a great deal used in India. Soak a quarter of a pound of rice in a pint of milk, with onion, pepper, and salt. When it is quite tender rub it through a sieve into a stewpan, and boil it. If too thick, thin with cream or milk.

SAUCES AND PICKLES. 59

WINE SAUCE.—One cup of butter and two cups of sugar stirred to a cream; one cup of wine added slowly. Set the bowl in a kettle of hot water three-quarters of an hour before you wish to use it. It must not be stirred or poured out of the bowl.

MADEIRA SAUCE.—Two cups of white sugar, three-quarters of a cup of butter; beat to a cream, and add by the teaspoonful, a cup of Madeira wine. Mix well, place the bowl containing the mixture in a vessel of boiling water, and stir to a cream. Serve hot.

PUDDING SAUCE, No. 1.—Beat to a cream one cup of butter with two cups of sugar, one cup of wine to be added slowly. Set the bowl it is in in a kettle of hot water three-quarters of an hour before you wish it for use. It must not be stirred before placing on the table, or poured out of the bowl.

PUDDING SAUCE, No. 2.—Dissolve two cups of sugar in a cup of butter, and add a wineglassful of wine; beat them well together, and flavor with nutmeg or mace to suit the taste.

LEMON SAUCE.—Melt two ounces of butter in a little water; put in two ounces of sugar, the juice and grated rind of half a lemon, and the pulp and juice of the other half. Boil together five minutes, and serve hot, for cold puddings.

ORANGE SAUCE.—Rub together one ounce of flour and two ounces of butter; put it into a saucepan, with the juice of four large oranges, the shred rind of half an orange, and two tablespoonfuls of loaf sugar. Stir gently over the fire until all is well mixed, and serve.

Sweet Egg Sauce.—Put the yelks of four hard boiled eggs into a mortar, with an equal weight of fresh butter and sugar; beat it smooth, then dilute with a sufficiency of either milk or white wine. Add the grated rind of half a lemon; boil five minutes, and serve.

Sweet Pudding Sauce.—Mix with half a pint of melted butter two dessertspoonfuls of pounded loaf-sugar (with or without a wineglass of sherry), make it quite hot, and pour it over and around the puddings when they are turned out into the dish.

PICKLES.

The general principle of pickling may be soon stated, although it is not universally applicable to all varieties. The vegetables are in the majority of cases placed in strong brine for some hours or days. This is done to extract part of the watery fluids they contain, for by a law well known to chemists, when two liquids are separated by an animal or vegetable membrane, an interchange takes place; but the lighter fluid is more rapidly attracted by the heavier. It follows, therefore, that if vegetables are put into strong brine, the more fluid parts are extracted, and the vegetable becomes less watery than before.

Great advantage, especially in wholesale manufacture, is taken of this circumstance, for, instead of placing the substances in the first instance, in vinegar, which would be so weakened that it would have to be renewed at a considerable cost, the vegetables are first pickled in strong brine, and, when the water is extracted, they are finally preserved in vinegar, and bottled. As an example of this method of proceeding we give the following:—

To Pickle String Beans.—String beans make a deservedly popular pickle, but they should not be more than half grown when gathered; have them as much of one size as possible, and let a little of the stalk remain upon each. Put them into a brine strong enough for an egg to float in; let them stay in it for three days, stirring occasionally; place them in a preserving pan, with plenty of vine leaves both over and under them; cover them in the brine in which they have steeped; put something over them to keep the steam from escaping, and set them over a very slow fire until they turn green, but they should not be allowed to boil; drain them in a sieve, and arrange them in a jar; pour upon them a pickle made by heating some of the best white wine vinegar, which you have flavored with mace, ginger, and pepper. If the beans are already properly greened, the pickle may be employed cold, otherwise use it hot.

It is needless to say that in following out these

directions the vinegar used should not be boiled in a copper, but, if possible, in an enamelled pan.

Sometimes the salt is more advantageously used dry, as extracting the moisture of the plant more rapidly. The following receipt is an example of this mode of procedure:—

To Pickle Red Cabbage.—Choose a medium-sized fresh red cabbage; tear off the coarse outer leaves, quarter it, remove the stalk, cut the cabbage into slices of about the third of an inch in thickness; place it in a bowl, strew amongst it two good handfuls of salt; let the whole stand for twenty-four hours; stirring it once or twice; drain it as dry as possible; place it loosely in wide-mouthed jars, and fill up with either the prepared vinegar given above, or use strong raw vinegar, adding peppercorns, capsicums, pieces of ginger, or what other spice you may fancy. This in a day or two will be of a splendid crimson color, and eat deliciously crisp. Those cooks who prefer to boil their vinegar and spices in an iron pot, and forthwith pour the pickle boiling hot upon the cabbage, may reasonably expect soon to find the latter limp, ill-flavored, and of a dismal purplish blue.

The caution here given respecting the boiling the vinegar in an iron vessel is perfectly correct. For, if done, a small quantity of the metal will be dissolved by the acid, and, although perfectly wholesome, alter materially the fine color which is so much esteemed in this pickle.

PICKLED NASTURTIUMS.—Very frequently nasturtiums are merely thrown into seasoned vinegar; they should be gathered in sunshiny weather. Although this method answers tolerably well, it is preferable to put the freshly pickled nasturtiums into a strong brine of salt and water, and let them remain in this till they grow somewhat soft; then cover them with strong vinegar, and they will keep for years.

TO PICKLE CABBAGE A GOOD COLOR.—Put a few slices of beet-root amongst it—will find it makes it a very beautiful color, besides being a nice addition to the pickles.

TO PICKLE MUSHROOMS.—Rub the buttons with flannel and salt, throw them into a stewpan with a little salt over them, then sprinkle them with some pepper and a small quantity of mace. As the liquor comes out shake them well, and keep them over a gentle fire until all is dried into them again, then put as much vinegar into the pan as will cover them. Give it a scald, and pour the whole into bottles.

SMALL ONION PICKLE.—Small onions, not larger than marbles, must be carefully peeled and thrown into strong brine. Let them remain eight days, changing the brine every other day. Dry in a cloth, place them in bottles, add spice, and fill up with strong distilled vinegar. A teaspoonful of olive oil will prevent the onions from turning yellow. Mustard seed, horseradish, allspice, cloves, black pepper-corns, and mace are all excellent spices for onions.

SPICED ONIONS.—Peel large onions and lay them in a jar. Put as much cider vinegar as will cover them in a pot, with cloves, allspice, cinnamon, mace, mustard seed, horseradish. When the vinegar boils pour it over the onions. Let them stand twelve hours. Pour off the vinegar, heat to boiling point, and pour on again until the vinegar has been heated three times, when the onions will be fit for use.

PICKLED ONIONS.—Have the onions gathered when quite dry and ripe, and with the fingers take off the thin outside skin, then with a knife remove one more skin, when the onion will look quite clear. Have ready some very dry bottles or jars, and as fast as the onions are peeled put them in. Pour over sufficient cold vinegar to cover them, add two teaspoonfuls of allspice and two teaspoonfuls of black pepper, taking care that each jar has its share of the latter ingredients. Tie down with bladder, and put them in a dry place, and in a fortnight they will be fit for use. This is a most simple receipt, and very delicious, the onions being nice and crisp. They should be eaten within six or eight months after being done, as the onions are liable to become soft.

TO PICKLE BEET-ROOT.—This vegetable makes an excellent pickle, and from the brightness of its color has a very pretty effect in a glass pickle dish or jar. Wash the beet perfectly. Do not cut off any of the fibrous roots, as this would allow the juice to escape, and thus the coloring would be lost. Put it into sufficient water to boil it, and when the skin will come off it will be sufficiently cooked, and may be taken out and laid upon a cloth to cool. Having rubbed off the skin cut the beet into thick slices, put it into a jar, and pour over it cold vinegar, prepared as follows: Boil a quart of vinegar with one ounce of whole black pepper, and an equal weight of dry ginger, and let it stand until quite cold. The jar should be kept closely corked.

CAROLINA CHOW-CHOW.—The evening before you wish to make your pickle take the cabbage, chop it up fine, say a water-pailful, put a layer of cabbage, sprinkle with salt, and so on until the vessel is full, place a plate on it to press it down, and let it stand until morning. Prepare ten large onions in the same way, spread the cabbage on a cloth, and let it remain while you are preparing your vinegar. Take one gallon of the best vinegar and sweeten to your taste, put into a bowl some mustard, two ounces of pulverized cinnamon, two ounces of turmeric, two ounces of white mustard seed, two ounces of celery seed, half a pint of grated horseradish, mix all well together in the vinegar, and let it come to a boil, then put in the cabbage and onions and let them boil about ten minutes. If too thick add vinegar. You can use salad oil, half a teacupful, if you like it, and other spices.

PICKLE CHOW-CHOW.—A quarter of a peck of green tomatoes, a quarter of a peck of white onions, a quarter of a peck of pickling beans, one dozen green cucumbers, one dozen green peppers, one large head of cabbage. Season with mustard, celery seed, salt, to suit the taste. Cover the mixture with the best vinegar. Boil two hours slowly, continually stirring, and add two tablespoonfuls of salad oil while hot.

CHOW-CHOW.—(EXCELLENT.)—To one peck of green tomatoes add three good sized onions, six peppers with the seeds taken out. Chop together and boil three minutes in three quarts of vinegar. Throw this vinegar away after straining. Then to three quarts of new vinegar, when scalding hot, add two cups of sugar, one cup of mixed mustard, one tablespoonful of cloves, one of allspice, two of cinnamon, three of salt. Pour over the tomatoes hot.

OLD VIRGINIA CHOW-CHOW.—Three pecks of ripe tomatoes, three of green tomatoes, five large heads of cabbage, one dozen large onions, one dozen ripe peppers, one dozen green peppers, half a pound of celery. Chop all very fine, cover with salt, and soak twenty-four hours. Then drain the brine off, thoroughly cover with strong vinegar, and add three pounds of sugar. Scald one hour, add one cup of grated horseradish, two tablespoonfuls of white mustard seed, one of cloves, two of allspice, two of ginger, and one of ground mustard. Cover close for one month, when it will be ready for use.

SAUCES AND PICKLES. 67

India Pickle.—Quarter of a pound of ginger, half an ounce of ground cloves, half an ounce of chillies, four ounces of black pepper, two of ground allspice, four of coarse salt, two of garlic, two of eschalots, quarter of a pound of mustard seed, and a small piece of alum, all put into two gallons of pure cider or white wine vinegar, and boiled half an hour. Mix half a pound of mustard and quarter of a pound of tannin, smoothe with a little vinegar, and add to the above pickle. Let it just come to a boil, then pour into a deep jar. Put into this pickle all vegetables as they come in their season, being careful to have them well dried. Let them remain in the pickle three weeks, then bottle for use. This will keep perfectly good three years.

Yellow Pickle.—Have firm white cabbages cut in quarters; put into strong brine for two or three days; then scald them in clear water until you can run a straw in them; take them out and dry them for twenty-four hours in the sun, or by the stove, as may be most convenient; then put them in strong cider vinegar, with powdered turmeric sufficient to color the cabbage, and let them remain in the vinegar about ten days. White onions managed the same way; also lemons whole. Cucumbers — white are the best — must not be scalded or dried, but only changed from the brine to the vinegar colored with the turmeric. After remaining in the turmeric vinegar ten or twelve days, take the fruit and vegetables out of it, and put them in a sieve or on a plank, and let all the vinegar drain from them for two or three hours. Have the following spices, etc., prepared ready, and pack them in a jar, a layer of fruit and vegetables and a layer of spices until the jar is three parts full; then fill up with vinegar—cider vinegar; after a day or two pour the vinegar from them, scald it, and to every gallon of vinegar add five pounds of sugar while the vinegar is boiling. Be sure to keep the pickle covered with the vinegar. For each gallon of pickle, three ounces of turmeric, two ounces of white ginger, two ounces of white pepper, quarter of an ounce of mace beaten fine, four ounces of horseradish shredded fine, four ounces of garlic, two ounces of white mustard seed, half an ounce of celery seed, whole. The pickle should have a tight cover at all times, and, during the warm weather, be frequently placed in the sun.

PICKLED RED CABBAGE.—Cut the red cabbage in thin slices, spread it on a sieve and sprinkle with salt. Let it drain for twenty-four hours, dry it, pack it in pickle jars, fill them with cold vinegar, put in spice to taste, and tie the jars up firmly with bladder. Open the jars in a few days, and if the cabbage has shrunk, fill up with vinegar.

ARTICHOKES PICKLED.—Boil the artichokes till you can pull the leaves off; take out the choke and cut away the stalk, but be careful that the knife does not touch the top; throw them into salt and water. When they have lain an hour, take them out and drain them; then put them into glasses or jars, and put a little mace and sliced nutmeg between; fill them with vinegar and spring water, and cover your jars close.

GHERKINS.—Steep them in strong brine for a week, then pour it off; heat it to the boiling point, and again pour it on the gherkins. In twenty-four hours drain the fruit on a sieve; put it in widemouthed bottles or jars; fill them up with strong pickling vinegar, boiling hot, bung them down at once and tie them over with bladder. When cold, dip the corks into melted bottle-wax. Spice is usually added to the bottles, or else steeped in the vinegar.

TO MAKE LEMON PICKLE.—Take some lemons and grate them slightly; cut them down at one end in four places, which fill up with salt; lay them at the bottom of a jar, and strew over them horseradish, (shred,) pepper, garlic, bruised ginger, Cayenne, a little turmeric, or, if preferred, half a spoonful of curry powder, and plenty of mustard seed; then add some more lemons again, and so on with the different ingredients until the lemons are all in the jar. Pour over some strong cold vinegar, as much as will cover the pickle; tie the jar over with a bladder, and set it in a pan of water. Let it boil slowly until the lemons become tender. The pickles will be fit for use in less than a week, if required.

TOMATO CATSUP, No. 1.—Scald ripe tomatoes, and remove the skin. Let them stand a day, covered with salt; strain thoroughly to remove the seeds. To every two quarts of the liquor add three ounces of cloves, two of black pepper, two grated nutmegs, a little Cayenne pepper, and salt. Boil all together for half an hour, then let the mixture cool and settle; add a pint of the best cider vinegar; bottle, cork tightly, and seal. Keep in a cool place.

TOMATO CATSUP, No. 2.—Boil one bushel of ripe tomatoes until perfectly soft; squeeze them through a fine wire sieve, add half a gallon of vinegar, one pint and a half of salt, two ounces of cloves, quarter of a pound of allspice, two ounces of Cayenne pepper, three teaspoonfuls of black pepper, five heads of garlic, skinned and separated. Mix together, and boil three hours; it should reduce to one-half. Bottle without straining.

TOMATO SOY.—To one peck of green tomatoes, sliced thin, add one pint of salt; stand twenty-four hours, strain, and put on the fire with twelve raw onions, an ounce of black pepper, one ounce of allspice, quarter of a pound of ground mustard, half a pound of white mustard seed, and a little Cayenne pepper. Cover with vinegar and boil till as thick as a jam, stirring occasionally with a wooden spoon, to prevent burning.

RIPE CUCUMBER PICKLE.—Pare them, take out

the seeds, cut in rings an inch thick; then simmer in weak alum water an hour; take them out, drain them, and lay them carefully in a jar; then prepare a syrup of one gallon good vinegar, two cups sugar, one ounce cinnamon, one ounce ginger-root; pour it hot over your pickles. This is a delightful pickle, and will keep sealed up a long time.

Green Cucumber Pickle.—Make a brine by putting one pint of rock-salt into a pail of boiling water, and pour it over the cucumbers; cover tight to keep in the steam, and let them remain all night and part of a day; make a second brine as above, and let them remain in it the same length of time; then scald and skim the brine, as it will answer for the third brine, and let them remain in it as above; then rinse and wipe them dry, and add boiling hot vinegar; throw in a lump of alum as large as a nut to every pail of pickles, and you will have a fine, hard, and green pickle. Add spices, if you like, and keep the pickles under the vinegar. A brick on the top of the cover, which keeps the pickles under, has a tendency to collect the scum which may arise.

Pickled Eggs, No. 1.—Obtain a moderate-sized, wide-mouthed earthen jar, sufficient to hold one dozen eggs; let the latter be boiled quite hard; when fully done, place the same, after taking them up, into a pan of cold water. Remove the shells from them, and deposit them carefully in the jar.

Have on the fire a quart (or more, if necessary) of good white wine vinegar, into which introduce one ounce of raw ginger, two or three blades of sweet mace, one ounce of allspice, half an ounce of whole black pepper, and salt, half an ounce of mustard seed, with four cloves of garlic. When it has simmered for half an hour take it up, and pour the contents into the jar, taking care to observe that the eggs are wholly covered. When quite cold, stopper it down for use. It will be ready after a month. When cut into quarters, they serve as a garnish, and afford a nice relish to cold meat of any kind.

PICKLED EGGS, No. 2.—Boil two or three dozen eggs for half an hour, then, after removing the shells, lay them carefully in large-mouthed jars, and pour over them scalding vinegar, well seasoned with whole pepper, allspice, a few races of ginger, and a few cloves of garlic. When cold, they are bunged down close, and in a month are fit for use. Where eggs are plentiful, the above pickle is by no means expensive, and, as an accompaniment to cold meat, it cannot be outrivalled for piquancy and *gout*.

PICCALILLI.—Take anything that can be pickled, such as onions, sliced cucumbers, cabbage, mangoes, peppers, squashes, small green tomatoes, cauliflowers, martenoes, celery, green beans, nasturtiums, radish pods, watermelon rinds, small green cucumbers, and Chili peppers. Lay them in salt and water, with enough turmeric to turn them yellow. Let them stand twenty-four hours, stirring frequently; then drain, and dry them and put them into the jars. To every quart of vinegar, allow a tablespoonful of mustard seed, one of turmeric, and a handful of whole black pepper, one clove of garlic. Spice to your taste with mace, ginger, cloves, red pepper, and horseradish. Boil all but the mustard seed in a bag in the vinegar. Let the vinegar stand till cold. Boil one dozen eggs quite hard, mash them in enough sweet oil to make a paste; then stir it in the vinegar, which pour over the pickles. Put one handful of salt in every jar. They should stand three days, well tied up, when they will be fit for use.

PICKLED WALNUTS, NO. 1.—One hundred walnuts, salt and water. To each quart of vinegar allow two ounces of whole black pepper, one ounce of allspice, one ounce of bruised ginger. Procure the walnuts while young, and prick them well with a fork. Prepare a strong brine of salt and water (four pounds of salt to each gallon of water), into which put the walnuts, letting them remain nine days, and changing the brine every third day. Drain them off, put them on a dish, and place it in the sun until they become perfectly black, which will be in two or three days. Have ready dry jars, into which place the walnuts, and do not quite fill the jars. Boil sufficient vinegar to cover them for ten minutes, with spices in the above proportion, and pour it hot over the walnuts, which must be quite covered with the pickle. Tie down with bladder and keep in a dry place. They will be fit for use in a month, and will keep good two or three years.

Pickled Walnuts, No. 2.—Take one hundred walnuts, soft enough to allow a needle to pass through them, lay them in water, with a good handful of salt, for two days, then change to fresh water and another handful of salt, for three days, then drain and lay them on some clean straw or a sieve in the sun until quite black and wrinkled; afterwards put into a clean, dry glass bottle or jar a quarter of an ounce of allspice, quarter of an ounce of mace, quarter of an ounce of ginger, half a pint of mustard seed, and half an ounce of pepper-corns; these to be mixed in layers with the walnuts until your walnuts are all used, then pour over them boiling vinegar to cover them. Ready for use in two months.

Sweet Peach Pickles.—To nine pounds of firm clingstone peaches (peeled) take three pounds of brown sugar and an ounce each of cinnamon bark, cloves, mace, and allspice, and a quart of good vinegar. Put the sugar, vinegar, and spices in a clean preserving kettle, and let it boil thoroughly. Have the peaches in a large jar, and when the vinegar, sugar, and spices have been skimmed, and while boiling, pour over the peaches. Do this for nine consecutive days, pouring off the liquid every morning, and boiling again and scalding the peaches. Tie and put in a cool place.

SWEET PICKLE.—Select fine cantaloupe or citron melons, ripe, but firm, pare and seed them, and slice or quarter them. Weigh the fruit, and to five pounds of melon allow two and a half pounds of white sugar and one quart of vinegar. The vinegar and sugar must be heated, well skimmed, and poured boiling over the fruit six times. In the last boiling of the syrup add the spices—stick cinnamon, white ginger, and a few cloves—and when the syrup boils put in the citron and let it boil for ten minutes, then put it in the jars, skim the syrup clear, and pour over it.

SWEET TOMATO PICKLES.—Chop one peck of green tomatoes, four onions, and six green peppers. Strew over them one cup of salt, and let them stand all night. Next day drain off the water from them, and add to them one cup of sugar (or more, if liked), one cup of grated horseradish, one tablespoonful of cinnamon, one of cloves, and one of allspice. Cover with vinegar and cook till tender.

GREEN TOMATO PICKLE.—Slice two gallons of green tomatoes, put them into a pan with a layer of salt, and then of tomatoes, with half a dozen of onions sliced, and alternately put with the tomatoes and salt, and let them remain in salt all night. The next morning rinse and drain well. Put them into a kettle with one gallon of strong cider vinegar, half a gallon of brown sugar, four tablespoonfuls of mustard, four of ground allspice, four of ground ginger, five of cinnamon, four of cloves, four of black pepper, four of celery seed, half a dozen red or green peppers, sliced fine, two teaspoonfuls of ground mace, and four tablespoonfuls of olive oil. Let it boil three or four hours, then, if the vinegar is not as strong as it should have been, while the pickles are still warm, add a quart of cold vinegar. This pickle has been considered as good as "chow chow," and will keep for years.

Tomatoes.—Always use those which are thoroughly ripe. The small round ones are decidedly the best. Do not prick them, as most receipt books direct. Let them lie in strong brine three or four days, then put them down in layers in your jars, mixing with them small onions and pieces of horseradish, then pour on the vinegar (cold), which should be first spiced as for peppers. Let there be a spice bag to throw into every pot. Cover them carefully, and set them by in the cellar for a full month before using.

Spiced Tomatoes.—Two pounds of tomatoes, one pound of brown sugar, half a pint of good cider vinegar, one dozen cloves, and two dozen grains of allspice. Put these ingredients into a preserving kettle, and stew them over a slow fire. When they have been in sufficiently long to cook the tomatoes tolerably well take them up and place them on a dish to cool, but continue slowly boiling the syrup. When the tomatoes become cool put them back into the syrup and boil them until they are of a dark red color; then take them out again, put them on a dish to cool, and continue boiling the syrup until it is as thick as molasses. When the tomatoes and syrup are both cool put it into jars and tie paper over the mouths.

MIXED PICKLE.—To each gallon of vinegar allow quarter pound of bruised ginger, quarter pound of mustard, quarter pound of salt, two ounces of mustard seed, one and a half ounce of turmeric, one ounce of ground black pepper, quarter ounce of Cayenne, cauliflowers, onions, celery, sliced cucumbers, gherkins, French beans, nasturtiums, capsicums. Have a large jar, with a tightly fitting lid, in which put as much vinegar as is required, reserving a little to mix the various powders to a smooth paste. Put into a basin the mustard, turmeric, pepper, and Cayenne. Mix them with vinegar, and stir well until no lumps remain; add all the ingredients to the vinegar, and mix well. Keep this liquor in a warm place, and thoroughly stir every morning for a month with a wooden spoon, when it will be ready for the different vegetables to be added to it. As these come into season have them gathered on a dry day, and, after merely wiping them with a cloth to free them from moisture, put them into the pickle. The cauliflowers, it may be said, must be divided into small bunches. Put all these into the pickle raw, and at the end of the season, when there have been added as many of the vegetables as could be procured, store it away in jars, and tie over with bladder. As none of the ingredients are boiled, this pickle will not be fit to eat till twelve months have elapsed. Whilst the pickle is being made, keep a wooden spoon tied to the jar; and its contents, it may be repeated, must be stirred every morning.

Cold Catsup.—One half peck of tomatoes, one half gallon of vinegar, half a teacup of salt, half a teacup of mustard seed, ground or broken, four pods of red pepper, cut very fine, one teacup of grated horseradish, two tablespoonfuls of ground pepper, two tablespoonfuls of celery seed. After peeling and mashing up the tomatoes the whole must be well mixed, put into bottles, and corked tightly. It is soon ready for use.

Pepper Catsup.—Fifty pods of large red peppers, with the seeds. Add a pint of vinegar, and boil until the pulp will mash through a sieve. Add to the pulp a second pint of vinegar, two spoonfuls of sugar, cloves, mace, spice, onions, and salt. Put all in a kettle and boil to a proper consistency.

CHAPTER IV.

MEATS.

STEWED BEEF.—A rump of ten pounds weight will require three hours' stewing. At first, it may be slowly but partly boiled, after which it is to simmer very slowly indeed. Have a saucepan, not over large, for the meat, and, at the bottom, fix two skewers, to prevent the meat touching the pan. Pour over it one pint and a half of cold water at the sides, two or three onions—if not very large—partly in pieces, and on the top put as many carrots as you may wish, cut into good-sized dice. Before dishing the meat, you must thicken the gravy as usual with flour and a little burnt sugar, to make the gravy (of which there should be a good deal) brown.

RUMP OF BEEF.—This is one of the most juicy of all the joints of beef, but is more frequently stewed than roasted. As it is generally too large to serve whole, cut as much from the chump end as will make a handsome roast. Manage it as the sirloin. When boned, roll it into the form of a fillet of veal, and bake.

SPANISH STEAK.—Cut some onions very fine

and put into a frying pan with plenty of butter, boiling hot. When fried quite tender, push to the back of the pan. Season a tender loin of beef with pepper and salt, put it on the pan, and cook till done. Put the onions over it, and pour in the pan sufficient boiling water to make a rich gravy. Let all stew five minutes, and serve.

BEEF STEWED WITH ONIONS.—Cut some tender beef into small pieces, and season with pepper and salt; slice some onions and add to it, with water enough in the stewpan to make a gravy. Let it stew slowly till the beef is thoroughly cooked, then add some pieces of butter rolled in flour, enough to make a rich gravy. Cold beef may be cooked in the same way, but the onions must then be cooked before adding them to the meat. Add more water if it dries too fast, but let it be boiling, when poured in.

BRISKET OF BEEF STUFFED.—A piece weighing eight pounds requires about five or six hours to boil. Make a dressing of bread crumbs, pepper, salt, sweet herbs, a little mace, and one onion chopped fine and mixed with an egg. Put the dressing between the fat and the lean of the beef, and sew it up tightly; flour a cloth, pin the beef in it, as closely pressed as possible, and boil five or six hours. Remove the cloth, and press the meat until it is cold. Cut in thin slices, and eat cold. Excellent for sandwiches.

A LA MODE BEEF.—Prepare a dressing with

bread or crackers, moisten with water seasoned with butter, pepper, salt, nutmeg, cloves, and, if relished, allspice; add two eggs, and mix the whole well together. Have ready a round of beef of the proper size for the family; cut gashes in it, and fill them with the dressing. Bind it together with skewers, and put it in a bake-pan with water enough to cover the bottom of the pan, in which is dissolved a little salt. Baste it three or four times with the salted water while cooking. Let it stew gently. When nearly done, cover it with dressing reserved for the purpose. Heat the lid to the pan sufficiently hot to brown it, cover and stew until done. It can be stewed in a dripping-pan, in a stove-oven, and browned when done by holding over it, if not already browned, a heated shovel. The dressing should be poured over it half an hour before taking it from the pan.

BEEF CUTLETS.—Cut the inside of a sirloin or rump in slices half an inch thick; trim them neatly; melt a little butter in a frying-pan; season the cutlets; fry them lightly; serve with tomato sauce.

FILLET OF BEEF WITH MUSHROOMS.—Cut the fillet into slices, and pour over them some melted butter, seasoned with pepper and salt; let them stand for an hour; then put them in a frying pan over a quick fire, to brown lightly; take them out, and put in the pan flour enough to thicken and brown, mix smoothly, add some stock, and some mushrooms half stewed or parboiled; put the fillet back and cook all together till done. When ready to serve, squeeze in the juice of a lemon. The gravy should be smooth and thick.

This dish is good substituting tomatoes for mushrooms, and may be varied by using wine instead of lemon-juice.

FILLET OF BEEF.—Take the sirloin or second cut of the ribs; take out the bones with a sharp knife, skewer it round in good shape; lay the bones in a large saucepan, with two onions, one carrot and a dozen cloves; add the meat, just covered with water. Let it cook slowly two hours; dish the meat; skim all the fat from the gravy, add some flour mixed with cold water, and two spoonfuls of walnut catsup; give all one boil. Turn part of the gravy over the meat, and serve the rest in a gravy tureen.

ENGLISH BEEF PIE.—Cut cold roast beef, or beefsteak into thin slices, and put a layer in a deep pie dish; shake in a little flour, pepper and salt; chop a tomato or an onion very fine, and spread on this. Another layer of beef and seasoning, another onion, and so on, until the dish is filled. Add beef gravy, or dripping, and water sufficient to make a gravy. Mash one dozen large potatoes, with half a teacup of milk or cream, and a little butter and salt. Spread this over the beef as a crust, an inch thick. Brush with beaten egg, and bake half an hour.

BEEFSTEAK PIE.—Cover the bottom of a deep plate with paste. Cut the beef in pieces convenient for the mouth; spread them evenly over the paste; then add butter, flour, pepper, salt and water; cover with paste, press the edges firmly, and cut a gash in the centre of the pie; it is good cold or hot. If to be used cold, make a gravy by boiling a bit of the bone, seasoning it the same as the pie; heat the gravy, and serve it with the pie. Potatoes are all the vegetables needed—they should be mashed. These pies can be made from cold beefsteak left the day before, but are not quite as good.

BEEFSTEAK PUDDING.—Prepare a good suet crust, and line a cake tin with it; put in layers of raw steak, with onions, tomatoes and mushrooms, chopped fine, a seasoning of pepper, salt and Cayenne, and half a cup of cold water. Cover with crust, and bake two hours. Serve very hot.

BEEFSTEAK SMOTHERED WITH ONIONS.—Cut up six onions very fine, put them into a saucepan with two cupfuls of hot water, about two ounces of good butter, some pepper and salt; dredge in a little flour. Let it stew until the onions are quite soft; then have the steak broiled; put it into the saucepan with the onions; let it simmer about ten minutes, and send to the table very hot.

MINCED BEEF.—Take the lean of some cold roast beef. Chop it very fine, adding a small minced onion; and season it with pepper and salt. Put it into a stewpan, with some of the gravy that has been left from the day before, and let it stew for a quarter of an hour. Then put it (two-thirds full) into a deep dish. Fill up the dish with mashed potatoes, heaped high in the centre, smoothed on the surface, and browned with a salamander or a red-hot shovel.

BEEF BALLS.—Mince very finely a piece of tender beef, fat and lean; mince an onion, with some boiled parsley; add grated bread crumbs, and season with pepper, salt, grated nutmeg, and lemon peel; mix all together, and moisten with a well-beaten egg; roll into balls; flour, and fry them in boiling beef dripping. Serve with fried bread crumbs, or a thickened beef gravy.

MOCK VENISON OF CORNED BEEF.—Cut the beef in thin slices, and freshen by soaking for three or four hours in tepid water. When sufficiently fresh, lay the slices on a gridiron, and heat through quickly. Make a gravy of drawn butter; add a little pepper, and the yelk of an egg chopped fine, and pour over the meat; or butter, pepper and salt, like beefsteak. This will be found a savory dish when only salt meat can be procured, but is better with fresh beef.

HASH BALLS OF CORNED BEEF.—Prepare the hash by mincing with potatoes; make it into flat cakes; heat the griddle, and grease it with plenty of sweet butter; brown the balls first on one side, and then on the other, and serve hot.

YORKSHIRE PUDDING, WITH ROAST BEEF.—Five tablespoonfuls of flour mixed with one of salt, one pint of milk, and three well-beaten eggs. Butter a square pan, and put the batter in it; set it in the oven until it rises and is slightly crusted on top; then place it under your beef roasting before the fire, or in the oven, and baste it as you do your meat.

CORNED BEEF, BOILED.—Wash it thoroughly, and put it in a pot that will hold plenty of water. The water should boil when the beef is put in, and great care should be taken to skim it often. Half an hour for every pound of meat is sufficient time. Corn beef, to be tender and juicy, should boil very gently and long. If it is to be eaten cold, take it from the pot when boiled, and lay it in an earthen dish or pan, with a piece of board upon it, the size of the meat. Upon this put a heavy stone or couple of flat irons. It greatly improves salt meat to press it.

CORNED BEEF HASH.—The best hash is made from boiled corned beef. It should be boiled very tender, and chopped fine when entirely cold. The potatoes for hash made of corned beef are the better for being boiled in the pot liquor. When taken from the pot, remove the skins from the potatoes, and when cold chop them fine. To a cup of chopped meat allow four of chopped potatoes; **stir the potatoes gradually into the meat, until the whole is mixed.** Do this at evening, and, if warm, set the hash in a cool place. In the morning put the pan on the fire with a lump of butter as large as the bowl of a tablespoon; add a dust of pepper, and if not sufficiently salt, add a little; usually none is needed. When the butter has melted, put the hash in the pan; add four tablespoons of water, and stir the whole together. After it has become really hot, stir it from the bottom, cover a plate over it, and set the pan where it will merely stew. This is a moist hash, and preferred by some to dry or browned hash.

PICKLING BEEF.—Rub a quarter of a pound of saltpetre and a little brown sugar on the beef; the following day season it with half a pound of bay salt, one ounce of black pepper, one ounce of allspice. Let the beef lie in pickle fourteen days, turning it every day, adding a little common salt three times per week; then wash it, and put it into a glazed earthen pipkin, deep enough to cover it. Lay beef suet under it; add one pint of water, cover the top with paste and then paper, or with a plate instead of paste. Bake seven hours in an oven; pour off the liquor, but do not cut till cold. Will keep three months.

POTTED OX-TONGUE.—Broil tender and unsmoked tongue of good flavor, and the following day cut from it the quantity desired for potting, or take for this purpose the remains of one which has already been served at table. Trim off the skin and rind, weigh the meat, mince it very small, then pound it as fine as possible, with four ounces of butter to each pound of tongue, a small teaspoonful of mace, half as much of nutmeg or cloves, and a tolerably high seasoning of Cayenne. After the spices are well beaten with the meat, taste it, and add more if required. A few ounces of any well-roasted meat mixed with the tongue, will give it firmness. The breasts of turkeys, fowls, partridges, or pheasants may be used for this purpose with good effect.

Tongue Toast.—Take cold tongue that has been well boiled, mince it fine, mix it with cream, or a little milk, if there is no cream at hand; add the beaten yelk of an egg, and give it a simmer over the fire. Toast nicely some thin slices of stale bread, and having buttered them, lay them in a flat dish that has been heated before the fire; then cover each slice with the tongue mixture, which should be kept quite hot, and serve up immediately.

Tongue, after it has been boiled, cut into thick slices, and stewed in a rich, brown gravy, makes a very nice corner-dish.

Spiced Tripe.—Take fresh tripe, cut it up in pieces four or five inches square; take an earthen jar, put in a layer of tripe, then sprinkle a few cloves, allspice, and peppers (whole) over it; then another layer of tripe, then spice, and so on till the jar is full; take good vinegar, scald it, pour over it, filling the jar full; cover it up and stand it away in a cool place for a few days, until it tastes of the spice, then serve it up cold for supper or any other meal. It is an excellent relish.

POTTED BEEF.—Salt three pounds of lean beef, with half a pound of salt, and half an ounce of saltpetre. Let it stand three days. Divide it into pieces weighing a pound each, and put it in an earthen pan of just sufficient size to contain it; pour over it half a pint of water, cover it close with paste, and set it in a slow oven for four hours. When taken from the oven, pour the gravy into a basin, shred the meat fine, moisten it with the gravy poured from the meat, and pound it thoroughly in a marble mortar, with fresh butter, until it becomes a fine paste; season it with black pepper and allspice, ground cloves, or grated nutmeg; put it in pots, press it down as closely as possible, put a weight on it, and let it stand all night; next day, cover it a quarter of an inch thick with clarified butter, and tie paper over it.

BUBBLE AND SQUEAK.—Take from a round of cold, boiled beef, one pound and a half of meat cut in thin slices, two carrots which have been boiled with the meat, cold, and the hearts of two boiled greens, cold. Cut the meat into small squares, and chop the vegetables together; pepper and salt the whole, and fry in a pan with a quarter of a pound of sweet butter. When fully cooked, toss into the pan half a gill of catsup, and serve, with mashed potatoes.

BEEF CAKES, No. 1.—Pound some beef that is under-done with a little fat bacon or ham; season with pepper, salt, and a little shallot or garlic; mix them well, and make into small cakes three inches long, and half as wide and thick; fry them a light brown, and serve them in a good thick gravy.

BEEF CAKES, No. 2.—Take the best sirloin of beef, one pound; boil it until soft; boil also a beef tongue until soft. Take one pound of tongue, chop it and the sirloin very fine, with quarter of a pound of suet, and quarter of a pound of raisins. After you have made them as fine as you can, add pepper and salt to taste, also one teaspoonful of cloves, one teaspoonful of allspice, one onion chopped fine, one tablespoonful of flour. Mix all well together, form into cakes, and fry in butter.

BEEF CROQUETTES.—Mince some dressed beef very fine; melt a piece of butter in a stewpan, add three or four onions chopped fine, and fried a light brown; add a spoonful of flour, and moisten with gravy or stock, season with pepper, salt, nutmeg and chopped parsley. When the sauce is cooked, put in the minced beef, stew ten minutes, or till the sauce is dry, form the meat into balls, dip each into beaten white of egg. Have some lard and butter hot, but not boiling or the balls will break. Put each ball gently into the frying-pan, shaking a little flour over them; roll them about gently in the pan, to brown evenly, and when a good color, drain and serve on dressed parsley.

To Roll Loin of Mutton.—Hang the mutton till tender, bone it, and lay a seasoning of pepper, allspice, mace, nutmeg, and a few cloves, all in fine powder over it. Next day prepare a stuffing; beat the meat, and cover it with the stuffing; roll it up tight and tie it. Half bake it in a slow oven; let it grow cold; take off the fat, and put the gravy into a stewpan; flour the meat, and put it in likewise; stew it till almost ready; and add a glass of port-wine, some catsup, and a little lemon pickle half an hour before serving; serve it in the gravy, with jelly sauce.

Panned Mutton.—Remove all the fat from mutton cutlets, and trim neatly. Set them in melted butter, luke-warm, with pepper and salt. Dip each into beaten yelk of egg, and afterwards in grated bread crumbs. Repeat the dipping till the cutlets are well covered with crumbs. Broil on a gridiron over a clear fire for ten minutes. Serve plain or with sauce, as preferred.

Mutton Cutlets.—The most economical way

of proceeding is to purchase a piece of the best end of a neck of mutton and divide and trim your chops at home. Every particle of gristle and almost all the fat should be removed from each cutlet, the bone or rib should not be more than two inches long, from the cutlet itself or "nut," and it should be scraped quite clean. Saw the bone at the end, as it looks badly chopped. Cut the meat about one-third of an inch thick, prepare neatly, and beat gently with the flat side of a meat chopper; you may cook them plain or crumbed.

The plain process consists in broiling them on the gridiron over or in front of a clear fire. The fire should be a brisk one, and the cutlets should be turned quickly and frequently while cooking. They should be thoroughly cooked, but not kept cooking till hard and tough.

Plain cutlets may also be fried in butter and lard. Crumbed cutlets require more trouble to prepare. The streak of meat with the fat and gristle which adheres to the bone need not be cut off, but detatched from the bone, and turned up on the side of the "nut." Smear the cutlet thickly with well beaten egg, and dip several times in bread crumbs till thickly covered. Fry in butter and lard.

Cutlets may be served in a plain, clear gravy, or with tomato or mushroom sauce.

Mutton cutlets may also be stewed in a variety of ways, of which the following may be taken as the common form: Put some butter in a stewpan, and place your cutlets in this, turning them over and over until they are well *saisies* (seized) by the butter; then add a small quantity of well-flavored stock or gravy, and let them simmer in this till done, when they are served with the gravy, which you thicken, if necessary, with a little flour, over them. Vegetables may be cooked with the cutlets, and served with them, or a garniture of vegetables, cooked separately, can be put round the dish.

MUTTON CUTLETS A LA BENE.—Take six chops from the best end of a neck of mutton, and after sawing off the ends, braise them until they are tender. Put them aside to cool. Make a thick, rich onion sauce, season it well, and run it through a sieve; then take the braised chops, when they are perfectly cold, and cut them into cutlets, and trim them into a proper shape. Dip each cutlet into the onion sauce, then into bread crumbs, and afterwards into egg and bread crumbs. Fry them in boiling lard, a light brown color; drain them well, and serve with or without tomato sauce.

SHOULDER OF MUTTON.—A shoulder of mutton weighing six pounds requires one hour and thirty minutes to roast; if stuffed, fifteen minutes longer. Before cooking, take out all the bone and fill the space with a dressing of bread crumbs, pepper, salt, parsley, sweet marjoram, one egg and a small piece of butter, all well mixed.

MUTTON PREPARED LIKE VENISON.—Choose a large leg of mutton, and let it hang in a cool place ten days. Prepare a good forcemeat, and make a deep slit near the bone at the fillet end. Put in the forcemeat and sew over it a piece of linen to keep it in. Roast for two hours and thirty minutes. Make a gravy with the shank bone, one pound of soup beef, one onion, a few whole peppers, salt, and a pint and a half of water. Let this simmer for two hours. Add a dessertspoonful of flour to thicken it; a little burnt sugar, if not dark enough in color, and more seasoning if necessary. When the meat is done, remove the linen cloth, strain part of the gravy over it, and serve. The remainder of the gravy should be served in a gravy-boat. Currant jelly should always be served with this dish.

SADDLE OF MUTTON, A LA PORTUGUESE.—To make this dish to look well, the saddle should be so carved as to have the sides left. When cold, the fillet, or undercut, and surplus meat is to be removed and cut small, and placed in a stewpan, with a little thickened gravy, mushroom catsup, pepper and salt. It should not be allowed to boil, but when hot should be placed on the saddle in the space from which the meat has been cut, and sprinkled over with bread crumbs. It must be levelled to the sides, and placed in the oven. If the bread crumbs are not brown enough, a salamander must be made hot, and placed over it; it should be served very hot with currant jelly.

COLD MUTTON.

There are not many people who object to eating cold beef, but there seems to be a popular prejudice against cold mutton. As far as looks go, when two or three persons have dined off a leg of mutton the day before, no amount of parsley, be it ever so curly and fresh, can make it look nice; but as a matter of taste cold meat, be it beef or mutton, is by no means devoid of merit at certain seasons, and with a proper accompaniment of salads, pickles, and sauces. Only to be perfect a cold joint should not be touched until it is cold; the joint of yesterday's dinner is quite a different affair. It is not everybody who can indulge, however, in such niceties of taste. Given a leg of mutton it must be used, and made to go as far as possible to furnish the second and even the third day's dinner.

If you wish to be very economical with a leg of mutton you should carve it pretty much as you do a ham, then the next day put it for twenty minutes into a vessel containing boiling water, take it out and sprinkle some salt and a little flour over it, and put it to roast for twenty minutes before a good fire, basting frequently with some dripping, melted for the purpose. The result will be a very fair second edition of roast leg of mutton. Some, however, may object to carving mutton after the fashion of ham, and in that case a hash or a mince are the only ways of turning cold mutton to account; but there are many ways of hashing mutton and other meats, and of mincing them, too.

The great desideratum of a second-hand dish, so to speak, is that it should not taste as such. Nothing is more abominable than the bad taste which is so prominent in the attempts at warming up cold meat, which your plain cook is pleased to call minced veal, hashed mutton, etc. The only means to avoid that taste is to remove carefully from the cold meat you are going to use every part that has seen the fire, as well as gristle and fat. Let every slice be carefully trimmed, and let them all be as near as possible similar in size and shape; then make your hash, and, even if you are not an expert at combining sauces and spices, at any rate it will not have a warmed-up taste. The following are various formulas for warming up mutton and other meats:

Cut an onion in slices and fry it in butter till it assumes a deep brown color, then put in a tablespoonful of floor, and when it is well amalgamated with the butter add a little less than half a pint of stock broth, or even water previously warmed. Stir a few minutes on the fire, and then proceed to flavor your sauce with walnut or mushroom catsup, tomato sauce, spices, and pepper and salt, in such proportions as taste may suggest and practice will teach. A little burnt onion browning may be put in if the sauce is not of a sufficiently deep color. When the flavoring is completed, strain the sauce through a fine colander into a saucepan and place in it your slices of meat. Keep the saucepan at a moderate heat till it is time to serve, and send up your hash with a garland of bread sippets fried in butter round it. The longer the meat lies in the sauce the better will your dish be.

Proceed as in the above receipt as far as the butter, flour, and onions are concerned; then add to your sauce a moderate allowance of mustard; then add the stock and a wineglassful of white or red wine. Season with catsup, spices, pepper, and salt. Strain and put in the meat, serving with pickles or not, according to taste. Beef and pork are best warmed up in this way.

A homely mode of warming cold meat is in this wise: Fry some slices of onion in butter, and when they begin to take color put in your slices of meat, pepper, salt, and a sprinkling of flour. Keep on frying till the onions are thoroughly done and the meat warmed, then add a small quantity of stock, broth, or water, with a small quantity of vinegar, and serve.

Minced parsley may be added to any of the above dishes with advantage.

If the state of the joint you have to work upon will allow it, cut your slices the thickness of your finger, trim them all nicely, as near as possible the same shape, then dip them in egg, and cover them with a mixture of bread crumbs, powdered, sweet herbs, pepper, and salt in due proportion. Let them rest a couple of hours, and egg and bread crumb them again; then fry them in plenty of lard till they are a nice color. Serve either alone with fried parsley as an ornament, or with any sauce, such as tomato, etc., which taste may suggest. Cold veal or pork treated in this way makes a very toothsome dish.

Of course it is necessary to carry out these warmings-up, that the cold joint should not have been too heavily punished when it first appeared on the dinner table. When a joint has not enough left upon it to cut nice slices, then mincing is the best way to utilize it.

MINCED MUTTON.—This is a very useful preparation of "cold mutton," and will be found an excellent mode. Cut slices off a cold roasted leg of mutton and mince it very fine; brown some flour in butter, and moisten it with some gravy; add salt and pepper to taste, and let it simmer about ten or fifteen minutes to take off the raw taste of the flour; add another lot of butter and some parsley chopped fine, then add the minced meat, and let it simmer slowly, but not to boil, or the meat will be hard.

BAKED MINCED MUTTON.—The remains of any joint of cold roast mutton, one or two onions, one bunch of savory herbs, pepper and salt to taste, two blades of pounded mace or nutmeg, one teacupful of gravy, mashed potatoes. Mince an onion rather fine, and fry it a light-brown color; add the herbs and mutton, both of which should be also finely minced and well mixed; season with pepper and salt, and a little pounded mace or nutmeg, and moisten with the above proportion of gravy. Put a layer of mashed potatoes at the bottom of a dish, then the mutton, and then another layer of potatoes, and bake for about half an hour. If there should be a large quantity of meat, use two onions instead of one.

Browned Minced Mutton.—Cut some lean meat from a roast leg of mutton, chop it fine, season it with pepper and salt, chopped parsley, and a little onion; mix all together with a quarter of a pound of grated bread, moisten with a tablespoonful of vinegar and a cup of good gravy; when put into the dish lay an ounce of butter in small bits on the top, grate bread over it, and add a little more butter; brown before the fire.

HOW TO COOK LAMB.

To Roast Lamb.—The hind quarter of lamb usually weighs from seven to ten pounds; this size will take about two hours to roast it. Have a brisk fire. It must be very frequently basted while roasting, and sprinkled with a little salt, and dredged all over with flour, about half an hour before it is done.

Fore Quarter of Lamb.—A fore quarter of a lamb is cooked the same way, but takes rather less time, if the same weight, than the hind quarter;

because it is a thinner joint; one of nine pounds ought to be allowed two hours.

LEG OF LAMB.—A leg of lamb of four pounds' weight will take about an hour and a quarter; if five pounds, nearly one hour and a half; a shoulder of four pounds will be roasted in an hour, or a very few minutes over.

RIBS OF LAMB.—Ribs of lamb are thin, and require great care to do gently at first, and brisker as it is finishing; sprinkle it with a little salt, and dredge it slightly with flour, about twenty minutes before it is done. It will take an hour or longer, according to thickness.

GARNISH AND VEGETABLES FOR ROAST LAMB.—All joints of roast lamb may be garnished with double parsley, and served up with either asparagus and new potatoes, spring spinach and new potatoes, green peas and new potatoes, or with cauliflowers or French beans and potatoes; and never forget to send up mint sauce. The following will be found an excellent receipt for mint sauce: With three heaped tablespoonfuls of finely-chopped young mint, mix two of pounded and sifted sugar, and six of the best vinegar; stir it until the sugar is dissolved.

TO STEW A BREAST OF LAMB.—Cut it into pieces, season them with pepper and salt, and stew them in weak gravy; when tender, thicken the sauce, and add a glass of white wine. Cucumbers, sliced and stewed in gravy, may be served with the lamb, the same being poured over it. Or, the lamb may be served in a dish of stewed mushrooms.

To Boil a Neck or Breast of Lamb.—These are small, delicate joints, and therefore suited only for a very small family. The neck must be washed in warm water, and all the blood carefully cleaned away. Either of these joints should be put into cold water, well skimmed, and very gently boiled till done. Half an hour will be about sufficient for either of them, reckoning from the time they come to a boil.

Lamb Chops.—Take a loin of lamb, cut chops from it half an inch thick, retaining the kidney in its place; dip them into egg and bread crumbs, fry and serve with fried parsley. When chops are made from a breast of lamb, the red bone at the edge of the breast should be cut off, and the breast parboiled in water or broth, with a sliced carrot and two or three onions, before it is divided into cutlets, which is done by cutting between every second or third bone, and preparing them, in every respect, as the last. If *house-lamb steaks* are to be done *white*—stew them in milk and water till very tender, with a bit of lemon-peel, a little salt, some pepper and mace. Have ready some veal gravy, and put the steaks into it; mix some mushroom-powder, a cup of cream, and the least bit of flour; shake the steaks in this liquor, stir it, and let it get quite hot, but not boil. Just before you take it up, put in a few white mushrooms.

LAMB CUTLETS AND SPINACH.—Eight cutlets, egg and bread crumbs, salt and pepper to taste, a little clarified butter. Take the cutlets from a neck of lamb, and shape them by cutting off the thick part of the chine-bone. Trim off most of the fat and all the skin, and scrape the top part of the bones quite clean. Brush the cutlets over with egg, sprinkle them with bread crumbs, and season with pepper and salt. Now dip them into clarified butter, sprinkle over a few more bread crumbs, and fry them over a sharp fire, turning them when required. Lay them before the fire to drain, and arrange them on a dish with spinach in the centre, which should be previously well boiled, drained, chopped, and seasoned. Peas, asparagus, or beans may be substituted for the spinach.

LOIN, NECK, AND BREAST OF LAMB.—A loin of lamb will be roasted in about an hour and a quarter; a neck in an hour; and a breast in three-quarters of an hour. Do not forget to salt and flour these joints about twenty minutes before they are done.

BROILED LAMB STEAK.—Broil slowly until quite done, then make a gravy with fresh butter melted by the steak, add a dust of pepper, and a little salt dissolved in a tablespoonful of water; serve with peas, potatoes, and salads.

Leg of Lamb to Boil.—It must be put into boiling water, then the saucepan (or deep fish-kettle with a drainer is best) drawn back, and the water allowed to simmer gently, reckoning eighteen minutes to each pound; if it boils fast, the meat will be hard and the skin broken. It should be lifted out of the water with the drainer, and no fork be stuck into it; if the scum has settled upon it, wash it off with some of the liquor before sending to table. Parsley and butter are served with this, or delicate caper sauce and young carrots.

Leg of Lamb to Roast.—All lamb should be very well cooked, and not put too near the fire at first; from eighteen to twenty minutes to the pound before a clear but not fierce heat. It may be served with spinach, peas, or asparagus.

Boned Quarter of Lamb.—Bone a quarter of lamb, taking care not to injure the skin. Make a seasoning in the following manner: Cut three onions and fry them in lard; when these are nearly done, add some parsley, chopped very fine, spice, two spoonfuls of cream, and four eggs. Simmer this mixture over the fire until quite thick, then stuff it into the meat in the spaces left by the bones, roll the meat up and roast it, basting with bread crumbs and butter. Serve with a rich sauce.

Fricassee of Lamb.—Cut the best part of a breast of lamb into square pieces of two inches each; wash, dry, and flour them. Boil together four ounces of butter, one of fat bacon, some parsley or sweet marjoram for ten minutes, and then add the meat; squeeze in the juice of half a lemon; chop an onion with pepper and salt and throw in. Simmer all for two hours; add the yelks of two eggs well beaten, shake over the fire two minutes, and serve.

SAVORY LAMB PIE.—Cut the meat into pieces, and season it with finely-beaten pepper, salt, mace, cloves, and nutmeg. Make a good puff-paste, and put the meat into it, adding some lambs' sweetbreads, seasoned in the same manner. Put in some oysters and forcemeat balls, some yelk of egg, and tops of asparagus, boiled green. Put butter all over the pie, and put on the covering paste, and let it bake for an hour and a half in a quick oven. Mix a pint of gravy, the oyster liquor, a gill of wine, and a little nutmeg, with the yelks of two or three eggs well beaten, and stir it in the same direction all the time. When it boils, take the cover off the pie, pour the mixture into it. Cover again and serve.

STEWED BREAST OF LAMB, WITH PEAS OR CUCUMBERS.—First roast the lamb to a nice brown color. Mix a tablespoonful of flour smoothly in cold water, burn a teaspoonful of sugar in an iron spoon, pour boiling water over it into the flour, mix all smoothly; strain it; add as much boiling water as will barely cover the meat, putting it into a stewpan with the bones upwards, add a blade of mace, and a little salt; let it stew for two hours, till the meat is very tender and the bones will slip; while the meat is cooking boil some peas, or, in their place, peel some small cucumbers, put them into boiling water, with a little salt and a small piece of butter, and boil for twenty minutes; drain them. When the meat is ready, thicken the gravy if necessary; add a little butter and a tablespoonful of catsup, place the meat on a dish, bones downward, strain the gravy over it. Drain the peas, or cut the cucumbers across in three pieces and place round the meat.

STEWED LEG OF LAMB.—Dredge the joint with flour, and put it in a stewpan with half a pound of butter, some parsley, pepper, and salt. Stew gently for half an hour. Choose some small, sound heads of lettuce and cut in small pieces; put them in a stewpan with a little sorrel, and stew with the mutton for another hour. Dish the joint, and add to the liquor in the stewpan half a pint of water. Boil up, pour over the meat, and serve.

LAMB SWEET-BREADS.—Blanch them, and put them into cold water. Soak five minutes; put them into a stewpan with a ladleful of broth, some pepper and salt, a small bunch of button onions, and a blade of mace; stir in a piece of butter braided in flour, and stew for half an hour. Have ready the yelks of three eggs well beaten in cream, with a little minced parsley and grated nutmeg. Add some boiled asparagus tops. After the cream is in, simmer, but do not boil, as it would curdle. French beans or peas, if very tender, are an improvement.

LARDED LAMB.—Lard the upper side of a fore quarter of lamb with lean bacon, and cover the lower side thickly with grated bread. Cover the whole with paper to prevent burning, and roast it. Take it from the fire when nearly done, and cover the lower side once more with grated bread; season it with salt, pepper, and finely-chopped parsley; put it before a brisk, clear fire to brown. Pour over all a little cider vinegar, and serve.

CHOPS, WITH CUCUMBERS.—Fry the chops of a light brown, and stew them for half an hour in good gravy; thicken and flavor the gravy, and add to it some cucumbers, thickly sliced and previously stewed. Boil them up together, and put the cucumbers on the dish, and the chops on them.

TO DRESS KIDNEYS.—Cut them through the centre; take out the core; pull the kernels apart; put them into the saucepan without any water, and set them on the fire where they may get hot, not boil; in half an hour put the kidneys into cold water, wash them clean, and put them back into the saucepan, with just enough water to cover them; boil them one hour, then take them up; clean off the fat and skin; put into the frying-pan some butter, pepper and salt; dredge in a little flour, half a pint of hot water, and the kidneys; let them simmer twenty minutes; stir them often; do not let them fry, because it hardens them. This is a very nice dish for breakfast.

Fried Sheep Kidneys.—Cut the kidneys open without quite dividing them, remove the skin, and put a small piece of butter in the frying-pan. When the butter is melted, lay in the kidneys the flat side downwards, and fry them for seven or eight minutes, turning them when they are half done. Serve on a piece of dry toast, season with pepper and salt, and put a small piece of butter in each kidney; pour the gravy from the pan over them, and serve very hot.

Mutton Kidneys Broiled.—Skin and split without parting asunder; skewer them through the outer edge and keep them flat; lay the opened sides first to the fire, which should be clear and brisk; in ten minutes turn them; sprinkle with salt and Cayenne, and when done, which will be in three minutes afterwards, take them from the fire, put a piece of butter inside them, squeeze some lemon-juice over them, and serve as hot as possible.

Kidney Omelette.—Remove all the fat and skin from six kidneys. Cut into very fine pieces, season with salt and pepper, and fry quickly in butter. Beat together two dozen eggs with a wine-glass of wine. Heat quarter of a pound of butter in a frying-pan, pour in the eggs, and just before they are set, put the kidneys in the middle. Turn over the ends of the omelette, and brown on top, before a clear fire, and serve, with thin slices of lemon on the edge of the dish.

KIDNEYS A LA BROCHETTE.—Remove the thin skin from the outside of the kidneys. Split in two, without entirely separating the halves. Lay flat with a little skewer passed through each to keep the halves apart. Powder with salt and pepper, put them on a gridiron, with the inner side of the kidneys next the fire. When one side is brown, turn them, and when the outside is done, the edges will turn up to form a cup; fill this with a little cold butter beaten with minced herbs; squeeze in a little lemon-juice, and serve.

ROAST VEAL.—Season a breast of veal with pepper and salt; skewer the sweet-bread firmly in its place, flour the meat and roast it slowly before a moderate fire for about four hours—it should be of a fine brown, but not dry; baste it with butter. When done, put the gravy in a stewpan, add a piece of butter rolled in browned flour, and if there should not be quite enough gravy, add a little more water, with pepper and salt to taste. The gravy should be brown.

SPICED VEAL.—Cut the thick portion of a loin of veal into small pieces, and cover it with hot spiced vinegar. To every half pint of vinegar put a teaspoonful of allspice, a little mace, salt and Cayenne pepper to taste. Stew till the meat is tender, adding more vinegar if it dries too fast.

CURRY OF VEAL.—Cut part of a breast of veal in moderate sized pieces; put it in a stewpan with an onion and a shalot sliced fine, a slice of lemon, one ounce of butter, a little parsley and thyme, and a tablespoonful of curry-powder mixed with the same quantity of flour; let the whole sweat together until the meat is slightly brown; add sufficient broth or water for the sauce; let it boil gently till the veal is done; strain the sauce through a sieve, pour it over the veal quite hot, and serve with rice in a separate dish.

FRICASSEE OF VEAL.—Cut in bits lean veal, and parboil in salted water. Drain off the water, dust the veal with flour, and brown in butter; add sufficient of the broth for the gravy to the browned butter, and thicken very little with flour. Toast bread, lay the slices on the platter, lay on each slice a part of the veal, and pour the gravy over the whole. Serve with mashed potatoes.

VEAL CUTLETS WITH SWEET HERBS.—Chop all sorts of sweet herbs, mushrooms, onions, pepper and salt, with a spoonful of butter; dip the cutlets in this, and reduce the sauce to make it stick; do them over with egg and bread crumbs, and set them in the oven to bake; then add a glass of white wine to the sauce, skim it well, and when the cutlets are done lay them on a dish, and send them to table with the sauce poured over.

CALF'S HEAD.—Split the head in two parts, and remove the brains, wash the brains in three waters, and lay them for an hour in cold salted water. Wash the head clean, and soak it in tepid water, until the blood is well drawn out. Put it in cold water; when it boils remove the scum, and simmer gently, until a straw can be run through it. A head with the skin will take three hours, if large, and without the skin two. Scald the brains, by pouring over them boiling water, take them out and remove the skin or film, put them in plenty of cold water, and simmer gently fifteen minutes. Chop them slightly, stew them in sweet butter; add a teaspoon half full of lemon-juice, or not, as desired, and a little salt; when done, skin the tongue, lay it in the centre of the dish, and the brains round it. Send the head to the table very hot, with drawn butter poured over it, and more in the tureen.

VEAL CHOPS, BREADED.—Take six or seven handsomely cut chops, season them with salt and pepper, and put them into melted butter. When sufficiently soaked put them into beaten eggs, take them out, and roll each separately in bread crumbs; make the chops as round as you can with your hand, and lay them in a dish. When all are breaded, broil them slowly over a moderate fire, that the bread may not be too highly colored. Serve with clear gravy.

VEAL CUTLETS, WITH RAGOUT.—Cut some large cutlets from the fillet, beat them flat, and lard them; strew over them pepper, salt, bread crumbs, and shred parsley; then make a ragout of veal sweetbreads and mushrooms; fry the cutlets of a nice brown in melted butter; lay them in a dish, and serve the ragout very hot over them.

FILLET OF VEAL, BOILED.—Choose a small, delicate fillet for this purpose; prepare as for roasting, or stuff with an oyster forcemeat; bind round with a tape; cover it with milk and water in equal quantities, and let it boil very gently for four hours, keeping it carefully skimmed. Send it to the table with a rich white sauce, or, if stuffed with oyster forcemeat, with oyster sauce; garnish with stewed celery, and slices of bacon.

BREAST OF VEAL, WITH OYSTER SAUCE.—Rub the veal all over with salt and pepper. Cover it with buttered paper and then with coarse paste, baste frequently, to prevent the paper and paste from burning; half an hour before serving, remove the paste and paper. Beat the white of an egg, add a very little loaf sugar, and wet the veal with the egg and sugar, without leaving any lumps of the glazing, and brown it nicely. Prepare drawn butter with oysters, and serve the sauce in a tureen. This sauce can be used with roast or boiled veal, to good advantage, if oysters are plenty. Serve with mashed potatoes and celery.

Shoulder of Veal.—Cut the veal into small, square pieces, and parboil them. Put the bones and trimmings into another pot, with a very little water, and stew them slowly, to make the gravy. Put the meat into a pie-dish, (deep) and season it with salt, Cayenne, the yellow rind of a large lemon grated, and some powdered mace or nutmeg. Add pieces of butter rolled in flour, or cold dripping of roast veal. Strain the gravy over the meat. Set in a hot oven, and bake brown. When nearly done, throw in a glass of wine, and serve hot.

Hashed Calf's Head.—Calf's head, one egg, a teaspoonful of flour, a grating of nutmeg, three tablespoonfuls of milk, some slices of bacon, a dozen forcemeat balls, pepper, salt, mace, an onion, bunch of herbs, one wineglassful of port wine, eight mushrooms, pint of gravy, lard. Carefully cleanse the head of a freshly killed calf, boil it three-quarters of an hour, let it stand till cold, then slice it up into nice looking pieces. Peel the tongue and cut it into thin slices; boil the brain in a cloth, chop it fine, and beat it up with the egg, flour, milk, and nutmeg. Have ready a frying-pan of boiling lard, and fry the mixture in fritters the size of a crown piece. Flavor the gravy with the whole pepper, mace, cloves, herbs, onion, and Cayenne pepper. Let it simmer ten minutes, strain, and add the wine and mushrooms. Place the sliced head in this, and let it heat gently for ten minutes. Serve in the centre

8

of the dish with the brain fritters, bacon, forcemeat balls, round. Strew little egg balls over the whole.

COLLARED CALF'S HEAD.—Boil half a calf's head in just enough water to cover it. Let it boil for two hours. Remove it from the broth and cut all the meat from the bones. Return the bones again to the broth and let them continue to stew. Put into the broth some sage leaves; take out the brains and put the meat into a jar with some slices of ham, pepper, and salt, and the tongue. Set the jar in a good oven for two hours; let it be closely covered. Beat up the brains with two eggs and pour them in. Remove the whole to a mould, and fill it with strained broth. Dish when quite cold.

TEA PIE OF VEAL.—The scrag, breast, or neck of veal will be suitable for this dish. Cut the meat into slices about an inch thick, fry some slices of salt pork in an iron pot, flour the slices of veal, put them in the hot fat, and brown them; cover them with water, and simmer half an hour. Season with salt and pepper, and dredge with flour. Make a common paste, roll half an inch thick, and cover the meat. Cover the pot with a hot iron cover; cook gently for an hour.

VEAL POT-PIE.—Cut any piece of veal into small pieces; wash and season it with pepper and salt. Line the sides of an iron pot with common paste. Put in the veal with some pieces of paste rolled thin and cut in squares, some pieces of butter rolled in flour, and as much water as will cover all. Cover with a sheet of paste, cutting a hole in the centre, put the lid on the pot, and cook slowly for two hours. Place the soft crust on a dish, put the meat on that, and on the top lay the hard crust with the brown side up. Serve the gravy separately. To have the crust of a pot-pie brown, set the pot for a few moments over a clear fire, after the meat is out.

VEAL MINCED.—Mince the veal as finely as possible, separating the skin, gristle, and bones, with which a gravy should be made. Put a small quantity of the gravy into a stewpan, with a little lemon-peel grated, and a spoonful of milk or cream. Thicken it with a little butter and flour, mixed gradually with the gravy; season it with salt and a little lemon-juice and Cayenne pepper. Put in the minced veal and let it simmer a few minutes. Serve it up with sippets of bread, and garnish with sliced lemon.

MINCED VEAL, WITH POACHED EGGS.—Mince part of a fillet of veal extremely fine, put it into a stewpan, and pour over it a sufficient quantity of good hot sauce to make it of a tolerable thickness; then have a stewpanful of water, with a little vinegar in it, and as soon as it boils break in two eggs, and keep boiling quickly, but not so as to boil over. When they are done take them out with a cullender spoon, put them into another stewpan with clear warm water, and so on till six are done. When you want to serve, squeeze a little lemon-juice in the mince, pour it on a hot dish, take the eggs out of the water, neatly trim them, lay them on some veal, and serve.

MINCED VEAL.—Take three or four pounds of the lean only of a fillet or loin of veal, and mince it very finely, adding a slice or two of cold ham, minced also; add three or four small young onions, chopped small, a teaspoonful of sweet marjoram leaves, rubbed from the stalks, the yellow rind of a small lemon, grated, and a teaspoonful of mixed mace and nutmeg, powdered; mix all well together, and dredge it with a little flour. Put it into a stewpan, with sufficient gravy of cold roast veal to moisten it, and a large tablespoonful or more of fresh butter. Stir it well, and let it stew till thoroughly done. If the veal has been previously cooked a quarter of an hour will be sufficient. It will be much improved by adding a pint or more of small button mushrooms, cut from the stems, and then put in whole; also, by stirring in two tablespoonfuls of cream about five minutes before it is taken from the fire.

FRIED PATTIES.—Mince a little cold veal and ham, allowing one-third ham and two-thirds veal. Add an egg, boiled hard and chopped, and a seasoning of pounded mace, salt, pepper, and lemon-peel; moisten with a little gravy and cream. Make a good puff-paste, roll rather thin, and cut it into round or square pieces; put the mince between two of them, pinch the edges to keep in the gravy, and fry a light brown. They may also be baked in patty-pans. In that case they should be brushed over with the yelk of an egg before they are put in the oven. To make a variety, oysters may be substituted for the ham. Fry the patties about fifteen minutes.

VEAL FORCEMEAT.—Free a piece of lean veal from skin and sinews. To one pound of meat put one pound of suet, chopped very fine, and one pound of grated bread crumbs, two drachms of chopped parsley, one drachm each of lemon-peel, sweet herbs, and onions, half a drachm of powdered allspice. Pound all in a mortar, adding a well-beaten egg or two if too dry. Rub all well together and season with pepper and salt.

VEAL CROQUETTES.—Half a pound of veal, minced fine, quarter of a pound of stale bread crumbs. Put on in a saucepan and moisten with the liquor the veal was boiled in, and the raw yelk of two eggs mixed in with the bread crumbs; cook it until it begins to leave the sides of the pan. Two teaspoonfuls of chopped parsley, one of thyme, one of chopped onions, half a nutmeg, quarter of a teaspoonful of Cayenne pepper, quarter of mace, a saltspoonful of salt, two ounces of butter; mix the above into the bread crumbs, then add the veal after well mixing. Roll out each croquette into the shape of a pear, then dip them into the white of an egg, and sprinkle with bread crumbs, and fry in hot lard. Sauce served with them should be brown sauce with spices and wine in it.

VEAL SAUSAGES.—Chop equal quantities of lean veal and fat bacon, a handful of sage, a little salt, pepper, and a few anchovies. Beat all in a mortar, and, when used, roll and fry it, and serve with fried sippets or on stewed vegetables.

VEAL ROLLS.—Cut thin slices, and spread on them a fine seasoning of a very few crumbs, a little chopped bacon or scraped ham, and a little suet and parsley, pepper, salt, and a small piece of pounded mace. This stuffing may either fill up the roll like a sausage, or rolled with the meat. In either case tie it up very tight and stew it very slowly in gravy. Serve it when tender, after skimming it nicely.

SUPERIOR VEAL ROLLS.—Cut a few slices from a cold fillet of veal half an inch thick; rub them over with egg; lay a thin slice of fat bacon over each piece of veal; brush these with the egg, and over this spread forcemeat thinly; roll up each piece tightly, egg and bread crumb them, and fry them a rich brown. Serve with mushroom sauce or brown gravy. Fry the roll from ten to fifteen minutes.

VEAL SWEET-BREAD.—Trim a fine sweet-bread; parboil it for five minutes, and throw it into a basin of cold water. Roast it plain, or beat up the yelk of an egg, and prepare some fine bread crumbs. When the sweet-bread is cold, dry it thoroughly in a cloth; run a skewer through it; egg it with a paste-brush, powder it well with bread crumbs, and roast it. For sauce, fried bread crumbs round it, and melted butter, with a little mushroom catsup and lemon-juice, or serve them on buttered toast, garnished with egg sauce or with gravy.

SWEET-BREADS.—Scald them in salt and water, and take out the stringy parts. Then put them in cold water for a few moments. Dry them in a towel, dip in egg and crumbs, and fry brown in butter. When they are done, take them on a dish, pour into the frying-pan a large cup of sweet cream, a little pepper and salt, and a little green parsley, chopped fine. Dust in a very little flour, and when it boils up pour it over the breads, and send to the table hot.

FRIED SWEET-BREAD.—Sweet-breads should always soak half an hour in tepid water with a pinch of salt in it, to make them white. Put them afterwards in cold water, and place over the fire to boil; boil ten minutes. Cut them into slices, brush them with beaten egg, and cover with grated bread crumbs. Fry each slice till brown, in butter. Serve with rich gravy.

VEAL OLIVES.—Cut two thin steaks from a fillet of veal; beat them, and rub them over with the yelk of an egg; cut them in strips four inches long. Over every strip lay a very thin piece of fat bacon, and strew each with grated bread crumbs, a little lemon-peel, and chopped parsley, and season with salt and Cayenne. Roll each strip up and fasten with a little wooden skewer. Dip each roll into egg, grated bread, and chopped parsley. Put some clarified beef dripping into a frying-pan, let it boil; then throw in the rolls, and fry light brown. To a pint of good gravy add a dessertspoonful of lemon pickle, a dessertspoonful of walnut catsup, and a teaspoonful of browning, Cayenne pepper and salt to taste, and thicken with butter rolled in flour. Place the fried olives on a dish, strain the gravy over them hot; garnish with lemon pickle and forced meat balls, and strew over all pickled mushrooms to flavor.

ROAST LEG OF PORK.—Cut a slit near the knuckle, and fill the space with sage and onion, chopped fine, and seasoned with pepper and salt, with or without bread crumbs. Rub sweet oil on the skin, to prevent it blistering and make the crackling crisp; and the outer rind may be scored with lines, about half an inch apart. If the leg weigh seven or eight pounds, it will require from two and a half to three hours' roasting before a strong fire. Serve with apple sauce and potatoes; which are likewise eaten with all joints of roasted pork.

If the stuffing be liked mild, scald the onions before chopping them. If pork is not stuffed, you may serve it up with sage and onion sauce, as well as apple sauce, which should always accompany roast pork, whether it is stuffed or not; and also with mustard. Roast leg of pork must always be served up with plenty of nicely boiled potatoes.

FRESH PORK POT-PIE.—Boil a spare-rib, after removing all the fat, and cracking the bones, until tender; remove the scum as it rises, and when tender, season with salt and pepper; half an hour before time for serving the dinner, thicken the gravy with a little flour, have ready another kettle into which remove all the bones and most of the gravy, leaving only sufficient to cover the pot half an inch above the rim that rests on the stove; put in the crust; cover tight, and boil steadily twenty-five minutes. To prepare the crust, work into light dough a small bit of butter, roll it out thin, cut it in small square cakes, and lay them on the moulding-board until very light; if made with brewers' yeast, the butter should be melted in the wetting of the crust, and rolled out before rising, as the first effervescence of brewers' yeast is the strongest; work the dough well before making up the cakes.

PORK CHOPS.—Cut the chops about half an inch thick; trim them neatly, (few cooks have any idea how much credit they get by this;) put a frying-pan on the fire, with a bit of butter; as soon as it is hot, put in your chops, turning them often till brown all over; they will be done enough in about fifteen minutes; take one upon a plate and try it; if done, season it with a little finely-minced onion, powdered sage, and pepper and salt. A little powdered sage, etc., strewed over them, will give them a nice relish.

PORK STEAK, BROILED.—The tenderloin is the best for steak, but any lean white meat is good. Broil slowly, after splitting it so as to allow it to cook through without drying or burning. When ready to turn over, dip the cooked side in a nice gravy of butter, pepper, and salt, which should be prepared on a plate, and kept hot without boiling. It must be well done. It requires slow broiling. It will take at least twenty minutes to broil a pork steak.

PORK CUTLETS.—Cut slices an inch thick from a delicate loin of pork, trim them neatly; take off a part of the fat, or if the fat is not liked, remove the whole of it. Dredge a little pepper and salt on the cutlets, and broil them over a clear fire about twenty minutes. They may be dipped in beaten egg and afterwards in grated bread crumbs flavored with minced sage, and then broil. If fried, they should be well seasoned with pepper and salt, and dredged with flour before being put in the fat. The best fat is fried from bacon or salt pork.

PORK AND APPLE FRITTERS.—Prepare a light batter, freshen or use cold boiled or baked pork; cut it fine enough for hash, and fry it a little to extract some of the fat for frying the fritters. Peel sour apples, and cut or chop them not quite as fine as the pork; mix first the pork and then the apples in the batter, and fry them brown. Potatoes, parsnips, salsify, or any vegetable desired, can be used in the same manner.

ENGLISH RAISED PORK PIE.—Put into a stewpan six ounces of lard, with a teacupful of cold water; let it stand by the fire till boiling, then put to it one pound of flour. Mix it well with a spoon till cool enough to raise. When you have raised your pies, let them stand for half an hour before you put in your meat; put on your cover and ornament to your fancy. To prepare the meat, cut up the pork to about the size of dice, add pepper and salt to your taste (but take care that the pepper be equally distributed), add one tablespoonful of water to each pound of meat. One pound of flour will bake three good-sized pies. They require three hours' baking in a very moderate oven.

FRESH PORK PIE.—Boil lean, fresh pork, and make the paste as for beefsteak pie; add to the pie, after putting in the meat, two potatoes cut fine, which have been before boiled; season with pepper, salt, and a dust of summer savory. If there is not fat enough in the pork, add butter; thicken the gravy with a little flour. The pie should contain as much gravy as possible. It is good cold or hot.

SCRAMBLED PORK.—Freshen nice salt pork, cut it in mouthfuls, and partly fry it. Just before it is done break into the pan with the pork from six to twelve eggs, break and mix the yelks with the whites, and stir them quickly with the pork. If the pork is fried brown before the egg is added, there may be too much fat for the egg; if so, put it in a gravy-boat if needed for the table, or save it for shortening. Baked potatoes are excellent with salt meats that have a gravy of their own.

To Cure Hams.—To each green ham of eighteen pounds, one dessertspoonful of saltpetre; quarter of a pound of brown sugar rubbed on the fleshy side of the ham, and round the hock. Cover the fleshy part with fine salt half an inch thick, and pack away in tubs; let them remain from three to six weeks, according to size. Before smoking, rub off any salt that may remain on the ham, and cover well with ground black pepper, especially on the bone and hock. Hang up to drain for two days; smoke with green wood for eight days, or until the rind is a light chestnut color. The pepper is a certain preventive of the fly.

Baked Ham.—Soak for an hour in water, and wipe very dry; cover with a thin batter, and put it in a deep dish, with a grate under it, to keep it up from the gravy. When fully done, take off the skin and batter. Cool and garnish as boiled ham; serve with wine sauce.

Ham Pie.—Make a crust the same as for soda biscuit; line your dish; then put in a layer of potatoes sliced thin, pepper, salt, and a little butter;

then a layer of lean ham; add considerable water, and you will have an excellent pie.

HAM OMELETTE.—Two eggs, four ounces of butter, half a saltspoonful of pepper, two tablespoonfuls of minced ham. Mince the ham very finely, without any fat, and fry it for two minutes in a little butter; then make the batter for the omelette, stir in the ham, and proceed as in the case of a plain omelette. Do not add any salt to the batter, as the ham is usually sufficiently salt to impart a flavor to the omelette. Good lean bacon, or tongue, answers equally well for this dish; but they must also be slightly cooked previously to mixing them with the batter. Serve very hot and quickly, without gravy.

HAM TOAST.—Grate a sufficiency of the lean of cold ham. Mix some beaten yelk of egg with a little cream, and thicken it with the grated ham. Then put the mixture into a saucepan over the fire, and let it simmer awhile. Have ready some slices of bread nicely toasted (all the crust being pared off) and well buttered. Spread it over thickly with the ham mixture, and send it to table warm.

OMELETTE OF HAM, TONGUE, OR SAUSAGE.—There are three methods of making a ham or tongue omelette: first, by simply cutting the meat into small dice, tossing it in butter, and pouring the well beaten and seasoned eggs upon it in the pan, and letting them remain until set, when serve; or pound the meat to a paste in a mortar, and beat it up with the eggs, and fry in the usual manner. The third method is to beat the eggs and fry them, then lay upon them the meat (which has been previously tossed in butter), fold in the ends of the omelette, and serve as hot as possible.

SAUSAGES, No. 1.—The proper seasoning is salt, pepper, sage, summer-savory, or thyme; they should be one-third fat, the remainder lean, finely chopped, and the seasonings well mixed, and proportioned so that one herb may not predominate over the others. If skins are used, they cannot be prepared with too much care; but they are about as well made into cakes; spread the cakes on a clean whitewood board, and keep them in a dry cool place; fry them long and gently.

SAUSAGES No. 2 are best when quite fresh made. Put a bit of butter or dripping into a clean frying-pan; as soon as it is melted (before it gets hot) put in the sausages, and shake the pan for a minute, and keep turning them (be careful not to break or prick them in so doing); fry them over a very slow fire till they are nicely browned on all sides; when they are done, lay them on a hair sieve, placed before the fire for a couple of minutes to drain the fat from them. The secret of frying sausages is, to let them get hot very gradually; they then will not burst, if they are not stale. The common practice to prevent their bursting is to prick them with a fork; but this lets the gravy out.

MEATS. 125

Sausage Dumplings.—Make one pound of flour and two ounces of dripping, or chopped suet, into a firm paste, by adding just enough water to enable you to knead the whole together. Divide this paste into twelve equal parts, roll each of these out sufficiently large to be able to fold up one of the beef sausages in it, wet the edge of the paste to fasten the sausage securely in it, and, as you finish off each sausage dumpling, drop it gently into a large enough saucepan, containing plenty of *boiling* water, and when the whole are finished, allow them to boil gently by the side of the fire for one hour, and then take up the dumplings with a spoon free from water, on to a dish, and eat them while they are hot.

Sausage Cakes.—Chop a pound of good pork fine; add half a teaspoonful of pepper, half a spoonful of cloves, half a spoonful of coriander seed, and four tablespoonfuls of cold water. Mix all well together, form them into small cakes, and fry in a hot pan.

Scrapple.—Take eight pounds of scrap pork, that will not do for sausage, boil it in four gallons of water; when tender, chop it fine, strain the liquor and pour it back into the pot; put in the meat, season it with sage, summer savory, salt and pepper to taste, stir in a quart of corn meal; after simmering a few minutes, thicken it with buckwheat flour very thick; it requires very little cooking after it is thickened, but must be stirred constantly.

To Prepare Fowls for Cooking.—Professor Blot, in his lectures on cooking, gives the following directions for preparing fowls: Never wash meat or fowls. Wipe them dry if you choose, and if there is anything unacceptable it can be sliced off thinly. In cooking a chicken whole, no washing is to be done, except the gall-bladder be broken, when it is best to cut the chicken up and wash it thoroughly. Again, in cleansing chickens, never cut the breast; make a slit down the back of the neck, and take out the crop that way. Then cut the neck-bone close, and after the bird is stuffed the skin of the neck can be turned up over the back, sewed down, and the crop will look full and round. Further, the breast-bone should be struck smartly with the back of a heavy knife, or with a rolling-pin, to break it. This will make the chicken lie rounder and fuller after it is stuffed. The legs and wings should also be fastened with thread close to the side, running a long needle through the body for that purpose. A good stuffing for baked or roast chicken may be made by chopping an onion fine, and stirring it with two ounces of butter in a saucepan on the fire. It is taken off a moment, and bread, which has been soaked in water and the water squeezed out, is added, with salt, pepper, a little nutmeg, and some parsley, chopped fine. Then one yelk of an egg, mixed in thoroughly on the fire for half a minute. This stuffing is then inserted in the chicken.

It is important in choosing poultry to ascertain, if possible, its age. A young fowl has smooth legs and combs. When old they are rough, and have long hairs on the breast. They should be plump-breasted, with fat backs, and have white or light yellow legs.

Fowl Stewed with Onions.—Wash it clean, dry and truss it as for boiling; put a little pepper and salt into it, rub it with butter; butter a saucepan; put the fowl in the pan with a pint of veal stock, or water, seasoned with pepper and salt. Turn it while stewing, and when quite tender add a dozen small onions, split. Stew all together for half an hour. A young fowl will take one hour, an old one three hours to stew.

Steamed Fowls.—Fowls are better steamed than boiled, especially when there is no veal stock on hand to boil them in. When steamed, the juices, should be saved by placing a pan under the strainer to catch all the drips. Drawn butter, plain or seasoned with parsley or celery, is the most common sauce used for boiled fowls. Liver sauce is good; but when oysters can be had, oyster sauce is to be preferred above all others.

Fowl Cutlets.—One fowl, one egg, pinch of pepper and salt, a tablespoonful of gravy. Cut up a fowl, and bone it, form the legs, wings, breast, and merry-thought into six cutlets, flattening and giving them a good shape; take the meat from the remainder of the fowl, and the liver, pound it in a mortar with pepper, salt, and a spoonful of gravy; brush the cutlet over with an egg, spread the forcemeat over them, egg again, and cover with fried bread crumbs, and fry them a light brown color; serve with lemon rind and gravy in a separate dish.

CHOICE FOWL PUDDING.—Take a cold fowl and mince it, cutting it into small square pieces. Make a white sauce with a small piece of butter, some flour, and cream or milk. Put the mince into the white sauce, and set it aside to cool. When quite cold, make up into balls. Cover them with egg and bread crumbs; do this twice, to prevent them from bursting. At dinner-time, fry them in hot lard or dripping; serve them up on a serviette; garnish with parsley.

TO BONE FOWLS FOR FRICASSEES, CURRIES, AND PIES.—First carve them entirely into joints, then remove the bones, beginning with the legs and wings, at the head of the largest bone; hold this with the fingers, and work the knife carefully all round it. The remainder of the birds is too easily done to require any instructions.

TO ROAST A FOWL.—Having nicely dressed the fowl, have ready a dressing seasoned with pepper, salt, and summer savory; fill the body of the bird, sew up the opening, truss it nicely, oil it with butter, and put it before a moderately hot but bright fire; heat the skin evenly as soon as possible, cover it with paper if there is the least danger of its browning too soon, roast pretty fast, without scorching, the first half hour, and baste the fowl all over every five minutes; after this let it roast steadily, but rather slowly, three-quarters of an hour, when, if young and tender, it will be done quite through. Stick a fork through the breast and thighs, and if the fluid which follows the fork is entirely free from blood, it is done. If not browned, replenish the fire, wet the fowl over with very little yelk of egg, dust it lightly with flour, and let it brown evenly all over. Remove the skewers and strings before sending it to the table.

To Bake a Fowl.—Prepare a fowl as for roasting; have the oven of good but not a raging heat. Lay the fowl on skewers; baste every five minutes, and manage the same as the roast. If young, it will bake in one hour.

To Roast a Turkey.—Proceed as directed in roast fowls; allow from two and a half to three hours for a good-sized tender turkey. The dressings of fowls can be varied by using oysters, etc.

To Bake a Turkey.—Follow the directions for baking fowls, and allow from two to two and a half hours steady baking for a common-sized young turkey; serve with a browned gravy. All roast fowls should be served with dressed vegetables, currant, grape, or cranberry jelly, and a baked pudding or pie.

STUFFING FOR A TURKEY.—Take some bread crumbs and turn on just enough hot water to soften them; put in a piece of butter, not melted, the size of a hen's egg, and a spoonful of pulverized sage, a teaspoonful of ground pepper, and a teaspoonful of salt; there may be some of the bread crumbs that need to be chopped; then mix thoroughly and stuff your turkey.

BAKED TURKEY.—Let the turkey be picked, singed, and washed and wiped dry, inside and out; joint only to the first joints in the legs, and cut some of the neck off if it is all bloody; then cut one dozen small gashes in the fleshy parts of the turkey, on the outside and in different parts of the turkey, and press one whole oyster in each gash; then close the skin and flesh over each oyster as tightly as possible; then stuff your turkey, leaving a little room for the stuffing to swell. When stuffed sew it up with a stout cord, rub over lightly with flour, sprinkle a little salt and pepper on it, put some water in your dripping pan, put in your turkey, baste it often with its own drippings; bake to a nice brown; thicken your gravy with a little flour and water. Be sure and keep the bottom of the dripping pan covered with water, or it will burn the gravy and make it bitter.

GIBLET PIE.—Wash and clean your giblets, put

them in a stewpan, season with pepper, salt, and a little butter rolled in flour, cover them with water, stew them till they are very tender. Line the sides of your pie-dish with paste, put in the giblets, and if the gravy is not quite thick enough, add a little more butter rolled in flour. Let it boil once, pour in the gravy, put on the top crust, leaving an opening in the centre of it in the form of a square; ornament this with leaves of the paste. Set the pie in the oven, and when the crust is done take it out.

To Fricassee Small Chickens.—Cut off the wings and legs of four chickens; separate the breasts from the backs; divide the backs crosswise; cut off the necks; clean the gizzards; put them with the livers and other parts of the chickens, after being thoroughly washed, into a saucepan; add salt, pepper, and a little mace; cover with water, and stew till tender. Take them up; thicken half a pint of water with two spoonfuls of flour rubbed into four ounces of butter; add a tumbler of new milk; boil all together a few minutes, then add eight spoonfuls of white wine, stirring it in carefully, so as not to curdle; put in the chickens, and shake the pan until they are sufficiently heated; then serve them up.

To Broil Chickens without Burning.—Remove occasionally from the fire and baste with a gravy prepared as follows: Simmer together one-half cup of vinegar, a piece of butter the size of an egg, and salt and pepper to the taste. Keep it hot to use.

CHICKEN POT-PIE.—Clean, singe, and joint a pair of chickens. Pare and slice eight white potatoes; wash the slices and put with the pieces of chicken into a stewpan lined with pie-crust; season with salt and pepper, dredge with flour, and cover with water. Cover with paste, making a hole in the centre; cover the kettle, and either hang it over the fire or set it in the oven. If in the oven, turn occasionally to brown evenly. Two hours' cooking is sufficient. When done, cut the upper crust into moderate-sized pieces and place them on a large dish; with a perforated ladle take up the potato and chicken, put it upon the crust; cut the lower crust and put on the top. Serve the gravy hot in a gravy tureen.

WHITE FRICASSEE.—Boil a chicken; joint it; lay it in a saucepan with a piece of butter the size of an egg, a tablespoonful of flour, a little mace or nutmeg, white pepper, and salt. Add a pint of cream, and let it boil up once. Serve hot on toast.

TO FRY COLD CHICKEN.—Cut up the chicken, and take off the skin, rub it with egg, cover it with seasoned bread crumbs and chopped parsley, and fry in butter. Serve with brown gravy, thickened with flour and butter, and seasoned with Cayenne, mushroom catsup, and lemon pickle. Or, the chicken may be seasoned, and fried in plain butter.

Chicken Baked in Rice.—Cut a chicken into joints, as for fricassee, season it well with pepper and salt, lay it in a pudding-dish lined with slices of ham or bacon, add a pint of veal gravy, and an onion finely minced; fill up the dish with boiled rice, well pressed, and piled as high as the dish will allow; cover with a paste; bake one hour, and serve.

Chicken Puffs.—Mince up together the breast of a chicken, some lean ham, half an anchovy, a little parsley, some shalot, and lemon-peel, and season these with pepper, salt, Cayenne, and beaten mace. Let this be on the fire for a few minutes, in a little good white sauce. Cut some thinly-rolled-out puff-paste into squares, putting on each some of the mince, turn the paste over, fry them in boiling lard, and serve them. These puffs are very good cold, and they form a convenient supper dish.

To Boil a Goose.—After it is well dressed, singe it thoroughly. Have ready a dressing prepared of bread crumbs, seasoned with pepper, salt and butter, with the addition of two finely-chopped onions, a little sage, and more pepper than would be used for turkey. Fill the body and close it firmly; put it in cold water, and boil it gently an hour, if tender; if not longer; serve with giblet sauce. The onion can be omitted if not relished.

TO COOK PARTRIDGES.

In making partridges ready for roasting leave the heads on, and turn them under the left wings; cut off the tops of the toes, but do not remove the legs; before a proper fire, twenty minutes' roasting will be ample for young partridges. After being shot, these birds should not be kept longer than from two days to a week. The plumage is occasionally allowed to remain upon the heads of the red partridges, in which case the heads require to be wrapped in paper.

To ROAST PARTRIDGES.—Rightly to look well there should be a leash (three birds) in the dish; pluck, singe, draw, and truss them; roast them for about twenty minutes; baste them with butter, and when the gravy begins to run from them you may safely assume that the partridges are done; place them in a dish, together with bread crumbs, fried nicely brown and arranged in small heaps. Gravy should be served in a tureen apart.

To BROIL PARTRIDGES.—Split them in half; do not wash them, but wipe their insides with a cloth; dip them into liquid butter, then roll them in bread crumbs; repeat this process; lay them inside downwards, upon a well-heated gridiron, turn them but once, and when done serve them with a piquante sauce. If you do not employ butter and bread crumbs, a little Cayenne and butter should be rubbed upon them before they are served. Cold roasted birds eat well if nicely broiled, and sent to table with a highly-seasoned sauce.

PARTRIDGE PIE.—Two braces of partridges are required to make a handsome pie; truss them as for boiling; pound in a mortar the livers of the birds, a quarter of a pound of fat bacon, and some shred parsley; lay part of this forcemeat at the bottom of a raised crust put in the partridges, add the remainder of the forcemeat and a few mushrooms; put some slices of bacon fat on the top, cover with a lid of crust, and bake it for two hours and a half. Before serving the pie remove the lid, take out the bacon, and add sufficient rich gravy and orange juice. Partridge pie may also be made in a dish in the ordinary way.

TO BOIL PARTRIDGES.—Properly prepare the birds; put them into plenty of boiling water; do them quickly for fifteen minutes; make a rich sauce by adding an ounce of butter to half a pint of good thick cream; stir it one way over the fire till it is quite hot, and pour it into the dish with the partridges.

TO STEW PARTRIDGES.—Cut up the birds, after seeing that they are properly plucked, singed, etc.; shake the following mixture over the fire until it boils; an onion, sliced and pulled into rings, a piece of butter rolled in flour, and a tablespoonful each of water, wine, and vinegar; put in the partridge;

let it simmer very gently till done; decorate the dish with small slices of toast; put into it the partridge, and pour the sauce over it.

To Fry Partridges.—Take a brace of cold partridges that have been either roasted or braised; cut them into quarters; dip them into beaten and seasoned yelk of eggs; make some butter or friture perfectly hot in a frying-pan; put into it the birds, and do them over a moderately hot fire until they are beautifully browned.

Quails Cured in Oil.—Procure a sufficient number of fine, plump quails. Pluck them, draw them, clean them thoroughly, cut them open so that they will lie flat, as for broiling, and rub them over with salt. Let them lie in the salt, turning them every morning, for three days. Let them dry; and then pack them down close in a stone jar, covering each layer of quails tightly with fresh gathered vine leaves. Fill the jar with pure salad oil, and cover it securely with bladder, so as quite to exclude the air. When they are wanted, take them out and broil them. They make a delicious dish for breakfast.

Woodcock.—Woodcocks should not be drawn, as the trail is considered a "*bonne bouche;*" truss their legs close to the body, and run an iron skewer through each thigh, close to the body, and tie them on a small bird spit; put them to roast at a clear fire; cut as many slices of bread as you have birds, toast or fry them a delicate brown, and lay them in the dripping-pan under the birds to catch the trail; baste them with butter, and froth them with flour; lay the toast on a hot dish, and the birds on the toast; pour some good beef gravy into the dish, and serve.

SNIPES differ little from woodcocks, unless in size; they are to be dressed in the same way, but require about five minutes less time to roast them.

WILD DUCKS.—For roasting a wild duck you must have a clear, brisk fire and a hot spit. It must be browned upon the outside without being sodden within. To have it well frothed and full of gravy is the nicety. Prepare the fire by stirring and raking it just before the bird is laid down, and fifteen or twenty minutes will do it in the fashionable way; but if you like it a little more done allow it a few minutes longer; if it is too much it will lose its flavor.

TO KEEP GAME.—If there be any danger of birds not keeping, pick and draw them, wash them well in water, and rub them with salt. Plunge them singly into a large saucepan of boiling water, draw them up and down by the legs to let the water pass through them. After they have been in the water for five minutes hang them up to dry in a cold place, sprinkle them with pepper and salt well inside. Before dressing them they must be again washed. By this means the most delicate birds may be preserved, with the exception of those which live by suction, as they are never drawn; but they may be kept a long time by putting lumps of charcoal, or placing a small quantity of mould in muslin bags in their insides.

VENISON STEAKS.—Cut them from the neck; season them with pepper and salt. When the gridiron has been well heated over a bed of bright coals, grease the bars and lay the steaks upon it. Broil them well, turning them once, and taking care to save as much of the gravy as possible. Serve them up with some currant jelly laid on each steak.

RABBIT PIE.—Cut the rabbit into joints. Take out the leg bones, which, with the head and breast bones well stewed, will make a good gravy. Put the joints of the rabbit into a pie-dish, with half a pound of salt pork in rashers, or a little ham or bacon, if preferred to the pork. Mix in a saucer a little flour, pepper and salt, pounded mace, and grated nutmeg. Sprinkle this mixture in, add half a pint of water, and cover with a suet, dripping, or butter crust, as you please. You may improve the pie by putting in forcemeat balls and hard-boiled eggs. Bake about an hour and a half; pour in the gravy you have made before serving.

ROMAN PIE.—Boil a rabbit; cut all the meat as thin as possible. Boil two ounces of macaroni very tender, two ounces of Parmesan or common cheese, grated, a little onion, chopped fine, pepper and salt to taste, not quite half a pint of cream. Line a mould, sprinkled with vermicelli, with a good paste. Bake an hour and serve it either with or without brown sauce. Cold chicken or cold game may be used for this pie instead of a rabbit.

POTTED FISH AND MEATS.

The preservation of potted meats is mainly due to the exclusion of the air by the vessels in which they are inclosed, and the layer of fat with which the meat is covered.

For home purposes we should always recommend butter to be employed for this purpose, and hence the first operation necessary in potting is the purification of that substance.

Butter, as ordinarily made, contains a considerable quantity of curdy matter, derived from the cream. This, after a time, turns rancid, even in spite of all the salt that may be added; and consequently the length of time that butter will keep is limited. By removing the curd, butter will keep a very great length of time without change. The only method by which this can be done is by clarifying. In some parts of Switzerland they put the butter into earthenware glazed vessels, these are placed in large saucepans of water and heated very gently until the contents melt, the greatest care being taken not to overheat the butter, and as soon as it becomes liquid the vessels are allowed to cool with the slightest agitation. In this manner all the impurities are got rid of, some being lighter rise to the top, others, as the curd, sink to the bottom. The pure butter so clarified will keep sweet for a long time, and it is in this condition that it should always be used in potting. If butter is clarified in a saucepan over a fire, the curdy matter is certain to be overheated, and the whole mass becomes unpleasantly flavored.

Clarified butter is better than suet or melted fat to pour over the top of the potted meats, as the suet in cooling cracks away from the pot and admits the air. This evil does not generally happen when butter is used. Having made these preliminary observations we will now give some receipts for potting meats, premising that small pots should generally be used for two reasons—firstly, the covering of butter is less likely to crack when small pots are used than when large ones are employed; and secondly, the contents are sooner eaten when opened, so that there is less chance of their being spoiled by exposure to the air.

Any kind of meat—as beef, tongue, ham, chicken, etc.,—may be potted if first baked or stewed until tender, and the fleshy parts pounded in a mortar with salt, such spices as may be approved, and a proportion of clarified butter. It should then be pressed firmly into the pots, melted clarified butter poured over it, and the pot tied down when cold In most cookery books a marble mortar is recommended. This is a mistake. There cannot be a much worse material used for mortars than marble.

It is soft, and, what is still worse, readily absorbent of grease and flavors, so after having been used for one substance, if high flavored, cannot be safely used for another. A good wedgewood-ware mortar, such as used by chemists, is the cheapest and best that can be employed.

Many potted articles require special treatment, the directions for which we subjoin:

POTTED SALMON.—Split a salmon down the back, and divide it into two pieces, removing the backbone, head, and tail. Wipe the two sides with a clean napkin, but do not wash them. Salt them slightly, and let them drain. Put the drained pieces into a baking pan, after having well rubbed them all over with a mixture of powdered cloves and mace and four or five bay leaves and some whole pepper. Cover the fish with cold clarified butter, and the pan with strong paper. When baked take the salmon out and let it drain from the gravy. Take off the skin and put the fish into the pots. Sprinkle the upper surface of the potted salmon with a little spice, and pour clarified butter over it when cold; then close the pots.

POTTED LOBSTER.—Boil the lobsters yourself. Choose hens in preference, on account of the spawn. When the lobsters are cold pick out all the parts that are eatable. Beat the flesh in a mortar, seasoning it with salt and a mixture of pepper, mace, and nutmeg, finely powdered. As you beat and mix it, incorporate with the paste a small quantity of clarified butter. Press the meat strongly into the potting pots, and pour over it hot clarified butter. Lobsters may also be potted by putting into the pots lumps of the meat, and pounding only the spawn, and filling up with clarified butter.

POTTED RABBIT.—Take off the legs and shoulders of the rabbits, also the fleshy parts of the back. Cut off the leg bones at the first joint, and the shoulder bones at the blades, but without cutting off the meat. Take also the livers, season these limbs and livers, put plenty of butter over them, and bake them gently; then stow them lightly into pots, covering them with clarified butter. The remainder of the rabbits may serve for any other purpose in the culinary arrangements of the day.

POTTED PIGEONS.—Clean them well, bone them, season them in the usual manner, and lay them very close in a baking-pan. Cover them with butter, tie very thick paper over them, and put the pan into the oven. When cold put them, closely packed side by side, into pots that will hold three each, and cover them with clarified butter.

POTTED BIRDS.—Bake them in a pan under a crust, with plenty of seasoning and butter. When they are cold put as many in a pot as can be forced in side by side, and cover them with clarified butter.

TO POT VEAL.—Cold fillet makes the finest potted veal, or it may be done as follows: Season a large slice of the fillet before it is dressed with some mace, pepper-corns, and two or three cloves; lay it close into a potting-pan that will just hold it, fill it up with water, and bake it three hours. Then pound it quite small in a mortar, and salt to taste; put a little gravy that was baked to it in pounding, if to be eaten soon, otherwise only a little butter just melted; when done, cover it over with butter.

POTTED CALVES' FEET.—Boil the feet for five hours; flavor half a pint of the jelley in which they are boiled with nutmeg, garlic, and pounded ham, and let them simmer together for a few minutes; cut up the feet into small pieces and season them; dip a mould into cold water, and put in the meat, mixed with a little grated lemon-peel and minced parsley. Some persons add beet-root, baked or boiled, cut in slices and mixed with the meat, when this is arranged in the mould, fill up with the flavored jelley. Turn out when quite cold. The remainder of the jelly in which the feet were boiled can be used as a sweet jelly.

POTTED VEAL AND BACON.—Cut equal quantities of veal and bacon into thin slices. Rub together some dried sweet-basil or summer-savory, very fine; lay in a stewpan a layer of bacon and a layer of veal, and on these sprinkle the powdered herbs, a little grated horseradish, pepper and salt. Put layers in the same order, seasoned, till all the meat is in the pan. Squeeze over all the juice of a lemon, and grate on it the yellow rind. Cover very tightly and bake for three hours in a moderate oven, then take out and drain off all the gravy. Shake over the meat a little catsup, press under heavy weights for three hours, and put away in a tightly covered **pot.**

CHAPTER V.

VEGETABLES AND SALADS.

VEGETABLES.

VEGETABLES should be carefully cleaned from insects and nicely washed. Boil them in plenty of water, and drain them the moment they are done enough. If over-boiled they will lose their beauty and crispness. Bad cooks sometimes dress them with meat, which is wrong, except carrots or cabbage with boiling beef.

In order to boil vegetables of a good green color, take care that the water boils when they are put in. Make them boil very fast. Do not cover, but watch them, and if the water has not slackened you may be sure they are done when they begin to sink. Then take them out immediately, or the color will change. Hard water, especially if chalybeate, spoils the color of such vegetables as should be green. To boil them green in hard water, put a teaspoonful of carbonate of soda or potash into the water when it boils, before the vegetables are put in.

TO BOIL POTATOES.—Pare or merely wash them, as preferred, and put them in a covered saucepan of cold water, with a teaspoonful of salt; boil them till they are done (which can be ascertained by running a fork into them) and begin to break a little; then pour the water from them, and hold the saucepan with the lid off, over the fire for two or three minutes, shaking well at the end of the time; put the lid loosely on so as to allow the steam to escape, and sprinkle a very little salt over them; let them stand till wanted (the sooner the better), but they may remain in this way, if necessary, half an hour or more. Time, twenty to thirty minutes, or longer if very large.

To Broil Potatoes.—Parboil, then slice and broil them. Or, parboil, and then set them whole on the gridiron over a very slow fire, and when thoroughly done send them up with their skins on. This last way is practised in many Irish families.

Potato Chips.—Wash and peel some potatoes, then pare them, ribbon-like, into long lengths; put them into cold water to remove the strong potato flavor; drain them, and throw them into a pan with a little butter, and fry them a light brown. Take them out of the pan, and place them close to the fire on a sieve, lined with clean writing-paper, to dry, before they are served up. A little salt may be sprinkled over them.

Steamed Potatoes.—Either peel them or not, according to their quality, but any rate wash them thoroughly; put them into a steamer, cover them down closely, and place them over a saucepan of boiling water. Endeavor not to lift the lid until you have reason to suppose the potatoes are done. Unless of a very small size, potatoes usually require forty minutes or an hour's steaming.

BAKED POTATOES.—Potatoes are either baked in their jackets or peeled; in either case they should not be exposed to a fierce heat, which is wasteful, inasmuch as thereby a great deal of the vegetable is scorched and rendered uneatable. They should be frequently turned while being baked, and kept from touching each other in the oven or dish. When done in their skins be particular to wash and brush them before baking them. If convenient, they may be baked in wood-ashes, or in a Dutch oven in front of the fire; serve them in damask napkin. When pared they should be baked in a dish, and fat of some kind added to prevent their outsides from becoming burnt; they are ordinarily baked thus as an accessory to baked meat.

POMMES DE TERRE A LA DANOIES.—Peel six good large mealy potatoes, cut them into rather thin slices, and throw them into a saucepan of boiling water, do them quickly until they are tender enough to mash; strain off the water and mash them smooth with a spoon, add some fresh butter or oil, salt, pepper, chopped parsley, and grated nutmeg, together with two new-laid eggs. Stir all well, heat some very good butter or salad oil in a frying-pan, place in it spoonfuls of the potato, turn them as they become brown, drain them from fat, and serve very hot. When preferred, spoonfuls may be arranged upon a buttered dish and baked.

POTATO SURPRISE.—Take some good-sized cold, boiled potatoes, cut a piece from the end of each, and with a round-topped knife remove a good deal of the inside of the potatoes; fill them with oysters, bearded, chopped, peppered, and mixed with raw egg; replace the tops upon the potatoes, moistening the edges with raw egg to make them adhere together, and place the potatoes in a slack oven, while you prepare a batter, into which dip them, and afterwards fry them in lard; when very nicely browned serve hot. Some pickled sauce may take the place of the oysters, if more convenient, or a few bread crumbs soaked in beaten egg.

MIROTON OF POTATOES.—Peel and nicely steam eight good mealy potatoes; when done, mash them and season them with pepper; chop up one medium-sized onion and the yelks of two hard-boiled eggs, fry them in plenty of oil or butter; when the onion is quite tender drain it and the eggs from all fat, add them to the mashed potato, mix with them two raw eggs, and a dessertspoonful of catsup; place all together in a mould buttered and sprinkled with bread crumbs; bake for half an hour, and turn out of the mould to serve.

POTATOES MASHED AND FRIED.—What are called mashed potatoes should, to be properly made, be passed through the hair sieve, and then stirred up in a saucepan with milk, butter, and salt; by this process you avoid coming upon pieces of hard potato.

Another simpler mode is to pass the potatoes through the sieve, and, before they have time to cool, put them into a vegetable dish, with a lump of butter under them, keeping them hot till the time of serving.

With some dishes fried potatoes are *de rigueur*. To fry them well you must attend to the following points: Plenty of fat. Wait till the fat is very hot before you throw them in. Let them be thoroughly dry, for, if at all damp, they will never be crisp. When they have got a fine golden tinge, take them out and lay them on a piece of blotting paper before the fire, giving them a good sprinkling of salt. Do not attempt to fry boiled potatoes; they must be raw, and you can cut them either in dices the thickness of a shilling, or in pieces about the size of a French Bean and the length of the potato.

Boiled potatoes can be warmed up by frying, and one very good way is to fry some shalots or onions, and, when they begin to take color, throw in the potatoes, any how, and keep turning them until warm.

Cold mashed potatoes make excellent little side

dishes, the simplest of which is this: Stir an egg or two with your potatoes; add a few finely-powdered spices, pepper and salt to taste, and some minced parsley; mix well, and roll the mixture into balls, or any shape you like; cover with fine. bread crumbs, fry a nice golden color, and serve garnished with fried parsley. This dish can be varied *ad infinitum,* by either inserting in the middle of each ball, or incorporating with the mixture, any of the following: The flesh of fowls or game, any kind of fish, lobsters, crabs, etc., all finely minced. If you have some very rich stock, moisten the minced meat or fish with it, and your dish will be improved; only, in that case, you must put a small portion of the mixture in each ball, and not mix it up with the potatoes. The above combinations can be erected into a more imposing dish by placing the minced fish or meat in a pie-dish, and covering over with potatoes, then baking until the top is of the desired color; in this case, however, a regular ragout should be made for the animal part of the dish, and the potatoes only play second fiddle.

A favorite way of dressing potatoes is this: Cut them up into quarters; rub a saucepan with a piece of garlic, put into it a goodly piece of butter, and when it is melted throw in your potatoes; add a very little water, pepper and salt, and a small quantity of grated nutmeg; let the whole simmer till done, and, before serving, add some minced parsley and a little lemon-juice. Cooked in this way they can be eaten as a separate dish.

Boiled potatoes cut up into quarters, and with a white sauce, with minced parsley put over them, make a very nice dish.

A delicious way of eating new potatoes is to put them into a saucepan with plenty of butter; toss them about till done, sprinkling with salt, and serving very hot.

With potatoes a most excellent good, sweet dish can be made. It is made thus: Boil and pass through a hair sieve three or four potatoes; stir to them powdered sugar and the yelks of two eggs; add a few drops of essence of vanilla, or any other essence; beat up the whites of the two eggs into a froth, mix quickly and thoroughly with the pudding, pour into a shape (previously buttered and bread-crumbed) and bake in a quick oven for twenty minutes or less. This will be found a very effective dish. The only difficulty about it is the timing of the cooking thereof, as it requires to be taken up to table as soon as it is done, and the cook must know her company well to be able to judge how long they will take over the previous dishes. The preparing of this dish is very good practice for making *soufflés;* and, in fact, if less potatoes are used and more eggs, you produce, without knowing it, a *soufflé* of *pommes de terre,* as it is called.

POTATO ROLLS.—Wash some potatoes of a medium size, pare them, and cut them in the form of small rolls of about three inches in length and an inch and a half across; dip them into beaten egg, have some thin slices of fat bacon large enough to envelop a potato; wrap one in each rasher, arrange them in a small baking dish, put them into a moderately hot oven, and bake them until the potatoes are done; rasp a little toast upon them, and serve them directly.

STEWED POTATOES.—Cut into slices four cold potatoes that have either been boiled or steamed; season them, dredge them with flour, and put them into a stewpan with some fresh butter or olive oil; fry them slightly on both sides for five minutes, drain off the fat, pour upon them half a pint of good gravy nicely flavored, and let them stew by the side of the fire for twenty minutes. Serve together with the sauce in which they were stewed.

BROWNED POTATOES.—Steam or boil some rather small-sized potatoes, peel them, and throw them into a stewpan of boiling butter; shake them occasionally, and when done and well browned, serve them upon a thin slice of toast which has been dipped into either essence of anchovy, or catsup.

POTATO FRITTERS.—Take seventeen large-sized Mercer potatoes, grate them finely; when all are grated, add three eggs, three tablespoonfuls of flour, and one tablespoonful of salt; mix it well. Drop into hot lard or butter and bake until done.

New Potatoes—To Boil.—Procure them of equal size, and if very young, wash them only; if older, rub off the skins with a scrubbing-brush or coarse cloth. Put them into boiling water till tender, and sprinkle a little salt over them, and put a lump of butter in; shake up and serve. Time, fifteen to twenty minutes.

Potato Salad is made with vinegar in the following manner, viz.: Boil your potatoes, (select the smallest,) and, as soon as they are done, peel them as quick as you can; cut them in small slices, and after seasoning them with salt and pepper, pour over them (while hot) five or six tablespoonfuls of vinegar to about one quart of potatoes, and turn them thoroughly. Cut a large onion very fine and put it in, still turning. Half an hour after, add three or four tablespoonfuls of sweet oil, and after turning again, serve.

Potato Patties.—Butter some small patty-pans; strew bread crumbs over the insides and fill them with some nicely-mashed potatoes, flavored with either mushroom catsup, grated lemon-peel, or savory herbs, chopped fine; add sufficient lard or fresh butter, and sift more bread crumbs on the tops; place them in an oven till properly browned, lift them out of the patty-pans to serve.

Potato Scones.—Mash boiled potatoes till they are quite smooth, adding a little salt; then knead out with flour, to the thickness required; toast, pricking them with a fork to prevent them blistering. When eaten with fresh butter, they are very nutritious.

POTATOES IN MEAT, PUDDINGS, AND PIES.—The introduction of a potato or two into family puddings is a generally acknowledged improvement, inasmuch as the farinaceous nature of the potato causes it to absorb fat, and thereby act as a corrective to the over richness of most meat pies and puddings. Potatoes are especially of advantage with beef or mutton, one or two to an ordinary sized pasty being sufficient.

ROASTED POTATOES.—Wash some good sized potatoes and boil them for ten minutes. Take them up and peel them, well butter them outside, sprinkle some salt and pepper upon them, and dredge them with a little flour; arrange them in an oven and roast them before the fire, turning them as they require it. When thoroughly brown serve in a hot dish.

JURY PIE.—Steam or boil some mealy potatoes, mash them together with some butter or cream, season them, and place a layer at the bottom of the pie-dish, upon this place a layer of finely chopped cold meat or fish of any kind, well seasoned, then add another layer of potatoes, and continue alternating these with more chopped meat until the dish be filled. Smooth down the top, strew bread crumbs upon it, and bake until it is well browned. A very small quantity of meat serves in this manner to make a nice presentable little dish. A sprinkling of chopped pickles may be added if handy, and when fish is employed it eats better if first beaten up with raw egg. Some dressed spinach, tomatoes, asparagus tops, etc., may be made use of in place of the meat, if convenient, but the potatoes should predominate three-fourths more than the other ingredient introduced.

POTATO CROQUETTES, A SWEET DISH.—Take some nicely baked potatoes, scoop out the mealy part, and mash it thoroughly smooth; press it through a sieve, make it into stiff paste with some cream, butter, orange flower water, powdered loaf-sugar, and raw eggs well beaten. Make it into croquettes by rolling portions in sifted bread crumbs, and dipping them in white of egg whipped to a snow. Fry them in plenty of lard or fresh butter.

POTATO PONE.—This is a favorite dish in the West India Islands. Wash, peel, and grate two pounds of potatoes, add four ounces each of sugar and butter (or beef dripping), melted, one teaspoonful each of salt and pepper, mix well together, place it in a baking-dish, and put it into a brisk oven until it is done and becomes nicely browned.

STUFFED POTATOES.—Take five large potatoes, wash and peel them, and scoop them out, so as to have them hollow from end to end; fill the holes with sausage or forcemeat, dip the potatoes into dissolved butter, and arrange them in a baking-dish. Put them into a moderately hot oven for about thirty or forty minutes. Serve directly after they are done. They may be accompanied by a sauce or not, according to choice.

Pommes de Terre en Pyramide.—Either steam or boil some very good mealy potatoes, mash them and put them into a stewpan, together with some butter, a little salt, and milk. As the mixture becomes stiff add more milk, but let it be of the desired consistency to arrange it in the form of a pyramid in a buttered dish. Place it in a hot oven, or brown with a salamander, and serve.

Potatoes Fried with Batter.—Nicely wash and pare some floury potatoes. Cut each into any form you fancy, such as a large lozenge, etc., then thinly slice them, so that the pieces may be of a uniform shape. Dip them into either a sweet or savory batter, fry them in plenty of butter, and serve them quite hot, with either salt or pounded loaf-sugar strewn upon them.

Potatoes a la Creme.—Put into a saucepan about two ounces of butter, a dessertspoonful of flour, some parsley, chopped small, salt, and pepper. Stir them up together, add a wineglassful of cream, and set it on the fire, stirring continually until it boils. Cut some boiled potatoes into slices and put them into the saucepan with the mixture, boil all together, and serve them very hot.

FRENCH MASHED POTATOES.—After well boiling some potatoes in their jackets peel, and mash them with a fork. Put them into a stewpan with some butter and salt, moisten them with fresh cream, and let them grow dry while stirring them over the fire; add more cream, and so continue for nearly an hour. Dish them, and brown them on the top with a salamander. Serve directly.

SAVORY POTATO CAKES.—Quarter of a pound of grated ham, one pound of mashed potatoes, and a little suet, mixed with the yelks of two eggs, pepper, salt, and nutmeg. Roll it into little balls or cakes, and fry it a light brown. Sweet herbs may be used in the place of ham. Plain potato cakes are made with potatoes and eggs only.

CAULIFLOWER.

One of the prettiest dishes of vegetables we know consists of a cauliflower of ivory whiteness resting upon a bed of well made tomato sauce. To insure the immaculate appearance of the cauliflower, a moderate quantity of flour should be put in the water it is boiled in, and the cauliflower should only be put in when the water is boiling fast. When two or more cauliflowers are used, they should be moulded into one to serve them. To do this, when they are boiled, cut off the stalk, and dispose the pieces of cauliflower head downwards in a basin; press them gently together, turn them out dexterously on a dish, and two or three small cauliflowers will by this means present the appearance of one large one. Care must be taken to have the basin quite hot and to operate quickly. This cannot very well be done with the small purple cauliflower or brocoli; but all the formulas given for cauliflowers proper may be applied to brocoli likewise.

The sauce should be put into the dish and the cauliflowers over it; but if the moulding process has not been successful, or if the cauliflowers are not very nice looking ones, then pour the sauce over them, so as to hide their deformity.

The very best way, however, to treat cauliflowers is *au gratin*, and this has the advantage that it may be applied to the remains of the cauliflowers served at the dinner of the day before. This is the simplest form of it: Dispose the pieces of cauliflowers on a dish, pour a good supply of liquified butter over them, and plenty of grated cheese, with a judicious admixture of powdered white pepper, salt, and nutmeg. Put the dish into the oven for a few minutes, or brown with a red-hot salamander, and serve.

Here are other modes of proceeding: Rub the dish very slightly with garlic, mould your cauliflowers in a basin, and pour into them, before turning them out, some melted butter, into which you have dissolved a good allowance of cheese; turn them out on the dish, strew plentifully with grated cheese, a few bread crumbs, pepper, and salt, pouring the remainder of the sauce over. Brown and serve.

Instead of moulding the cauliflowers, dip each piece in the sauce, and dispose them flat on the dish, filling up the interstices with bread crumbs and cheese in equal parts; pepper and salt according to taste; brown and serve.

The great thing to be avoided is not to make these preparations too dry, and yet there should not be over much butter. The browning must be carefully done, so as to produce a surface of a uniform golden color—not in patches, some burnt black, and others not browned at all, as is too often the case in the preparations of the careless and hasty operators who preside in kitchens.

To such people as may object to cheese, I can recommend the following receipt, which has great merit of its own: Dispose your pieces of boiled cauliflower upon a dish well rubbed with garlic, over them strew a mixture of bread crumbs and anchovies, capers, and olives, mixed fine pepper, and salt; over all pour a judicious quantity of fine salad oil. Bake for about ten minutes, and serve.

Celery may be dressed according to the above formulas also; but we prefer treating the latter in the same way as asparagus, which it emulates in delicacy of flavor—*i. e.*, by plain boiling in salt and water, and serving with some simple sauce.

BOILED CAULIFLOWER.—Soak the head two hours in salt water, and cook until tender in milk and water; drain and serve whole with drawn butter. This makes the best appearance, but it will be found to suit the taste better cut up and seasoned richly with butter and a little salt and pepper. In either case it must be well drained.

CAULIFLOWER OMELETTE.—After boiling a firm head of cauliflower allow it to grow cold, chop it very fine, mix it with sufficient well beaten egg to make a very thick batter. Fry brown in fresh butter, and serve hot.

CAULIFLOWER IN MILK.—Choose those that are close and white, cut off the green leaves, and look carefully that there are no caterpillars about the stalk; soak an hour in cold water, with a handful of salt in it; then boil them in milk and water, and take care to skim the saucepan, that not the least foulness may fall on the flower. It must be served very white and rather crimp.

FRIED CAULIFLOWER.—Having laid a fine cauliflower in cold water for an hour, put it into a pot of boiling water that has been slightly salted (milk and water will be still better,) and boil it twenty-five minutes, or till the large stalk is perfectly tender. Then divide it equally into small tufts, and spread it on a dish to cool. Prepare a sufficient quantity of batter made in the proportion of a tablespoonful of flour, and two tablespoonfuls of milk to each egg. Beat the eggs very light; then stir into them the flour and milk alternately; a spoonful of flour, and one of milk and eggs; season with pepper and salt. Dip the cold cauliflower into the batter, and fry each piece in butter and lard until brown.

CORN BALLS.—Grate five ears of partly dried corn, and powder it in a mortar. Roll the powder into small balls and boil them twenty minutes. Take them out of the water; cool them; mash them with some crushed white sugar and two eggs. Form again in balls and fry in boiling lard and butter. Sprinkle them with finely powdered sugar, and serve hot.

CORN OYSTERS.—Grate the corn. To every pint, take three well beaten eggs, and sufficient flour to bind the mixture together. Season with salt, form in the shape of oysters, and fry brown in butter and lard.

CORN IN CANS.—Dissolve one ounce and a quarter of tartaric acid in half a pint of water. Cut the corn from the cob, and add sufficient water to cook it properly. When cooked, add two tablespoonfuls of the acid solution to every quart of corn. Can it immediately; seal securely, and put it away in a cool, but not damp place. When wanted for use, stir half a teaspoonful of soda through two quarts of corn, and let it stand three or four hours before cooking. This will remove all the acid taste, and render the corn as fresh as when cooked in the summer.

CORN PORRIDGE.—Take young corn, and cut the grains from the cob. Measure it, and to each heaping pint of corn allow not quite a quart of milk. Put the corn and milk into a pot, stir them well together, and boil them till the corn is perfectly soft. Then add some bits of fresh butter dredged with flour, and let it boil five minutes longer. Stir in at the last some beaten yelk of egg, and in three minutes remove it from the fire. Take up the porridge, and send it to table hot, and stir some fresh butter into it. You may add sugar and nutmeg.

SUCCOTASH.—If old beans are used, they must be soaked over night, and parboiled in two waters before putting in the pork. The corn should be added to the beans and pork about fifteen minutes before the hour for serving the dinner. It is well to boil the cobs with the beans and pork in the last water. Remove them before adding the corn. For using beans not fully ripe, one change of water is sufficient; the pork can be parboiled at the same time. Beans for succotash should remain whole; care must be taken that they boil gently, so as not to break them. Considerable water is generally used in boiling the beans, that no more need be added when the corn is put in; most persons like considerable soup in this dish. Families can be governed by taste in this. Dish the corn and beans in a deep dish with the froth, and season with butter and a very little salt: use no pepper; if any person desires it, it is easily added. Serve the pork on a platter, after taking off the skin and dotting it with pepper, by dipping the little finger in ground pepper and pressing it on the pork.

GREEN CORN DUMPLINGS.—A quart of young corn grated from the cob, half a pint of wheat flour sifted, half a pint of milk, six tablespoonfuls of butter, two eggs, a saltspoonful of salt, a saltspoonful of pepper, and butter for frying. Having grated as fine as possible sufficient young fresh corn to make a quart, mix with it the wheat flour, and add the salt and pepper. Warm the milk in a small saucepan, and soften the butter in it. Then add them gradually to the pan of corn stirring very hard, and set it away to cool. Beat the eggs light, and stir them into the mixture when it has cooled. Flour your hands and make it into little dumplings. Put into a frying-pan a sufficiency of fresh butter (or lard and butter, in equal proportions), and when it is boiling hot, and has been skimmed, put in the dumplings, and fry them ten minutes or more, in proportion to their thickness. Then drain them, and send them hot to the dinner table.

CORN FRITTERS.—One dozen ears of young corn grated; one pint of new milk or rich cream, two eggs, a little salt and flour sufficient for a stiff batter. Fry brown in butter and lard.

BROILED TOMATOES.—Wash and wipe the tomatoes, and put them on the gridiron stem down. Set the gridiron over a clear fire. When brown on one side, turn them; let them cook through. Pepper, salt, and serve on a hot dish, with a small piece of butter on each tomato.

Tomato Fritters.—Take one quart of stewed tomatoes, stir in one egg, one small teaspoonful of saleratus or soda, and flour enough to make it the consistency of pancakes.

Browned Tomatoes.—Take large round tomatoes and halve them; place them, the skin side down, in a frying-pan in which a very small quantity of butter or lard has been previously melted; sprinkle them with salt and pepper and dredge them well with flour; place the pan on a hot part of the fire, and let them *brown thoroughly;* then stir them and let them brown again, and so on until they are quite done. They lose their acidity, and the flavor is superior to stewed tomatoes.

Tomato Soup.—Wash, scrape, and cut small the red part of three large carrots, three heads of celery, four large onions, and two large turnips; put them into a saucepan, with a tablespoonful of butter and half a pound of lean new ham; let them stew very gently for an hour; then add three quarts of brown gravy soup and some whole black pepper, with eight or ten ripe tomatoes; let it boil an hour and a half, and pulp it through a sieve; serve it with fried bread cut in dice.

Tomato Toast.—Remove the stem and all the

seeds from the tomatoes; they must be ripe—but not over ripe; stew them to a pulp, season with butter, pepper and salt; toast some bread, butter it, and then spread the tomato on each side, and send it up to table two slices on each dish, the slices cut in two, and the person who helps it must serve with two half slices, not attempt to lift the top slice, otherwise the appearance of the under slice will be destroyed.

To Bake Tomatoes.—Season them with salt and pepper; flour them over, put them in a deep plate with a little butter, and bake in a stove.

Breakfast Tomatoes.—This is a nice breakfast dish; prepare the tomatoes, and stew them. Toast a slice of light bread for each member of the family, and spread the stewed tomatoes evenly on each slice. If any is left, pour it over the whole; serve immediately.

Chinese Rice.—The process of boiling one pound of rice is as follows: Take a clean stewpan, with a close-fitting top, then take a clean piece of white muslin, large enough to cover over the top of the pan and hang down inside nearly to, but not in contact with, the bottom. Into the sack so formed place the rice, pour over it two cupfuls of water, and put on the top of the stewpan, so as to hold up the muslin bag inside, and fit tight all round. Place the pan on a slow fire, and the steam generated from the water will cook the rice. Each grain, it is stated, will come out of the boiler as dry and distinct as if just taken from the hull. More water may be poured into the pan if necessary, but only sufficient to keep up the steam till the rice is cooked. The pan must not be heated so hot as to cause the steam to blow off the lid.

CAROLINA RICE.—Pick the rice carefully, and wash it through two or three cold waters till it is quite clean. Then (having drained off all the water through a colander) put the rice into a pot of boiling water, with a very little salt, allowing as much as a quart of water to half a pint of rice; boil it twenty minutes or more. Then pour off the water, draining the rice as dry as possible. Lastly, set it on hot coals with the lid off, that the steam may not condense upon it and render the rice watery. Keep it dry thus for a quarter of an hour. Put it into a deep dish, and loosen and toss it up from the bottom with two forks, one in each hand, so that the grains may appear to stand alone.

RICE AND MILK.—To every quart of good milk allow two ounces of rice; wash it well in several waters; put it with the milk into a closely-covered saucepan, and set it over a slow fire; when it boils, take it off; let it stand till it is cold, and simmer it about an hour and a quarter before sending it to table, and serve it in a tureen. .

STRING BEANS FOR WINTER USE.—String them and cut them in small pieces as if for boiling; put them raw in stone jars, in alternate layers, with coarse table salt, each layer about one inch in thickness, leaving a layer of salt at the top, tying paper over the whole. During the winter use the beans, (boiling and seasoning them in the ordinary way, after soaking them in cold water for twelve hours,) and they prove quite equal to the best beans cooked fresh from the vine. The appearance and flavor are precisely the same.

To Cook Beans in a French Style.—Choose small young beans, and strip off the ends and stalks, throwing them, as prepared, into a dish full of cold spring water, and, when all are finished, wash and drain them well. Boil them in salted boiling water, in a large saucepan, and drain them, after which put them into an enamelled stewpan, and shake them over the fire until they are quite hot and dry; then add about three ounces of fresh butter, and a tablespoonful of veal or chicken broth; the butter must be broken up into small lumps. Season with white pepper, salt, and the juice of half a lemon strained. Stir them well over a hot fire for five minutes, and serve them in a vegetable dish very hot.

String Beans.—Gather them while young enough to break crispy; break of both ends, and string them; break in halves, and boil in water with a little salt, until tender; drain free from water, and season with butter.

Boiled Beans.—Soak over night any small white beans in soft water, put them in a strong bag, leaving room to swell; let them boil in a potful of water until done; hang them up to let all the water drain off, and season with butter, pepper, and salt, to the taste.

Parsnips require a good deal of boiling. When young wipe off the skin after they are boiled; when old boil them with salt meat, and scrape them first. (Parsnips should always be scraped.) Average time, from twenty to forty-five minutes.

Broiled Parsnips.—After they are boiled tender let them become perfectly cold. Slice thin lengthwise, and broil until nicely browned; spread them with butter, and season with pepper and salt. To be served with roast, broiled, or fried meats.

Parsnip Cutlet.—Slice boiled parsnips lengthwise, and brown them in lard, after rubbing them with pepper and salt. When browned on both sides, dip one side in batter made of egg and flour, let them brown, not burn, then dip the other side, and brown in the same manner; spread over them a little butter, or not, as desired. Serve with roasts, etc.

Parsnip Fritters, No. 1.—Boil and peel two large parsnips, scrape them to a fine pulp, beat them up with the whites of two and the yelks of four eggs, two spoonfuls of cream, half a glass of sherry, and a little grated nutmeg. Beat all together for nearly half an hour until the batter becomes light. Fry them well covered with lard, and serve with lemon or orange-juice and sugar, or with sweet or wine sauce.

PARSNIP FRITTERS, No. 2.—Boil the parsnips in salted water, so as to flavor them through. Make a light batter, cut them round, and dip them in the batter. Have ready hot lard, take them up with a a tablespoon, and drop them in while the lard is boiling. When they rise to the surface turn them; when browned on both sides take them out. Let them drain, and set them in the oven to keep hot. Serve with broiled, fried, or roast meats or fowls.

FRICASSEE OF PARSNIPS.—Boil in milk till they are soft, then cut them lengthwise into bits two or three inches long, and simmer in a white sauce made of two spoonfuls of broth, a bit of mace, half a cupful of cream, a bit of butter, and some flour, pepper and salt.

FRIED PLANTAINS OR BANANAS.—Buy some sweet plantains, or bananas. If not thoroughly ripe, hang them up in the room to ripen. Take off the skins, cut in slices, and fry in hot lard until browned. The long, green, hard, plantains are peeled and roasted in the ashes, when it closely resembles bread. It is also cut in slices and fried a nice brown in hot lard. They are also boiled in soups, stews, hashes, etc.

VEGETABLES AND SAUCES.—Potatoes are good

with all meats. With fowls they are nicest mashed. Carrots, parsnips, turnips, greens, and cabbage are eaten with boiled meat; and beets, peas, and beans are appropriate to either boiled or roasted meat. Mashed turnip is good with roasted pork. Tomatoes are good with every kind of meat, but especially so with roast; apple sauce with roast pork; cranberry sauce with beef, fowls, veal, and ham. Currant jelly is used by many persons with roast mutton. Pickles are good with all roast meats, and capers or nasturtiums with boiled lamb or mutton. Horseradish and lemons are excellent with veal.

CARROTS.—Let them be well washed and brushed, not scraped. An hour is enough for young spring carrots. Grown carrots must be cut in half, and will take from an hour and a half to two hours and a half. When done rub off the peels with a clean, coarse cloth, and slice them in two or four, according to their size. The best way to try if they are done enough is to pierce them with a fork.

CARROT FRITTERS.—These very nice fritters are simply made, and we can recommend them as being an agreeable variety for a side dish at a small party. Beat two small boiled carrots to a pulp with a spoon, add three or four eggs, and half a handful of flour. Moisten with cream, milk, or a little white wine, and sweeten to taste; beat all well together, and fry them in boiling lard. When of good color take them off and serve, having squeezed over them the juice of an orange, and strewed them over with finely sifted sugar.

PARSLEY AND BUTTER.—Wash and tie up a bunch of parsley. Put it in boiling water, and let it boil for five minutes. Drain it, cut off the stalks, and chop the leaves very fine. Put it into the melted butter, which may be made by smoothly mixing a tablespoonful of flour with half a pint of water and two ounces of butter. Stir all one way; let it boil about two minutes.

FRIED ARTICHOKES.—Cut the artichokes into six or eight pieces, according to their size, remove the choke and the large leaves which will not become tender, and trim off the tops of the remainder of the leaves with a pair of scissors. Wash them in several waters, drain them, and dip them in a batter made with flour, a little cream, and the yelk of an egg. Let the artichokes be well covered with the batter, and fry them in lard. Sprinkle a little salt over them, and serve them on a bed of parsley fried in the lard which remains in the pan.

SUMMER SQUASHES.—When these vegetables are fresh, the rind will be crisp when cut by the nail. If very young and tender they may be boiled whole, if not pare them. Extract the seeds and strings, cut them small, put them in a stewpan with water enough just to cover them, add one teaspoonful of salt to each common sized squash, boil them till the pieces break, half an hour is generally enough, and then press them through a colander with a skimmer. Mix them with butter to your taste, and a little salt if necessary.

STEWED SPINACH.—Pick the spinach very clean, and wash thoroughly through several waters. Drain it and put it in a saucepan with only the water that clings to it. Add salt and pepper and stew for twenty minutes, or till quite tender. Turn it often while stewing and press it down with a wooden spoon or ladle. When done, drain and press as dry as possible; chop it up fine; set it again over the fire; add to it some pieces of butter rolled in flour, and the beaten yelks of two eggs. Simmer five minutes, and take it off without allowing it to boil. Serve upon thin slices of well-buttered toast cut in small squares.

SPINACH TO BOIL.—Spinach requires a great deal of water to free it from the grit in which it is covered from its low growth. The stalks should be broken off, and the spinach washed well with the hand. Put it into a saucepan with a little salt. A very large quantity of uncooked spinach is needed to make a dish, as it wastes considerably in cooking. Boil it for about twelve minutes, pressing it down when quite tender. Drain it thoroughly and squeeze out the water. Chop it quite small. Put it into a fresh saucepan with some butter, and stir it till it is hot. Spinach is frequently dished around minced meats; it is also sometimes served with poached eggs upon it.

BOILED ONIONS.—Take the outside skin from white onions as uniform in size as possible, lay them in cold salt and water one hour, boil them in milk and water until thoroughly tender; lay them in a deep dish, and pour over them melted butter.

BUTTERED ONIONS.—Peel enough small onions to fill a vegetable dish; throw them into a stewpan of boiling water; add a little salt and a piece of fresh butter. Stew for five minutes. Drain them; put them into a saucepan with a large piece of butter, some pepper, nutmeg and salt. Toss them about over a clear fire until they begin to brown; add a tablespoonful of gravy, and a dessertspoonful of chopped herbs. Stew gently for fifteen minutes, and serve upon cream toast.

ROASTED ONIONS.—These should be cooked in their skins; but before putting them into the oven, brush off all grittiness. Place in a moderate oven, cooking gradually until nearly done, then quicken the oven and brown. Serve with plenty of fresh butter.

FLAKED ONIONS.—Boil two good-sized Spanish onions in plain water, put aside until cold. Flake on two forks; season to taste. Make some butter very hot in a frying-pan, put the onions into it, and toss over the fire till brown. Drain, and serve on toast with parsley.

ONIONS AND CAPER SAUCE.—Boil a dozen large onions in milk, do not press them, but simply drain them; put them immediately into a vegetable dish, and pour over them a good caper sauce made quite hot. This is the proper way of serving onions with a dish of boiled mutton.

STEWED CELERY.—Wash the celery very clean, and cut it to the length that it will lie evenly in a saucepan. Cover it with water, but do not use more than necessary. Salt the water rather freely. Let the celery boil from a quarter of an hour to twenty-five minutes, according to the size of the heads. Drain it, and serve it on toast as you would asparagus. A tureen of melted butter should be served with it, or some persons prefer white sauce.

FRIED CELERY.—Is prepared as follows: Cut off the green tops of six or eight heads of celery, and remove the outside stalks. Wash them well and pare the roots clean. Have ready half a pint of white wine, the yelks of three eggs finely beaten, and a little salt and nutmeg, and mix them all well together with some flour into a batter. Dip every head into this batter, and fry them in butter. When sufficiently done, lay them in a dish and pour melted butter over them.

ESSENCE OF CELERY.—This is prepared by soaking for a fortnight a half ounce of the seeds of celery in a quarter of a pint of brandy. A few drops will flavor a pint of soup or broth, equal to a head of celery.

VEGETABLE OYSTER CAKES.— Select good, large-sized oyster plant roots, grate them, and add milk and flour sufficient to make a stiff batter, about a gill of grated oyster plant, two eggs, one pint of milk, and flour to make the batter, and salt. Drop it by tablespoonfuls into hot lard. Bake till brown.

EGG PLANT.—Select long purple if possible; the next best is the round kind with prickles on the stem. Peel and slice them, spread salt on each separate piece, and lay them in a colander to drain; let them lie one hour, parboil, and fry them, until thoroughly cooked, in pork fat or butter; egg plants, unless well cooked, are insipid, and even disgusting; they must be cooked through and browned.

BOILED BEETS.—Beets must not be cut before boiling, as the juice will escape and the sweetness be destroyed. Select small-sized, smooth roots, wash them nicely, and boil in clear water until tender. When sufficiently cooked, skim them into a pan of cold water, and slip off the skin. Cut them in thin slices, and while hot, season with butter, salt, pepper and vinegar, and serve. If preferred cold, slice lengthwise and lay in strong cold vinegar.

ASPARAGUS.—Set a stewpan with plenty of water in it on the fire; sprinkle a handful of salt in it;

let it boil, and skim it; then put in your asparagus, prepared thus: Scrape all the stalks till they are perfectly clean; throw them into a pan of cold water as you scrape them; when they are all done, tie them up in little bundles, of about a quarter of a hundred each; cut off the stalks at the bottom that they may be all of a length, leaving only just enough to serve as a handle for the green part; when they are tender at the stalk, which will be from twenty to thirty minutes, they are done enough. Great care must be taken to watch the exact time of their becoming tender; take them up just at that instant, and they will have their true flavor and color; a minute or two more boiling destroys both. While the asparagus is boiling, toast some bread about half an inch thick; brown it delicately on both sides; dip it lightly in the liquor the asparagus was boiled in, and lay it in the middle of a dish; melt some butter, then lay in the asparagus upon the toast, which must project beyond the asparagus, that the company may see there is a toast. Pour no butter over them, but send some up in a deep dish.

Stewed Asparagus.—Use it as soon as possible after cutting; there are several ways of cooking this; each of which is good. Discard all not brittle enough to break easily, tie it in small bunches, and boil it in very little water, slightly salted, until tender; take off the strings, put it in a covered dish, add butter to the water sufficient to make a rich gravy, and thicken it with very little flour, and pour the gravy over the asparagus; be careful to lay the heads all one way.

ASPARAGUS SOUP.—Cut the asparagus in pieces a half inch long, boil in water with a little salt, and add rich sweet cream to thicken the soup.

ASPARAGUS TOAST.—Tie the stalks in small bunches, boil them in very little salted water until tender; toast as many slices of bread as there are bunches of asparagus, butter them while hot, lay a bunch on each slice of toast, add a little butter to the water, and pour it over the whole.

ASPARAGUS OMELETTE.—Boil some tender, freshly-cut asparagus in a very little water, slightly salted, or steam till tender. Chop up very fine; beat with it the yelks of six and the whites of three eggs, (which must be beaten separately till light;) add two tablespoonfuls of sweet cream. Fry in butter, and serve hot.

TURNIPS A LA POULETTE.—Cut the turnips into dice in a saucepan; boil till tender, and drain. Put in the saucepan a piece of butter rolled in flour, and stir gently over the fire; add a gill of milk, stir again; put in the turnips, pepper, and salt. Stew five minutes, and serve.

TURNIPS.—Full-grown turnips will take about an hour and a half gentle boiling; if you slice them, which most people do, they will be done sooner; try them with a fork; when tender, take them up, and lay them on a sieve till the water is thoroughly drained from them. Send them up whole; do not slice them.

Turnip Tops.—Boil thoroughly, with plenty of water, salt, and soda in due proportions; drain and pass through a hair sieve. Melt a piece of butter, to which add a little flour and the pulp of your turnip tops; stir on the fire a few minutes, adding a little milk or cream, and a little broth or stock, with pepper or grated nutmeg to taste. When a nice consistency, not too thick, dress on a dish as you would spinach, and serve with fried sippets of bread around it. If properly cooked, this dish has a better color than spinach, and a very pleasant, nutty, bitter taste.

To Boil Peas.—They should be young and of a good sort. Must not be over-done, nor in much water. Boil some mint with them, and chop it to garnish them, and stir a piece of butter in with them. If either too young or too old, a little sugar boiled with them is an improvement.

Green Peas.—Put into a stewpan a quart of peas, one onion, two ounces of butter, a sprig of mint, a teaspoonful of white sugar, and two tablespoonfuls of gravy; stew till soft, when take out the onion and mint, and thicken with flour and butter. A lettuce is sometimes stewed with them.

Lettuce Peas.—Having washed four lettuces and stripped off the outside leaves, take the hearts and chop them up very fine; put them into a stew-pan with two quarts of freshly-shelled green peas, a few lumps of loaf sugar and a few leaves of green mint, finely minced. Add a slice of cold ham, and a quarter of a pound of butter, divided into four pieces and rolled in flour, two tablespoonfuls of water and a pinch of black pepper. Let all stew for half an hour, or longer, if the peas are not tender. Take out the ham and add half a pint of cream. Stew five minutes longer, and serve hot.

To Stew Peas.—Take a quart of shelled peas, a large onion, or two of middling size, and two lettuces cut small; put them into a saucepan with half a pint of water; season them with a little salt, a little pepper, mace, and nutmeg. Cover them close, and let them stew a quarter of an hour, then put in a quarter of a pound of fresh butter rolled in a little flour, a spoonful of catsup, and a small piece of butter as big as a nutmeg; cover them close, and simmer gently an hour, often shaking the pan.

Peas au Sucre.—Boil the peas and throw into cold water, then put them in a pan with a little butter, a tablespoonful and a half of sugar, a tablespoonful of broth, one yelk of egg; stir fast, and they are done.

Cabbage Boiled with Meat.—Select for boiling, small white cabbages with firm heads; cut these in quarters, and wash perfectly clean. Lay the pieces in salted water for an hour. Skin the fat from the pot when the meat is boiling, and put in the cabbage, an hour before the meat is done; drain well before serving.

To Stew Cabbage.—Parboil in milk and water, and drain it, then shred it, put it into a stewpan, with a small piece of butter, a small teacupful of cream, and seasoning, and stew tender. Or, it may be stewed in white or brown gravy.

Cold Cabbage.—Chop fine and heat it in vinegar, season with pepper and salt; if not boiled with meats, add a little butter. It can also be fried; cauliflower and brocoli can be prepared in the same manner.

Dressing for Cold Slaw.—To the well-beaten yelk of one egg, add a little milk, two or three tablespoonfuls of vinegar and a small piece of butter. Stir it over the fire till it comes to a boil.

Red Cabbage Stewed.—After slicing a small red cabbage, and washing it perfectly clean, put it into a saucepan with pepper, salt and butter, and whatever water clings to the leaves from washing. Let it stew until perfectly tender; add two spoonfuls of vinegar and boil up once. Or, shred the cabbage, wash it, and put it in a saucepan over a slow fire, with slices of onion, a little gravy, pepper and salt. When quite tender, add a piece of butter rolled in flour, three spoonfuls of vinegar, and boil up once before serving.

STEWED CABBAGE.—Parboil in milk and water drain, shred, put it in a stewpan with a small piece of butter rolled in flour, a small teacup of cream; season and stew till tender. Or, stew in meat gravy.

CABBAGE JELLY.—Boil cabbage in the usual way; squeeze it in a colander till dry, and chop very fine. Add a little butter, pepper, and salt. Press all closely into an earthen mould, and bake one hour. Turn out of the mould and serve.

HOT SLAW.—Cut cabbage into fine shreds; boil it in clear water until it is perfectly tender. Mix in a saucepan a teacupful of sharp vinegar, a piece of butter, salt and pepper; stew gently for five minutes. Drain the cabbage, place it in a deep dish, pour the dressing over it, and serve hot.

BROILED MUSHROOMS.—*A Breakfast, Luncheon, or Supper Dish.* Mushroom-flaps, pepper and salt to taste, butter, lemon-juice. Cleanse the mushrooms by wiping them with a piece of flannel and a little salt; cut off a portion of the stalk, and peel the tops; broil them over a clear fire, turning them once, and arrange them on a very hot dish. Put a small piece of butter on each mushroom, season with pepper and salt, and squeeze over them a few drops of lemon-juice. Place the dish before the fire, and when the butter is melted, serve very hot and quickly. Moderate-sized flaps are better suited to this mode of cooking than the buttons; the latter are better in stews.

STEWED MUSHROOMS.—One pint of mushroom buttons, three ounces of fresh butter, white pepper and salt to taste, lemon-juice, one teaspoonful of flour, cream or milk, quarter of a teaspoonful of grated nutmeg. Cut off the ends of the stalks, and pare neatly a pint of mushroom buttons; put them into a basin of water, with a little lemon-juice, as they are done. When all are prepared, take them from the water with the hands, to avoid the sediment, and put them into a stewpan with the fresh butter, white pepper, salt, and the juice of half a lemon; cover the pan closely, and let the mushrooms stew gently from twenty to twenty-five minutes; then thicken the butter with the above proportion of flour, add gradually sufficient cream, or cream and milk, to make the sauce of a proper consistency, and put in the grated nutmeg. If the mushrooms are not perfectly tender, stew them for five minutes longer, remove every particle of butter which may be floating on the top, and serve.

TO DRY MUSHROOMS.—Wipe them clean, take away the brown part and peel off the skin; lay them on sheets of paper to dry, in a cool oven, when they will shrivel considerably. Keep them in paper bags, which hang in a dry place. When wanted for use, put them into cold gravy, bring them gradually to simmer, and it will be found that they will regain nearly their usual size.

PRESERVING MUSHROOMS FOR WINTER USE.—

Peel small some freshly-gathered mushrooms, cut off the stems, and scrape out the whole of the fur, then arrange the mushrooms singly on tins or dishes, and dry them as gradually as possible in a moderately-heated oven; put them into tin canisters and store them in a dry place.

Another way.—Wash large buttons, lay them on sieves, with the stalks upwards, sprinkle salt over them to extract the water; when they are drained put them into a saucepan and set them in a cool oven for an hour, then take them out carefully and lay them by to cool and drain; boil the liquor which comes out of them with a little sauce until reduced to half the quantity. Put the mushrooms into a clean, dry jar, and when the liquor is cold, cover the mushroom in the jar with it and pour boiling suet over it; tie the jar well down with bladder and store it in a dry closet.

Okra Stewed.—Cut into small, round slices, and to a quart add a wineglass of hot water, a tablespoonful of butter, into which has been rubbed a teaspoonful of flour; salt and pepper to taste; put into a covered stewpan and stew until tender, shaking occasionally.

Okra Fried.—Strain a quart already boiled, mash it smooth, and season with salt and pepper; beat in one or two eggs and add flour enough to thicken into a paste; fried as fritters, and served upon a napkin hot, as fried.

OKRA TO DRY FOR WINTER USE.—Use only the young and tender ones, quarter and string them in a dry place, they must be soaked half a day before cooking.

CUCUMBER SALAD.—To one hundred cucumbers add a quarter of a peck of small onions. Peel both and cut them into thin slices; cover with salt, and stand in the sun for six hours; rinse clean, and stand in clear cold water for one hour. For the dressing take a box of the best mustard, put into it a little salt, pour in sufficient olive oil to stir it easily, add vinegar, and oil alternately till thin enough to pour smoothly. Put the cucumbers in jars, cover with the dressing, and cover closely. Seal the jars.

SALAD DRESSING WITHOUT OIL.—Take the yelks of two fresh eggs, boiled hard, mash them in a plate with a silver fork, and a saltspoonful of salt, and two spoonfuls of mustard; rub the whole well together. Add by degrees three spoonfuls of fresh cream and two of good vinegar, stirring all the time until quite smooth.

SALAD DRESSING.—Beat together one raw egg and a saltspoonful of salt until smooth. Then incorporate with it a teaspoonful of mustard, made rather thicker than usual. When these are quite smooth add, by degrees, one, two, or three tablespoonfuls, or even more, of good salad-oil, taking care to blend each portion of it with the egg before adding more. This ought to make any quantity, up to a teacupful, of a tenacious mass so thick that a teaspoon will stand up in it, and as smooth as honey. Dilute it with vinegar till it assumes the consistence of thick cream. No salad mixture is so smooth and rich as this, and at the same time the original oily flavor is completely lost, from the *raw* egg converting the oil into an emulsion. A little anchovy may be added if desired.

ITALIAN SALAD DRESSING.—Peel two well boiled potatoes and rub through a sieve, add a few shreds of raw onion, and the pounded yelks of two hard-boiled eggs. Mix these ingredients on a deep plate with two teaspoonfuls of salt, one of made mustard, three tablespoonfuls of olive oil, and one tablespoonful of vinegar; add, lastly, a teaspoonful of essence of anchovy, mash and mix the whole together thoroughly. Having cut up a sufficiency of lettuce (previously well washed in cold water and drained), add to it the dressing immediately before dinner, mixing with a wooden fork.

SALAD.—Look over carefully the tender half blanched leaves of head-lettuce, and cut them slightly. Make a dressing of the yelks of hard-boiled eggs, mixed mustard; black pepper, butter, and vinegar. Slice three hard-boiled eggs, lay them upon the lettuce, and pour the sauce over the whole.

POTATO SALAD.—To make a potato salad the potatoes must be boiled and cold, cut in slices **with** salt, pepper, oil, vinegar, and a little parsley. Mix the sauce, stew gently five minutes, and pour over the potatoes.

CHICKEN SALAD.—Mince the white meat of a chicken fine, or pull it in bits; chop the white parts of celery; prepare a salad dressing thus: Rub the yelks of hard-boiled eggs smooth with a spoon, put to each yelk a teaspoonful of made mustard, half as much salt, a tablespoonful of oil, and a wineglass of strong vinegar; put the celery on a large dish, lay the chicken on that, then pour it over the dressing. Lettuce, cut small, in the place of celery, may be used. Cut the whites of the eggs in rings to garnish the salad. Turkey meat prepared in the same way makes almost as good a dish.

LOBSTER SALAD.—Boil the fish for half an hour, afterwards rubbing the shell with oil; preserve this with the coral to garnish the dish. Extract the meat, and lay carefully on some nice white lettuce in the centre of the dish. Make a dressing of two hard-boiled eggs rubbed smooth in two tablespoonfuls of vinegar; add one tablespoonful of English mustard, three of salad oil, one of white powdered sugar, a teaspoonful of salt, some of black pepper, one pinch of Cayenne, and the yelks of two raw eggs; mix together and pour over the fish, dressing with cut hard-boiled eggs, the coral, and the claws and selected parts of the shell.

ENGLISH SALAD SAUCE.—Pound in a mortar the hard-boiled yelk of an egg; mix with it a saltspoonful of salt, a tablespoonful of ground mustard, a mashed mealy potato, two dessertspoonfuls of cream, a tablespoonful of olive oil, and a tablespoonful of vinegar.

SWEET SALAD SAUCE.—Mix together two tablespoonfuls of olive oil, the raw yelk of an egg, a little pepper, one tablespoonful of the best vinegar, a pinch of salt, and a dessertspoonful of moist sugar.

SWISS SALAD DRESSING.—Pound in a mortar two ounces of cheese, add a tablespoonful of vinegar, a small quantity of salt and pepper, and, by degrees, dilute it with olive oil.

PIQUANTE SAUCE FOR SALADS.—Two hard-boiled yelks of eggs, two raw yelks of eggs, mashed smooth, with a tablespoonful each of cream and olive oil; add sufficient vinegar to make it pretty sharp.

MAYOUNAISE FOR SALAD.—Beat together the juice of a lemon and the raw yelks of two eggs; then slowly drop in enough olive oil to make a thick cream, stirring gently and continuously while adding the oil. Vinegar may be used instead of lemon-juice.

CHAPTER VI.

PUDDINGS AND PASTRY.

PUDDINGS.

A few general remarks respecting the various ingredients of which puddings are composed, may be acceptable as preliminary to the receipts in this department.

Flour should be of the best quality, and perfectly dry, and sifted before being used; if in the least damp, the paste made from it will certainly be heavy.

Butter, unless fresh is used, should be washed from the salt, and well squeezed and wrung in a cloth, to get out all the water and buttermilk, which, if left in, assists to make the paste heavy.

Lard should be perfectly sweet, which may be ascertained by cutting the bladder through, and, if the knife smells sweet, the lard is good.

Suet should be finely chopped, perfectly free from skin, and quite sweet; during the process of chopping, it should be lightly dredged with flour, which prevents the pieces from sticking together. Beef suet is considered the best, but veal suet, or the outside fat of a loin or neck of mutton, makes good crusts, as also the skimmings in which a joint of mutton has been boiled, but *without* vegetables.

Clarified Beef Dripping answers very well for kitchen pies, puddings, cakes, or for family use. A very good short crust may be made by mixing with it a small quantity of moist sugar; but care must be taken to use the dripping sparingly, or a very disagreeable flavor will be imparted to the paste.

The freshness of all pudding ingredients is of much importance, as one bad article will taint the whole mixture.

When the *freshness* of eggs is *doubtful*, break each one separately in a cup before mixing them all together. Should there be a bad one amongst them, it can be thrown away; whereas, if mixed with the good ones, the entire quantity would be spoiled. The yelks and whites beaten separately make the articles they are put into much lighter.

Raisins and dried fruits for puddings should be carefully picked, and, in many cases, stoned. Currants should be well washed, pressed in a cloth, and placed on a dish before the fire to get thoroughly dry; they should then be picked carefully over, and *every piece of grit or stone* removed from amongst them. To plump them, some cooks pour boiling water over them, and then dry them before the fire.

Batter pudding should be smoothly mixed and free from lumps. To insure this, first mix the flour with a very small proportion of milk, and add the remainder by degrees. Should the pudding be very lumpy, it may be strained through a hair sieve.

All boiled puddings should be put on in *boiling water*, which must not be allowed to stop simmering, and the pudding must always be covered with the water; if requisite, the saucepan should be kept filled up.

To prevent a pudding boiled in a cloth from sticking to the bottom of the saucepan, place a small plate or saucer underneath it, and set the pan *on a trivet* over the fire. If a mould is used, this precaution is not necessary, but care must be taken to keep the pudding well covered with water.

For dishing a boiled pudding as soon as it comes out of the pot, dip it into a basin of cold water, and the cloth will then not adhere to it. Great expedition is necessary in sending puddings to table, as, by standing, they quickly become heavy, batter puddings particularly.

For baked or boiled puddings, the moulds, cups, or basins should be always buttered before the mixture is put in them, and they should be put into the saucepan directly after they are filled.

Scrupulous attention should be paid to the cleanliness of pudding-cloths, as, from neglect in this particular, the outsides of boiled puddings frequently taste very disagreeable. As soon as possible after it is taken off the pudding, it should be soaked in water, and then well washed without soap, unless it be very greasy. It should be dried out of doors, then folded up, and kept in a dry place. When wanted for use, dip it in boiling water, and dredge it slightly with flour.

The dry ingredients for puddings are better for being mixed some time before they are wanted; the liquid portion should only be added just before the pudding is put into the saucepan.

A pinch of salt is an improvement to the generality of puddings; but this ingredient should be added very sparingly, as the flavor should not be detected.

When baked puddings are sufficiently solid, turn them out of the dish they were baked in, bottom uppermost, and strew over them, fine sifted sugar.

When baked puddings are not done through, and yet the outside is sufficiently brown, cover them over with a piece of white paper until thoroughly cooked; this prevents them from getting burnt.

All batter puddings fall soon after they are baked. They ought to be served immediately after they are done. Indian puddings require long and slow baking. Rice should be baked quickly. Tapioca and other puddings of the kind should bake in a moderate oven like custards. All cake puddings should be baked in the same manner as cakes of nearly the same composition; as, for instance, sponge puddings quick, and plum puddings a long time.

ST. CLAIRE PUDDING.—Boil one quart of milk with sugar and lemon-peel to taste, and a pinch of powdered cinnamon; add one ounce of dissolved isinglass or gelatine. When boiling, add the yelks of four eggs, well beaten. Fill a mould; stand it in water and boil fifteen minutes. Put it on the ice for two hours. Make a sauce of sugar and wine, thickened with a little arrowroot, and stand also on the ice. Pour over the pudding when it is turned out of the mould.

ICE PUDDING.—Take one pint of cream, half a pint of milk, the yelks of four eggs, one ounce of sweet almonds pounded, and half a pound of sugar; put them in a stewpan on a gentle fire, and stir the mixture until the cream sets about the consistency of custard. When cold, add two wineglasses of brandy; freeze, and when sufficiently congealed, add one pound of preserved fruits, with a few currants; cut the fruit small, and mix well with the ice. Let it remain to set in the moulding pots, and keep it in ice till required for the table.

HALF-PAY PUDDING.—Quarter pound of suet, quarter pound of currants, quarter pound of raisins, quarter pound of flour, quarter pound of bread crumbs, two tablespoonfuls of molasses, half a pint of milk. Chop the suet finely; mix with it the currants (which should be nicely washed and dried), the raisins (which should be stoned), the flour, bread crumbs, and molasses; moisten with the milk, beat up the ingredients until all are thoroughly mixed, put them into a buttered basin, and boil the pudding for three and a half hours.

Minute Pudding.—Mix five tablespoonfuls of flour with half a pint of cold sweet milk, a very little salt, one-fourth of a nutmeg; stir it into a pint and a half of boiling sweet milk; boil one minute, stirring constantly; set it off from the fire until it gets lukewarm; add three beaten eggs; stir until it boils, and eat with cream and sugar.

Queen Pudding.—One pint of nice fine bread crumbs, one quart of milk, one cup of sugar, the yelks of four eggs beaten, the grated rind of a lemon, a piece of butter the size of an egg. Bake until done, but not watery. Whip the whites of the eggs stiff, beat in a teacupful of sugar in which has been strained the juice of the lemon, spread over the pudding a layer of jelly, pour the whites of the eggs over this; replace in the oven; bake lightly. To be eaten cold, with cream, if preferred.

Gray Pudding.—Take three eggs, weigh them in the shell; take an equal weight of sugar and of butter, and two-thirds of the weight of flour. Half melt the butter, and beat it to a cream; beat the eggs also, and mix them with the butter and sugar, beating the whole to a froth; then add the flour and the rind of a lemon, grated; beat all together and pour it into a mould. An hour will boil it.

Cottage Pudding.—A pound and a quarter of flour, fourteen ounces of suet, a pound and a quarter of stoned raisins, four ounces of currants, five of sugar, a quarter pound of potatoes smoothly mashed, half a nutmeg, a quarter teaspoonful of ginger, the same of salt, and of cloves in powder; mix the ingredients thoroughly; add four well beaten eggs with a quarter pint of milk, tie the pudding in a well-floured cloth, and boil it for four hours.

SOYER'S NEW CHRISTMAS PUDDING.—This receipt, if closely followed, would, at this festive season of the year, save tons of fruit and other expensive ingredients, which are partly wasted for the want of knowing how to turn them to the best advantage. This pudding will be found sufficient for eight persons after a Christmas dinner. Carefully prepare the following, previous to mixing the pudding: Four ounces of stoned raisins, four ounces of sultanas, half a pound of well-cleaned currants, half a pound of beef suet chopped fine, two ounces of powdered white sugar, two ounces of flour, half a pound of bread crumbs, twelve bitter almonds blanched, chopped small, half a nutmeg grated, two ounces of candied citron, the peel of half a small lemon chopped fine, separately, put in a basin, break over four eggs, and add half a gill of brandy. Mix these all well the evening before wanted, cover over till the morning, and when all is prepared, add half a gill of milk, again well stir your pudding; slightly butter a cloth, sprinkle a little flour over, put it in a basin, pour in the mixture, tie your cloth in the usual way, not too tight; put in half a gallon of boiling water, add more now and then, if required; let it simmer two hours and thirty minutes, turn out of the cloth and serve on a hot dish. Serve plain, if preferred, or with the sauce only. After which, when at the dining-room door, pour round a gill of either brandy or rum, which set on fire with a piece of paper; place the dish on the table, let burn half a minute, and pour the following sauce over from the sauce-boat; after which cut seven or eight slices from the pudding crosswise, or according to number, when help, and serve very hot. The sauce I prefer with it is as follows: Make half a pint of ordinary plain melted butter, rather thick, add to it two teaspoonfuls of sugar, the juice of half a lemon, and a pat of butter; stir quickly, pour over your pudding when very hot, or serve the sauce separately in a sauce-boat. Though the above pudding is not very expensive, it requires a little time and attention to do it properly; and well will be repaid the housewife who will take the trouble, as above described. In the event of some of the ingredients, such as almonds, candied orange or lemon-peel, not being obtainable in some country places, the pudding will still be good, although not so delicate in flavor.

CHRISTMAS PUDDING.—One pound of raisins, one pound of currants, one pound of suet, three-quarters of a pound of bread crumbs, one pint of milk, ten eggs, three-quarters of a pound of citron and orange-peel mixed, one small nutmeg, one glass of brandy. Stone the raisins and divide them, wash and dry the currants, and cut the peel into slices. Mix all these with the bread crumbs, flour and suet, chopped very fine; add the grated nutmeg, and then stir in the eggs well beaten, the brandy, and the milk. When the ingredients are well blended, put it into a mould, tie a floured cloth over it, and boil it six hours. When done turn it out, and serve it with brandy and arrowroot sauce.

PLUM PUDDING.—Four eggs, about one dozen crackers, one pint of new milk, one teacup of butter, half a pound of sugar, one pound of raisins, one pound of prunes, a grated nutmeg. Bake about an hour.

SUET PLUM PUDDING.—One cup of molasses, one cup of finely-chopped suet, one cup of milk, three cups of flour, one cup of stoned raisins; add currants and citron, if liked; one teaspoonful of soda, one teaspoonful of ground cloves and cinnamon, one nutmeg. Tie up loosely in your pudding-bag, and boil three or four hours. Eat with wine sauce.

BARBARA'S PLUM PUDDING.—One cup of chopped suet, one cup of chopped apples, one cup of molasses, two cups of raisins, one cup of sweet or sour milk, four cups of flour, quarter of a teaspoonful of saleratus, and a little salt. Boil or steam five hours.

RICH PLUM PUDDING WITHOUT FLOUR.—One

pound and a half of grated bread, one pound and a half of raisins, one pound and a half of currants, one pound of beef suet, peel of one large lemon, three ounces of almonds, a little nutmeg or mixed spice, sugar to taste, three-quarters of a pound of candied orange, lemon, and citron, eight or nine eggs, half a pint of milk, two wineglassfuls of brandy. Stone the raisins, wash and pick the currants, chop the suet very fine, and mix with them a pound and a half of grated bread; add the candied peel cut into shreds, the almonds blanched and minced, and the mixed spice and sugar to taste. When all are thoroughly blended, stir it well together with eight or nine well beaten eggs, two glassfuls of brandy, and half a pint of milk, tie it in a cloth, and boil it for five hours or five hours and a half, or divide it into equal parts, and boil it in moulds or basins for half the time.

Cottage Plum Pudding.—A pound and a half of flour, four or five eggs, a pinch of salt, a little nutmeg, one pound of raisins, half a pound of currants, sugar to taste, and a little milk. Make a thick batter with five well beaten eggs, a pound and a half of flour, and a sufficient quantity of milk. Then add the currants, washed and picked, the raisins stoned, a little nutmeg, and sugar to taste. Mix all well together, and boil it in a basin or floured cloth for quite five hours. The peel of a lemon grated, and a few pieces of citron cut thin may be added.

UNRIVALLED PLUM PUDDING.—Two and a half pounds of raisins, one and three-quarters of a pound of currants, two pounds of the finest moist sugar, two pounds of bread crumbs, sixteen eggs, two pounds of finely-chopped suet, six ounces of mix candied peel, the rind of two lemons, one ounce of ground nutmeg, one ounce of ground cinnamon, half an ounce of pounded bitter almonds, quarter of a pint of brandy. Stone and cut up the raisins, but do not chop them; wash and dry the currants, and cut the candied peel into thin slices. Mix all the dry ingredients well together, and moisten them with the eggs, which should be well beaten and strained; then stir in the brandy, and, when all is thoroughly mixed, well butter and flour a stout new pudding cloth; put in the pudding, tie it down very tightly and closely, boil from six to eight hours, and serve with brandy sauce. This quantity may be divided and boiled in buttered moulds. For small families this is the most desirable way, as the above will be found to make a pudding of large dimensions.

CHRISTMAS PLUM PUDDING.—A pound of suet, cut in pieces not too fine, a pound of currants, and a pound of raisins stoned, four eggs, half a grated nutmeg, an ounce of citron and lemon-peel, shred fine, a teaspoonful of beaten ginger, half a pound of bread crumbs, half a pound of flour, and a pint of milk; beat the eggs first, add half the milk, beat them together, and by degrees stir in the flour, then the suet, spice, and fruit, and as much milk as will mix it together very thick; then take a clean cloth, dip in boiling water, and squeeze dry. While the water is boiling fast, put in your pudding, which should boil at least five hours.

APPLE PUDDING.—Pare four or five large tart apples, grate them fine; then make the following custard, into which stir the grated apple: Flour, four tablespoonfuls; one pint of milk, five eggs, and a little grated orange-peel. After you have these ingredients well mixed, pour them into your pudding-dish, and bake about one hour and a quarter.

BOILED APPLE PUDDING.—Make a butter-crust, or a suet one, using for a moderate-sized pudding from three-quarters to one pound of flour, with the other ingredients in proportion. Butter a basin; line it with some of the paste; pare, core and cut the apples into slices, and fill the basin with these; add sugar to taste, flavor with lemon-peel and juice, and cover with crust; pinch the edges together, flour the cloth, place it over the pudding, tie it securely, and put it into plenty of fast-boiling water. Let it boil from one and a half to two and a half hours, according to the size; then turn it out of the basin, and send it to table quickly. Apple puddings may also be boiled in a cloth without a basin; but, when made in this way, must be served without the least delay, as the crust so soon becomes heavy.

BAKED APPLE PUDDING.—Four large apples boiled, some grated bread, four ounces of butter, four yelks and two whites of eggs well beaten, sugar to taste; edge a dish with puff-paste, and bake half an hour.

RICH SWEET APPLE PUDDING.—Half a pound of bread crumbs, half a pound of suet, half a pound of currants, half a pound of apples, half a pound of moist sugar, six eggs, twelve sweet almonds, half a saltspoonful of grated nutmeg, one wineglassful of brandy. Chop the suet very fine; wash the currants, dry them, and pick away the stalks and pieces of grit; pare, core and chop the apple, and grate the bread into fine crumbs, and mince the almonds. Mix all these ingredients together, adding the sugar and nutmeg; beat up the eggs, omitting the whites of three; stir these to the pudding, and when all is well mixed add the brandy, and put the pudding into a buttered mould; tie down with a cloth, put it into boiling water, and let it boil for three hours.

PIPPIN PUDDING.—Boil six apples well; take out the cores, put in half a pint of milk thickened with three eggs, a little lemon-peel, and sugar to the taste; put puff-paste around your dish, bake it in a slow oven, grate sugar over it and serve it hot.

ANOTHER.—Take the pulp of two large roasted apples, the peel and juice of one lemon, the yelks of six eggs, two Savoy biscuits grated, a quarter of a pound of butter melted, and sugar to your taste. Beat the ingredients together, put a puff-paste around your dish, and bake it.

APPLE ROLL.—Make a paste with one-fourth of a pound of butter to one of flour mixed with water, not very stiff. Peel and slice rather thick, tart apples, roll the paste very thin, or as thin as the bottom crust of a pie; spread the apples on the crust, so as to cover it, dredge on a little flour, and roll it as tight as possible. Cut the ends even, and put it in the steamer, or wrap it in thick cloth and boil it. It will take one hour steady cooking. Serve with butter and sugar; cut it in thin slices from the end when serving.

COCOANUT PUDDING—Half a pound of loaf-sugar, half a pound of butter, half a cocoanut, grated, the whites of six eggs, one tablespoonful of rose water, two tablespoonfuls of brandy. Pare the brown skin off the nut, wash it in cold water, wipe it dry, and grate it. After the butter has been prepared as for lady-cake, and the sugar pounded fine, beat them to a cream; whisk the whites of the eggs until stiff and dry, and add to the butter and sugar; *stir the whole well together*, and add gradually the nut, brandy and rose-water—then *stir well*, but do not *beat* it. Bake on *rich* pastry, without a top crust.

FINE COCOANUT PUDDING.—Pare the dark rind from one cocoanut and grate the meat. Break into a bowl six eggs, adding a heavy tablespoonful of sugar for each egg. When very light, pour in a pint of cream or milk to stir in the cocoanut. Melt a teacup half full of butter and add to it, with a small portion of soda. Put a puff-paste into your dish, and fill it with the mixture.

Cocoanut Custard Pudding.—Grate half a cocoanut meat; stir it into a good custard, and bake in a buttered basin. Make the custard of four eggs to a quart of milk. This may be baked with an under crust. A quick oven for this—thirty or forty minutes. Serve with the following wine sauce: One cup of butter, one cup of sugar; stir to a cream; then one cup of wine added slowly. Put the bowl into a vessel of hot water, one half hour before using it. It must not be stirred.

Cocoanut Cup Puddings.—Melt two ounces of butter, cut small, stirring in two ounces of sifted sugar; boil up for a minute. When cool, grate in two ounces of cocoanut, add two ounces of shred citron, the grated rind of a lemon, and four eggs; beat with the juice of half a lemon. Mix, and put into well-buttered coffee cups, and bake half an hour. The same may be made as one pudding in a dish, and baked longer.

Lemon Pudding.—To a pint of new milk boiled, add two spoonfuls of flour, and boil till smooth; then stir in a quarter of a pound of butter and four well beaten eggs, add the peel of a lemon shred very fine, and sweeten to your taste; line a dish with very light puff-paste, pour in the mixture, and bake half an hour.

EXCELLENT LEMON PUDDING.—Beat the yelks of four eggs; add four ounces of white sugar, the rind of a lemon being rubbed with some lumps of it to take the essence; then peel, and beat it in a mortar with the juice of a lemon, and mix all with four or five ounces of butter warmed. Put a crust into a shallow dish, nick the edges, and put the above into it. When served, turn the pudding out of the dish.

ICED LEMON PUDDING.—Quarter of a pound of butter, half a pound of sugar, the yelks of five eggs, one quart of milk, one lemon, the rind grated and juice pressed out, six tablespoonfuls of grated bread or cracker. When the pudding is baked, take the whites of the eggs and sugar and beat for icing. Spread over the top and brown in the oven; it will brown in a few minutes.

BAKED LEMON PUDDING.—One teacupful of boiling water, one tablespoonful of corn-flour, mixed with a little water, one teacupful of sifted sugar, one tablespoonful of butter, one egg, juice and rind of one lemon. Pour this mixture into the boiling water; then pour it on to the butter and sugar; beat the egg, and, when cool, put it in; have the paste ready in the dishes, and pour it in and bake.

Sponge Pudding.—Butter a mould thickly and fill it three parts full with small sponge cakes, soaked through with wine; fill up the mould with a rich cold custard. Butter a paper and put on the mould, then tie a floured cloth over it quite close, and boil it an hour. Turn out the pudding carefully, and pour some cold custard over it; or bake it and serve with wine sauce instead of custard.

Baked Sponge Pudding.—Cream together a quarter of a pound of butter and two ounces of powdered white sugar, then add four eggs and two tablespoonfuls of flour; beat it slowly. Fill six small cups and bake them twenty minutes.

Clara's Sponge Pudding.—One cup of sugar, one egg, one cup of sweet milk, three cups of flour, one teaspoonful of soda, two of cream of tartar, half a one of salt. Steam two and a half hours.

Boiled Fig Pudding.—A quarter of a pound of figs, half a pound of suet, a cupful of bread crumbs, four eggs, a breakfastcupful of milk. Mix the suet, figs, and bread together; boil the milk and pour over them. Now beat the eggs and pour over the other ingredients. Let the mixture stand a little while, then put it into shape, boil it for two hours, and serve with cream or sweet sauce.

Fig Pudding.—Procure one pound of good figs, and chop them very fine, and also a quarter pound of suet, likewise chopped as fine as possible. Dust them both with a little flour as you proceed, it helps to bind the pudding together. Then take one pound of fine bread crumbs, and not quite a quarter pound of sugar; beat two eggs in a teacupful of milk, and mix all well together; boil four hours. If you choose, serve it with wine or brandy sauce, and ornament it with blanched almonds. Simply cooked, however, it is better where there are children, with whom it is generally a favorite. We forgot to say, flavor with a little allspice or nutmeg, as you like; but add the spice before the milk and eggs.

RAISIN PUDDING.—Soak two ounces of raisins in enough brandy to cover them. Take half a pound of flour, half a pound of chopped suet, a dessertspoonful of ground ginger, two eggs, four ounces of white sugar, and enough milk to make it a pretty light paste; add the raisins and brandy, put it into a cloth or basin, boil it for two hours, and serve with what pudding sauce you please.

BOILED RAISIN PUDDING.—Mix together half a pound each of stoned raisins, chopped suet, and bread crumbs; add four well beaten eggs, a teacupful of milk, a little salt, and a spoonful of grated ginger. Boil it for four hours in a buttered mould or floured cloth. Pour a little brandy over it before serving.

PLAIN RAISIN PUDDING.—One pound of raisins, stoned, one pound of beef-suet, shred fine, eight eggs, quarter pound of flour, two spoonfuls of milk, a little ginger and salt; brandy to your taste. Mix all well together, tie up in a cloth, and boil four hours.

FRUIT RAISED PUDDING.—When baking take two and a half cups of light dough, one of sugar, hardly three-fourths of a cup of butter, two eggs, half a teaspoonful of soda, one glass of wine or brandy, cinnamon, cloves, and nutmeg, being careful not to let one spice predominate; a half pound of washed currants, the same of stoned raisins, and a quarter of a pound of citron, chopped fine. Let it stand until light in the pudding-dish; bake carefully, so as not to form a heavy crust; turn it out when baked, and pour over it while hot a rich wine sauce. This will be found excellent. It must be started very early in the morning. If home-made yeast is used the dough can be saved until the next day. Sweeten it with soda before mixing in the other ingredients, and allow it to rise again.

TOMATO PUDDING.—Pour boiling water on tomatoes, remove the skins, put in the bottom of the pudding-dish some bread crumbs, then slice the tomatoes on them, season with sugar, butter, pepper, and salt; add some more bread crumbs, then the sliced tomatoes and seasoning, and if the tomato does not wet the bread crumbs add a little water; then, for a small pudding, beat up two eggs and pour over the top. Bake about twenty minutes.

CAROMEL PUDDING.—Seven ounces of sugar dissolved in a pan in water and burnt. Line the inside of a well buttered new tin with a coating of this. In another pan, one pint of sweetened new milk, the yelks of seven eggs, and the whites of two, beaten together; boil the milk, pour it upon the eggs, and stir well together. Pour this into the sugar-lined tin, put the tin into a pan with three inches of water, and steam it for three-quarters of an hour. When quite cold turn out into a dish, and serve.

CASSANDRA PUDDING.—Three tablespoonfuls of flour, three eggs, quarter of a pound of moist sugar, three-quarters of a pound of raisins, stewed and chopped fine, and half a pound of chopped suet. Mix well and boil three hours and a half in a well floured bag.

BRIGHTON PUDDING.—Three eggs, quarter of a pound of sugar, quarter of a pound of flour, quarter of a pound of butter, and the peel of a lemon, finely minced or grated. Beat the sugar and eggs for twenty minutes, oil the butter and beat in gradually, and sift in the flour slowly, beating steadily while mixing. Steam the pudding for one hour, and serve with preserved fruit.

GOLDEN PUDDING.—Quarter of a pound of bread crumbs, quarter of a pound of suet, quarter of a pound of marmalade, quarter of a pound of sugar, four eggs. Put the bread crumbs into a basin, mix with them the suet, which should be finely minced, the marmalade, and the sugar. Stir all these ingredients well together, beat the eggs to a froth, moisten the pudding with these, and when mixed put it into a mould or buttered basin; tie down with a floured cloth, and boil for two hours. When turned out, strew a little fine sifted sugar over the top and serve. The mould may be ornamented with stoned raisins, arranged in any fanciful pattern, before the mixture is poured in, which would add very much to the appearance of the pudding. For a plainer pudding double the quantities of the bread crumbs; and if the eggs do not moisten sufficiently use a little milk.

LUNCHEON PUDDING.—A teacupful of cream, the same of butter, well beaten, and a little salt, made into a stiff batter with flour, so that it will just pour out; tie it in a cloth, and boil two hours.

MOULDED PUDDING.—Beat lightly the yelks of ten eggs and the whites of six with three-quarters of a pound of sugar, the rind of an orange, or two lemons grated, six and a half ounces of flour; add one pint of boiling milk. When nearly cold, mix in the eggs and sugar, and add a wineglassful of brandy, and half a pound of melted butter. Bake it an hour and a quarter, and turn it out.

STALE LOAF PUDDING.—Take a three quart pudding-dish, fill two-thirds full of broken bread, pour boiling water over it, and let it stand till soft enough to stir up fine; then add three well beaten eggs, salt to taste; fill up the pan with water and bake. When done, make a sauce with butter and sugar mashed together and flavored with lemon or nutmeg. It is very nice made with the sweetening and rice baked in. Indian and rice are good made in the same way. Milk is quite unnecessary for such things when you can get eggs.

FARMER'S PUDDING.—Take one pint of bread crumbs, one quart of milk, half a cup of sugar, four eggs, taking only the yelks, butter the size of a walnut, one lemon, grated; bake until done, but not watery; then spread a layer of currant-jelly or any preserved fruit over it. Take the whites of the eggs and sugar, in which has been stirred the juice of the lemon, beat to a stiff froth, pour it over the pudding, and brown it. Serve cold with cream. It can be made without a lemon. Flavor with nutmeg.

STEAMBOAT PUDDING.—One quart of milk, six eggs, quarter of a pound of seeded raisins, quarter of a pound of currants, sugar to the taste. Beat the eggs and add them to the milk with the fruit; pour it in a pudding-dish, cover the top with slices of bread, well buttered. First dip the bread in the milk, so as it may be brown when it is baked. This is generally eaten cold. It may be flavored with lemon or vanilla.

TREACLE PUDDING.—Four ounces each of flour, suet, currants, raisins, and bread crumbs, two tablespoonfuls of treacle, and half a pint of milk. Mix all well together, and boil in a mould three hours. Serve with wine or brandy sauce.

Rich Pudding.—Line a deep pie-dish with puff-paste, having first buttered it thoroughly, place on this a layer of jam, then a layer of custard, then jam, then custard, until the dish is nearly full, leaving the custard layer at the top. Slice the minced peel and cut it into diamonds and arrange on the top. Bake for twenty minutes in a quiet oven, let the pudding cool, beat up the whites of the eggs that were used for the custard into a stiff whip with a little powdered sugar; pile the whip on as high as possible, and serve.

Economical Pudding.—Take two tablespoonfuls of rice, put it into a small saucepan with as much water as the rice will absorb. When boiled enough add a pinch of salt, then set it by the fire until the rice is quite soft and dry. Throw it up in a dish, add two ounces of butter, four tablespoonfuls of tapioca, a pint and a half of milk, sugar to the taste, a little grated nutmeg, and two eggs beaten up. Let it all be well stirred together and baked an hour.

Family Pudding.—One pound of flour, one pound of suet, chopped fine, three-quarters of a pound of sugar, one pound each of carrots and potatoes, well boiled and mashed together, half a pound of raisins, three-quarters of a pound of bread crumbs; spice, flavoring, and peel optional. Mix the whole well together with a little water. It must not be too stiff, and certainly not too moist. Rub a basin well with dripping, and boil for eight hours.

Flour Pudding.—Four spoonfuls of flour, six eggs, two pints of milk. Line a basin with buttered paper, and boil an hour.

Simple Pudding.—Three-quarters of a pound of flour, one pint of new milk, four eggs, whites well beaten, a pinch of salt. Boil it for one hour and a half.

Suet Pudding.—One pint of sweet milk, one cup of sour milk, four eggs, one cup of sugar, two cups of chipped suet, one teaspoonful of soda, a piece of butter the size of a small egg, raisins or currants or dried fruit, flour to make a stiff batter. Boil three hours. Liquid sauce.

Boiled Suet Pudding.—One cup of finely chopped suet, one of molasses, one of milk, sweet or sour, one of raisins or currants, three cups of flour, one teaspoonful of salt, one teaspoonful and a half of soda, one of every kind of spice, part of nutmeg. Boil four hours; tie up loosely. Wine sauce.

Tapioca Pudding.—Four large tablespoonfuls of tapioca soaked over night in one quart of new milk, grated rind of one lemon, one tumbler of sweet cream, one half of a tumbler of wine, with sugar enough in it to fill the glass. Stir the tapioca and milk over the fire until it comes to a boil, before adding any of the other ingredients; four eggs, beaten separately, and added just before baking; bakes in about five minutes. To be eaten cold.

ARROWROOT PUDDING.—Mix a tablespoonful of arrowroot in two of cold milk; pour it into a pint of boiling milk, in which dissolve a teacupful of white sugar; stir it constantly, and add a little mace, or any other kind of spice, and four eggs; bake it half an hour in a dish lined with paste. If it is preferred to look clear, substitute water instead of milk, and add one more egg.

POTATO SUET PUDDING.—Take a pound of mealy potatoes, boiled and mashed smooth; add four ounces of chopped beef suet, three eggs, a little milk, sugar to taste, and a good dessertspoonful of powdered ginger. Put it into a well floured cloth and boil for an hour. Serve, turned into a dish, with saffron or sweet sauce poured over it.

BOILED INDIAN PUDDING.—Take sweet milk of sufficient quantity for the pudding desired; salt to the taste, and stir in Indian meal till a little milk will rise on the top by standing. If too thick it will be hard. Fill a pudding crock, and tie a cloth tightly over it. Put into boiling water sufficient to keep it covered, and boil steadily three hours. Fruit may be added, if desired. Serve with sweetened cream. This is an old-fashioned Connecticut pudding.

CORN-MEAL PUDDING.—Two quarts of sweet milk, one pint of corn-meal, one-half pint of beef suet or fat pork, chopped fine, three eggs, and a little nutmeg and salt; sweeten to your taste with sugar. Heat the milk, and, while hot, stir in the meal; after this, set it where it will cool, and then add the eggs. Bake from three to fours in a slow oven.

INDIAN-MEAL PUDDING.—Into one quart of boiling milk stir one quart of sifted fine meal; then add one quart of cold milk, two well beaten eggs, one-half cup of sugar, one cup of flour, and a little salt and spice. Stir it well and pour it into a buttered dish. Bake two hours, and serve with butter.

POUND PUDDING.—Take half a pound of fresh butter and an equal weight of sugar, beat the butter to a cream, then add six very well whisked eggs, half a pound of flour, four ounces of currants, two ounces of candied lemon-peel, shred fine, and a little lemon-juice. Beat all together for a quarter of an hour, put it into a buttered mould, and boil it for two hours and a half.

POTATO PUDDING. — One pound of potatoes, boiled, half a pound of fresh butter, half a pound of sugar, the yelks of six eggs, and whites of three, one gill of cream, one gill of wine, one teaspoonful of mace, and one nutmeg. Bake in puff-paste.

BISCUIT PUDDING.—Crumble four moderate-sized biscuits in two pints of sweet milk, take a piece of butter the size of an egg, one cup of sugar, three eggs, beat them separate, and pour the white on top. Add a little nutmeg; bake half an hour.

Macaroni Pudding.—Take three-quarters of a pound of macaroni, boil it till quite soft. Add half a pound of sugar, a quarter of a pound of currants, and juice of one lemon; bake till browned. A simple mode of cooking macaroni, or tapioca, is to sweeten and boil till soft. Add the juice of a lemon, and turn into a mould till cool.

Cake Pudding.—One cup of butter, two of sugar, one of milk, five eggs, two teaspoonfuls of cream of tartar, one of soda, three and a half cups of flour. Flavor to taste.

Sago Pudding.—One pint of milk, three tablespoonfuls of sago, one half cup of butter, one cup of sugar, four eggs. Soak the sago in water two hours; then put the milk on the stove and stir the sago in; add the butter and sugar after it is cold; stir in the whites and yelks of the eggs beaten separately.

Crumb Pudding.—The yelks and whites of three eggs, beaten separately, one ounce of moist sugar, and sufficient bread crumbs to make it into a thick, but not stiff mixture; a little powdered cinnamon. Beat all together for five minutes, and bake in a buttered tin. When baked, turn it out of the tin, pour two glasses of boiling wine over it, and serve. Cherries, either fresh or preserved, are very nice mixed in the pudding.

Custard Pudding.—One quart of new milk, three eggs, half a pound of sugar, a little salt, pour these into your pudding-dish, mix well, slice some bread, and butter it, and lay the thin slices over the top of your pudding. Bake about one hour.

Cup Puddings (without Eggs).—Beat three ounces of fresh butter to cream, mix with it three ounces of baked flour, three ounces of sifted loaf-sugar, three ounces of currants, and three tablespoons of cream; beat the whole for ten minutes. Butter six or seven small moulds, pour the mixture in till they are three parts full, and bake them in a quick oven for twenty minutes. Serve with wine sauce.

Cold Cup Puddings.—Grate the rind of a lemon into a pint of cream (or new milk), let it just boil, and strain it. When cool, beat the yelks of six eggs, and add them to the above, with crushed lump sugar to sweeten it. Pour the mixture into six cups, and steam for half an hour. Next day turn out and garnish with currant jelly or other preserves.

Green Corn Pudding.—One dozen ears of corn, grated, three eggs, well beaten, one pint of sweet milk, half a cupful of butter, one large spoonful of sugar, pepper and salt. Bake in a large pudding-pan two hours.

Carrot Pudding, Baked.—Take half a pound of grated raw carrot, half a pound of bread crumbs, the yelks of four eggs and the whites of two, a little sugar and nutmeg, a gill each of white wine and cream; mix all well together, lay a puff-paste over your dish; put in your pudding and bake for an hour.

CHOCOLATE PUDDING.—Put one quart of milk on to boil; take an ounce and a half of chocolate and grate it, mix it with a little cold milk. Then take the boiled milk and stir into it the chocolate, and set it to cool; when nearly cool stir in the beaten yelks of six eggs. Flavor with vanilla sweetened to taste, and bake until of the consistency of custard. Beat the whites of the eggs to a froth with six spoonfuls of powdered sugar, pile it lightly on top of the pudding, replace in the oven, and brown.

RICE PUDDING.—To one cup of boiled rice add half a cup of butter, five eggs, sugar to taste, and cream enough to make it liquid. Flavor with essence of lemon, and bake in rich paste in deep pudding dishes.

BOILED BATTER PUDDING.—Three eggs, one ounce of butter, one pint of milk, three tablespoonfuls of flour, a little salt. Put the flour into a basin, and add sufficient milk to moisten it. Carefully rub down all the lumps with a spoon, then pour in the remainder of the milk, and stir in the butter, which should be previously melted. Keep beating the mixture, add the eggs and a pinch of salt, and when the batter is quite smooth put into a well buttered basin, tie it down very tightly, and put it into boiling water. Move the basin about for a few minutes after it is put into the water, to prevent the flour settling in any part, and boil for one hour and a quarter. This pudding may also be boiled in a floured cloth that has been wetted in hot water; it will then take a few minutes less than when boiled in a basin. Send these puddings very quickly to table, and serve with sweet sauce, wine sauce, stewed fruit, or jam of any kind. When the latter is used, a little of it may be placed around the dish in small quantities as a garnish.

QUAKING PUDDING.—Well beat eight eggs, add to them the grated crumbs of a stale bread roll, two spoonfuls of ground rice, a little nutmeg, and orange flower water. Mix it smoothly together with a quart of new milk, put it into a floured cloth, tie it rather loose, plunge it into boiling water, and boil it briskly for one hour. Serve with red or white wine sauce.

PENNSYLVANIA PUDDING.—Three eggs, one teacupful of sugar, quarter of a pound of butter, three-quarters of a cup of new milk, two cups of flour, one yeast powder. Bake in a quick oven three-quarters of an hour.

VARIETY PUDDINGS.—Take a quarter pound of fresh butter and beat it to a thick cream, add four tablespoonfuls of fine flour, two ounces of loaf sugar, one ounce of candied peel, cut into thick slices, six sweet and six bitter almonds, blanched and **cut** lengtnways. Mix these ingredients together, form them into rounds, and bake them in six patty-pans.

BLACKBERRY PUDDING.—One quart of blackberries, six large apples, pared and cut in thin slices, half a pound of sugar, and three or four slices of lemon-peel. Make a light paste, line a deep dish, fill it with the fruit and sugar, and boil it slowly and steadily for one hour. Serve with grated nutmeg, sugar, and sweet cream.

RIPE GOOSEBERRY PUDDING.—Scald a pint of ripe gooseberries in very little water, when tender mash them in the liquor in which they were boiled, pulp them through a sieve, and add to them the beaten yelks of four eggs, a quarter of a pound of sugar, and a quarter of a pound of blanched sweet almonds, lightly chopped. Mix all very well together, and bake it in a pie-dish, edged with a rim of puff-paste. Half an hour's baking will do it. Serve with cream.

GREEN CURRANT PUDDING.—Take the currants as soon as they are large enough, pick them from their stalks, put them into a pudding-basin lined with a light suet crust, add plenty of sugar, cover them with a paste, and, if it is a pint pudding, boil it for two hours. A larger size requires to be boiled longer.

ORANGE PUDDING.—Pound in a mortar three ounces of fresh butter and four ounces of lump sugar, grate in the rinds of two oranges (taking care not to allow any of the juice to escape); also the whole of a large or two small apples, also grated. When thoroughly mixed, add four eggs, well beaten. Spread it to the thickness of half an inch of puff-paste. Bake quickly.

ALMOND PUDDING.—Half a pound of blanched almonds, four ounces of white sugar, six tablespoonfuls of rose water, half a pint of sweet cream, three eggs, a little grated lemon-peel. Put the almonds in a mortar and put a few spoonfuls of sugar on them, and rub them fine; then add the rosewater, beat the remaining sugar and the eggs together separate, and then add them to the mixture in the mortar. When all are well mixed, warm a little, then put a little crust around the edges or sides, and bake half an hour.

CITRON PUDDING.—Take one half pint of cream, one tablespoonful of flour, two ounces of white sugar, and a little grated nutmeg. Mix all these ingredients together with the well beaten yelks of three eggs. Cut two ounces of citron into thin slices, place pieces of it in small buttered moulds or cups, fill them with the mixture, and bake until the pudding assumes a light brown color. This quantity will make five puddings, which are sufficient for a side dish.

SUPPER PUDDING.—Line a basin with slices of stale bread, cut half an inch thick; boil some fruit (currants are the best, mixed with raspberries) with sugar as for compote, pour it boiling into the basin, cover it with bread, and place a plate with a weight upon it, let it stand in a cold place all night; serve as soon as turned out. Cream may be eaten with it, or a whipped cream poured over it.

PERIPATETIC PUDDING.—Six sponge cakes, six eggs, a quarter of a pound of sifted sugar, half a pound of fresh butter, half a pound of marmalade, two glasses of sweet wine. Well mix these ingredients, paper the tin, and bake it about half an hour.

FORTUNATUS PUDDING.—Two eggs and their weight in butter and loaf sugar, melt the butter a little, and beat well together. Line the dish with puff-paste and lay some fruit jam upon it; pour the batter in, and bake a quarter of an hour or twenty minutes.

TRANSPARENT PUDDING.—Beat eight eggs very well, put them into a stewpan with half a pound of sugar, pounded fine, the same quantity of butter, and some nutmeg, grated. Set it on the fire, and keep stirring it till it thickens. Then set it in a basin to cool, put a rich puff-paste round the edge of the dish, pour in your pudding, and bake it in a moderate oven. It will eat light and clear. You may add candied orange or citron, if preferred.

CREAM PUDDING.—Boil a quart of cream with a blade of mace and half a nutmeg, grated; let it cool, and beat up eight eggs and three whites. Strain them well, and mix a spoonful of flour into them; also a quarter of a pound of almonds, blanched and beaten fine, with a spoonful of orange flower or rose water. Then by degrees mix in the cream and beat all well together. Take a thick cloth, wet it, and flour it well, pour in the mixture, tie it close, and boil in half an hour. Let the water boil fast. When it is done, turn it into the dish, pour melted butter over with a little sack, and throw fine sugar all over.

CHOCOLATE CREAM CUSTARD PUDDING.—Scrape a quarter of a pound of the best chocolate, pour on it a teacupful of boiling water, and let it stand by the fire until it is quite dissolved. Beat eight eggs lightly, omitting the whites of two. Stir them by degrees into a quart of rich cream, alternately with the chocolate and three tablespoonfuls of white sugar. Put the mixture into a dish and bake it ten minutes.

CREAM TAPIOCA PUDDING.—Soak three tablespoonfuls of tapioca in water three hours, put the same in a quart of boiling milk, boil fifteen minutes. Beat the yelks of four eggs in one cup of sugar, stir them into the pudding five minutes before it is done, flavor with lemon or vanilla. Beat the whites of four eggs to a stiff froth with three tablespoonfuls of sugar, put this over the pudding, and bake five minutes. A spoonful or two of prepared cocoanut in with the yelks and sugar is very good; the cocoanut can also be sprinkled over the top, on the whites, before putting in to brown.

Railway Pudding.—Flour, suet, sugar, currants, and raisins, of each ten ounces, grated potatoes and carrots, together ten ounces, one nutmeg, and two ounces of candied orange-peel, well mixed together and boiled for several hours. To be served with brandy sauce.

Simple Bread Pudding.—Take the crumbs of a stale roll, pour over it one pint of boiling milk, and set it by to cool. When quite cold, beat it up very fine with two ounces of butter, sifted sugar sufficient to sweeten it, grate in half a nutmeg, and add half a pound of well washed currants. Beat up four eggs separately, and then mix them up with the rest, adding, if desired, a few strips of candied orange-peel. All the ingredients must be beaten up together for about half an hour, as the lightness of the pudding depends upon that. Tie it up in a cloth and boil for an hour. When it is dished, pour a little white wine sauce over the top.

Bread Pudding.—One pint of grated bread crumbs, one quart of milk, yelks of six eggs, well beaten, one grated lemon, and sugar to taste. Bake. When cold spread a layer of jelly over the top, then make an icing of the whites of the eggs and white sugar, and spread smoothly over the jelly. To be eaten cold without sauce.

Brown Bread Pudding.—Take half a pound of good brown bread without crust, cut it into moderately thin slices, spread them over with cream, lay them in a buttered dish, strew finely shred candied citron-peel between each slice, boil half a pint of new milk, add some sugar and cinnamon, pour it over the bread, and when nearly cold, beat three eggs and pour into the dish. Bake for half an hour in a moderately heated oven.

STEAMED BREAD AND BUTTER PUDDING.—Lay your bread and butter in a pudding-basin, with layers of fruit jam between; add a custard as for a baked pudding, and then steam it. When served pour a custard over it.

SOUFFLÉ PUDDING.—Put six ounces of corn flour into a stewpan with eight ounces of pounded loaf sugar, mix these smoothly together, add four ounces of fresh butter and a few drops of essence of vanilla; stir briskly over the fire until it boils, and then work in vigorously six yelks of eggs and the six whites whisked into a firm froth. They are to be slightly incorporated with the batter, which must then be poured into a buttered dish.

PRINCE ALBERT PUDDING.—Half a pound of bread crumbs, half a pound of sugar, half a pound of butter, six eggs, beaten separately, juice of one lemon, rinds of two, grated, one wineglass of brandy, four tablespoonfuls of any kind of preserves. Steam the pudding in a mould one hour and a half. Wine sauce.

GERMAN PUDDING.—Boil twelve good-sized potatoes, peel them, and crush them thoroughly. Put them into a saucepan, with salt and a little lemon-peel; put it on the fire and stir all well whilst you add a piece of fresh butter and a little cream and sugar. When quite hot, take the saucepan from the fire, let the mixture cool a little, and then add a tablespoonful of orange flower water, four whole eggs, and the yelks of four more. Mix all well together, and put into a mould which has previously had a slight coating of butter and bread crumbs. Bake it, and bring it hot to table.

Syllabub Pudding.—Well beat your eggs, add to them six ounces of pounded and sifted loaf sugar, a glass of brandy, a glass of white wine, and sufficient flour to make it a very stiff batter. Have a quart of milk, warm from the cow, poured upon it while you continue beating, and when it is well frothed, put it into a buttered dish, place it in a quick oven, and bake it for a quarter of an hour. Serve immediately.

Bird's Nest Pudding.—Peel tart apples, take out the cores, leaving the apples whole. Make a custard of eight well beaten eggs, half a pint of cream, and a pint and a half of scalded milk, thickened with a heaping tablespoonful of flour and a little salt, but no sugar; pour it over the apples. Bake twenty minutes. When the apples are tender the pudding is done. Serve immediately with butter and sugar, stirred to a cream.

Omnibus Pudding.—Half a pound of flour, half

a pound of beef suet, half a pound of currants, half a pound of raisins, stoned, half a pound of sugar, half a pound of scraped raw potatoes, and quarter of a pound of scraped carrots, mixed together, and spice to taste. Boil four hours.

BIDDLE PUDDING.—One pint of milk, four large tablespoonfuls of flour, four eggs. Butter the bake-dish, put it in the oven when you are about to dish the dinner, allowing twenty-five minutes for baking. Bring it directly from the oven to the table, or it falls.

SAUCE FOR THE ABOVE.—One cup of brown sugar, two tablespoonfuls of cream, one ounce of butter. Stir the butter and sugar thoroughly, then add a little of the cream at a time, to keep from separating; add wine to the taste in the same manner (not quite a wineglass). Let the mixture melt. It will be a white froth when done.

BIRTHDAY PUDDING WITHOUT EGGS.—One pound of suet shred fine, half a pint of molasses, one pound of currants, one pound of flour; to be mixed with boiling milk; add candied lemon, raisins, nutmeg, and bitter almonds to taste; tie in a cloth, and boil five hours.

ORRIS PUDDING.—Boil one quart of milk and add five tablespoonfuls of flour, a little salt, seven eggs (reserving the whites of three for the sauce), and one-half a cup of sugar. Bake about half an hour.

SAUCE FOR THE ABOVE.—Whites of three eggs beaten with one and a half cup of powdered sugar and a glass of wine. If persons are averse to using wine to flavor the sauce for puddings, they will find that any well-flavored jelly or preserve is a great addition to the sauce for plain puddings.

GRANDMAMMA'S PUDDING.—Cut some moderately thin slices of bread; butter a mould and line it with the bread. Next, cover the bread with jam or marmalade. Fill up the mould with slices of bread, candied-peel, or marmalade, and raisins, or jam, whichever may be preferred. Beat two or three eggs, according to the size of the mould. Mix with a little sugar and sufficient milk to fill the mould. Cover with a cloth, and boil for an hour and a half. Serve with wine or sweet sauce.

WEST-POINT PUDDING.—One pound sheep's-tongue chopped fine, half pound suet chopped fine, five ounces of sugar, one tablespoonful of butter, one pound of potatoes, boiled. Mix all well together and bake about four hours.

UNION PUDDING.—Take one cup of white sugar, three tablespoonfuls of flour, two eggs, one grated nutmeg, and one good-sized cocoanut grated fine, two teacupfuls of new milk and a tablespoonful of good fresh butter. Bake like tarts, *without an upper crust.*

SNOW PUDDING.—Half an ounce of gelatine, one pint of boiling water, three-quarters of a pound of white sugar, the juice of two lemons. After it is thoroughly dissolved, strain it; as soon as it begins to thicken, add the well-beaten whites of two eggs; beat it for half an hour, and set it on ice, after putting in a mould or bowl. Make a rich, soft custard, flavored with the lemon-rinds grated. Send it to table in the middle of the custard.

PERSIAN PUDDING.—Take the pulp of six baked apples; add to them one ounce of rice previously boiled in milk, and beaten smooth, one ounce of sifted sugar, the grated rind of a lemon, and a teaspoonful of lemon-juice; mix these well together; then beat the whites of four eggs to a fine froth, put in the other ingredients, whisk it all up quickly, put it into a warm mould, and place it in a tolerably quick oven; when properly set, turn it out and pour around it a custard made with the yelks of the eggs remaining from the pudding.

VARIOUS KINDS OF PASTRY.

In making pastry the cook should be particularly clean and neat. Her utensils should be kept in order, and when they are done with they should be carefully cleaned and put in their places Her paste-board and rolling-pin, let it be remembered, should, after using, be well scoured with hot water alone. She should not use soap or sand. A marble slab is preferable to a board for rolling paste. Both are generally made too small to be convenient. Three feet long by two feet wide is a good size. In making a paste a good cook will have no waste of any kind, and particularly she will not make more at one time than she wants, under the idea that she can keep it in flour till the next time of making; for it is ten to one but that the old paste will spoil the new. No flour except the very best can be used for fine descriptions of pastry, and in damp weather it should be dried before the fire. Clarified dripping, good lard, marrow, salt butter, well washed, may be used for ordinary pastry; indeed, if they are pure and sweet they will form good pastry, with good flour and good management. In wealthy families, however, where economy is not an object, and everything for the table is required to be of the first quality, the safest plan is to use the best fresh butter. The fat that settles on stews, and on the broth in which meat has been boiled, may be used for pastry, that is, provided it is tasteless. Suet is sometimes used for meat pies, but though it makes a light crust, when hot, it does not eat well when cold.

A great deal more butter, or fat of some kind or other, was formerly directed to be used in making pastry than at present. For ordinary purposes, half the weight of lard or butter is sufficient, but in the richest crusts the quantity should never exceed the weight of flour. Eggs may be added to enrich the crust. Use no more water or other liquid in making paste than is absolutely necessary, or, in other words, take care not to "put out the miller's eye," that is, to make the paste too moist. The great thing is to incorporate the flour well with the fat, which you cannot do if you allow too much water or milk in the first instance.

The under or side crust, which should be thin, should not be made so rich as the top crust, as otherwise it will make the gravy or syrup greasy. All dishes in which pies are to be baked should be buttered or greased round the edges to prevent the crust from sticking, and if there be an under crust, all over the inside, and the same must be done with tins or saucers.

There is a number of other little things to be attended to in making pastry, which we will enumerate in as few words as we can. Fruit pies or large tarts should have a hole made in the middle of the crust.

FLAKY AND SHORT CRUSTS.—In making a flaky crust a part of the fat should be worked with the hand to a cream, and then the whole of the flour well rubbed into it before any water or milk is added. The remaining fat must be stuck on the paste and be rolled out. For crisp crust, by far the most wholesome, the whole of the fat should be rubbed in and thoroughly incorporated with the flour. Water or milk must be added when this is done, and the dough, or rather paste, made up. The pie-board and rolling-pin should be well dusted with flour, and the dough should be well beaten with the pin to thoroughly mix it, and render it light. Mind, in rolling out paste do not drive the pin backwards and forwards, but always keep rolling from you. In making flaky crusts the paste must be rolled out thin, and the fat or butter laid all over it; then roll it up and beat it till it puffs up in little bladders; it should be then finally rolled out and put in the oven as quickly as possible.

RAISED CRUST.—Put two pounds and a half of flour on the paste-board, and put on the fire in a saucepan three-quarters of a pint of water and half a pound of good lard; when the water boils, make a hole in the middle of the flour, pour in the water and lard by degrees, gently mix it with a spoon, and when it is well mixed, then knead it with your hands till it becomes stiff; dredge a little flour to prevent it sticking to the board, or you cannot make it smooth; then set it aside for an hour, and keep it cool; do not roll it with your rolling-pin, but roll it with your hands, about the thickness of a quart pot; cut it into six pieces, leaving a little for the covers; put the left hand, clenched, in the middle of one of the pieces, and with the other on the outside, work it up against the back of the left to a round or oval shape. It is now ready for the meat, which must be cut into small pieces with some fat, and pressed into the pie; then cover it with the paste previously rolled out to a proper thickness, and of the size of the pie; put this lid on the pie and press it together with your thumb and finger, cut it all around with a pair of scissors, and bake for an hour and a half. Our good old country housewives pride themselves very much upon being able to raise a large and high pork pie. This crust will answer for many meat and other pies baked in dishes or tins.

Puff-Paste.—This paste is nearly the same as what we have called flaky crust, and of course made upon the same principles. If eggs are desired, allow three yelks to a pound of butter or lard. Rub a fourth part of the fat to a cream, then mix the eggs with it, and afterwards the flour. A very little water will suffice to wet it. Beat it with the pin to make it flaky; roll it out thin three times, putting in a portion of the fat each time, and roll it from you; after each rolling beat it well.

Superior Puff-Paste.—One pound of flour, one pound of good butter, the yelk of an egg well beaten, and the juice of half a lemon. The paste must be made with cool hands, and in a cool place. Put the flour into a pan, make a hole in the middle, and put in the egg and lemon-juice, then cold water—enough, together, to make a tolerably stiff, but not too stiff, paste. Roll it out, and put a layer of butter over it in patches, sprinkle some dry flour over this (not that of the pound first weighed; that should all be wetted), fold over the paste, flour your paste-board and rolling-pin, and roll lightly on one side until butter and paste are amalgamated. In this manner continue to put on the butter, and roll out the paste until all the butter is used. The paste should be put on to the dishes in about three layers, and should be put into a quick oven to bake.

SWEET PASTE.—This is suitable to fruit tarts generally, apples, perhaps, excepted, for which we recommend a puff paste. To three-quarters of a pound of butter put a pound and a half of flour, three or four ounces of sifted loaf sugar, the yelks of two eggs, and half a pint of new milk. Bake it in a moderate oven.

CRUST FOR SAVORY PIES.—To two pounds of flour, one and a half of butter or lard, and the yelks of three eggs; rub part of the fat to a cream with the eggs, then rub in the flour; wet with cold water, and roll out with the remainder of the butter. This crust is suitable for pigeon, rabbit, hare, and other savory pies.

ICING PASTRY.—When nearly baked enough, take the pastry out of the oven and sift fine powdered sugar over it. Replace it in the oven, and hold over it till the sugar is melted a hot iron shovel. The above method is preferred for pastry to be eaten hot; for cold, beat up the whites of two eggs well, wash over the tops of the pies with a brush, and sift over this a good coating of sugar; cause it to adhere to the egg and pie-crust; trundle over it a clean brush dipped in water till the sugar is all moistened. Bake again for about ten minutes.

FRENCH CRUST FOR RAISED PIES.—To every pound of flour allow half a saltspoonful of salt, two eggs, third of a pint of water, six ounces of butter. Spread the flour, which should be sifted and thoroughly dry, on the paste-board; make a hole in the centre, into which put the butter; work it lightly into the flour, and when quite fine, add the salt; work the whole into a smooth paste with the eggs (yelks and whites) and water, and make it very firm. Knead the paste well, and let it be rather stiff, that the sides of the pie may be easily raised, and that they do not afterwards tumble or shrink.

PIE CRUST.—*For Meat Pies:* Take one pound of dried flour and rub into it six ounces of lard, six ounces of butter, a small quantity of salt, and a half teaspoonful of baking powder. Mix all these ingredients well together, and then use as much water as will make them into a nice stiff paste. Roll it out, let it stand for about ten minutes and then roll it once more before putting it on the meat. The pie should be baked in a moderately quick oven. *For Fruit Pies:* Take one pound of dried flour, and one pound of butter, well squeezed in a clean cloth, to get the salt out. Break the butter with your fingers amongst the flour, as fine as possible, and then with a little cold water mix into a tolerably stiff paste. Gently roll it, passing the roller in one direction only—from you. After this, lightly fold it over, and set it aside for a quarter of an hour in a cool place; then repeat the rolling in the same manner, and let it stand another quarter of an hour. This is to be repeated once more. Be sure to handle it as little as possible, and to keep it cool. Bake in a quick oven.

FARMERS' PIE.—Grate a good sweet pumpkin; add to it sufficient milk to thin it like custard; add four eggs, one teacupful of sugar, or sufficient to sweeten it to your taste; add a little ground cinnamon and a little cinnamon water; mix all well together; make a crust like for pies, fill your shells, sprinkle them over thickly with pulverized cinnamon. Bake with a moderate heat.

CRACKER PIES.—Six soda crackers pounded and mashed in two cups of cold water for twenty minutes, the rind and juice of two lemons, two and a half cups of white sugar; mix well together; bake in puff-paste; this quantity will make three pies, and taste like green apples.

SODA CRACKER PIE.—Take four soda crackers, grated fine, three cupfuls of warm water, quarter of a teaspoonful of tartaric acid, the grated rind of an orange, three cupfuls of sugar, three tablespoonfuls of butter, a little salt; make a good short crust, fill it with this mixture, and bake in a quick oven.

ORANGE PIE.—Take the juice and pulp of six

large sour oranges, and the grated rind of four, a little salt, three cupfuls of sugar, three eggs, four cupfuls of water, six spoonfuls of rice flour; mix these ingredients well together; make a good short crust, and bake like other pies.

AUNT HARRIET'S PIE.—To make the crust, take eight tablespoonfuls of fine flour, and four large spoonfuls of butter, and a little salt. Rub it finely like for other pies, then wet it up with water sufficient to make a crust or dough, roll out, and cover your pie plates, fill them with the following mixture: Take six tablespoonfuls of rice flour, mix it into a paste, with cold water, then add six tablespoonfuls of white sugar, twelve spoonfuls of warm water, and as much tartaric acid as will lay on a ten-cent-piece, and five drops of essence of lemon, make a thin top crust; and bake like other pies.

WASHINGTON PIE.—One cup of sugar, one egg, one-third of a cup of butter, half a cup of sweet milk, half a teaspoonful of soda, one teaspoonful of cream of tartar, one and a third cup of flour; flavor with lemon. Grease two round tins, and put this cake in. It will bake in a short time. When done, put on a dinner plate, and spread with nice, fine apple-sauce, then put the other cake on the top. This is very nice without sauce, still sauce improves it.

GERMAN PUFFS.—One ounce of sweet almonds, blanched and pounded, with a dessertspoonful of orange-flower water. Then add two tablespoonfuls of flour, four eggs (but the whites of only two) beaten separately, one pint of cream, sweetened to taste with white sugar, and beat all very well. Bake this quantity in six large teacups, and serve very hot with butter and sugar sauce.

LEMON PUFFS.—Take a pound of finely-powdered loaf sugar, and mix it with the juice of two lemons, beat the white of an egg to a complete froth, then add it to the lemon and sugar, and beat the whole for half an hour, then well beat three more eggs, and grate the outside rind very fine from the peel of the two lemons you have used the juice of; add this and the eggs to the previous mixture, and well mix the whole. Sprinkle some finely-powdered sugar on a sheet of writing paper, and drop the mixture upon it. A moderate oven will bake them in a few minutes.

SPICED PUFFS.—Beat up any quantity of whites of eggs, adding white sifted sugar with any spices; the puffs to be flavored with mace, cinnamon or cloves; drop them from the point of a knife, in a little high towering form, upon damp wafer sheets, and put them into a very slow oven.

PRESERVE PUFFS.—Roll out puff-paste very thinly, cut it into round pieces, and lay jam on each; fold over the paste, wet the edges with egg, and close them; lay them on a baking sheet, ice them, and bake about a quarter of an hour.

APPLE PUFF.—Prepare some apples in the same way as for sauce; while hot, beat them up with a small quantity of butter and a very little sugar; lemon-juice and sugar to taste. Take the whites of two eggs and beat them up with two spoonfuls of wine, one of cream, one of pounded sugar, and one of lemon-juice; when beaten to a froth, put it on the apples.

EGG PUFFS.—Six eggs, one pint of milk, three spoonfuls of flour, four ounces of butter melted, and a spoonful of yeast; mix, and fill cups half full; bake fifteen minutes; wine sauce.

LEMON CUSTARD TART.—Squeeze the juice of two lemons upon half a pound of loaf sugar; add the rind grated or pared as thin as possible. Boil the pulp of the lemons until tender in clear water. Beat and rub them through a sieve; add them to the other ingredients; pour in half a pint of white wine. Simmer all together for one hour; gradually mix in the beaten yelks of four eggs and whites of two. Strain into a tart dish edged with a rim of puff-paste, and bake for twenty minutes.

LEMON PIE, No. 1.—The proportions are two lemons, four eggs, two tablespoonfuls of melted butter, ten tablespoonfuls of loaf sugar. Grate the yellow rind of the lemon, beat together the rind, juice, sugar, and the yelks of the eggs until very light. Prepare a large tart pie, fill the pie with the mixture before baking the paste, and bake until the paste is done. Beat the whites stiff, and stir into them little by little one-fourth of a pound of sugar; spread it over the top, and bake a light brown.

LEMON PIE, No. 2 (*easily made*).—Two lemons; squeeze out the juice, and chop the lemons fine (take out the seeds); three cups of water, three cups of sugar, one egg, two-thirds of a cup of flour; beat the egg well with half a cup of water and the flour; then stir lemons, juice, and all together; this will fill three pies.

CUSTARD CREAM PIE.—This is baked like a custard, but to be very nice, the edge of the plate should be layered with puff-paste; make a custard of thin cream instead of milk, and bake it as a custard. It must be eaten the same day it is baked.

CREAM PIE.—Take as much thick, sweet cream as will fill your pie-dish, to which add the whites of two fresh eggs beaten to a froth, and sugar enough to suit your taste. Flavor with lemon.

CORN STARCH PIE.—Boil six tablespoonfuls of corn starch in three pints of water; let it cool, then add one cup of butter, one cup of sugar, one small cup of vinegar, and three eggs. Flavor with essence of lemon, and bake between two crusts.

FROSTED PIE.—Seven soda crackers soaked in cold water, three pints of milk, one whole egg and yelks of three, two or three lemons, peel grated, and juice; sweeten to the taste before adding the lemons. Beat the whites of three eggs with powdered sugar for the frosting, to be spread on and browned after the pies are baked.

MACARONI PIE.—Boil the macaroni in water until quite tender; drain the water off, put into the baking-pan; add a tablespoonful of butter, half a pound of grated cheese, a pint of milk, salt, pepper, and mustard to taste; if desired, the pan can be lined with a rich paste and an over crust.

SUPERIOR PEACH PIES.—Take good ripe peaches, halve and stone them; make a good short crust, and lay it in your pie-plates. Lay your peaches evenly to cover it; then add to each moderate-sized pie about three spoonfuls of white sugar, and a few drops of essence of lemon, or rose, and half a teacupful of water; cover, and bake like other pies.

CRANBERRY TART.—Take half a pint of cranberries, pick them from the stems and throw them into a saucepan with half a pound of white sugar and a spoonful of water; let them come to a boil; then retire them to stand on the hob while you peel and cut up four large apples; put a rim of light paste around your dish; strew in the apples; pour the cranberries over them; cover with a lid of crust, and bake for an hour. For a pudding, proceed in the same manner with the fruit, and boil it in a basin or cloth.

SAND TART.—One teacup of butter, one and a

half of sugar, two well-beaten eggs, half a teaspoonful of saleratus, three teaspoonfuls of water, flour to make them stiff enough to roll out thin; cut them out with a tumbler. Bathe the top with the white of an egg, and sprinkle on sugar. They will keep well for four or five months.

BLACK CURRANT TART.—Lightly stem and top the currants, being careful not to bruise them; put them into a tart-dish with a rim of paste, and, as they are considered to be too rich by themselves, it is advisable to add a little white currant juice or cider to dilute their flavor; throw in a good deal of sugar, cover them with a top crust, and bake rather more than an hour.

CHERRY AND CURRANT TART.—Stem and stone your cherries; take an equal weight of very ripe red currants, press them through a sieve, add the juice to your cherries with the crumb of two sponge-cakes, a quarter of a pound of sugar, and a wineglassful of brandy. Put it into a tart-dish lined with a rim of paste, cover it with a top crust, and bake it for an hour.

RASPBERRY CREAM TART.—This is a delicious summer dish, and is prepared as follows: Roll out some thin puff-paste, and lay it in a patty-pan; put in some raspberries, and strew over them some very finely pounded sugar. Put on the covering paste, and bake the tart. Cut it open, and put in half a pint of cream, the yelks of two or three eggs, well beaten, and a little sugar. Let it stand till cold before it is sent to table.

ORANGE TART.—Grate the peel of one orange, and put the juice with it (keeping away the pips), also the juice and peel of half a lemon, a quarter of a pound of sugar, two ounces of butter carefully melted, two eggs, leaving out one of the whites; beat them well together, and having lined a tart-tin with thin paste, fill it with the mixture, and bake it a quarter of an hour, or a little more, if requisite.

LEMON TART.—Mix well together the juice and grated rinds of two large lemons, half a pound of powdered loaf sugar, two eggs, and the crumb of two sponge-cakes; beat it thoroughly smooth, and put it into twelve patty-pans, lined with a light puff-paste; bake them until the crust is done.

ALMOND TART.—Make a very fine paste with half a pound of blanched almonds beaten in a mortar, a quarter of a pound of powdered loaf sugar, a tablespoonful each of brandy and cream, a little nutmeg, the crumb of two stale sponge-cakes, and, if you can procure it, a little spinach-juice to color it green. When perfectly smooth, lay it either in patty-pans, or in a tart mould lined with a light paste; bake for a quarter of an hour in a gentle oven, and before serving, decorate the top with small pieces of candied orange-chips. It may be eaten hot or cold.

RHUBARB TART.—Take your stalks of rhubarb,

peel off the outer skin and cut them into pieces of about three inches long; pack them closely into a pie-dish lined with a rim of light paste; add a good deal of sugar, put on a top crust, and bake it for an hour in a gentle oven. No water should be put to a rhubarb tart, for the vegetable is of so juicy a nature that most epicures evaporate it by keeping the stalks some days before using them.

Greengage Tart.—Take some greengage plums, not over-ripe; do not stone them, but lay them either in a basin lined, or pie-dish edged, with a rich crust; add a good quantity of white sugar, cover with a top crust, and boil or bake for an hour and a half.

Rich Mince Pie.—One fresh tongue, boiled, four pounds of suet, twenty-five large apples, seven pounds of currants, three and a half pounds of raisins, five pounds of sugar, the grated rinds of two lemons and juice of four, citron and candied lemon-peel to your taste, three nutmegs, grated, one-eighth of an ounce of mace, a little ground cloves and salt, one quart of brandy, one quart of Madeira wine.

Mock Mince Pie.—Four Boston crackers, rolled, two-thirds of a teacup of cold water, one cup of molasses, half a cup of sugar, half a cup of vinegar, one egg, raisins, and spices, as for mince pies.

Mincemeat.—Six pounds of currants, three pounds of raisins, stoned, three pounds of apples, chopped fine, four pounds of suet, two pounds of sugar, two pounds of beef, the peel and juice of two lemons, a pint of sweet wine, a quarter of a pint of brandy, half an ounce of mixed spice. Press the whole into a deep pan well mixed.

ANOTHER WAY.—Two pounds of raisins, three pounds of currants, three pounds of beef suet, two pounds of moist sugar, two ounces of citron, one ounce of orange-peel, one small nutmeg, one pottle of apples, chopped fine, the rind of two lemons and juice of one, half a pint of brandy; mix well together. This should be made a little time before wanted for use.

PASTRY SANDWICHES.—Puff-paste, jam of any kind, the white of an egg, sifted sugar. Roll the paste out thin, put half of it on a baking-sheet or tin, and spread equally over it any preserve that may be preferred. Lay over this preserve another thin paste, press the edges together all round, and mark the paste in lines with a knife on the surface, to show where to cut it when baked. Bake from twenty minutes to half an hour, and, a short time before being done, take the pastry out of the oven, brush it over with the white of an egg, sift over pounded sugar, and put it back in the oven to color. When cold, cut it into strips, pile these on a dish pyramidically, and serve. These strips, cut about two inches long, piled in circular rows, and a plateful of flavored whipped cream poured in the middle, make a very pretty dish.

FLORENTINES.—Roll puff-paste to the thickness of the eighth of an inch, and lay it on a thin baking-tin. Spread over it a layer of greengage or any other preserve or jam, and bake it in a moderate oven. Take it out, and when partially cool, having whipped some whites of eggs with sugar, put the whip over the preserve, and strew some minced almonds all over the surface, finishing with sifted sugar. Put it once more into the oven until the whip is quite stiff. The florentines should be of a pale color, and a few minutes after the paste is finally removed from the oven, it should be cut into diamonds and served up.

RHUBARB PIE.—Cut up in small pieces, skinning the older stalks; add a little water and sugar before the crust is put on; flavor with lemon. All juicy fruits can be made in this way.

CHAPTER VII.

CREAMS AND DESSERTS.

CHOCOLATE CREAMS.—Take fresh milk enough to fill twelve glasses, and boil with it two ounces of grated chocolate and six ounces of white sugar; then beat the yelks of six eggs, to which add slowly the chocolate milk, turning slowly one way. Flavor with vanilla boiled in milk. When quite mixed, fill your cups and place in water and boil for an hour. Serve when cold.

SCOTCH CREAM.—Put to a quart of cream the whites of three eggs well-beaten, four spoonfuls of sweet wine, sugar to taste, and a bit of lemon-peel; whip it to a froth, remove the peel, and serve in a dish.

CALEDONIAN CREAM.—The whites of two eggs, two spoonfuls of loaf-sugar, two of raspberry jam, two of currant jelly; all to be beaten together with a silver spoon till so thick that the spoon will stand upright in it.

ORANGE CREAM.—Pare the rind of an orange very thin, and squeeze the juice of four oranges, and put it, with the peel, into a saucepan with one pint of water, eight ounces of sugar, and the whites of five eggs well beaten. Mix all together, place it over a slow fire, stir it in one direction until it looks thick and white, strain it through a gauze sieve, and stir it till cold. Beat the yelks of the five eggs very thoroughly, and add them to the contents of the saucepan, with some cream. Stir all together over the fire till ready to boil, pour it into a basin, and again stir it till quite cold before putting it into glasses.

SNOW CREAM.—Put in a stewpan four ounces of ground rice, two ounces of sugar, a few drops of the essence of almonds, or any other essence you choose, with two ounces of fresh butter. Add a quart of milk, boil from fifteen to twenty minutes, till it forms a smooth substance, though not too thick; then pour into a mould previously buttered, and serve when cold and well set. If the mould be dipped in warm water, the cream will turn out like a jelly. If no mould, put either in cups or a pie-dish. The rice had better be done a little too much than under.

FRENCH CREAM.—Half an ounce of gelatine, soaked in a cup of light wine, let it boil over the fire, then stir in one pint of sweet cream. Let it nearly boil again, sweeten to your taste, and cool in a mould. To be eaten with cream. To be made the day before using.

VELVET CREAM.—To a pint of cream put a very little sugar, keep stirring it over the fire till the sugar is dissolved, and then take it off; but keep on stirring it till it is about the warmth of new milk, after which pour it through a fine colander into a dish containing three spoonfuls of lemon or orange juice, a little grated peel, and a little fruit marmalade, chopped small, with two spoonfuls of white wine. This should be prepared the evening before it is wanted.

APPLE CREAM.—Boil twelve apples in water till soft, take off the peel and press the pulp through a hair sieve upon half a pound of pounded sugar; whip the whites of two eggs, add them to the apples, and beat all together till it becomes very stiff and looks quite white. Serve it heaped up on a dish.

ITALIAN CREAM.—Take one pint of cream and half a pint of milk, make it hot, sweetening it to taste, and flavoring it with lemon-peel. Beat up the yelks of eight eggs, beat up all together, and set it over a slow fire to thicken. Have ready an ounce of isinglass, melted and strained, which add to the cream. Whip it well, and pour it into the mould.

MADEIRA CREAM.—Take seven sponge cakes, split them in halves, line a glass dish with the pieces, mix together two wineglassfuls of Madeira wine or sherry, and one wineglassful of brandy. With a teaspoon pour a little of this mixture over the layer of pieces, on this again put a layer of raspberry jelly, which can readily be made by putting a pot of raspberry jam in the oven; in a few minutes it will be warm, when the liquid, which is the jelly, can be strained from it and poured over the pieces. Now put the other layer of pieces, soak this with wine, as before, but omit the raspberry; make a custard as directed for boiled custard. When cold, and just as the dish is going to table, pour the cold custard over, and sprinkle some ratafias on the top.

SPANISH CREAM.—Half a pint of cream, same of new milk, three ounces of rice flour, a tablespoonful of peach or orange flower water; sweeten it to taste. Boil till it is stiff, stirring it constantly, and when it will leave the side of the pan, put it into a mould which has first been put in cold water.

LEMON CREAM.—To one quart of new milk add the whites of ten eggs, beat to a stiff froth, and to each egg add a tablespoonful of white sugar. Beat well together, and add to the milk while boiling. Boil a few minutes, take it off, stir it until it cools, and flavor with lemon. Make in a tin vessel.

LEMON RICE.—Wash some rice thoroughly in cold water, boil it in as much milk as it will absorb, sweeten it to taste and turn it into a mould. Peel a lemon, cut the peel into shreds three-quarters of an inch in length, and put them into a little water. Boil up, and drain; put them into a teacupful of fresh water. Squeeze the juice from a large lemon, put it with some white sugar upon the shreds, and stew gently for two hours. When cold it should be a thick syrup. Turn out the rice, and pour the syrup over it, spreading the shreds equally over the surface.

LEMON FLUMMERY.—Squeeze four lemons into a basin, throwing in the rinds, but not the seeds; add half a pint of water, half a pound of loaf-sugar, and cover close for an hour; take out the lemon-rinds, and again cover, and let it stand all night. Then strain through a cloth, and add one ounce of isinglass, and put it in a saucepan with six eggs well beaten; set over the fire, and keep stirring one way till it is as thick as cream. When milk-warm, put into moulds previously dipped in cold water.

MERINGUES.—The whites of six eggs and one pound of sifted pounded white sugar. Procure a board about an inch in thickness, and of a convenient size for the oven. Cover this with foolscap or thin cartridge paper, proceed to beat the whites of eggs to a substantial froth, remove the whisk and stir the sugar in lightly with a spoon; do not stir it too much, as it would lose its firmness. With a dessertspoon drop the mixture out on the papered board in masses about the size of an egg, about an inch and a half apart; in dropping them turn the spoon over as they fall, so as to produce as round an appearance as possible; then dust them over with sifted sugar, and blow off the loose sugar from the paper. Put them in a moderately-heated oven, and bake a very light brown color. When done, each piece must be carefully removed from the paper, the inside scraped out with a dessertspoon, leaving the shell about a quarter of an inch thick; place them in order on a papered baking sheet, the hollow side upwards, and put again in the oven, taking care they do not acquire any more color; they should be dried so as to be quite crisp; they may be put in the oven at night when the fire is out and the heat subsided, and remain until the morning, when they may be packed in a tin box and used when required.

TRIFLE.—Arrange macaroons and sponge cakes in a deep glass dish; place about them slices of currant jelly and little lumps of apricot jam, and pour as much white wine or brandy over them as they will drink. Take a quart of cream, flavor some sugar by rubbing it on a lemon until it takes the essence of the peel, and with it sweeten the cream to taste. Mill your cream to a strong froth; lay as much froth on a sieve as will fill the dish intended for the trifle. Put the remainder of the cream into a tossing-pan, with a stick of cinnamon, the yelks of four eggs, well beaten, and sugar to taste, and stir it over a slow fire until it is thick; pour it over the macaroons, and when it is cold put the frothed cream on the top, and decorate it with sweetmeats of various colors. Another good trifle is made by placing the cakes, and saturating them as above, and then pouring over them a *very thick* custard; this is left some hours to become firm, and is then covered with a layer of rich jam first and whipped cream.

SWEET SOUFFLÉ.—Thicken to a stiff paste over the stove, one pint of milk, with sifted flour; stir while heating; add the well beaten yelks of six eggs, a pinch of salt, and sugar to sweeten. Beat the whites of eight eggs to a froth; stir into the mixture. Bake in a quick oven fifteen minutes. Glaze with finely powdered sugar, and send to the table quickly as it will soon fall. Ground rice may be used instead of flour, and lemon-juice or grated lemon-peel used for flavoring.

SWEET DISH OF MACARONI.—Quarter of a pound of macaroni, a pint and a half of milk, the rind of half a lemon, three ounces of lump sugar, three-quarters of a pint of custard. Put the milk into a saucepan, with the lemon-peel and sugar, bring it to the boiling point; drop in the macaroni, and let it gradually swell over a gentle fire, but do not allow the pipes to break; the form should be entirely preserved, and though tender should be firm and not soft, with no part beginning to melt. Should the milk dry away before the macaroni is swelled, add a little more. Place the macaroni on a dish, pour the custard over the hot macaroni, grate over it a little nutmeg, and when cold, garnish the dish with slices of candied citron-peel.

LEMON HONEYCOMB.—This is a very simple

dish, and one that makes a pleasant variety on the supper-table. The juice of a lemon should be sweetened to the taste, and put into the dish in which it will be served up. The white of an egg is beaten into a pint of rich cream, with a little sugar, and whisked. As the froth rises, it should be placed on the lemon-juice, and has a very light and pretty appearance. It is desirable to prepare this dish the day before it is required, and a few pieces of sponge cake may be strewed over it just before it is sent up.

BIBAVOE.—One pint of cream whipped until stiff, one ounce of isinglass boiled and strained in about one pint of water until reduced to a half pint. Four ounces of sugar, one vanilla bean; stir in the cream when the isinglass gets blood heat. Then mould and cut with whipped cream.

DELICATE DESSERT.—Lay half a dozen crackers in a tureen, pour on enough boiling water to cover them. In a few moments they will be swollen to three or four times their original size. Now grate loaf sugar and a little nutmeg over them, and dip on enough sweet cream to make a nice sauce, and you will have a simple and delicious dessert that will rest lightly on the stomach—and it is easily prepared. Leave out the cream, and it is a valuable receipt for "sick-room cookery."

GERMAN FLOTTKRENGEL.—Take one pound of dry flour, three-quarters of a pound of well-washed butter, ten tablespoonfuls of cream. For the top of these cakes melted butter or egg, powdered sugar and cinnamon. Break the butter into small pieces, and mix with the flour, then adding the cream; mix quickly into a light paste. From this break pieces, and roll them out with the hand about a quarter of a yard long, and join the two ends in the middle, to give them the form of a B. When all are done, grease them on top with egg or melted butter, strewing sugar and cinnamon over it. Those who like almonds will find them with the above very delicious. These cakes require to be baked quickly.

CUSTARD AND WHEY.—Beat six eggs with sugar and add them to a quart of milk, bake hard until the custard separates; pour it into cups, and serve warm.

FINE FLOATING ISLAND.—The juice of two lemons, the whites of two eggs, three tablespoonfuls of currant jelly, and twenty medium-sized lumps of loaf-sugar; mix and beat these to a stiff froth. Put it into the middle of the dish, and dress it with sweetmeats. Just before it is to be served, pour cream enough in the dish to float it.

FLOATING ISLAND.—Take six eggs, separate them; beat the yelks, and stir into a quart of milk; sweeten to taste; flavor with lemon or nutmeg. Put this mixture in a pan. Put some water in a saucepan, and set it on the fire. When boiling, put in your pan, which ought to be half immersed. Keep stirring it until the custard gets thick, which will be in about thirty minutes. Whip the whites of the eggs to a strong froth. When the custard is done, put into a deep dish, and heap the frothed eggs upon it. Serve cold.

FRENCH ISLAND.—Take a pint of rich cream and dissolve in it two tablespoonfuls of currant or plum jelly; to this add a large wineglassful of white wine, and then sweeten the whole to taste. Take a half pint of rich cream, sweeten and flavor it, and beat it to a stiff froth. Place the first mixture in a glass bowl, and the whipped cream to float on top. This is a very nice and delicate dessert.

FLOATS.—Break the whites of six eggs into a flat dish, beating as for icing; add a tablespoonful of pounded loaf-sugar for each egg. When quite stiff beat into it a tablespoonful (or more, according to taste) of currant, strawberry, or any other fruit jelly. Pour cream into saucers and drop the float on it.

TAPIOCA BLANC MANGE.—Half a pound of tapioca soaked for an hour in a pint of milk, and boiled till tender; sweeten to taste, and put it into a mould. When cold turn it out, and serve in a dish with strawberry or raspberry jam around it, and a little cream.

BLANC MANGE.—Four or five tablespoonfuls of corn starch, to a quart of milk; beat the starch thoroughly with two eggs, and add to the milk while boiling, with a little salt; boil a few minutes, stirring briskly; flavor with rose, lemon, or vanilla, and pour into a mould. Sweeten it while cooking, or pour over it a sauce, or some of the lemon cream.

CHOCOLATE BLANC MANGE.—A quarter of a pound of sweet German chocolate, half a box of gelatine, one quart of milk, one coffeecupful of sugar. Put it all in a dish set in a kettle of water, and let it boil an hour. When nearly cold, turn into the mould.

CORN STARCH BLANC MANGE.—Boil one quart of sweet milk, stir into it gradually five tablespoonfuls of corn starch, mixed with milk, add salt, and only two large spoonfuls of loaf sugar, stir until thoroughly cooked. When done, take it from the fire, and, when cooled, add lemon and vanilla, and pour it into moulds. Serve with jelly or fresh fruit, and whipped cream, flavored like the pudding.

PEACH ROLLS.—Take a peck or two of soft freestone peaches, pound them, pass the pulp through a coarse sieve, and to four quarts of pulp add one quart of good brown sugar, mix well together, and boil for about two minutes. Spread the paste on plates, and put them in the sun every day until the cakes look dry, and will leave the plates readily by passing a knife round the edges of the cakes. Dust some white sugar over the rough sides, and roll them up like sweet wafers. If kept in a dry place, they will continue sound for some months. If the weather is fine, three days will be enough to dry them.

Spiced Sugar for Fritters, etc.—This is simply one dessertspoonful of very finely powdered and sifted mixed spice, mixed with three dessertspoonfuls of powdered sugar.

Snowballs.—Take half a pound of the best rice, put it into a saucepan with a quart of new milk, simmer it slowly, so that it may not burn. When it has absorbed all the milk, let it cool; then mix in the whites of two eggs, pare and core some middling-sized apples, put a little sugar into each, then envelop them in rice, tie them in cloths, and boil them for twenty minutes or half an hour, according to the quality of the apples used. Turn them into a dish to serve, and dust them thickly over with loaf sugar.

Suet Dumplings with Currants.—Scald a pint of new milk and let it grow cold, then stir into it a pound of chopped suet, two eggs, four ounces of cleaned currants, a little nutmeg and salt, two teaspoonfuls of powdered ginger, and flour sufficient to make the whole into a light batter-paste. Form it into dumplings, flour them well outside, throw them into your saucepan, being careful that the water is boiling, and that they do not stick to the bottom. Half an hour's boiling will cook them.

OXFORD DUMPLINGS.—Mix well together the following ingredients: Two ounces of grated bread, four ounces of currants, four ounces of shred suet, a tablespoonful of sifted sugar, a little allspice, and plenty of grated lemon-peel. Beat up well two eggs, add a little milk, and divide the mixture into five dumplings. Fry them in butter to a light brown color, and serve them with wine sauce.

SUET DUMPLINGS.—To one quart of flour add half a pound of beef suet, broken in small pieces, one cupful of peach marmalade, a little salt, one teaspoonful of soda. Knead it with buttermilk, and make the dough out in dumplings larger than biscuit, and boil them till done. Serve up while hot with a rich sauce.

APPLE CUSTARD.—One pint of *good* stewed apples, a quarter pound of butter, half a pint of cream, three eggs, beaten light, sugar and grated nutmeg to taste. Mix the ingredients together, and bake in a puff-paste in a moderate stove.

SOLID CUSTARD.—One ounce isinglass, two pints of new milk, one dozen of bitter almonds, pounded, the yelks of four eggs, sugar to taste. Dissolve the isinglass in the milk, add the pounded almonds, put the mixture on the fire, and let it boil a few minutes. Pour it through a sieve, then add the yelks of the eggs, well beaten; sweeten to your taste. Put it on the fire until it thickens, stir it till nearly cold, and put it into a mould.

ORANGE CUSTARD.—Boil till tender half the rind of an orange, beat it fine in a mortar, put to it a spoonful of brandy, the juice of an orange, four ounces of loaf sugar, and the yelks of four eggs. Beat all well together for ten minutes, pour in a pint of boiling cream by degrees, keep beating till cold, then put them in cups, and place them in an earthen dish of hot water till set. Stick preserved orange on the top, and serve either hot or cold.

FRENCH CUSTARD.—Take one quart of milk, flavor it with the peel of about half a small lemon, pared very thin, and sweetened to taste with white sugar. Boil it, and leave it to get quite cold, then blend with it three dessertspoonfuls of fine flour, and two eggs, well beaten. Simmer it until it is of the proper thickness, stirring it in the whole time. Pour into cups or a custard-dish.

MILK PANCAKES.—Put four yelks and two whites of eggs into a pint of milk, and dredge in flour until you have a smooth light batter; add a teaspoonful of grated ginger and a glass of brandy. Well heat some fritures in your frying-pan, and fry your pancakes of a nice brown color. Drain them carefully from the fat, and serve with pounded and sifted sugar strewn over them. Garnish the dish with sliced lemon.

CREAM PANCAKES.—Mix the yelks of two eggs, well beaten, with a pint of cream, two ounces of sifted sugar, a little nutmeg, cinnamon, and mace.

Rub the pan with a piece of butter, and fry the pancakes thin.

ORANGE NUTS.—Take seven ounces of flour, seven of sugar, and three eggs, one ounce and a half of orange-peel, and the same of lemon-peel. Beat the eggs with the sugar for a quarter of an hour, add the flour and peels, beating it till no flour is visible. Form them into little balls, and bake them like the others.

COMPOTE AUX CONFITURES.—Peel some apples, leave them whole, but take out the cores. Put a little water in the preserving pan and let the apples cook, with a large lump of sugar, taking great care that they do not break. Place the apples in a glass dish, and when they are cold fill the centre of each with apricot jam, or any other *recherché* preserve. Boil the liquid until it jellies, pour it into a dish, that it may take its form, let it cool, and then put it over the apples without breaking it. The French receipt adds that the jelly will leave the dish easily if it be dipped for an instant into hot water, but as this would be likely to dull the jelly, it is a better plan to just dip, shape, jelly, and all into cold water, a plan followed by good confectioners.

WASHINGTON, OR CREAM PIE.—One cup of sugar, one cup of milk, two and a half cups of flour, half a cup of butter, one egg, one teaspoonful of cream of tartar. Bake in round jelly tins, and split when cold. *For the cream:* One pint of milk, four tablespoonfuls of sugar, one tablespoonful of flour, one egg, and a lump of butter the size of a walnut. Flavor with lemon or vanilla, boil the milk, stir in the butter, sugar, etc., when boiling, and let it boil two or three minutes. Flavor when cold, pour the cream on the cake, and put together like jelly cake. This makes two cakes.

CUSTARD FRITTERS.—Beat the yelks of four eggs with a dessertspoonful of flour, a little nutmeg, salt and brandy; add half a pint of cream; sweeten it to taste, and bake it in a small dish for a quarter of an hour. When cold, cut it into quarters, and dip them into a batter made with a quarter of a pint each of milk and cream, the whites of the four eggs, a little flour, and a good bit of grated ginger; fry them brown; grate sugar over them, and serve them as hot as possible.

BUN FRITTERS.—Dip stale sliced sugar-biscuit in milk, with two or three eggs beaten light and stirred in, till completely saturated, then fry them a light brown, and dip them immediately in pounded cinnamon and sugar. Serve them very hot.

APPLE FRITTERS.—Pare and core some fine large pippins, and cut them into round slices. Soak them in wine, sugar and nutmeg for two or three hours. Make a batter of four eggs, a tablespoonful of rose-water, one of wine, and one of milk; thicken with enough flour, stirred in by degrees, to make a batter; mix it two or three hours before it is wanted, that it may be light. Heat some butter in a frying-pan; dip each slice of apple separately in the batter, and fry them brown; sift pounded sugar, and grate nutmeg over them.

CHERRY FRITTERS.—Take half a pound of ripe Mayduke cherries; stone and halve them; make a pint of new milk pretty hot, sweeten it, and pour it upon your cherries, then well beat four eggs, put them with the cherries, stir all well together, add a little flour to bind it; put it into a frying-pan, a spoonful at a time, and when the fritters are done, serve with sugar sifted over them.

ELEGANT FRITTERS.—Take eight eggs, sixteen tablespoonfuls of flour, a little salt, and milk sufficient to make a batter, mix and fry in butter. Eat with sugar and cinnamon.

SNITZ AND KNEP.—Take of sweet dried apples (dried with the skins on, if you can get them) about one quart. Put them in the bottom of a porcelain or tin-lined boiler with a cover. Take a nice piece of smoked ham washed very clean, and lay on top; add enough water to cook them nicely. About twenty minutes before dishing up, add the following dumplings.—*Dumplings*—Mix a cup of warm milk with one egg, a little salt, and a little yeast, and enough flour to make a sponge. When light, work into a loaf. Let stand until about twenty minutes before dinner, then cut off slices or lumps, and lay on the apples, and let steam through.

STEWED PEARS.—Take six large and ripe pears, peel, core and cut them lengthways. Put them into a very clean stewpan, cover them with the sugar. Peel the lemon very finely, cut the rind into long strips, and squeeze the juice of the lemon on the sugar. Gently shake the pan until the sugar is dissolved, place the stewpan on a very slow fire for fifteen minutes, shake it again once or twice, and turn each piece with a fork. Let it stew slowly again for ten minutes. Place on a dish to cool. Dress them on a flat china or glass dish, pour the syrup over, and serve.

CHOCOLATE CARAMEL.—Half a pound of chocolate, three pounds of *dark* brown sugar, one-eighth of a pound of butter, a small teacup of milk; season with vanilla, or grated lemon or orange-peel. Boil it very quickly over a hot fire, stirring constantly. When it becomes hard on being dropped in water, take it off the fire and stir for a few moments before pouring into buttered dishes. Before it is quite cool cut into little squares. Those who like the craramel very hard need not stir it, as this makes it "sugary." The grated peel should not be put in till the caramel is taken from the fire.

CARAMELS.—Two cups of brown sugar, one cup of molasses, a piece of butter the size of an egg; three tablespoonfuls of flour. Boil these together for twenty-five minutes. Then add half a pound of grated chocolate dissolved in one cup of sweet milk. Let it boil until it will harden when dropped into water (stirring constantly); take it from the fire and add one teaspoonful of vanilla; pour it in buttered plates to cool; just before it is hard mark it into small squares.

BURNT SUGAR.—Take one and a half tablespoonfuls of white sugar and put it in a ladle over the fire, and stir with a wooden spoon. When the sugar is black, add of water one gill and a half; let it cool, strain, and keep it in a bottle. It is used for coloring soup, gravy, and other dishes, and can be put in ice cream to color it.

FRIAR'S OMELETTE.—Boil a dozen apples as for sauce, stir in a quarter of a pound of butter, and the same of white sugar; when cold, add four well-beaten eggs; put it into a baking-dish strewn thickly with crumbs of bread, so as to stick to the bottom and sides; strew crumbs of bread plentifully over the apple mixture when in the baking-dish; bake, turn out, and grate sugar over it.

ANGEL'S FOOD. *A New Dish.*—Make a rich custard, pour it in a glass bowl, and put a layer of sliced cake on it. Stir some finely-powdered sugar into quince or apple jelly, and drop it on the cake. Pour syllabub on the cake, and then put on another layer of cake, and icing.

CHOCOLATE BUTTER.—Stir quarter of a pound of butter over the fire until quite soft and creamy; put two cakes of good vanilla-flavored chocolate on a tin plate, and add cream until they are soft enough to mix with the butter. Stir all well together. Serve cold, to use like butter with bread or biscuit.

CHOCOLATE CHARLOTTE RUSSE.—Having soaked in cold water an ounce of isinglass, or of gelatine, shave down three ounces of the best chocolate, which must have no spice or sugar in it, and mix it gradually into a pint of cream, adding the soaked isinglass. Set the cream, chocolate, and isinglass over the fire, in a porcelain kettle, and boil it slowly till the isinglass is dissolved thoroughly, and the whole is well mixed. Then take it off the fire and let it cool. Have ready eight yelks of eggs and four whites, beaten all together till very light; and stir them gradually into the mixture, in turn with half a pound of powdered loaf sugar. Simmer the whole over the fire, but do not let it quite boil. Then take it off, and whip it to a strong froth. Line your moulds with sponge cake, and set them on ice. If you like a strong chocolate flavor, take four ounces of the cocoa.

CHARLOTTE RUSSE.—Take an ounce of isinglass or of gelatine, and soften it by soaking it awhile in cold water. Then boil it slowly in a pint of cream, sweetened with a quarter of a pound of fine loaf sugar (adding a handful of fresh rose-leaves, if convenient, tied in a thin muslin bag), till it is thoroughly dissolved, and well mixed. Take it off the fire; set it to cool; and beat together till very light and thick, four whole eggs, and the yelks only of four others. Stir the beaten eggs gradually into the mixture of cream, sugar, and isinglass, and set it again over the fire. Stir it well, and see that it only simmers; taking it off before it comes quite to a boil. Then, while it is warm, stir in sufficient extract of roses to give it a high rose-flavor and a fragrant smell. Have ready two moulds lined with lady cake, or almond sponge cake. Fill them with the mixture, and set them on ice. Before they go to table, ice the tops of the charlotte, flavoring the icing with rose.

CHARLOTTE DE RUSSE.—Take a little less than one ounce of gelatine, and dissolve in one pint of new milk. Strain into one pint of thick cream made very sweet, and set this in a cool place or on the ice. Take the whites of seven eggs, and beat to a froth; then add them to the cream, and beat light. Flavor with vanilla, and keep on the ice until wanted. Line the moulds with very light sponge cake, and fill with the above when wanted.

JAM· OR MARMALADE CHARLOTTE (*without Eggs*).—Cut five slices of bread a quarter of an inch thick, trim off the crust, lay them in a dish, and pour over six ounces of dissolved fresh butter. Put it in the oven for ten minutes, and, when the bread is cold and the butter all absorbed, spread each piece of bread a quarter of an inch thick with any kind of jam or marmalade, and over that put a teaspoonful of powdered loaf sugar. Blanch and chop two ounces of sweet almonds, butter a plain mould, strew the almonds over, lay in the slices of bread and jam; place a dish over the mould, and bake in a quick oven.

BUTTERED ORANGE JUICE, A COLD DISH.—Mix the juice of seven Seville oranges with four spoonfuls of rose-water, and add the whole to the yelks of eight and whites of four eggs, well beaten; then strain the liquors to half a pound of sugar pounded, stir it over a gentle fire, and when it begins to thicken put about the size of a small walnut of butter; keep it over the fire a few minutes longer, then pour it into a flat dish, and serve to eat cold. It may be done in a china basin in a saucepan of boiling water, the top of which will just receive the basin.

CAKES FOR DESSERT.—Four eggs, half a pound of butter, half a pound of sugar, half a pound of flour. Mix the butter, sugar, and yelks of the eggs thoroughly, then add the flour and mix again, then the whites of the eggs beaten to a thick froth. Grate in a little lemon rind. Put in little dishes, filling each about one-third full, and bake till done.

APPLE CHARLOTTE.—Take any number of apples you may desire to use; peel them, cut them into quarters, and take out the core. Cut the quarters into slices, and let them cook over a brisk fire, with butter, sugar, and powdered cinnamon, until they are *en marmalade*. Cut thin slices of crumb of bread, dip them in butter, and with them line the sides and bottom of a tin shape. Fill the middle of the shape with alternate layers of the apple and any preserve you may choose, and cover it with more thin slices of bread. Then place the shape in an oven, or before the fire, until the outside is a fine brown, and turn it out upon a dish, and serve it either hot or cold. For *croquettes de pommes* you cook the apple just as for the Charlotte; but instead of putting it into the jelly shape you roll into balls, or rather cakes, which you cover with egg and bread crumbs, and fry of a rich brown.

POMMES AU RIZ.—Peel a number of apples of a good sort, take out the cores, and let them simmer in a syrup of clarified sugar, with a little lemon-peel. Wash and pick some rice, and cook it in milk, moistening it therewith by little and little, so that the grains may remain whole. Sweeten it to taste, and add a little salt and a taste of lemon-peel. Spread the rice upon a dish, mixing some apple preserve with it, and place the apples upon it, and fill up the vacancies between the apples with some of the rice. Place the dish in the oven until the surface gets brown, and garnish with spoonfuls of bright-colored preserve or jelly.

DELICIOUS DISH OF APPLES.—Take two pounds of apples, pare and core them, slice them into a pan; add one pound of loaf sugar, the juice of three lemons, and the grated rind of one. Let these boil about two hours. Turn it into a mould, and serve it with thick custard or cream.

GATEAU DE POMMES.—Take a few apples, boil them with as little water as possible, and make them into apple sauce, then add a pound and a half of sugar, and the juice of a lemon; boil all together till quite firm, and put it into a mould. Garnish it with almonds stuck over it. It will keep for many months if allowed to remain in the mould.

APPLE SOUFFLÉ.—Stew the apples with a little lemon-peel; sweeten them, then lay them pretty high round the inside of a dish. Make a custard of the yelks of two eggs, a little cinnamon, sugar, and milk. Let it thicken over a slow fire, but not boil; when ready, pour it in the inside of the apple. Beat the whites of the eggs to a strong froth, and cover the whole. Throw over it a good deal of pounded sugar, and brown it of a fine brown.

APPLE IN JELLY.—Peel and quarter some good apples, and take out the core. Cook them with just water enough to cover them, some slices of lemon, and clarified sugar, until they are soft. Take out the pieces of apple with great care not to break the pieces, and arrange them in the jars. Then boil the syrup until it will jelly, and pour it over the pieces of apple.

APPLE FLOAT.—Take six large apples, pare, slice, and stew them in as much water as will cover them. When well done, press them through a sieve, and make very sweet with crushed or loaf sugar. While cooling, beat the whites of four eggs to a stiff froth, and stir in the apples; flavor with lemon or vanilla. Serve with sweet cream. Quite as good as peaches and cream.

APPLE SNOW.—Put twelve good tart apples in cold water, and set them on a slow fire; when soft, drain off the water, strip the skins from the apples, core and lay them in a large glass dish. Beat the whites of twelve eggs to a stiff froth, put half a pound of powdered white sugar to the apples; beat them, and add the eggs. Beat the whole to a stiff snow, and turn into a dessert-dish.

FLOATING ISLAND OF APPLES.—Bake or scald eight or nine large apples; when cold, pare them and pulp them through a sieve. Beat up this pulp with sugar, and add to it the whites of four or five eggs previously beaten up with a small quantity of rose-water. Mix this into the pulp a little at a time, and beat it until quite light. Heap it up on a dish, with a rich custard or jelly round it.

APPLE ISLAND.—Make some good apple sauce, which has been flavored with lemon and clove, beat it up very fine, with loaf sugar enough to taste sweet; add two glasses of sherry, then beat the whites of four eggs separately till they are of a light froth, strain them into a large basin, beat them up again; now add two tablespoonfuls of cream, or a little milk, and a quarter of an ounce of isinglass, dissolved in a little water, and added to the milk and egg froth. Beat it well up, take off the froth with a spoon, and lay it on an inverted sieve over a dish. When sufficient froth is made, beat the remainder up with the apples till the whole is very light and frothy. Place the apples piled high in a glass dish, pour some cold custard *around*, not on it, then take off the froth and put on the top of the apples.

APPLE CHEESE CAKES.—Half a pound of apple pulp, quarter of a pound of sifted sugar, quarter of a pound of butter, four eggs, the rind and juice of one lemon. Pare, core, and boil sufficient apples to make half a pound when cooked; add to these the sugar, the butter, which should be melted, the eggs, leaving out two of the whites, and the grated rind and juice of one lemon; stir the mixture well. Line some patty-pans with puff-paste, put in the mixture, and bake about twenty minutes.

APPLE PIQUE.—Peel and stew some apples, but do not let them break. Place them in a glass dish half full of syrup, and put a piece of currant jelly on the top of each apple.

SPONGE CAKE FOR DESSERT.—One pound of sugar, ten eggs, *half* the weight of the sugar and eggs in flour. Beat the yelks of the eggs, flour, and sugar together, then add the whites, beaten to a froth, when just ready for the oven. Butter square tins, put in the mixture one inch deep. This will make two cakes. Take one of them, blanche almonds, and stick the small ends of them in the cake, just so far that they will stand up, putting them in about an inch apart. Then make a custard of three eggs to a pint of milk; sweeten to taste. Pour the custard over the cake just before serving.

A Dish of Snow.—Pare and core a dozen of large apples, put them into cold water and stew them till soft, then pulp through a sieve, and sweeten it to the taste with loaf-sugar. Lay it on the dish on which it is to be sent to table, then beat the whites of twelve eggs to a strong froth, with half a pound of sifted white sugar, and a flavoring of vanilla or orange flower. Strew this over the apple pulp very high, and it will present all the appearance of a veritable dish of snow.

Sugar Drops.—Beat the whites and yelks of four eggs separately to a light foam, dilute the yelks with two teaspoonfuls of water, and turn them with the whites, and beat them some time; then add by degrees a pound of sugar in fine powder, and then four ounces of superfine flour, beating the mixture constantly. Drop the mixture on white paper, placed in a tin plate, in any shape you please, ice them over with sugar in powder, to prevent running, and bake about ten minutes in a moderate oven.

Ice Cream.—To two quarts of cream add one pound of white sugar, boil one tablespoonful of arrowroot in a tumbler of milk, mix all together and freeze. It will be found advisable to stir the mixture frequently. To give the vanilla flavor, put in with the boiled arrowroot half a vanilla bean, previously grated. For strawberry and other fruit creams, add a little larger proportion of sugar, and freeze as soon as possible to prevent curdling.

LEMON ICE CREAM.—To one quart of cream eight ounces sugar, one lemon. Grate the lemon-rind in the sugar, add the raw cream. Strain and freeze very soon.

WATER ICES.—Made with any desired fruit, such as lemon, currant, strawberry, raspberry, etc.; the same to be squeezed, sweetened to taste, and added to water. Strain thoroughly before freezing, and only use the pure liquid so obtained. Orange water ice should be nearly the pure juice of the orange.

CHAPTER VIII.

PRESERVES AND JELLIES.

DIRECTIONS FOR PRESERVING FRUITS, ETC.

PRESERVES of all kinds should be kept entirely secluded from the air and in a dry place. In ranging them on the shelves of a store-closet, they should not be suffered to come in contact with the wall. Moisture in winter and spring exudes from some of the driest walls, and preserves invariably imbibe it, both in dampness and taste. It is necessary occasionally to look at them, and if they have been attacked by mould, boil them up gently again. To prevent all risks, it is always as well to lay a brandy paper over the fruit before tying down. This may be renewed in the spring.

Fruit jellies are made in the ratio of a quart of fruit to two pounds of sugar. They must not be boiled quick nor very long. Practice and a general discretion will be found the best guides to regulate the exact time, which necessarily must be affected, more or less by local causes.

TO PRESERVE PEACHES.—The clear-stone, yellow peaches, white at the stone, are the best. Weigh the fruit after it is pared. To each pound of fruit allow a pound of loaf sugar. Put a layer of sugar at the bottom of the preserving-kettle, and then a layer of fruit, and so on until the fruit is all in. Stand it over the fire until the sugar is entirely dissolved; then boil them until they are clear; take them out piece by piece, and spread them on a dish free from syrup. Boil the syrup in the pan until it jellies; when the peaches are cold, fill the jars half full with them, and fill up with boiling syrup. Let them stand a short time covered with a thin cloth, then put on brandy paper, and cover them close with corks, skin, or paper. From twenty to thirty minutes will generally be sufficient to preserve them.

PEACH MARMALADE.—Prepare peaches as for jam, boil one hour; mix equal parts of sugar with the jam; when dissolved, pass the whole through a sieve; boil slowly two hours, being very careful not to burn; spread it on plates and set it in a cool oven, where it will dry but not burn, for a half day, when it will be ready to pack into moulds; cover the moulds with paper dipped into the white of eggs, beaten as stiff as possible; it must be entirely free from juice, of a dark mahogany color, and clear when finished, sufficiently stiff to cut with a knife; keep it cool; it is liable to mould, which can be the more readily removed if a piece of paper, closely fitting the edges of the jar, is pressed firmly on the marmalade before covering with the egg paper. No air should be allowed to remain in the fruit, which should be packed very closely; and, as marmalade is very thick, it will require some care to accomplish it.

PEACH JAM.—This confection should be made of the cling-stone peach in preference, it being more juicy and of a higher flavor than the other kind of peach, the stone of which separates from the pulp. Treat the peaches exactly in the manner directed for apricots, using the same quantity of sugar.

RASPBERRY FOOL.—Put your fruit for a quarter of an hour into an oven; when tender, pulp it through a sieve, sugar it, add the crumb of sufficient sponge-cake to thicken it; put it into a glass mould, or into custard-cups, and lay some thick cream on the top. If for immediate use, the cream may be beaten up with the fruit.

RASPBERRY JAM.—Let the raspberries be thoroughly ripe. Mash them with a wooden spoon. To every pound of raspberries add a pound of sifted sugar. Boil this well together during half an hour, stirring it continually, lest it should burn. When of a good thickness, put it into pots, let it cool thoroughly, and cover with brandied paper.

CELERY PRESERVE.—Cut the blanched part of the celery in pieces, and boil it in water with a large quantity of ginger until it is quite tender, then throw it into cold water and allow it to remain for an hour. Put it over a slow fire in good syrup, with some pieces of ginger, and let it remain simmering for an hour. Cool it again, and in the meantime thicken the syrup by further evaporation. Put the celery in again, and repeat the same process. After a third simmering in this way, taking care to keep the syrup thick, put the celery into pots, and cover with a syrup.

PRESERVED LETTUCE STALKS.—Peel large lettuce stalks that have run to seed, cut them in pieces, boil them gently till tender, but not too soft, putting half a dozen whole red peppers in the water; put them to drain; make a syrup and boil the stalks up in it just once a day for a week; then make a good rich syrup, well skimmed and boiled, scraping in some best white ginger; pour hot over the stalks; keep in a covered jar.

TO PRESERVE WATERMELON RINDS.—Do not cut your rinds too thin; pare off the outside green rind; soak them two days in clean soft water, and then drain them. Take six pounds of sugar and three pints of water, boil to a thick syrup; then add your watermelon rinds; boil until they are clear; flavor with orange flower water; cool, and put away in jars for use.

PRESERVED CITRON.—Take some fine citron melons, pare, core, and cut them into slices, then weigh them, and to every pound of fruit allow three-quarters of a pound of the best refined sugar. Make a syrup, skim it clear, then put in the citron and ginger, and boil until the citron is quite tender and clear. Allow a quarter of a pound of green ginger to two good sized melons. When the citron is done, put it in the jars, boil the syrup a few minutes longer, skim it till perfectly clear, and pour it over the fruit. Fine fresh lemons can be used instead of the ginger, if preferred. Four large ones will be sufficient for two melons. Slice and boil them with the fruit the same as the ginger. Lay upon the top of the syrup a double white tissue-paper, cut exactly to fit the surface, and paste paper over the top of each jar.

APRICOT JAM.—Let the fruit be just in maturity, but not over ripe. Remove the skins, then cut the apricots in halves. Crack the stones, take out the kernels, bleach them in boiling water, and then pound them in a mortar. Boil the broken stones, skins, and parings in double the quantity of water required for the jam. Reduce it in the boiling to one-half of its original quantity, then strain it through a jelly-bag. To each pound of prepared apricots put a quarter of a pint of this juice, a pound of sifted loaf sugar, and the pounded kernels. Put it on the fire, which should be brisk, and stir the whole with a wooden spoon until it is of a nice consistence, but without being very stiff, or it would have a bad flavor. Put it immediately into pots, and let these stand uncovered during twenty-four hours, then strew a little sifted sugar over the upper surface of the jam in each pot, and tie egged paper over each pot.

To Preserve Hedge Pears.—Take four pounds of sugar and two pounds of water, boil to a middling thick syrup. Pare six pounds of good ripe hedge pears, and leave them whole. Boil these in your syrup until done; cool, flavor with orange flower water, and put away in jars for use.

Pears for the Tea Table.—Take ripe pears and wipe them carefully, place a layer, stem upward, in a stone jar, sprinkle over sugar, then set in another layer of pears, and so on till the jar is filled. To every gallon put in one and a half pints of water. Cover the top of the jar with pie crust, and set it in a slow oven for two hours.

Preserving Pears.—Gather the fruit when not too ripe, peel, then cut them into halves or quarters, weigh them, and to every pound of fruit allow one pound of the best white sugar. Put the fruit in a stone jar with a layer of fruit and one of sugar until you get all the fruit covered. Let them remain in the jar one night, then take your fruit out and lay them on dishes. Put the sugar into a brass or bell metal kettle and make a thick syrup, then put your pears into the syrup, and let them boil until they look clear, and they are ready for use.

Blackberry Jelly.—Gather the fruit when perfectly ripe, and in very dry weather. Put the blackberries into a jar and place the jar in hot water, keeping it boiling until the juice is extracted from the fruit. Pass it through a fine sieve or jelly-bag without much pressure. For every pint of juice add fourteen ounces of sugar, and boil in a clean preserving-pan about five and twenty minutes, carefully taking off the scum as it rises to the surface. Place it hot in small jars and cover it down with thin tissue-paper, dipped in brandy, and brown paper over it. Keep it in a cool, dry place.

BLACKBERRIES.—Preserve these as strawberries or currants, either liquid, or jam, or jelly. Blackberry jelly or jam is an excellent medicine in summer complaints or dysentery. To make it, crush a quart of fully ripe blackberries with a pound of the best loaf sugar, put it over a gentle fire, and cook it until thick, then put to it a gill of the best fourth-proof brandy. Stir it awhile over the fire, then put it in pots.

GREENGAGE JAM.—To every pound of fruit, weighed before being stoned, allow three-quarters of a pound of lump sugar. Divide the greengages, take out the stones, and put them in a preserving-pan. Bring the fruit to a boil, then add the sugar, and keep stirring it over a gentle fire until it is melted. Remove the scum as it rises, and just before the jam is done, boil it rapidly for five minutes. To ascertain when it is sufficiently boiled, pour a little on a plate, and if the syrup thickens and appears firm it is done. Have ready all the kernels blanched, put them into the jam, give them one boil, and pour the preserve into pots. When cold, cover down with oiled papers, and over these tissue-paper, brushed over on both sides with the white of an egg.

GREENGAGES.—Weigh a pound of sugar to a pound of fruit, the largest, when they begin to get soft, are the best. Split them and take out the kernels and stew them in part of the sugar. Take out the kernels from the shells and blanch them. The next day strain off the syrup and boil it with the remaining sugar about ten minutes. Skim it and add the fruit and kernels; skim it until clear, then put into small pots with syrup and kernels.

BOTTLED GREEN GOOSEBERRIES.—Cut off the tops and stalks of some gooseberries which have not attained their full growth, and put them into wide-necked bottles which have been well washed and dried. Cork them loosely, and set them in a pan of cold water, which should be brought to boil very gradually. Leave the gooseberries to simmer until they assume a shrunken appearance, when take the bottles out. If they are not full, take the contents of one bottle to fill up the rest, and pour sufficient boiling water into each bottle as will cover the gooseberries. Cork the bottle close, and tie a bladder over the tops, keeping them in a dry, cool place until wanted. When required for tarts or puddings, pour the water away, and add as much sugar as would be necessary for fresh fruit, which they closely resemble, both in flavor and appearance.

Gooseberry Jelly.—This is made exactly as black currant jelly; use no water with the fruit, but press it firmly, and make the remains of the pulp into jam; if desired to remove the skins, pass the pulp through a colander, allow one pound of sugar for one of jam.

Gooseberry and Raspberry Jelly.—Take any quantity of fine red gooseberries, a quarter as many white ones, and half a quarter as many raspberries; pick the fruits, and put them in a kettle for preserves, with as many pounds of sugar in pieces as you have pounds of fruit. Boil over a quick fire, skimming carefully, and continue boiling until your jelly, turned upon a napkin, fixes or congeals in a moment. This is a proof that your jelly is sufficiently cooked. Remove it from the fire, and turn it through a hair sieve. Let it drain without squeezing, and turn the first results into your pots. This will be a jelly of the first quality, of a beautiful ruby tint, and perfectly transparent. Afterwards squeeze and express the remainder into another vase. This second part is as good as the first, but it has not its transparency.

Red Gooseberry Jam.—Take the eyes and tails from a quantity of red, hairy gooseberries, quite ripe, and put them into a preserving-pan with half a pint of red currant juice to each half-a-dozen pounds. Let them boil until they are all broken and mashed, which you must aid with a wooden spoon. Then for every pound of gooseberries add a pound of sugar, sprinkling it over the fruit. Let the whole simmer until reduced to the proper consistence of jam, taking care that it does not burn during the operation. Then put it into pots.

GREEN GOOSEBERRY JAM.—Gather the finest green gooseberries when quite ripe; take off the tails and eyes. Put the berries into a jar, and set them in a kettle of boiling water over the fire, until they begin to break. Then put them into a preserving pan. Use a pound of sugar for each pound of gooseberries. Add it to the fruit, which you must break as it boils. When of the consistence of jam, put it into pots.

WHITE GOOSEBERRY JAM.—This jam is made with the large white gooseberry, which must be quite ripe and fresh-gathered. Treat it exactly in the same manner as directed for red gooseberry jam, omitting the red currant juice.

DRIED STRAWBERRIES.—Put three pounds of strawberries into a large dish, and sprinkle six pounds of white sugar over them. Let them stand until the next day, then scald them and put them back into the dish. On the third day place another pound of sugar over them, and scald them again. In two days more repeat the process. After this, place the strawberries on a hair-sieve to drain, and then on fresh plates every day, until they are dried. They must be kept in tin canisters.

To Preserve Strawberries.—To two pounds of fine large strawberries, add two pounds of powdered sugar, and put them in a preserving kettle, over a slow fire, till the sugar is melted; then boil them precisely twenty minutes, as fast as possible; have ready a number of *small* jars, and put the fruit in boiling hot. Cork and seal the jars immediately, and keep them through the summer in a cold, dry place. The jars must be heated before the hot fruit is poured in, otherwise they will break.

Strawberry Jelly.—Express the juice from the fruit through a cloth, strain it clear, weigh, and stir to it an equal proportion of the finest sugar dried and reduced to powder; when this is dissolved, place the preserving-pan over a very clear fire, and stir the jelly often until it boils; clear it carefully from scum, and boil it quickly from fifteen to twenty-five minutes. This receipt is for a moderate quantity of the preserve; a very small portion will require much less time.

Strawberry Jam.—Put the fruit into a jar, and stand this in a pan of boiling water over the fire. As the boiling proceeds, keep mashing the strawberries with a wooden spoon until they are all bruised to a pulp. Then put them into a preserving-pan, and to every pound add three-quarters of a pound of sugar. Boil the whole until of due consistence, which will occupy more than half an hour; keeping the jam in constant agitation, lest the bottom should burn. When done enough, take it off the fire and put it into pots.

PRESERVED PINEAPPLE.—Twist out the crown of the pineapple, and pare off the hard yellow rind; next slice the fruit about half an inch thick, and trim it quite clean around the edges, taking care of the trimmings. Put them into a preserving pan with one quart of cold water, and boil till reduced to half a pint; strain it, then put the slices on the fire with the juice and equal weight of fine white sugar; boil gently half an hour.

Or: Make a thin syrup, a quart of water to two pounds of sugar. While this is dissolving, prepare the pineapples, eight medium-sized ones, by removing the skin, and cutting the flesh into slices, about half an inch thick. When the sugar is dissolved, and while the syrup is still hot, throw in the fruit. Give one boil up; let it boil for a quarter of an hour, and put it aside to cool. When cool, boil up again, and repeat this three times. This is some trouble; but the pineapple will not be enough cooked with less than three-quarters of an hour's boiling, and if boiled for that time without a break, it is apt to get pappy. Lastly, make a thick syrup of four pounds of sugar to a quart of water, and add this to the other while both are hot. Boil up once more for a few minutes, and put away in a well-corked or stoppered bottle with a wide mouth. The preserve made as above is most delicious.

PINEAPPLES WITHOUT COOKING.—Peel very ripe pineapples, cut them in slices, take out the cores, and weigh the fruit; allow a pound of double-refined loaf sugar to every pound of fruit. Spread the sugar evenly over the fruit; pack it in layers, and let it stand twenty-four hours; then drain off the syrup, and boil it as long as any impurities rise to the surface; skim it constantly, and pour it over the fruit boiling hot.

PINEAPPLE JELLY.—This is set with isinglass. To every quart of syrup allow one ounce of shred isinglass. To make the syrup, allow to a pint of juice a pound of the best loaf sugar.

PINEAPPLE MARMALADE.—To every pound of grated pineapple allow a pound of double-refined loaf sugar. Boil until thick; then pack in tumblers, and paste over them papers wet with the beaten whites of eggs. Keep in a dry, cool place until wanted.

PINEAPPLE PRESERVE.—Twist off the top and bottom, and pare off the rough outside of pineapples; then weigh them, and cut them in slices, chips, or quarters, or cut them into four or six, and shape each piece like a whole pineapple; to each pound of fruit put a teacup of water; put it in a preserving kettle; cover it, and set it over the fire, and let them boil gently until they are tender and clear; then take them from the water by sticking a fork in the centre of each slice, or with a skimmer, into a dish.

Put to the water white sugar, a pound for each pound of fruit; stir it until it is all dissolved; then put in the pineapple, cover the kettle, and let it boil gently until transparent throughout; when it is so, take it out, let it cool, and put it into glass jars; as soon as the syrup is a little cooled, pour it over them; let them remain in a cool place until the next day, then secure the jars, by tying them over in the usual manner. Pineapple done in this way is a delicious preserve, but in preserving it, by putting it into the syrup without first boiling it, makes it little better than sweetened leather.

Rhubarb Jam.—Cut into pieces about an inch long (not peeled), put three-quarters of a pound of powdered lump sugar to every pound of rhubarb, and leave till morning; pour the syrup from it and boil till it thickens, then add the rhubarb and boil gently a quarter of an hour; tie down with tissue-paper dipped in white of egg. It will keep good for a year, and is excellent.

Rhubarb Preserve.—To every six pounds of rhubarb add six pounds of sugar and a quarter of a pound of bruised ginger; the rhubarb to be cut into pieces two inches long and put into a stone jar, with the sugar in layers, till the sugar is dissolved; take the juice or syrup and boil it with the ginger for half an hour, then add the rhubarb and boil another half hour.

Plums.—Prick them with a needle to prevent

bursting, simmer them very gently in thin syrup, put them into a china bowl, and, when cold, pour the syrup over. Let them lie three days, then make a syrup of three pounds of sugar to five pounds of fruit, with no more water than hangs to large lumps of the sugar dipped quickly and instantly brought out. Boil the plums in this fresh syrup, after draining them from the first; do them very gently till they are clear and the syrup adheres to them; put them one by one into small pots, and pour the liquor over them.

To Preserve Purple Plums.—Make a syrup of clean brown sugar; clarify it; when perfectly clear and boiling hot, pour it over the plums, having picked out all unsound ones and stems; let them remain in the syrup two days, then drain it off, make it boiling hot, skim it, and pour it over again; let them remain another day or two, then put them in a preserving-kettle over the fire, and simmer gently until the syrup is reduced, and thick or rich. One pound of sugar for each pound of plums.

Preserved Cherries.—Take large cherries not very ripe; stew and stone them; save what juice runs from them; take an equal weight of white sugar; make the syrup of a teacup of water for each pound, set it over the fruit until it is dissolved and boiling hot, then put in the juice and cherries, boil them gently until clear throughout; take them from the syrup with a skimmer, and spread them on flat dishes to cool; let the syrup boil until it is rich and quite thick; set it to cool and settle; take the fruit into jars and pots, and pour the syrup carefully over; let them remain open till the next day; then cover as directed. Sweet cherries are improved by the addition of a pint of red currant-juice, and half a pound of sugar to it, for four or five pounds of cherries.

CHERRY MARMALADE OR JAM.—Take out the stones and stalks from some fine cherries, and pulp them through a cane sieve; to every three pounds of pulp add half a pint of currant-juice, and three-quarters of a pound of sugar to each pound of fruit; mix together, and boil until it will jelly. Put it into pots or glasses.

SPICED CHERRIES.—Seven pounds of sour cherries seeded, three pounds of sugar, one pint of vinegar, cinnamon, cloves, and mace. Boil six times; last time put cherries in and let it come to a boil.

BOTTLING CHERRIES.—To every pound of fruit add six ounces of powdered lump sugar. Fill the jars with fruit, shake the sugar over, and tie each jar down with two bladders, as there is danger of one bursting during the boiling. Place the jars in a boiler of cold water, and after the water has boiled, let them remain three hours; take them out, and when cool, put them in a dry place, where they will keep over a year.

CHERRY OR STRAWBERRY FOOL.—Pick the

stems from your fruit; if cherries, stone them, bruise them to a pulp, add a sufficiency of loaf sugar pounded and sifted, and half a pint of cream to a pint of pulp; put it into custard-glasses with a layer of raw cream upon the top, and serve. Some housekeepers, to avoid the trouble of frequent bakings, line several tart-dishes with an edge of crust; bake them and keep them for use as required, when some preserve or raw fruit as above may be simply laid in, and an easy-made tart produced upon an emergency.

CHERRY JAM.—To every pound of fruit, weighed before stoning, allow half a pound of sugar; to every six pounds of fruit allow one pint of red currant-juice, and to every pint, one pound of sugar. Weigh the fruit before stoning, and allow half the weight of sugar; stone the cherries, and boil them in a preserving-pan until nearly all the juice is dried up; then add the sugar, which should be crushed to powder, and the currant-juice, allowing one pint to every six pounds of cherries, (original weight,) and one pound of sugar to every pint of juice. Boil all together until it jellies, which will be in from twenty minutes to half an hour; skim the jam well, keep it well stirred, and, a few minutes before it is done, crack some of the stones and add the kernels.

CURRANT JELLY.—Pick fine red, but long ripe currants from the stems; bruise them, and strain the juice from a quart at a time through a thin muslin; wring it gently, to get all the liquid; put a pound of white sugar to each pound of juice; stir it until it is all dissolved; set it over a gentle fire; let it become hot, and boil for fifteen minutes; then try it by taking a spoonful into a saucer; when cold, if it is not quite firm enough, boil it for a few minutes longer.

BLACK CURRANT JELLY.—It is necessary to add a little water to the fruit, in order to strain it, it is so very thick, unless jam is made at the same time, when a part can be strained for the jelly, and the remainder used for jam. After it is boiled so as to heat the fruit through, press it little by little until all the juice is extracted; measure the juice, and allow one pound of sugar to every pint of juice; mix the juice and sugar, and boil ten minutes gently, stirring constantly, when it will be ready to put in moulds. Cover with paper wet with brandy.

BLACK CURRANT JAM.—To every pound of black currants pulped, put a pound of sugar. Boil up the fruit, stirring it continually, until reduced by evaporation to the proper consistence. Jams may also be made of red and white currants, but as they are scarcely ever used, the jelly being so much preferred, few persons make them. The black currant is one of the most wholesome of jams, and certainly very useful. It has many medicinal virtues, in addition to its agreeable flavor. As a foundation in a glass of whipped cream, it is delicious.

To Can Fruit and Vegetables.—Peaches should be skinned and cut in halves if clingstones, or quartered if freestone, and thrown into water to keep fresh. Put them in a can, adding half as much sugar as fruit, in alternate layers. Let stand until the sugar is dissolved, then put in a preserving kettle and let boil until the fruit is boiling-hot. At once fill the cans and seal tight.

Raspberries, and such other small fruit, are done as follows: Pick and wash the fruit carefully, and to every pound of fruit add half a pound of sugar. Put in a vessel in alternate layers and let stand for one hour. Boil in preserving-kettle for ten minutes, can whilst hot. No water need be used, as the fruit yields sufficient juice.

Corn, peas, okra, etc.: Boil for half an hour, with just sufficient water to cover them; can whilst hot. The corn, of course, should be cobbed before boiling.

Tomatoes: Scald only enough to remove the skins, boil for half an hour in their own juice. Can boiling-hot.

To seal hermetically, place the jars in a pan of hot water, which will expel the air, seal at once, and the fruit will keep an indefinite period.

Brandy Peaches.—Four pounds of ripe peaches, two pounds of powdered loaf sugar. Put the fruit over the fire in cold water, simmer, but not boil, till the skins will rub off easily; stone them, if liked.

Put the sugar and fruit in alternate layers in the jars till filled, then pour in white brandy, and cover the whole. Cork tightly.

QUINCES PRESERVED WHOLE.—Pare and put them into a saucepan, with the parings at the top, then fill it with hard water, cover it close, set it over a gentle fire till they turn reddish. Let them stand till cold, put them into a clear, thick syrup, boil them for a few minutes; set them on one side till quite cold, boil them again in the same manner. The next day boil them until they look clear. If the syrup is not thick enough, boil it more. When cold, put brandied paper over them. The quinces may be halved or quartered.

QUINCE MARMALADE.—To one gallon of quinces three pounds of good loaf sugar. Pare the quinces and cut them in halves, scoop out the cores and the hard strip that unites the core with the string. Put the cores and some of the parings in a saucepan with about a quart of water; put the halves of quinces in a steamer that fits the saucepan, boil them until the quinces are softened by the steam, then mash them with a wooden spoon in a dish and pour the water from the saucepan on them, which is now of a thick glutinous substance. Put them with the sugar in a stewpan or enamelled saucepan, and let them boil for about half an hour, keeping them well stirred.

QUINCE JELLY. — Take some sound, yellow

quinces, which are not over ripe; peel them, cut them in quarters, and boil them in as much water as will cover them. When they have been well boiled, squeeze them through a linen cloth, clarify the juice in a filtering-bag, weigh it, and put it with three-quarters of its weight of sugar in a brass kettle. Do not forget to put in a piece of cinnamon. Cook the whole together until it has become a jelly. Take it from the fire, and tie up in pots when it is cold.

QUINCES FOR THE TEA TABLE.—Bake ripe quinces thoroughly. When cold, strip off the skins, place them in a glass dish, and sprinkle with white sugar, and serve them with cream. They make a fine looking dish for the tea table, and a more luscious and inexpensive one than the same fruit made into sweetmeats. Those who once taste the fruit thus prepared will probably desire to store away a few bushels in the fall to use in the above manner.

QUINCE AND APPLE JELLY.—Cut small and core an equal weight of tart apples and quinces. Put the quinces in a preserving-kettle, with water to cover them, and boil till soft; add the apples, still keeping water to cover them, and boil till the whole is nearly a pulp. Put the whole into a jelly-bag and strain without pressing. To each quart of juice allow two pounds of lump sugar. Boil together half an hour.

APPLE JELLY.—Cut off all spots and decayed

places on the apples, quarter them, but do not pare or core them. Put in the peel of as many lemons as you like, about two to six or eight dozen of the apples. Fill the preserving-pan, and cover the fruit with spring water. Boil them till they are in pulp, then pour them into a jelly-bag; let them strain all night; do not squeeze them. To every pint of juice put one pound of white sugar. Put in the juice of the lemons you had before pared, but strain it through muslin. You may also put in about a teaspoonful of essence of lemon, let it boil for at least twenty minutes; it will look redder than at first; skim it well all the time. Put it either in shapes or pots, and cover it the next day. It ought to be quite stiff and very clear.

APPLE JAM.—The apples, which should be ripe, and of the best eating sort, being pared and quartered, are put into a pan with just water to cover them, and boiled until they can be reduced to a mash. Then, for each pound of the pared apples, a pound of sifted sugar is added, being sprinkled over the boiling mixture. Boil and stir it well until reduced to a jam; then put it into pots.

The above is the most simple way of making it; but to have it of the best possible clearness, make a thick syrup with three pounds of sugar to each pint of water, and clarify it with an egg, as before directed. Then add one pint of this syrup for every three pounds of apples, and boil the jam to a proper thickness.

PRESERVES AND JELLIES.

APPLE MARMALADE.—This is a useful thing to make, as it may be put aside for future use, and will keep a long time. Pare, core, and cut your apples into small pieces, put them into water with a little lemon-juice to keep them white; take them out after a short time and drain them, weigh and put them into a stewpan, with an equal quantity of sugar, a stick of cinnamon, and the juice of a lemon. Place the stewpan over a brisk fire and cover it. When the apples are pulped, stir the mixture until it becomes of a proper consistency, and put the marmalade into pots.

APPLE PRESERVE.—Procure fresh gathered ripe apples of a fine sort, peel them, take out the cores, and cut them in quarters. Place them in a preserving-pan, with a glass of water, a little lemon or orange-peel, and a pound of sugar to a pound and a half of fruit. Let it boil thoroughly, and then put t out into preserve pots.

CRAB APPLE JAM.—Pare the crab apples when quite ripe, put them into a stone jar, cover it well, and put it in a pan of boiling water for an hour and a half. Then prepare the syrup with two pounds of sugar in half a pint of water for every pound of the apples. Clarify the syrup. Then put the apples into it and boil the whole to a jam.

CHAPTER IX.

BUTTER, CHEESE AND EGGS.

BUTTER THAT THREATENS TO TURN RANCID.—Butter that has not been properly churned, or that has not been carefully separated from the buttermilk, has been improperly packed, or from any other cause threatens to turn rancid, should be immediately washed and kneaded in spring water, changing the water several times, then resalted with salt pounded as fine as possible, and sifted through a hair sieve.

BUTTER MAKING.—Strain away the milk in *flat, stone* jars nicely cleaned and scalded. Skim the cream off when it rises. In the summer season the cream should not be kept longer than twenty-four hours before it is churned. After churning take the butter up in a wooden bowl without any water at all, and let it set by over night, and in the morning, while cool and pleasant, beat it well and season with salt to taste. After a day or two it should be beaten over again to get all the milk out of it (for this is the true secret of keeping butter well). Season it with a little more salt, and pack.

To Preserve Butter.—Take good, sweet, June butter, work the buttermilk carefully out; then add a handful of salt to a pound of butter; pack a good layer of butter in your stone jar, then a layer of salt; repeat until the jar is full; then place a good weight on top, and stand in a good cool place; cover with brine, to bear an egg.

Curled Butter.—Tie a strong cloth by two of the corners to an iron hook in the wall; make a knot with the other two ends so that a stick might pass through. Put the butter into the cloth; twist it tightly over a dish, into which the butter will fall through the knot, so forming small and pretty little strings. The butter may then be garnished with parsley, if to serve with a cheese course; or it may be sent to table plain for breakfast in an ornamental dish. Squirted butter for garnishing hams, salads, eggs, etc., is made by forming a piece of stiff paper in the shape of a cornet, and squeezing the butter in fine strings from the hole at the bottom. Scooped butter is made by dipping a teaspoon or scooper in warm water, and then scooping the butter quickly and thin. In warm weather, it would not be necessary to heat the spoon.

Rancid Butter, boiled in water with a portion of charcoal (say a tenth part), will be entirely divested of its rancidity, and may be used for cooking purposes, although its fine flavor will not be restored for the table.

MANUFACTURE OF PINEAPPLE AND POTATO CHEESES.

The Netherlanders supply the market with what is popularly known as "pineapple" cheese. Very excellent cheese it is, too—this Dutch pineapple—keeping in all climates capitally, and always commanding ready sale at good prices. This is the Hollanders' formula for making Edam or pineapple cheese. It is simple enough, and the Holland "pine-apples" may just as easily be made in America, wherever four or five cows are kept, as it is in the Netherlands.

The fresh sweet milk is curdled with muriatic acid or spirits of salt, and the curd cut and chopped and manipulated in the most thorough manner in order to expel every particle of whey. The curd is then soaked in a brine of sufficient strength to float an egg for an hour. The brine is then worked out, and the curd subjected to a heavy pressure in iron moulds, that give the pineapple form to the cheese. After from four to five hours' pressing, the cheese is taken from the form and anointed with soft butter, having as much fine salt worked into it as it will hold. Thus finished up they set singly in rows on shelves in a cool, airy place, and with a month's curing are in a fit condition to send abroad, and will keep for years in any climate.

The largest of these Dutch cheeses never exceed four and a half pounds weight, to make one of which requires about six gallons of milk. So at any farm-house, where three or four cows only are kept, an Edam cheese may be made every day without interfering with other duties, and the aggregate for a year would make a very respectable increase of income.

In Saxony the smaller farmers manufacture very palatable cheese from the milk of a single cow by the addition of potatoes. The potatoes are boiled until perfectly cooked, then mashed, and to four pounds of potatoes one quart of thick sour milk is added, with salt enough to season, and the mass kneaded as thoroughly as bread dough. In four days it receives another vigorous kneading, and is divided into balls of three to five pounds weight, pressed with the hand as compact as possible into small baskets, and dried, in summer, in the shade; in winter, by the fire or stove. When thoroughly dry, the cheese is put into tin cans, sealed up, and set by for use in a cool, dry place.

CHEESE BISCUIT.—Two ounces of butter, two ounces of flour, two ounces of grated cheese, a little Cayenne, and salt. To be made into a thin paste and rolled out very thin, then cut in pieces four inches long and one inch broad, bake a very light brown, and send to table as hot as possible.

CHEESECAKE.—Bruise one cottage cheese with one-eighth of a pound of butter, add four eggs and milk enough to render it the consistency of thick gruel; sweeten to taste; add one-half a lemon and spice to your liking. Bake with bottom crust.

BUTTERMILK CHEESE.—Scald the buttermilk; then set it over the fire to boil; skim the top, and put it in a jug to drain; add a little salt, and it is ready for use.

POTTED CHEESE.—This is a useful luncheon dish, and, being in a glass jar, it looks light and pretty on the table. One pound of cheese must be well beaten in a mortar, and to it must be added two ounces of liquid butter, one glass of sherry, and a very small quantity of Cayenne pepper, mace, and salt. All should be well beaten together and put into a pretty-shaped glass potting-jar, with a layer of butter at the top. It makes a delicious relish for bread or toast.

CHEESE STRAWS, No. 1.—Half a pound of puff-paste, three ounces of Parmesan cheese, grated, a little Cayenne pepper, salt, and black pepper, roll it very thin, cut it in narrow strips, bake in a moderate oven, and serve hot.

2. Quarter of a pound of flour, and two ounces of butter worked through the flour with the fingers, and rubbed till quite smooth; two ounces of grated cheese, the yelks of two eggs, and the white of one. Season to taste with Cayenne pepper and a small pinch of salt. Mix all together, roll it out thin,

place it on a well-buttered tin pan; cut into narrow strips about five inches long. Remove from the tin carefully, after baking ten minutes.

3. Quarter of a pound of puff-paste, a quarter of an ounce of Parmesan (or any other good cheese) grated very fine, a little salt and Cayenne pepper mixed, sprinkle the cheese, salt and pepper over the paste, and roll it two or three times; cut it into narrow strips about five inches long. Bake them in a slow oven, and serve hot.

CREAM CHEESE.—The cream cheese we make at home is much admired. We put a quart of cream into a clean jug, with half a teaspoonful of salt stirred in, and let it stand a day or two till thickish. Then we fold an ordinary grass cloth about six or eight times, and sprinkle it with salt, then lay it in a sieve about eight inches in diameter. The sides of the cloth should come up well over the sieve. Then pour in the cream, and sprinkle a little salt on it. Change the cloth as often as it becomes moist, and as the cheese dries press it with the cloth and sieve. In about a week or nine days it will be prime and fit to eat. The air alone suffices to turn the cream into cheese.

Another: Take about half a pint of cream, tie it up in a piece of thin muslin, and suspend it in a cool place. After five or six days take it out of the muslin, and put it between two plates, with a small weight on the upper one. This will make it a good shape for the table, and also help to ripen the cheese, which will be fit to use in about eight days from the commencement of the making.

HOW TO COOK AND SERVE EGGS.

When we inform our readers that in the wide and ever-extending circle of French cookery, no less than six hundred and eighty-five ways of preparing eggs are recognized, it will be obvious to them that our chief difficulty has been, in preparing this collection, what to choose, and what to avoid. Our principle has been to present to our readers the choicest, the most useful, and palatable varieties.

Eggs, Plain Boiled.—This being beyond question the most popular way of serving eggs, we must commence by giving it in the approved French method. Get ready a saucepan of boiling water, place in it some fresh eggs, immediately remove the saucepan from the fire, put on the lid, and let the eggs remain exactly four minutes. Take them up, and serve them, well warmed, in a dish. The eggs, if so preferred, may be put into cold water over a quick fire, and when the water comes to a boil, they are done.

Eggs sur le Plat.—Heat some butter upon a tin or pewter dish; carefully break into it as many eggs as you think sufficient; arranging them neatly; season with salt and pepper; add a few teaspoonfuls of good, thick cream, and place the dish for six minutes over a clear fire, and serve directly.

EGG-BALLS.—Take the yelks of six hard-boiled eggs; pound them in a mortar, together with a little salt, one dessertspoonful of flour, and a small quantity of pepper. When a smooth, but stiff paste is formed, add as much raw yelk of egg as will serve to mix it of the consistency required. Make it into balls, and serve them upon buttered toast.

LAIT DE POULE.—Beat until light the yelks of two fresh eggs, add two teaspoonfuls of powdered loaf sugar, and the same quantity of orange flower water. Stir quickly and add a teacupful of boiling water. Drink while hot.

EGGS A L'ARDENNAISE.—Break the shells of one dozen eggs. Separate the yelks from the whites and keep each yelk by itself. Beat the whites to a froth; add to them a little salt, pepper and thick cream. Pour the mixture into a well-buttered deep dish, and arrange the yelks upon the top. Put the dish into a gentle oven, and, when set, serve hot.

EGGS A L'AURORE.—Boil some eggs until they are hard. Remove the shells; cut each egg in half and scoop out the yelks, put these into a mortar with some pepper, salt, savory herbs and cream. Beat all to a paste; place some of it in each halved white of egg, and lay the remainder in a buttered dish. Arrange the stuffed eggs on the top with the forced meat uppermost. Brown in a moderate oven, and serve hot.

BROILED EGGS.—Cut a large round of bread; toast it on both sides, and butter it. Carefully break six eggs, and arrange them upon the toast; sprinkle over them some salt and pepper, and slowly pass a red-hot shovel up and down over them until they are well set. Squeeze upon them the juice of an orange, and strew over a little grated nutmeg. Serve as quickly as possible. If preferred, the toasted bread may be dipped into some warmed cream, and some poached eggs placed upon it, and then glazed with a red-hot shovel.

MINCED EGGS.—Shell four or five hard-boiled eggs, and mince them; but not very fine. Thicken a breakfastcupful of gravy or milk, with sufficient flour rolled in butter; add some savory herbs, chopped small; season with Cayenne or white pepper, a little nutmeg, and salt; simmer it for ten minutes, put in the eggs, shake it gently round and round over the fire for a few moments, and serve garnished with sippets of toast and small pieces of sliced lemon. Any particular flavor may be given to this dish, to suit the taste.

BROWN EGGS.—Hard boil some eggs, put them into cold water, shell them and slice them; lay them upon hot buttered toast, and season them according to taste. Strew fried bread crumbs over them, then sprinkle them with catsup and brown them.

Egg Dumplings.—Make a batter of a pint of milk, two well-beaten eggs, a teaspoonful of salt, and flour enough to make a batter as thick as for pound cake. Have a clean saucepan of boiling water; let the water boil fast; drop in the batter with a tablespoon. Four or five minutes will boil them. Take them with a skimmer on a dish; put a bit of butter and pepper over them, and serve with boiled or cold meat. To serve sweet, put butter and grated nutmeg, with syrup or sugar over it.

Rumbled Eggs.—Very convenient for invalids, or, when required, a light dish for supper. Beat up three eggs with two ounces of fresh butter, or well-washed salt butter; add a teaspoonful of cream or new milk. Put all in a saucepan and keep stirring it over the fire for nearly five minutes, until it rises up like *soufflé*, when it should be immediately dished on buttered toast.

Omelette Soufflée.—Put three tablespoonfuls of sugar in a bowl with four yelks of eggs, and mix them well, adding a few drops of essence. (Omelette soufflée is an *entremét* and comes after the vegetables.) Then beat the whites, adding a pinch of salt, and mix with the rest, putting in two tablespoonfuls of the mixture with the whites at first, and then adding the rest. Stir gently until well mixed, and serve in the dish that it is cooked in. After putting it in the pan smooth with a knife, dust with powdered sugar and bake. The salt is added to the white of egg to prevent its curdling. The omelette is cooked at 310° Fahrenheit. For puff-paste, 500°. It must be served at once, as it falls rapidly. Powder with sugar and serve.

OMELETTE A LA CREPPE.—Put into a basin eight tablespoonfuls of flour; beat six eggs into it, with as much milk as will make it into a batter, with a pinch of salt. Bake till brown.

EGG CHEESECAKES.—Twelve eggs, boiled hard and rubbed through a sieve (while hot), with half a pound of butter; then add half a pound of pounded loaf sugar, half a pound of currants, and a little nutmeg. Brandy may be added, which flavors them nicely; or, if preferred, a few drops of essence of lemon or almonds.

EGG SANDWICHES.—Hard boil some very fresh eggs, and, when cold, cut them into moderately thin slices, and lay them between some bread and butter cut as thin as possible; season them well with pepper, salt, and nutmeg. For picnic parties, or when one is travelling, these sandwiches are far preferable to hard-boiled eggs *au naturel.*

PRESERVING EGGS.—In order to keep well, eggs must be perfectly fresh when packed. Take a stone pot which will hold three gallons; pack the eggs closely, sharp end down. Salt one pint of unslacked lime, and dissolve it in sufficient water to cover the eggs. When cold, pour it over them, being sure no eggs float.

Egg Omelette.—Scald one pint of new milk; into this stir the yelks of five eggs, and a tablespoonful each of sugar and flour. Beat the whites of the eggs till stiff, and add to the yelks; beat all well together, and bake in a quick oven.

Buttered Eggs.—Four eggs, well beaten; three tablespoonfuls of cream or rich unskimmed milk, a little grated tongue or ham, pepper, salt, and three ounces of butter. Put all the ingredients, excepting the eggs, into a stewpan and heat; when quite hot, add the eggs, and stir while cooking till quite thick. Spread upon buttered toast, and serve hot.

Bacon Omelette.—Either simply mince some cold boiled bacon, and mix it with eggs which have been spiced and well beaten; or take some raw bacon, chop it well, toss it in a frying-pan till nicely browned, and then pour the beaten eggs upon it; or, place the tossed bacon upon some eggs that you have just poured into a frying-pan; when set, fold the omelette, and serve with a tomato sauce in the dish.

Kidney Omelette.—Remove all skin, fat, and sinew from a fresh kidney, whether sheep's or calf's. Cut it small, season it well, and fry it quickly in hot butter. Beat six eggs together with a glassful of white wine; heat a little butter in the frying-pan, pour in the eggs, and before they are regularly set place the kidney in the middle; turn in the ends of the omelette and serve; garnish with thin slices of lemon quartered.

Omelette aux Croutons.—Beat the yelks of six and the whites of four eggs; season with salt and spice according to taste. Cut some nice little pieces of bread no larger than dice; fry them in butter till they are well browned, then throw them quickly into boiling gravy or milk, or sauce of any particular flavor; mix them with the beaten egg, and fry as an ordinary omelette.

CHAPTER X.

BREAD, BISCUIT, CAKES AND YEAST.

BREAD.—Set your sponge over night with one-half pint of lukewarm water, one teacupful of yeast, and one pint of flour (measure before sifting). In the morning warm half a cup of milk (or water with a little butter in it), and stir into the sponge with one tablespoonful of lime-water, and one and one-half pint of flour. Knead into two loaves and put them in your pans to rise, they will bake in about half an hour.

ROLLS AND BREAD (SUPERIOR).—Sift three quarts of flour. Take two eggs, one teacupful and a half of liquid yeast, two pints of lukewarm water, one tablespoonful of brown sugar, one of salt, and four handfuls of flour taken from the measured flour. Beat the eggs very light, and make these ingredients into a smooth batter. After the batter is well beaten, divide the remaining flour into two equal parts, and put one part of the flour into a tin pan or bucket, pour in the batter, and cover it with the remainder of the flour. Set it in a moderately warm place, and, in an hour and a half, or when light, turn the whole out and work it well. It may require more flour in kneading it. Work it quickly, but not until it is cold, and set it to rise again, rubbing a little lard over the top of the dough. In three or four hours it will be ready to knead over again, and, after it has risen a second time, it is ready for baking in a quick oven. If you wish rolls, work in a spoonful of lard during the last kneading, and mould the dough into small cakes. Do not keep the dough too warm, and it will be more flaky. If you wish a smaller loaf of bread, use only a pint and a half of water in making up the batter, but do not diminish the other ingredients.

BREAD RECEIPT.—Take three pints of warm water, one tablespoonful of lard, one teacupful of warm yeast; thicken with flour to form a dough. Let it stand to rise, then work into loaves. Let it rise fifteen or twenty minutes, then bake about three-quarters of an hour.

WHEATEN BREAD.—One spoonful of hop yeast, two potatoes boiled, and one pint of water; make a sponge, and when light, or sufficiently raised, mix hard and let rise, and when it is light again, mould it over, and bake while light.

ANOTHER WAY.—Grate half a dozen potatoes, and add one quart of water; put in one cup of hop yeast at night, and in the morning, when light, add three teaspoonfuls of sugar, and flour to form a dough. Let it rise; when light, put it in tins; let it rise again, and bake for half an hour.

POTATO BREAD.—Take four or five good mealy potatoes, and after boiling, peel and mash well; add a large spoonful of flour and enough hot water to make a thin batter; when cool enough, add a small quantity of good yeast and a spoonful of sugar; set to rise in a moderately warm place, say by the stove or fire-place; it rises very quickly. When risen, take two large spoonfuls of it for a pint and a half of flour, a small spoonful of lard or butter, a half pint of milk, and hot water enough to make into a stiff batter, (over night;) beat well; next morning work it well into a smooth dough and make into rolls or loaves; set in a warm place to rise again, and bake in a quick oven. Do not forget a teaspoonful of salt and one of yeast powders sifted in the dry flour that you work into the batter in the morning; a tin bucket is best, with a tight cover, and a towel between it and bucket. If your flour is good, there is no better receipt than this; no hops are needed.

HOMEMADE BREAD.—Save a gill of bread dough made with hop yeast, cover it tightly and place it in a cool room or cellar until baking day; then make a sponge of it by adding warm water and flour, and a good teaspoonful of sugar. This should be done early in the morning. When the sponge is very light, mix the bread as usual with warm milk, or water, and a teaspoonful of soda or saleratus, and when light, bake This always insures light, sweet bread, and entirely does away with yeast making. Of course, a piece of dough must be saved out each time.

PREMIUM RYE BREAD.—One quart of Indian meal, one quart of rye meal, one quart of wheat flour, one teacup of yeast, one teaspoon of salt. Make a thick batter with warm milk; pour into pans and let it rise. Bake until well done.

RICE BREAD.—Boil half a pound of rice in three pints of water till the whole becomes thick and pulpy. With this, and yeast, and six pounds of flour, make your dough. In this way, it is said, as much bread will be made as if eight pounds of flour, without rice, had been used.

CORN BREAD.—One quart of sour milk, one tablespoonful of soda, one teaspoonful of salt, one cup of molasses or brown sugar, three large cups of corn meal, and three of flour. Mix well, and bake in a slow oven at least two hours.

BROWN BREAD.—One quart of corn meal, wet thoroughly with boiling water; then add one quart of lukewarm water, one quart of raw corn meal, one quart of Graham flour, one tablespoonful of salt, four tablespoonfuls of good hop yeast, one teacupful of molasses; mix thoroughly; when light, bake two hours in a moderately heated oven.

LIGHT CORN BREAD.—One quart of boiled milk poured over one pint of corn meal, salt, three well beaten eggs, four tablespoonfuls of flour, half a spoonful of soda, one of cream of tartar, and a little butter.

CORN MEAL BREAD.—Beat two eggs very light and mix them with one pint of sour milk; add a teaspoonful of soda, and stir in one pint of corn meal and one tablespoonful of melted butter. Beat it well, and bake in a quick oven.

GRAHAM LOAF.—Take one quart of warm water, one teacupful of good yeast, and one tablespoonful of salt. Put into a pan, make a stiff batter with flour, which has been sifted, and keep it very warm until it is light; then take flour, which has been half sifted, to thicken it, knead it well, but do not let it get cold; let it rise again. Then work it down, and put in one teacupful of sugar and a piece of butter the size of an egg. Knead it half an hour, put it in pans, and let it rise very light. Bake three-quarters of an hour in a moderate oven.

GRAHAM BISCUIT.—Two pints of buttermilk, half a pound of butter or lard, one teaspoonful of finely pulverized soda in the flour; flour of desired quantity.

GRAHAM CRACKERS. — To flour sufficient to make a batter add two pints of cold water, quarter of a pound of butter, quarter of a teaspoonful of soda; mix as stiff as can be worked. Cut out, pick with a fork, bake in a moderately hot oven. These crackers, with a cup of sweet cream, make a very light, wholesome meal for dyspeptics.

GRAHAM BREAD.—Graham flour. The wheat must be of the best quality, and either run through a smut-mill, or washed and dried before grinding. It should be ground rather coarser than common flour, and used without bolting. It takes more wetting than fine flour. For every loaf allow three large tablespoonfuls of molasses, one quart of wetting, a teaspoonful of salt, three teaspoonfuls of brewer's yeast. Mix the yeast, molasses, and salt in the wetting, add a half teaspoonful of soda, and mix in as much coarse flour as can possibly be stirred in with a spoon. Now knead the bread briskly, until it cleaves from the hand. Put the loaves in the pan, and pat it in place and shape. If made with homemade yeast, sponge the bread, and add the molasses and other wetting after the sponge rises. Knead until the dough cleaves from the hands; set it in a warm place until it rises. When light, knead it again as before, and put it into the pans to rise. Add no flour after the first mixing; the dough will not be stiff enough to form into loaves. Shape the loaves after they are in the pan with the hand.

ITALIAN BREAD.—One pound of butter, one pound of powdered loaf sugar, one pound two ounces of flour, twelve eggs, half a pound of citron and lemon-peel. Mix as for pound cake. If the mixture begins to curdle, which it is most likely to do from the quantity of eggs, add a little of the flour. When the eggs are all used, and it is light, stir in the remainder of the flour lightly. Bake it in long narrow tins, either papered or buttered, first put in a layer of the mixture, and cover it with the peel, cut in large thin slices. Proceed in this way until it is three parts full, and bake it in a moderate oven.

POTATO BREAD.—There are many ways in which potato bread may be made, the most generally practiced being to add hot mashed potatoes with wheat flour; but potato bread proper is prepared by making use of potato meal and mashed potatoes only, adding one-fifth the quantity of water, with yeast and salt as for ordinary bread. This composition also makes excellent crumpets. A little butter introduced, and milk used instead of water, is a material improvement to potato bread.

INDIAN CORN BREAD.—One cup of sour milk, one cup of sweet milk, half a cup of lard, half a cup of molasses, one cup of wheat flour, four cups of Indian meal, one teaspoonful of saleratus, one teaspoonful of salt. Steam it three hours.

SCOTCH SHORTBREAD.—Take half a pound of fresh butter, one pound of flour, quarter of a pound of finely pounded loaf sugar; work the butter into the sugar by degrees, then add the flour in small quantities. Knead it with the hand into either a round or square tin about an inch thick. Prick all over with a fork, and mark neatly round the edges, and bake in rather a cool oven for half an hour.

COMMON CORN BREAD.—One pint of sifted corn

meal, a pinch of salt, two tablespoonfuls of butter, and a quarter of a cup of cream, two eggs. Add milk till it is a thin batter. Bake in deep tin pans.

Or: A pint of sifted meal, one egg, a teaspoonful of soda, and a heaped one of cream of tartar, a little salt, a bit of butter half the size of an egg, and the same of lard; thin this with milk, so that it will pour quite freely. Bake just twenty minutes.

GENUINE SCOTTISH SHORTBREAD.—Take two pounds fine flour, one pound fresh butter, half pound fine sifted sugar. Thoroughly knead these together without one drop of water (the prevailing mistake is to add more or less water), roll out the cake to half an inch in thickness, and place it over paper in a shallow tin, and fire slowly until of proper crispness. It is usual to insert in upper surface a few caraway confections and small pieces of orange-peel. Good cake should be most brittle—*Scotice,* "short," —hence its name.

SHORTBREAD.—One pound of flour, half a pound of fresh butter, three ounces of powdered lump sugar. Thoroughly mix the flour and sugar. Place your butter in the middle of the pasteboard, and pile round it the mixed flour and sugar, which you must gradually and thoroughly work into the butter. When you have worked it smooth, roll it out. Cut in the form you wish, pinch round the edges, and put some caraway comfits or citron on the top. Bake in a very slow oven.

DINNER ROLLS.—One pound of flour, a quarter of a pound of butter, one tablespoonful of good yeast, one egg, a little warm milk. Rub the butter into the flour, then add the yeast, breaking in one egg. Mix in with a little warm milk poured into the middle of the flour; stir all well together, and set it by the fire to rise; then make it into light dough, and again set it by the fire. Make up the rolls, lay them on a tin, and set them in front of the fire for ten minutes before you put them into the oven, brushing them over with egg.

FRENCH ROLLS.—Work one pound of butter into a pound of flour; put to it one beaten egg, two tablespoonfuls of yeast, one teaspoonful of salt, and as much warm milk as will make a soft dough; strew flour over it; cover it with a cloth and set it in a warm place for an hour or more, until light; flour your hands well; make it in small rolls; bake in a quick oven.

PENNSYLVANIA RUSK.—Two pounds of flour, one pint of good new milk, two spoonfuls of good yeast; set the sponge to rise over night. Early in the morning add a little salt, two large spoonfuls of pulverized white sugar (brown will answer), three large spoonfuls of butter, two well-beaten eggs, and half a nutmeg; add flour until it is the consistency of bread. Knead it well for fifteen or twenty minutes; set it to rise again. When it has risen mould it out into cakes about the size of a small hen's egg;

place them in a large iron pan a little distance apart; set them to rise. When they are well raised, beat the white of an egg with a little sugar, and brush them over the top. Bake them fifteen or twenty minutes, not longer. If you do not have the very nicest of rusks after trying this receipt, you must try it over again, as it will certainly be your own fault.

TEA RUSKS.—Half a pint of new milk, and one cup of hop yeast; add flour to make a batter, and set the sponge at night. In the morning add half a pint of milk, one cup of sugar, one of butter, one egg, one nutmeg, and flour to make it sufficiently stiff. Let it rise, then roll it, and cut it out; let it rise again, and then bake.

RUSK.—One pint of milk, one teacupful of butter, one cup of sugar, one cup of yeast; mix stiff, and set in a warm place to rise three hours.

LIGHT BISCUITS.—Put half a pound of butter into a basin and turn it about well with a spoon. Whisk six eggs well, add half a pound of powdered sugar, whisk another ten minutes, and then mix with the butter, after which stir in six ounces of currants, and an equal quantity of dried flour. After mixing these all well together, drop the mixture on paper, each about the size of a shilling, and bake in a quick oven, taking the biscuits off the paper while hot.

BISCUITS.—Take some of the bread dough in the

morning, as much as would make a loaf of bread and add one cup of butter; mix well, let it rise, and then make into biscuit. Let it rise again, and then bake.

BUTTER BISCUITS.—Dissolve half a pound of butter in half a pint of warm milk, and with four pounds of flour make up a smooth, stiff paste; roll it out very thin, and cut with a tin or the top of a tumbler into shape; prick the biscuits over with a fork, and bake on tins in a quick oven.

BISCUIT CAKES.—One pound of flour, five eggs, beaten and strained, eight ounces of sugar, a little rose or orange flower water; beat the whole well together, and bake it one hour.

CREAM BISCUITS.—Rub one pound of fresh butter into one pound of flour, make a hole in the centre, into which put half a pound of powdered sugar, upon which the rind of a lemon was rubbed previously to pounding, and three whole eggs. Mix the eggs well with the sugar, and then mix all together, forming a flexible paste. Cut it into round pieces, each nearly as large as a walnut, stamp them flat with a butter stamp of the size of a half dollar, and bake them in a slack oven.

GERMAN CREAM BISCUITS.—Take four ounces of butter, six ounces of powdered loaf sugar, seven ounces of flour, one tablespoonful of fresh cream, and one egg. Make the above into a dough, beating it well; then roll it out very thin, cutting it into square pieces two inches long and one broad Bake in a quick oven, and when done, they should be of a light yellow brown.

SOUR CREAM BISCUIT.—Sift a teaspoonful of salt and one of soda with a quart of flour in the bread-pan. Have ready a large pint of sour cream, beat one egg, add it to the cream, mix, roll, cut, and bake the biscuit as quickly as possible.

MILK BISCUIT.—Take one pound of flour, quarter of a pound of butter, eight tablespoonfuls of yeast, and half a pint of new milk. Melt the butter in the milk, put in the yeast and some salt, and work into a stiff paste. When light, knead it well, roll it out an inch thick, cut out with a tumbler, prick them with a fork, and bake in a quick oven. If butter is not abundant, you may take two ounces of lard and the rest butter.

SODA BISCUIT.—One pint of buttermilk, two tablespoonfuls of sour cream, one teaspoonful of soda, three-quarters of a cup of lard. Make a very soft dough, and bake quickly in a hot oven.

POTATO BISCUITS.—Nicely peel and steam four middling-sized potatoes, mash them, and pound them in a mortar. Moisten them with a little raw egg. When perfectly smooth, add to them sufficient loaf sugar to make them pretty sweet. Beat the whites of four eggs to a snow, mix it with the potatoes, etc., add a dessertspoonful of orange flower water, and when well mixed, place portions of the preparation upon paper, to form either round or oblong biscuits. Bake them slowly, and when of a fine color, they are done. Remove the paper when the biscuits are cold.

JUDGE'S BISCUITS.—Having broken six eggs into a basin, whisk them well for five minutes. Put in half a pound of powdered sugar, and whisk again for ten minutes; add some caraway seeds (if liked) and half a pound of dry, sifted flour, mixing all thoroughly with a wooden spoon. Drop the mixture on paper, each being about the size of a half dollar and high in the middle. Sift sugar over them and bake them. Remove them from the paper while they are hot.

ABERNETHY BISCUITS.—Dissolve a quarter of a pound of butter in half a pint of warm milk, and with four pounds of fine flour, a few caraways, and half a pound of sugar, make a stiff, smooth paste; and, to render the biscuits short and light, add half a drachm of powdered carbonate of soda. Roll out very thin, stamp the biscuit, prick each with a fork, and bake in tins in a quick oven.

SALLY LUNN.—Warm a quart of new milk with a quarter of a pound of butter and a tablespoonful of sugar, beat up three eggs and put them in, with a little salt, and flour enough to make the dough a little stiffer than pound cake. Beat all well together, add a teacupful of yeast. Let it rise eight hours, and bake in a quick oven.

SUPERIOR SALLY LUNN.—Three pints of flour, three teaspoonfuls of cream of tartar, three ounces of butter, one cup of sugar, and a saltspoonful of salt. Mix all together dry, add four well beaten eggs and a dessertspoonful of soda, dissolved in a pint and a half of milk. Bake in a quick oven.

LIGHT SALLY LUNN.—One pound of flour, one pint of milk, three well beaten eggs, salt, three ounces of butter, half a cup of baker's yeast. Set in pans to rise the usual time.

JOHNNY CAKES.—Scald a quart of Indian meal with water enough to make a very thick batter, add two or three teaspoonfuls of salt, and mould it into small cakes with the hands. The hands must be well floured, or the batter will stick. Fry them in nearly sufficient fat to cover them. When brown on the under side, turn them; cook them about twenty minutes. When done, split and butter them.

INDIAN CAKES.—Indian meal, two cupfuls; wheat flour, one cupful; cream, half gill; white sugar, half pound; five eggs; new milk, half pint, a little salt, and a little baking soda. Bake in a quick oven.

SHORT CAKE.—One pound of flour, one pound of butter, half a pound of sugar, and a teaspoonful of caraway seeds. Spread on a tin sheet with an edge, and bake slow. Sprinkle a little sugar over the top when it is taken from the oven.

CORN CAKE.—A pint of buttermilk or sour milk, a pint of corn meal, one egg, a teaspoonful of soda, one of salt, two of sugar or molasses. Dissolve the soda in a little warm water and add it the last thing. Bake half an hour in a quick oven.

GREEN CORN CAKES.—Grate the corn; make a rich batter with cream, or according to directions given for batter cakes. Use just enough of the batter to hold the corn together, and lay the cakes on the griddle as you would a common griddle cake. Serve with butter.

SODA CAKE.—One cup of sugar, one teaspoonful of soda, one cup of sweet milk, one egg, one tablespoonful of butter, two teaspoonfuls of cream of tartar.

RICE CAKES.—Take eight yelks and four whites of eggs, and beat to a foam; add six ounces of powdered sugar, and the peel of one lemon grated; then stir in half a pound of ground rice, and beat all together for half an hour. Put it into a buttered tin, and bake twenty minutes. This cake is recommended as very easy of digestion.

MUFFINS.—Strain into a pan a pint of warm milk and a quarter of a pint of thick yeast; add sufficient flour to make the whole into a batter, cover it over, and let it stand in a warm place to rise. Then add a quarter of a pint of warm milk and one ounce of butter rubbed in some flour quite fine. Mix these well together, and add flour enough to make into dough. Cover, and let it stand for half an hour. Next work it up again and break it into small pieces, roll them into a round form, and cover them for a quarter of an hour. Lay them on an iron plate to-bake, watching them carefully. When done on one side, turn to the other.

GERMAN WAFFLES.—Half a pound of butter stirred to a cream; the yelks of five eggs, stirred in a half pound of flour; half a pint of milk gradually stirred in, and lastly the white of the eggs beaten to a stiff froth, and beat into the batter. Very rich and delicious.

WAFFLES.—(Simple receipt.) One pint of sour cream, one pint of flour, three eggs, half a spoonful of soda. Thin with a little sweet milk.

RAISED WAFFLES.—One quart of sweet milk a little warmed, four eggs, a piece of butter the size of an egg, a teaspoonful of salt, a teacupful of yeast, flour enough to make a stiff batter; let it raise three hours; heat the iron hot before baking. Flannel cakes are baked the same way, but made thinner with milk and baked in small cakes on a griddle. Sometimes they are made with sour milk and soda in place of raising, but are neither as good nor healthy.

CRUMPETS.—Set two pounds of flour, with a little salt, before the fire till quite warm. Then mix it with warm milk and water till it is as stiff as it can be stirred; let the milk be as warm as it can be borne with the finger; put a cupful of this with three eggs well beaten and mixed with three spoonfuls of very thick yeast; then put this to the batter and beat them all together in a large pan or bowl; add as much milk and water as will make it into a thick batter; cover it close, and put it before the fire to rise; put a bit of butter in a piece of thin muslin, tie it up, and rub it lightly over the iron hearth or frying-pan; then pour on a sufficient quantity of batter at a time to make one crumpet; let it do slowly, and it will be very light. Bake them all the same way. They should not be brown, but of a fine yellow color.

CORN MEAL MUFFINS.—To one quart of corn meal add half a cup of melted lard, two eggs, a teaspoonful of soda, and salt to taste; beat it to a stiff batter with buttermilk, and bake in muffin rings by a brisk fire.

BUTTERMILK BREAKFAST CAKES.—Two cups of buttermilk, or sour milk, one cup of sugar, one piece of butter the sice of a walnut, a teaspoonful of saleratus, spice to taste, and as much flour as will make a thin batter. Bake on a griddle, or stiffen the batter and bake in a pan in a quick oven.

BREAKFAST SHORT CAKES.—One pound of flour, quarter of a pound of butter, a few caraway seeds, quarter of a pound of sifted sugar, a teaspoonful of carbonate of soda dissolved in a teacup of warm milk. Mix well; stand for fifteen minutes before the fire; roll out; cut into rounds; bake in a quick oven.

HOMINY BREAKFAST CAKES.—A pint of small hominy, a pint of white Indian meal, sifted, a salt-spoonful of salt, three large tablespoonfuls of fresh butter, three eggs, or three tablespoonfuls of strong yeast, one quart of milk. Soak the hominy all night, boil it till soft; drain; mix with the meal, and while hot add the salt and butter. Mix gradually in the milk and stand till cool. Beat the eggs light and stir in gradually. Beat all together to a stiff batter, and bake on a griddle.

BREAKFAST WAFFLES.—One quart of sweet milk, nine well beaten eggs, two tablespoonfuls of butter, a teaspoonful of soda dissolved in the milk and strained, and two of cream of tartar sifted with the flour. Make the batter as thick as pound cake. Serve with maple syrup, or cream and sugar.

BREAKFAST JOHNNY CAKE.—One cup of flour, three cups of meal, one cup of molasses, two cups of sweet milk, one of sour milk, one teaspoonful of soda, and one of salt. Bake one hour in a sponge cake tin.

FRIED BREAKFAST CAKES.—One and a half cup of sour milk, one cup of sugar, four tablespoonfuls of melted butter, three eggs, one tablespoonful of soda, flour enough to roll out. Fry in hot lard.

BREAKFAST PUFFS.—One teacupful of milk, one egg, a little salt, one teacupful of flour; bake in plain tins in a quick oven.

COFFEE CAKE.—Melted butter one pint, white sugar two pounds, mace quarter of an ounce, a teacupful of yeast, one quart of milk. Add flour sufficient to make a stiff batter. Beat a little, then set it in a warm place to rise; that is, make it up at night and let it rise until morning. Then add one pound of raisins, work well through, and half fill your cake moulds. Let them bake half an hour in a hot oven.

VIRGINIA BREAKFAST CAKES.—One pint of sweet milk, two eggs, one tablespoonful of yeast, one teaspoonful of salt, a piece of butter the size of an egg. Take two eggs and beat them well, melt the butter in the milk, then pour the eggs into the milk, add the salt and yeast. Beat enough Indian meal into it to make it the consistency of pound cake. Set them to rise two hours, and bake in bread pans.

BREAKFAST SODA CAKE.—One pound of flour, dried, quarter of a pound of butter, beaten to a cream, six ounces of moist sugar, half a pound of currants, two ounces of mixed peel, a few drops of essence of almonds, half a pint of milk. When these are well mixed, add a teaspoonful of carbonate of soda mixed with a tablespoonful of warm milk.

Give all a good stir. Put in a well-buttered tin; bake an hour and a half.

FRENCH BREAKFAST ROLLS.—Rub an ounce of butter into a pound of flour; mix one egg, beaten, a little yeast that is not bitter, and as much milk as will make a dough of a middling stiffness. Beat it well, but do not knead; let it rise and bake on tins.

BREAKFAST SALLY LUNN.—One quart of flour, four eggs, one gill of yeast, and a little salt; mix with milk to a stiff batter; add a piece of butter melted. Pour it into your baking tins and let it rise over night.

LIGHT BREAKFAST ROLLS.—Two quarts of flour, one pint of milk, one teaspoonful of soda, two teaspoonfuls of cream of tartar. Bake it immediately.

BREAKFAST ROLLS.—Take one pint and a half of flour, one large teaspoonful of soda, a small quantity of lard. Mix with sour buttermilk. Bake immediately.

FRENCH TEA CAKES.—Beat ten eggs to a high froth; dissolve half a teaspoonful of cream of tartar in hot water, and let it stand to cool; then put it with the eggs, and beat them for ten minutes; add four ounces of powdered loaf sugar and the same of fine flour; put the mixture in square tins, and bake in a quick oven.

TEA CAKES.—One pound of butter, one pound of

sugar, (mix butter and sugar together,) two eggs, two and a quarter pounds of flour, but if too thin, add a little more. Season to taste; roll thin, and bake brown.

GERMAN TEA CAKES.—Into eight ounces of flour rub four ounces of butter. Mix eight ounces of currants, six ounces of fine sugar, two yelks of eggs, one white of egg, and a teaspoonful of brandy; make a stiff paste of these ingredients and roll out the thickness of a biscuit. Cut into rounds with a wineglass, that they may round up on the top. Brush with the white of the second egg, well beaten, dust with sugar and bake.

PENNSYLVANIA TEA CAKE.—The yelks of six eggs, and whites of two; three quarters of a pound of loaf sugar, half a pound of butter, one teaspoonful of soda dissolved in a tablespoonful of vinegar. Beat all well together in a deep pan, then add sifted flour gradually till a stiff paste is formed, knead and roll out. Cut into biscuit and bake in a moderate oven.

PLAIN TEA CAKE.—A half cup of butter, two of sugar; work the sugar and butter together, add four beaten eggs; three teacups of sifted flour, an even teaspoonful of soda dissolved and strained, ground coriander seed, and lastly a teacup of sour milk.

SUPERIOR TEA CAKES.—To each pound of flour allow a dessertspoonful of bread-powder, one egg and half a pint of cream or new milk, half a teaspoonful of suet, and two teaspoonfuls of loaf sugar, powdered. Rub the dry things well together, then quickly mix in, first the cream and then the egg. Bake quickly in buttered tins. If yeast be preferred, the milk should be a little warmed, and strained through the yeast, as for bread. Add the egg last. Let the dough stand to rise, then bake half an hour in a quick oven.

SIMPLE TEA CAKES.—Two pounds of flour, two spoonfuls of yeast, made into a dough with warm milk. When ready (as for bread) to make into cakes, mix well two ounces of butter and two ounces of sifted sugar; let the cake stand to rise, brush over with milk, and bake in a quick oven.

LEMON TEA CAKES.—One pint of flour, into which put two teaspoonfuls of cream of tartar; one cup of sweet milk, into which put one teaspoonful of soda. Two tablespoonfuls of butter and one cup of sugar mixed well together; then break into it two eggs; add milk and flour; flavor with grated rind and juice of a lemon.

CAKES.

HINTS FOR MAKING AND BAKING SWEET CAKES.—Eggs should always be broken into a cup, the whites and yelks separated, and they should always be strained. Breaking the eggs thus, the bad ones may be easily rejected without spoiling the others, and so cause no waste. As eggs are used instead of yeast, they should be very thoroughly whisked; they are generally sufficiently beaten when thick enough to carry the drop that falls from the whisk.

Loaf sugar should be well pounded, then sifted through a fine sieve.

Currants should be nicely washed, picked, dried in a cloth, and then carefully examined, that no pieces of grit or stone may be left amongst them. They should then be laid on a dish before the fire, to become thoroughly dry; as, if added to the other damp ingredients, cakes will be liable to be heavy.

Good butter should always be used in the manufacture of cakes; and if beaten to a cream, it saves much time and labor to warm, but not melt, it before beating.

Less butter and eggs are required for cakes when yeast is mixed with the other ingredients.

The heat of the oven is of great importance, especially for large cakes. If the heat be not tolerably fierce, the butter will not rise. If the oven is too quick, and there is any danger of the cake burning or catching, put a sheet of clean paper over the top. Newspaper, or paper that has been printed on, should never be used for this purpose.

To know when a cake is sufficiently baked, plunge a clean knife into the middle of it; draw it quickly out, and if it looks in the least sticky, put the cake back, and close the oven door until the cake is done.

PLUM CAKE, RICH POUND CAKE, TWELFTH, OR BRIDE CAKES.—The following table will give the ingredients necessary for cakes of different sizes:—

Ingredients.	1 lb. oz.	2 lb. oz.	3 lb. oz.	4 lb. oz.	5 lb. oz.	6 lb. oz.
Butter	0 11	0 13	1 1	1 4	1 6	2 1
Sugar	0 7	0 8	0 10	0 12	1 0	1 6
Currants	1 4	1 6	1 10	2 0	2 8	3 12
Orange, lemon, and citron (mixed)	0 6	0 7	0 8	0 10	0 12	1 2
Almonds	0 1½	0 2	0 2	0 3	0 3	0 4
Mixed spices	0 0½		0 0¾		0 1	0 1½
Flour	0 11	0 13	1 1	1 4	1 6	2 1
Eggs (number)	6	7	9	10	12	18
Brandy, or brandy and wine	Wineglassful			¼pt.		

These proportions allow for the cake being iced. If more sugar is preferred, the quantity must be the same as the butter; but less is used in this instance, that the cake may be light, and also to allow for the fruit, which would make it too sweet. Double the quantity of almonds may be used if required, as some persons prefer more. Warm a smooth pan, large enough for the mixture; put in the butter, and reduce it to a fine cream, by working it about the pan with your hand. In summer the pan need not be warmed, as it can be reduced to a cream without; but in winter keep the mixture as warm as possible, without oiling the butter. Add the sugar and mix it well with butter, until it becomes white and feels light in the hand. Break in two or three eggs at a time, and work the mixture well, before any more is added. Continue doing this until they are all used and it becomes light; then add the spirit, currants, peel, spice, and almonds, some or most of these being previously cut in thin slices, the peel having also been cut into small thin strips and bits. When these are incorporated, mix in the flour lightly; put it in a hoop with paper over the bottom and round the sides, and place on a baking-plate. Large cakes require three or four pieces of stiff paper round the sides; and if the cake is very large, a pipe or funnel, made either of stiff paper or tin, and well buttered, should be put in the centre, and the mixture placed round it; this is to allow the middle of the cake to be well baked, otherwise the edge would be burnt two or three inches deep before it could be properly done. Place the tin plate containing the cake on another, the surface of which is covered an inch or two thick with sawdust or fine ashes to protect the bottom. Bake it in an oven at a moderate heat. The time required to bake it will depend on the state of the oven and the size of the cake. A large cake in an oven of a proper heat will take from four to five hours. When the cake is cold, proceed to ice it. Wedding cakes have generally, first, a coating on the top of almond icing; when this is dry, the sides and top are covered with royal or white icing. Fix on any gum paste or other ornaments whilst it is wet; and when dry, ornament it with piping, orange-blossoms, ribbon, etc.; the surface and sides are often covered with small knobs of white sugar candy whilst the icing is wet. Twelfth cakes are iced with white or colored icing, and decorated with gum paste, plaster ornaments, piping-paste, rings, knots, and fancy papers, etc., and piped.

ROCK CAKES.—A pound of currants cleaned and dried, the same quantity of flour well dried, half a pound of powdered sugar, half a pound of butter, the yelks of eight eggs and the whites of six. Mix the whole well together, having first beaten the batter to a cream; drop the paste in small quantities on buttered paper, and bake on tins in a quick oven.

LOVE CAKES.—Three eggs, five ounces of sugar, six ounces of flour, salt, mace, or rose water, to be dropped, and sugar sprinkled on before baking.

In cake making every article employed therein should be ready one hour previous to their being wanted, and should be placed before the fire or upon a stove, that they may become gently heated, without which no good cakes can be produced.

Cakes keep best in tin canisters; wooden boxes, unless well seasoned, are apt to give them a disagreeable taste; brown paper should be avoided for the same reason.

BUNS.—One pound of flour, quarter pound of sugar, quarter pound of butter, quarter pound of currants, a teaspoonful of cream of tartar, six eggs. The salts to be dissolved in a little cold milk, and put in last. Drop on tins and bake.

BATH BUNS.—Half a pound of flour, six ounces of butter, two eggs, and a little white sugar and yeast. Mix and bake in small tins; rub over with white of egg.

RICH BUNS.—Mix one pound and a half of flour with half a pound of sugar, melt a pound and two ounces of butter in a little warm water, add six spoonfuls of rose water, and knead the above into a light dough, with half a pint of yeast. Then mix five ounces of caraway comfits in, and put some on them.

GROUND RICE BUNS.—Beat three eggs well to a froth, quarter of a pound of butter, melted, half a pound of sugar, browned or crushed lump, quarter of a pound of ground rice, and a few drops of either essence of almonds or lemon. To be baked in small paste tins. They are soon baked.

SPANISH BUNS.—Take one pound of fine flour, rub into it half a pound of butter, add half a pound of sugar, the same of currants, a little nutmeg, mace, and cinnamon. Mix it with five eggs, well beaten. Make this up into small buns, and bake them on tins twenty minutes. When half done, brush them over with a little hot milk.

EXCELLENT SPANISH BUN.—Take one pound of fine flour, rub into it half a pound of butter, add half pound of sugar, the same of currants, a little nutmeg, mace, and cinnamon; mix it with five eggs, well beaten. Make this up into small buns, and bake them on tins twenty minutes. When half done, brush them over with a little hot milk.

CHILDREN'S CAKE.—Rub a quarter of a pound of butter, or good, fresh, clean beef dripping, into two pounds of flour; add half a pound of pounded sugar, one pound of currants, well washed and *dried*, half an ounce of caraway seeds, a quarter of an ounce of pudding spice or allspice, and mix all thoroughly. Make warm a pint of new milk, but do not let it get *hot*. Stir into it three tablespoonfuls of good yeast, and with this liquid make up your dough lightly, and knead it well. Line your cake tins with buttered paper, and put in the dough. Let it remain in a warm place to rise for an hour and a quarter, or more, if necessary, and then bake in a well heated oven. This quantity will make *two* moderately-sized cakes; thus divided, they will take from an hour and a half to two hours baking. N. B. Let the paper inside your tins be about six inches higher than the top of the tin itself.

MOLASSES DROP CAKES.—One cup of molasses, one half cup of butter, one half cup of water, three cups of flour, two teaspoonfuls of ginger, one of soda. Beat the ingredients well together, and drop with a spoon in a buttered tin. Bake quick.

MOLASSES CUP CAKE.—Two cups of molasses, **two cups of butter**, three eggs, one-third of a cup of cold water, and one tablespoonful of soda; then bake.

CORNSTARCH CAKE.—Stir to a froth three-quarters of a pound of butter and one pound of powdered sugar; add one half cup of sweet cream and the whites of nine eggs, beaten very light. Take from a pound package of cornstarch two tablespoonfuls, and replace it with the same quantity of wheat flour and add it to the above. Flavor with lemon.

SODA CAKE.—Half a pound of butter, half a pound of flour, three-quarters of a pound of loaf sugar, four eggs, one teaspoonful of soda, and the rind of one lemon, grated. Beat the eggs for twenty minutes, the yelks and whites separately, melt the butter, and add the ingredients to it separately, heating them all the time. Bake for two and a half hours in a moderate oven.

RYE DROP CAKES.—One pint of milk, three eggs, one tablespoonful of sugar, and a little salt. Stir in rye flour till about the consistency of pancakes. Bake in buttered cups or saucers half an hour.

GOOD PLAIN CAKE.—Two pounds of flour, three dessertspoonfuls of baking powder, one pound of loaf sugar, powdered, one pound of currants, quarter of a pound of raisins, cut small, twelve ounces of butter, four eggs, and a pint of milk; candied orange and lemon-peel to taste. Bake two hours and a half in rather a slow oven.

CHILDREN'S LOAF CAKE.—Five cups of dough, two of sugar, one of butter, caraway seed, ground, and two eggs. Line pans with buttered paper, and bake as soon as light. Use homemade yeast.

CHEAP CAKE.—One pint of flour, one egg, one cup of sugar, butter as large as the bowl of a spoon, milk to make stiff as pound cake, one teaspoonful of cream of tartar, half teaspoonful of soda.

FRENCH CAKE.—Five eggs, weight of five eggs in flour, weight of five eggs in sugar, weight of three eggs in butter. Beat until light, then add one teacupful of raisins. Bake in a quick oven.

THICK GINGERBREAD.—One quart of molasses, quarter of a pound of butter, quarter of a pound of coarse brown sugar, a pound and a half of flour, one ounce of ginger, half an ounce of ground allspice, a teaspoonful of carbonate of soda, quarter of a pint of warm milk, and three eggs. Put the flour into a bread-pan with the sugar, ginger and allspice; mix these together; warm the butter, and add it with the molasses, to the other ingredients. Stir well; warm the milk and dissolve the carbonate of soda in it; beat the eggs light, and mix the whole into a smooth dough. Pour the mixture into a buttered tin and bake about one hour in a moderate oven. Just before it is done, brush the top with the yelk of an egg beaten in a little milk, and replace it in the oven to glaze.

SOFT GINGERBREAD.—Two cups of butter, two

cups of sugar, two cups of molasses, one cup of milk, four eggs, a teaspoonful of pearlash, five cups of flour, two tablespoonfuls of ginger, two teaspoonfuls of allspice, one teaspoonful of cinnamon.

GINGER BISCUITS.—Rub half a pound of fresh butter into two pounds of fine flour, add half a pound of sifted sugar, and three ounces of pounded ginger. Beat up the yelks of three eggs, and take a little milk, with which make the above ingredients into a paste. Knead it all well together, and roll it out extremely thin, and cut it into the form of round biscuits with a paste-cutter. Bake them in a slow oven until crisp, taking care that they are a pale brown color.

GINGERSNAPS.—One quarter of a pound of butter, and the same of lard, mixed in a quarter of a pound of brown sugar, a pint of West India molasses, ginger according to its strength, and cinnamon according to taste; add one quart of flour, two teaspoonfuls of soda, dissolved in a wineglass of milk and flour, to enable you to roll it thin. Bake in a moderate oven.

GINGERBREAD.—One cup of molasses, one of sugar, one of milk, three eggs, four cups of flour, one small cup of butter, two teaspoonfuls of cream of tartar, one of soda, ginger, and cloves.

ALMOND PEPPERNUTS.—Half a pound of loaf sugar, and three eggs; beat together half an hour.

Pound two ounces of blanched almonds very fine, chop an ounce of citron as fine as possible, grate in the yellow rind of a lemon, add cinnamon, nutmeg, and a quarter of a teaspoonful of black pepper, half a teaspoonful of cloves, and seven and a half ounces of flour. Measure and shape the dough in a teaspoon, and bake in a moderate oven.

Peppernuts.—Take four eggs, beat them light, with one pound of sugar; then take half a pound of butter, beat it up with the eggs and sugar; one gill of milk, one nutmeg, half an ounce of saleratus, and flour enough to make a dough stiff to roll out.

Lemon Drop Cakes.—One pound and a quarter of flour, three-quarters of a pound of loaf sugar, six ounces of fresh butter, four eggs, one ounce of lemon-peel, two dessertspoonfuls of lemon-juice. Rub the flour and butter well together; powder the sugar and stir it in with the lemon-peel grated; when these ingredients are thoroughly mixed, add the eggs, beaten light, and lastly the lemon-juice. Beat the mixture well together; drop it from a spoon on a buttered sheet of tin, leaving two inches space for each cake to spread; when warm place the tin in the oven, and bake twenty minutes. The cakes should be a pale brown.

Superior Lemon Cake.—One cup of butter, three cups of sugar, the yelks of three eggs; dissolve a teaspoonful of saleratus in a teacup of milk; add the grated peel of one lemon, and the whites of three eggs, and sift in, as light as possible, four teacups of flour.

LEMON CAKE.—Beat six eggs, the yelks and whites separately, till in a solid froth; add to the yelks the grated rind of a fine lemon and six ounces of sugar dried and sifted; beat this a quarter of an hour; shake in with the left hand six ounces of dried flour; then add the whites of the eggs and the juice of the lemon; when these are well beaten in, put it immediately into tins, and bake it about an hour in a moderately hot oven.

LEMON CHEESECAKES.—Rasp the rind of a large lemon with four ounces of fine sugar, then crush and mix it with the yelks of three eggs, and half the quantity of whites, well whisked; beat these together thoroughly; add to them four tablespoonfuls of cream, a quarter of a pound of oiled butter, the strained juice of the lemon, which must be stirred quickly in by degrees, and a little orange flower brandy. Line some patty-pans with the puff-paste, half fill them with the mixture, and bake them thirty minutes in a moderate oven.

ORANGE CHEESECAKES are made as in the last receipt, except that oranges are substituted for the lemons. A few thin slices of candied lemon or orange-peel may be laid on the cheesecakes before baking.

SWEET MACAROON.—One pound and a half of

crushed sugar, one pound and a half of grated almonds, the whites of four eggs, and the skin of a lemon. The almonds, sugar, and peel are beaten for some time with the thick froth of the eggs; in the meantime have ready a hot tin plate greased, and put on the tin a quantity as large as a walnut. Bake them in a slow oven to a light-straw color; they can be baked on wafer-paper.

ANOTHER WAY.—Seven ounces of sweet almonds, seven ounces of crushed sugar, two whites of eggs, and a little lemon-juice. Half the quantity of almonds are grated, and the other half cut into long pieces. The sugar, lemon-juice, and eggs are whisked till in bubbles; then mix the almonds in, and bake as above. This quantity makes forty cakes.

BITTER MACAROON.—These are made in the same way, but two-thirds are sweet and one-third are bitter almonds, and to one pound of these, one pound and three-quarters of sugar.

POP OVERS.—One cup of milk, one of flour, one egg, a little salt. Bake in cups or pop-over irons.

GINGER SPONGE CAKE.—One cup of molasses, one cup of butter, two cups of sugar, four eggs, three cups of flour, one cup of milk, soda, and ginger.

GINGER LOAF CAKE.—Flour, one pound four ounces; butter, four ounces; pulverized ginger, one and a half tablespoonful; pulverized cloves, one and a half tablespoonful; dissolve one teaspoonful of soda in a little warm milk; then add it, and also molasses sufficient to wet up the dough. Bake in a quick oven.

GINGER JUMBLES.—Two pounds of flour, one pound of moist sugar, one and a half pound of treacle, ten ounces of ginger, half a pound of butter, a little lemon-peel, and a little brandy; make it over night. Drop it on tins.

CONNECTICUT LOAF CAKE.—Six pounds of flour, four and a half of butter, four and a half of sugar, four and a half of raisins and currants, one and a half of citron, one pint of brandy, one pint of wine, half a pint of homemade yeast, one ounce of mace, six nutmegs, twenty eggs. Beat all together and put into pans over night.

NEW ENGLAND LOAF CAKE.—Four pounds of flour, two of butter; put in more yeast than for bread; make soft with milk, and let it stand over night. When light, add twelve eggs well beaten, two and a quarter pounds of sugar, two pounds of raisins, quarter pound of citron, mixed spice. Beat well and put into pans; let it rise, then bake one hour and a quarter.

CLAY CAKE.—One pound of flour, one pound of sugar, half a pound of butter, six eggs, half a pint of milk, one teaspoonful of soda, two of cream tartar; flavor with bitter almonds or lemon.

OLD-FASHIONED DOUGHNUTS.—Take one pound of butter, (half lard is better,) a pound and a quarter of sugar, one quart of warm milk, four eggs, one nutmeg. Take the milk, half the sugar, the lard, and a teacupful of good baker's yeast, with flour enough to make a nice sponge. When light, warm the butter; take the rest of the sugar and eggs, and beat well together nutmeg and flour enough to knead very soft dough. Keep it pretty warm, as the quicker you can get them light the better. This receipt is an excellent one.

DOUGHNUTS.—Half a cup of butter, two and a half cups of sugar well rolled and sifted, four eggs, one teaspoonful of saleratus, one cup of sour milk, one nutmeg, flour enough to roll; cut in any shape desired, either in strips or twisted; have the lard hot enough for the cakes to rise to the surface as soon as put in. This is an excellent fried cake.

CRULLERS.—Half a pound of butter, three-quarters of a pound of sugar, two pounds of flour, one nutmeg, half a teaspoonful of soda dissolved in half a teacup of water or milk, six eggs.

BORDEAUX CAKES.—Make a mixture as for pound cakes, leaving out the fruit, peel, spices, etc.; bake it in a round or oval hoop. When baked and cold, cut it into slices half an inch thick; spread each slice over with jam or marmalade. The outside of the cake may be cut round, or fluted to form a star, and the centre of the cake is occasionally cut out to about an inch and a half from the edge, leaving the bottom slice whole; this may be filled with preserved wet or dry fruits, creams, or a trifle. The top is ornamented with piping, wet or dry fruits, and peels, or piped with jam and icing.

CHRISTMAS CAKE.—Wash one pound and a quarter of butter in water, beat it to a cream; beat ten eggs, yelks and whites separately, half an hour each; have ready a pound and a quarter of flour well dried and kept hot, also three-quarters of a pound of sugar, half an ounce of pounded mixed spice, a pound and a half of currants washed, picked, and dried, a quarter of a pound of almonds, blanched and sliced, and four ounces of candied peel, also sliced. Mix all these, and keep them by the fire. Strain the eggs, and mix them with the butter; add to them a teacupful of sweet wine, and a wineglassful of brandy. Then add the dry ingredients by degrees, and a quarter of a pound of chopped raisins. Beat all together for a full hour. Butter a piece of white paper, and line the moulds with it, and fill them about three parts full. Bake in a quick oven two hours.

YULE-TIDE CAKE.—Place a pound of fresh butter in a pan; keep it near the fire till melted; stir into it a pound of powdered loaf sugar, a good tablespoonful each of beaten allspice and cinnamon; by degrees put in the yelks of ten eggs and their whites separately whisked to a froth; add one pound of candied citron-peel sliced thin, two pounds of currants cleaned and dried, two ounces of blanched sweet almonds, a pound and a half of flour, and four ounces of brandy; mix all well together and bake it for three hours.

Jelly Cake.—To three well beaten eggs add one cup of powdered sugar, one of flour; stir well, and add one teaspoonful of cream of tartar, half a teaspoonful of saleratus, dissolved in three teaspoonfuls of water. Bake in two pie-pans; spread as even as possible. Have ready a towel, and as soon as done, turn the cake on it, bottom side up; then spread evenly with jelly, roll up quickly, and wrap in a towel.

Rose Water Cake.—One coffeecupful and a quarter of sugar, one of butter, four eggs, one teaspoonful of brandy, two of rose water, one-third of a cup of sweet milk, and flour to suit.

Almond Jelly Cake.—One cup of sugar, one egg, a little salt, one pound of flour, one grated nutmeg, one teaspoonful of soda. Add warm milk sufficient to make a stiff dough, roll out like thick pie-crust. Bake in a quick oven. When done, spread it thick with some good fruit jelly, and strew some powdered sweet almonds over it.

Army Cake.—Half a cup of butter, two cups of sugar, three of flour, three eggs, one cup of milk or cream, one teaspoonful of cream of tartar, half a teaspoonful of soda.

Navy Cake.—Three and a half cups of flour, two of sugar, one of milk, three eggs, half a cup of butter, one teaspoonful of cream of tartar, and one of soda.

FRUIT CAKE.—Two and a half cups dried apples, stewed until soft; add one cup of sugar, stew a while longer, and chop the mixture, to which add one half cup of cold coffee, one of sugar, two eggs, a half cup of butter, one nutmeg, one teaspoonful of soda, and cinnamon and spices to taste.

FRUIT CAKE WITHOUT EGGS.—Two-thirds of a cup of butter, two cups of sugar, two of raisins, two of currants, two of sweet milk, two teaspoonfuls of cream of tartar, one of soda in the milk, six cups of flour, one nutmeg, one tablespoonful of cinnamon, one of allspice, one of cloves. Half a pound of citron improves it. Bake slowly.

GOOD FRUIT CAKE.—One quart of flour, one of sugar, ten eggs, beat separately, two pounds of raisins, two of currants, three-quarters of a pound of citron, the same of butter, half a pint of brandy, one tablespoonful of cinnamon, one teaspoonful of cloves, one of soda, one nutmeg. Bake three hours.

SODA FRUIT CAKE.—Five cups of flour, five eggs, three cups of sugar, nearly two of butter, one of milk, two teaspoonfuls of soda, one pound of currants, one pound of raisins; flour the raisins; put the fruit in last. Bake three-quarters of an hour.

MOLASSES FRUIT CAKE.—Two cups of butter, three of sugar, one of molasses, two pounds of raisins, two pounds of currants, one pound of citron, ten eggs, one tumbler of cream, one half tumbler of brandy, one teaspoonful of saleratus, spice of all kinds.

Pound Cake.—Beat one pound of butter to a cream, and mix with it the whites and yelks of eight eggs, beaten apart. Have ready warm by the fire one pound of flour, and the same of sifted sugar. Mix them and a few cloves, a little nutmeg and cinnamon, in fine powder together; then by degrees work the dry ingredients into the butter and eggs. When well beaten, add a glass of wine and some caraways. It must be beaten a full hour. Butter a pan and bake it an hour in a quick oven.

The above proportions, leaving out four ounces of the butter, and the same of sugar, make a less luscious cake, and to most tastes a more pleasant one.

Rice Pound Cake.—One pound of butter, one pound of powdered loaf sugar, twelve ounces of flour, half a pound of ground rice, and twelve eggs. Mix as Italian bread, and bake it in a papered hoop. If it is required with fruit, put two pounds of currants, three-quarters of a pound of peel, one nutmeg, grated, and a little pounded mace.

Almond Cake.—Blanch, dry, and pound to the finest possible paste half a pound of fresh almonds, moisten with a few drops of water to prevent their oiling, then mix with them gradually twelve fresh eggs, which have been whisked until they are exceedingly light. Strew in by degrees one pound of dry and sifted sugar, keeping the mixture light by constant beating with a large wooden spoon as the separate ingredients are added. Mix in by degrees three-quarters of a pound of sifted flour, then pour gently from the sediment one pound of butter, melted, but not allowed to become hot; beat it very gradually, but very thoroughly into the cake, letting one portion disappear before another is thrown in. Add the rasped or finely grated rinds of two lemons, fill a well buttered mould rather more than half full. Bake from an hour till an hour and a half. Lay paper over when browned.

ALMOND CUP CAKE.—One cup of sugar, one of flour, three eggs, beaten light, one teaspoonful of cream of tartar, half a teaspoonful of soda, one pound of almonds. Mix the sugar, flour, and cream of tartar together, then add the eggs. Blanch and chop the almonds and mix them in, and lastly stir in the soda, dissolved in as little hot water as possible. Bake immediately.

SWEET ALMOND CAKE.—Work two cups of sugar into one cup of butter; one cup of sweet milk, into which dissolve one teaspoonful of soda; four cups of flour, into which put two teaspoonfuls of cream of tartar. Put in the milk and flour alternately. Flavor with essence of almond.

SEED CAKE.—Beat one pound of fresh butter to cream add one pound of loaf sugar, and beat both together until they become white, then add two eggs, beat for some time, add two more, and so on until you have added twelve. Have one and three-quarters of a pound of flour sifted, mix among it half a pound of orange-peel and one pound of citron-peel, cut small, half a pound of almonds, blanched and cut small, then mix all together, but stir as little as possible. Have a mould prepared, put the cake in, smooth with a knife, and scatter a few caraways at the top. Bake two hours and a half in a moderate oven.

CARAWAY CAKE.—Two cups of sugar, one cup of butter, one cup of sour milk, two eggs, one grated nutmeg, a teaspoonful of soda, and two of cream of tartar. Flour enough to roll out. Caraway seed to taste.

FROSTED LOAF CAKE.—Nearly three cups of flour, two of sugar, three-fourths of sweet milk, whites of six eggs, half a cup of butter, half a teaspoonful of soda, and one of cream of tartar; flavoring. Be careful not to get in too full measures of butter and soda; be sure to beat the eggs well, and your cake will be delicious.

MAXIMILLIAN CAKE.—One pound of pulverized loaf sugar, and one pound of sweet butter, free from salt and water, worked with the sugar to a light cream; one teaspoonful extract of lemon, and the same of vanilla, the whites of twenty eggs, beat stiff, and lastly one pound of flour, stirred in lightly.

Bake immediately in round pans, and frost it before cold. The frosting, if flavored, should have the same extracts as the cake. It should not be cut fresh.

BITTER ALMOND CAKE.—Three cups of sugar, one cup of butter, one of sweet milk, five of flour, the whites of twelve eggs, one teaspoonful of cream of tartar, half a teaspoonful of soda; flavor with bitter almonds; to be frosted or not.

STEVENS CAKE.—Six cups flour, four of molasses, one and a half cup butter, two and one-third cups milk, two cups currants, four eggs, two nutmegs, one large spoonful saleratus, and a little cinnamon.

GOOD BOY'S CAKE.—One cup of butter beaten to a cream, two cups of light sugar, four eggs beaten separate, three cups of flour, one cup of sweet milk, one teaspoonful of soda dissolved in the milk, add a little extract of lemon; bake one hour.

CUP CAKE.—One cup of butter, two cups of white sugar, four of flour, one cup of sweet milk, five eggs, one teaspoonful of soda, two of cream of tartar.

TRAVELLER'S CAKE.—One coffeecup of sugar, two tablespoonfuls of butter (not melted), one teacup of sweet milk, the whites of two eggs (or one whole egg, if you do not want it very delicate), two coffeecups of flour, one teaspoonful of cream of tartar, half teaspoonful of soda.

23

APPLE CAKE.—Take two cups of dried apples, stew just enough to cut easily, chop about as fine as raisins, and simmer in two cups of molasses three hours, one cup of sugar, one cup of sour milk, one of butter, two eggs, five cups of flour, two teaspoonfuls of soda, some salt, cloves, and cinnamon. Mix with molasses warm. Put apples and molasses in before the flour. Bake in large cake dishes; it makes one large one, or two small ones.

PIPPIN CAKE.—Flour one pound, sugar half a pound, two eggs, a little salt, and one yeast powder. Grate six large apples, and rub them well into the other ingredients; add milk sufficient to make a dough, cut into thin cakes, and bake quickly.

GATEAU DE POMMES.—Take a few apples, boil them with as little water as possible, and make them into apple-sauce, then add one and a half pound of sugar and the juice of a lemon; boil all together till quite firm, and put it into a mould. Garnish it with almonds stuck over it. It will keep for many months if allowed to remain in the mould.

SCHOOL CAKE.—Half pound dried flour, one-fourth pound fresh butter, one-fourth pound sifted loaf sugar; mix the flour and sugar together, then rub in the butter and yelk of an egg beaten with a tablespoon to a cream; make into a paste, roll and cut into small round cake; bake upon floured tin.

SUGAR CAKE.—Three pounds of flour, one pound of butter, one teaspoonful of pearlash dissolved in half a pint of water. Put in the water a pound and a half of sugar, rub the flour and butter together, roll thin, and bake in a quick oven.

BLACK CAKE.—One pound of sugar, one of browned flour, three-quarters of a pound of butter, twelve eggs, one pint of molasses, one glass of wine, one of brandy, one tablespoonful of cinnamon, one teaspoonful of cloves, one of mace, two nutmegs, two pounds of raisins, two of currants, one of citron, one tablespoonful of soda, two tablespoonfuls of cream of tartar, one pinch of black pepper. Dredge the fruit in flour and put in last.

ARROWROOT BISCUITS.—Rub together three-quarters of a pound of sugar, the same weight of butter. Beat three eggs well and mix with this; stir in two cups of sifted arrowroot, and two cups of sifted flour. When well kneaded, roll out thin, cut round, and bake on buttered tins in a slow oven.

MARBLE CAKE—*The White Cake.*—Whites of seven eggs, one cup of butter, two cups of sugar, half a cup of sweet milk, half a teaspoonful of soda, one of cream of tartar, three cups of flour. Bake two hours in a slow oven.

The Dark Cake.—The yelks of seven eggs, one cup of molasses, two cups of brown sugar, half a cup of butter, spice to taste, one cup of sweet milk, one teaspoonful of soda, two of cream of tartar, five cups of flour.

This makes two good-sized cakes by putting in

first a spoonful of white and then a spoonful of black, and the next layer alternate.

RAILROAD CAKE.—One cup of white sugar, one cup of flour, two tablespoonfuls of melted butter, three eggs, one teaspoonful of essence of lemon. All ingredients stirred in together, and baked in a long narrow tin.

JOSEPHINE CAKE.—Two tablespoonfuls of sugar, one nutmeg grated, a little lemon-peel, three tablespoonfuls of butter, two tablespoonfuls of cream, two cups of milk, four cupfuls of flour, four eggs, one teaspoonful of soda, two teaspoonfuls of cream of tartar. Bake half an hour. Eat hot, with fresh butter.

JENNY LIND CAKE.—Half cup of sugar, three cups of flour, two of milk, one teaspoonful of cream of tartar, one of soda, a little salt. Bake twenty minutes.

JEFFERSON CAKE.—Butter, one pound; sugar, one pound; flour, two pounds; a little salt; soda, quarter of an ounce; one grated nutmeg, a little cinnamon, and milk sufficient to form a dough. Cut into cakes, and bake.

APPLE CHEESECAKE.—Peel, core, and boil some apples till they are quite soft, with a few cloves and some lemon-peel. The saucepan in which they are boiled will only require about a tablespoonful of water at the bottom to keep the apples from burning. When they are soft, remove the lemon-peel and cloves, and beat them up in the saucepan with moist sugar and a little piece of butter. Cut up some candied peel, and add to the apples with currants in the proportion of a quarter of a pound to one pound of apples. Mix well together, and let the mixture stand till quite cold. Line a dish or patty-pan with light paste, fill with the apple, and bake.

COCOANUT CHEESECAKES.—Grate the cocoanut according to the quantity you wish to make (on a fine grater,) weigh it, and add the same quantity of butter, with two ounces of loaf sugar, and the yelk of an egg to every ounce of the cocoanut, a large wineglassful of brandy, the same quantity of rose water, and half a nutmeg. Line your pans with a rich puff-paste, fill them, grate a little sugar on the top of them, and bake in a quick oven.

CITRON CHEESECAKES.—Beat up the yelks of four eggs; mix them with a quart of boiling cream; when cold put it on the fire, and let it boil till it curdles. Blanch some almonds, beat them with orange flower water, and put them into cream, with a few Naples biscuits, and green citron shred fine. Sweeten to taste and bake them.

BLACKBERRY CAKE.—One cup of sugar, three-quarters of a cup of butter, one and a half cup of flour, one cup of blackberry jam, three eggs, three tablespoonfuls of milk, one teaspoonful of soda;

nutmeg, cinnamon, and allspice to taste. Bake in two sheets.

PRUNE CAKE.—Flour, three pounds; butter, one pound; sugar, half pound; raisins, two pounds; dried prunes, chopped fine, one pound; eight eggs; best brandy, one gill; one teacupful of yeast, one teacupful of cinnamon water, half ounce of pulverized cinnamon; form into loaves, and let it rise. Bake in a moderate oven one hour.

FRENCH JUMBLES.—One pound and a half of flour, one pound of sugar, three-quarters of a pound of butter, three eggs; dissolve one teaspoonful of soda in one-half cup of milk; add this, also one nutmeg, and roll out the dough, and cut into small cakes of any shape, and bake them in a quick oven.

SOFT JUMBLES.—One pound and a quarter of flour, one pound of butter, one pound of pulverized loaf sugar, six eggs, and nutmegs.

JUMBLES.—Take a pound and a half of flour, one pound of sugar, three-quarters of a pound of butter, four yelks and two whites of eggs, with a wineglass of rose water; roll them thick with fine powdered sugar, and bake on tins.

COCOANUT JUMBLES.—Cut the meat of a large cocoanut in slices and grate them. Beat up the white of five eggs, and the yelks of three, and mix with them a few drops of the essence of lemon.

Mix the grated cocoanut with a small portion of flour, roll it lightly on a floured paste-board, cut it into rings with a tumbler, the edge of which is floured. Butter the pans into which the cakes are to be laid, and after sifting a little loaf sugar over the cakes, bake them in a quick oven. When they begin to brown they are done.

COOKIES (FINE).—One bowl of sugar, one-half pound of butter, four eggs, one teaspoonful of soda, half a nutmeg. Roll thin, and bake in a quick oven.

BUTTER COOKIES.—Half cup of sugar, one cup of butter, and three eggs; roll thin and bake in a moderate oven. These cookies improve with age.

GOOD COOKIES.—Five cups of flour, two of sugar, one of butter, one egg, one teaspoonful of saleratus; cut it into small cakes.

GROUND RICE CAKE.—Four eggs, eight ounces of ground rice, eight of sugar, eight of butter, four of flour, the juice of half a lemon, the rind of a lemon, grated, and half a teaspoonful of carbonate of soda. Pound the sugar, mix it with the ground rice, flour, and lemon-peel. Beat the butter to a cream, add it and the eggs, well beaten. Next put the lemon-juice, and last the soda, mixed with a tablespoonful of milk; beat all together for a quarter of an hour, and bake in a tin or mould lined with buttered paper. It will take about an hour to bake. The oven must be very hot.

BRIDE CAKE.—One pound of flour, eight ounces of butter, one and a quarter pound of sugar, six ounces of candied peel, eight ounces of almonds, nine eggs, two pounds and a quarter of currants. Flour, currants, almonds, and candied peel, mix together on a dish, and let them be thoroughly dried. Beat the butter to a cream, add the sugar, then the eggs, having previously beaten them in a pitcher. After beating the butter, etc., well, add the flour and fruit, and bake four or five hours. The almonds for the top must be prepared as follows: Blanch half a pound of sweet almonds, and beat them in a mortar until very fine, with half a pound of grated loaf sugar, the white of one egg, and a little rose water. Lay it on the top of the cake when it is warm, and let it set in a very slow oven previous to putting on the icing.

WINE BISCUITS.—Take two pounds of flour, two pounds of butter, and four ounces of sifted loaf sugar. Rub the sugar and the butter into the flour, and make it into a stiff paste with milk, pound it in a mortar, roll it out thin, and cut into sizes or shapes to fancy. Lay them on buttered paper in a warm oven, on iron plates, having first brushed them over with a little milk. When done, you can give them a gloss by brushing them over with a brush dipped in egg. A few caraway seeds may be added, if thought proper.

ROCK BISCUITS.—Six eggs, one pound of sifted

sugar, half a pound of flour, a few currants. Break the eggs into a basin, beat them well until very light, add the pounded sugar, and when this is well mixed with the eggs, dredge in the flour gradually and add the currants. Mix all well together, and put the dough with a fork on the tins, making it look as rough as possible. Bake the cakes in a moderate oven from twenty minutes to a half an hour. When they are done, allow them to get cool, and store them away in a tin canister in a dry place.

ROUGH BISCUITS.—One pound of flour, five eggs, leaving out two of the whites, one pound of sugar. Beat the eggs and sugar together half an hour, mix with the flour one ounce of ground ginger, and one ounce of caraway seeds, then mix all together, drop upon tins, so as to look rough when baked.

ALMOND BISCUITS.—To one pound of loaf sugar, *roughly* crushed, add two ounces of sweet almonds, chopped (not too fine), two eggs, well beaten, and a little essence of almonds. Mix with as much flour, added gradually, as will make it into a stiff paste, that can be stirred with a spoon. Drop on tins, floured, but not buttered, and bake in a *very* slow oven. These biscuits are an excellent substitute for macaroons.

BISCUITS.—One pound of flour, half a pound of sugar, two eggs, beaten, a teaspoonful of caraway seeds, and a quarter of a pound of butter. Mix all well together, roll the paste thin, and cut it into round biscuits. Prick them, and bake them upon tins.

SWEET BISCUITS.—Rub four ounces of butter well into eight ounces of flour, add six ounces of loaf sugar, the yelks of two eggs, the white of one, and a tablespoonful of brandy. Roll the paste thin, and cut it with a wineglass or cutter. Egg over the tops of each with the remaining white, and sift on white sugar. Bake in a warm oven.

LADY FINGERS.—Four eggs, four ounces of sugar, two ounces of flour. Beat the yelks and sugar together, and then add the whites and the flour. Flavor with orange flower, rose water, or lemon. Drop on paper with a paper or tin funnel, then lay the paper on pans and bake. Sprinkle the cakes with sugar before baking.

GERMAN LADIES' FINGERS.—Beat one hour the yelks of five eggs with half a pound of sugar, add half a pound of blanched almonds, pounded fine, the yellow part of one lemon, grated. Mix well, add half a pound of flour very gradually. Roll out the paste, and cut it in strips the length and size of the forefinger. Beat lightly the whites of two eggs, and wet the fingers.

LADIES' FINGERS.—Beat the whites of six eggs lightly as possible, beat the yelks the same, add to the whites, little by little, half a pound of best pulverized sugar; have the yelks beating all the time. When the eggs have been beaten one hour, mix them very gradually by using the top of the yelks until the whole is added. Squeeze in half the juice of a lemon, and add gradually, beating lightly, one-fourth of a pound of arrowroot or flour. Have ready buttered paper, spread the batter in small oval cakes, joining in the middle to represent the joint of a finger. Bake quickly, and leave the cakes on the paper until wanted. For parties frost them.

CAKE SANDWICHES.—Four eggs, half a pound of pounded lump sugar, half a pound of fresh butter, half a pound of flour. Beat the butter to cream, dust in the flour, and add the eggs, well whisked; beat with a fork for a quarter of an hour, butter a tin, and pour in half of the mixture. Bake from a quarter of an hour to twenty minutes. Remove from the tin, butter again, and add the other half of the mixture. Bake as before. When cool, spread jam thickly over one portion of the cake, place the other part over it, and cut into whatever shape you please.

COCOANUT CAKE.—Two-thirds of a cup of butter, two cups of sugar, five eggs, half a cup of milk, half a teaspoonful of soda, one teaspoonful of cream of tartar, three and a half cups of flour, and two cups of grated cocoanut.

GRATED COCOANUT CAKE.—One cup of butter, three cups of sugar, one of sweet milk, four of flour, and teaspoonful of soda, two of cream of tartar, five eggs, one cocoanut grated. Put half the cocoanut in cake and half in icing. *Icing for cake,* half a pound of white pulverized sugar to the whites of two eggs; ice the cake and sprinkle grated cocoanut on the top of the cake.

WHITE COCOANUT CAKE.—The whites of eight eggs, one cup of butter, two cups of sugar, three cups of flour, one teaspoonful of cream of tartar, half a teaspoonful of soda dissolved in milk. This makes a delicious *White Cake,* and if you want *Cocoanut Cake,* just add to the above one and a half cup more sugar, one cup of flour, and a little more butter, with a small cocoanut grated.

COCOANUT LOAF CAKE.—Four cups of flour, three cups of sugar, one cup of milk, five eggs, beaten separately, one cup of butter, two teaspoonfuls of cream of tartar, one teaspoonful of soda, the half of a cocoanut grated and put into the cake. The other half put with the whites of three eggs and half a cup of sugar, and put on the top to form an icing. Bake in two pans two inches thick.

CHOCOLATE CAKE.—One cup of sugar, half a cup of butter, two eggs, half a cup of milk, one teaspoonful of cream of tartar, half a teaspoonful of soda, two cups of flour. Bake in very thin layers. For the *Chocolate:* Grate a half cake of sweet chocolate, half a cup of milk, yelk of one egg, one teaspoonful of vanilla, sweeten to taste. Boil until stiff like a jelly, and when cool spread it between the layers of cake.

CHOCOLATE DROP CAKE.—Beat the whites of two eggs with a quarter of a pound of pounded sugar into a frothy cream, add the juice of half a lemon and six ounces of finely-grated chocolate. Drop this mixture in spoonfuls on a flat tin, and bake them slowly.

CHOCOLATE PASTE CAKE.—Two cups of sugar, one cup of butter, three eggs, three cups of flour, three-quarters of a cup of milk, half a teaspoonful of soda, one teaspoonful of cream of tartar. *Paste:* Chocolate two ounces, one cup of sugar, three-quarters of a cup of sweet milk; boil half down. This makes one cake of four layers with paste between.

CURRANT LOAF CAKE.—One cup of butter, four of flour, four eggs, three cups of sugar, one of sweet milk, one of currants, one teaspoonful of cream of tartar, half teaspoonful of soda, nutmeg, lemon, or vanilla. This makes two loaves; two cups of sugar will do.

BACHELOR BUTTONS.—These delicious little cakes are prepared by rubbing two ounces of butter into five ounces of flour; add five ounces of white sugar; beat an egg with half the sugar, then put it to the other ingredients; add almond, flavoring according to taste; roll them in the hand about the size of a large nut, sprinkle them with white sugar, and place them on tins with buttered paper. They should be slightly baked.

PRINCESS CAKES.—Butter, half a pound; sugar,

half a pound; rice flour, one pound; six eggs, one gill of sweet wine, one teaspoonful of caraway seeds, one teaspoonful of soda, quarter of a pound of raisins; add water sufficient to form a batter, drop into buttered pans and bake until done.

QUEEN'S BISCUIT.—Make a soft paste by mixing together thoroughly one and a half pound of flour, the same quantity of fine loaf sugar, the whites of twenty-four eggs, and the yelks of eighteen, and a small quantity of coriander seed beaten small. Place this paste on paper, cut it into pieces about two inches broad and four inches long, put them in a moderate oven, and when they begin to turn brown take them out, and put them on paper in a dry place.

LINCOLN CAKE.—Two eggs, two cups of sugar, a half cup of butter, one of sweet milk, three of flour, one teaspoonful of cream of tartar, half a teaspoonful of soda, and one of lemon essence.

BOSTON CAKE.—One pound of sugar and half a pound of butter stirred together, three eggs beaten lightly, one glass of wine, half a pint of milk mixed with the wine, and an even teaspoonful of soda sifted with one pound of flour. Bake in a rather quick oven.

GOLD CAKE.—Yelks of eight eggs beaten to a froth; mix with them one cup of sugar, three-fourths of a cup of butter previously stirred to a cream, add two cups of flour, a half teaspoonful of soda dissolved in half a cup of milk. When well mixed, stir in a teaspoonful of cream of tartar.

SILVER CAKE.—Two teacupfuls of white sugar, three-fourths of a cup of butter, one cup of sweet milk, four cups of flour, whites of four eggs beaten to a stiff froth, one teaspoonful of soda, two of cream of tartar; flavor with vanilla, nutmeg, or lemon. First rub the butter and sugar to a cream, and then add the other ingredients; bake in a quick oven.

WHITE CAKE.—Three-quarters of a pound of best white flour, well dried, one pound of white sugar, six ounces of butter, whites of fourteen eggs, one teaspoonful of cream of tartar, sprinkled into the flour; rub the butter and sugar well, then add the eggs alternately with the flour into the butter. Bake in a quick oven.

MRS. W.'s SNOW CAKE.—The whites of ten eggs, one cup and a half of fine white sugar, one cup of flour, a small teaspoonful of cream of tartar. Beat the whites to a stiff froth, sift on them the sugar; put the cream tartar in the flour, and sift it in; beat well; bake half an hour, this makes one cake.

SNOW CAKE.—One pound of arrowroot, half a pound of pounded white sugar, half a pound of butter, the whites of six eggs; flavoring to taste of essence of almonds, or vanilla, or lemon. Beat the butter to a cream; stir in the sugar and arrowroot gradually, at the same time beating the mixture.

Whisk the whites of the eggs to a stiff froth, add them to the other ingredients, and beat well for twenty minutes. Put in whichever of the above flavorings may be preferred, pour the cake into a buttered mould or tin, and bake it in a moderate oven from one hour to an hour and a half.

Scotch Cake.—One pound of flour, one pound of sugar, half a pound of butter, three eggs, well mixed together, a little dried and pounded orange-peel, and cinnamon. Roll on a tin sheet with an edge, and bake.

Dutch Cake.—Six ounces of butter and lard mixed, four eggs, half a pound of flour, half a pound of sugar. Beat the butter and lard to a cream, mix it with the eggs well beaten; then add the flour and sugar, both warmed, and a little nutmeg and cinnamon; when well beaten, add a spoonful of brandy, and bake a full hour, in a buttered mould, in a quick oven.

Derby Short Cake.—Rub half a pound of butter into one pound of flour, and mix one egg, a quarter of a pound of sifted sugar, and as much milk as will make a paste. Roll this out thin, and cut the cakes with any fancy shapes or the top of a wineglass. Place on tin plates; strew over with sugar, or cover the top of each with icing, and bake for ten minutes.

Queen Cake.—Mix one pound of dried flour, the same of sifted sugar and of washed currants;

wash one pound of butter in rose water, beat it well, then mix with it eight eggs, yelks and whites beaten separately, and put in the dry ingredients by degrees; beat the whole an hour; butter little tins, teacups, or saucers, filling them only half full; sift a little fine sugar over just as you put them into the oven.

MEDLEY CAKE.—Work together until light, three-quarters of a pound of butter with one and a quarter pound of nice sugar, add four well beaten eggs, half a pint of milk, one wineglassful of wine, one and three-quarters of a pound of flour, one nutmeg, one pound of raisins, half a pint of cream, and one teaspoonful of saleratus; more fruit may be used if desired; when no cream can be had, use a pint of milk, and a teaspoonful more of butter.

CONGRESS CAKE.—Flour two pounds, sugar half a pound, butter half a pound, cream one teacupful, best brandy half a pint, four eggs, soda one scruple; flavor with orange flower water; mix into a stiff dough with warm water; form into loaves, and bake in a moderate oven.

GERMAN SPONGE CAKE.—One pint of milk, one pound of sugar, one dozen eggs, juice and grated rind of one lemon. Beat the whites and yelks of the eggs separately; add the sugar to the yelks; beat well together; add the lemon, then the whites of egg, and lastly the flour. Beat till mixed, and bake till light and a pale brown. Garnish with preserved fruit.

SPONGE CAKE.—Beat twelve eggs as light as possible (for sponge and almond cake they require more beating than for anything else); beat one pound of loaf sugar, powdered and sifted by degrees, into the eggs, continuing to beat some time very hard after all the sugar is in (none but loaf sugar will make light sponge cake). Stir in gradually a teaspoonful of powdered mixed cinnamon and mace, a grated nutmeg, and twelve drops of lemon essence; lastly, by degrees, put in ten ounces of sifted flour, dried near the fire, stirring round the mixture very slowly with a knife. If the flour is stirred too hard the cake will be tough. It must be done gently and lightly, so that the top of the mixture wil be covered with bubbles. As soon as the flour is all in, begin to bake, as setting will hurt it. Put it in small tins, well buttered, or in one large tin pan. The thinner the pans the better the sponge cake. Fill the small tins about half full. Grate loaf sugar over the top of each before setting it in the oven.

SPONGE BISCUITS.—Beat the yelks of twelve eggs for half an hour, and beat in a pound and a half of sugar, very finely sifted. Beat it well until it rises in bubbles. Beat the whites to a strong froth, continue to beat them, adding them to the yelks and sugar, and add by degrees fourteen ounces of flour; grate in the rinds of two lemons, put them in long tin moulds, buttered, and bake them. Just before putting them in the oven dust sugar over them. They will require a moderately hot oven, and will take half an hour to bake.

BERWICK SPONGE CAKE.—Three eggs, beat two minutes; add one and a half cup sugar, beat five minutes; add one cup flour, one teaspoonful cream of tartar, and beat two minutes; add half cup cold water, half teaspoonful soda, beat one minute; add cup of flour, a little salt, rose or lemon.

SUPERIOR SPONGE CAKE.—One cup of white sugar, three-quarters of a cup of sweet milk, two eggs, one teaspoonful of cream of tartar, half a teaspoonful of soda, butter, a quarter of a cup. Flour to thicken, and bake on pie pans.

FINE SPONGE CAKE.—Whites of twelve eggs, yelks of ten eggs, one pound of sugar, three-quarters of a pound of flour. Then take out one large tablespoonful and not use; one tablespoonful of vinegar. Flavor with lemon. Stir the flour in lightly.

FRENCH CREAM CAKE.—*Cream.* Boil nearly a pint of sweet milk; take two small tablespoonfuls of corn-starch beaten with a little milk; to this add two eggs, whites and yelks. When the milk has boiled, stir this in slowly with one scant teacupful of sugar. When almost done, add one half cup of butter, and two teaspoonfuls of lemon essence.

Cake.—Three eggs, one cup of white sugar, one and a half cup of flour, one teaspoonful of baking powder in the flour, two tablespoonfuls of cold water. This will make two cakes; put it in two pie-pans, and bake in a quick oven; split the cakes while warm, and spread with the cream. The amount of cream mentioned is sufficient for both cakes. The cakes are better for standing a day or two.

CREAM CAKE.—Boil one pint of sweet milk. Take two tablespoonfuls of corn-starch beaten with a little milk, add two eggs; when the milk comes to a boil, stir this in slowly, with one small teacupful of white sugar; when almost done add half a teacupful of butter, and one teaspoonful of lemon. The cake is composed of six eggs, two cupfuls of white sugar, two tablespoonfuls of water, one cupful of flour, two teaspoonfuls of baking powder in the flour. The cake must be baked in four pie-pans, then split, and spread with the above cream, and then lay together again.

CREAM BISCUITS.—Rub one pound of fresh butter into one pound of flour, make a hole in the centre, into which put half a pound of powdered sugar upon which the rind of a lemon was rubbed previously to pounding, and three whole eggs; mix the eggs well with the sugar, and then mix all together, forming a flexible paste; cut it into round pieces, each nearly as large as a walnut, stamp them flat with a butter stamp, and bake them in a slack oven.

WASHINGTON CAKE.—Three-quarters of a pound of butter, and the same of sugar worked to a cream, five eggs well beaten, nutmeg and cinnamon, one pound of sifted flour, one gill of wine, half a teaspoonful of soda dissolved in one gill of cream, one pound of currants or raisins. Bake in a moderately quick oven.

WASHINGTON PIE CAKE.—Half a teacup of butter, two cups of sugar, three cups of flour, four eggs. Mix the butter and sugar together, add the yelks, then the whites beaten to a froth. Mix one teaspoonful of cream of tartar in the flour, add one-half a teacupful of milk, in which is dissolved a half teaspoonful of soda. Bake like a loaf of jelly cake.

The Jelly Part.—One pint of sweet milk sweetened and flavored, one egg beaten, two tablespoonfuls of corn-starch. Cooked like blanc mange.

GERMAN CORNUCOPIA CAKES.—Beat the whites of four eggs to snow, add gradually one pound of loaf sugar, and beat one hour. Mix in half a pound of blanched almonds pounded fine, with the white of an egg, to prevent their oiling; add half an ounce of cinnamon; grease the paper with butter, put for each cake a heaping spoonful of the mixture, and spread it round until it is as large as the top of a half-pint tumbler; as soon as they are baked a light brown take them up, and while soft roll them in the shape of a cornucopia. Sift over them sugar and cinnamon mixed.

SWISS CAKE.—Take butter, flour and sugar, of each the weight of four eggs. Beat the yelks with the sugar and some grated lemon-peel, or ten drops of essence of lemon, and one large teaspoonful of rose water, orange flower water if preferred. Add the butter just melted, and slowly shake in the flour, beating it until well mixed. Beat the whites of the eggs to a froth, mix the whole together, and beat on for a few minutes after the whites are added. Butter a tin and bake the cake half an hour.

MOLLY'S CAKE.—Four eggs, three cups of flour, two of sugar, one of sweet milk, half a pound of butter, one teaspoonful of cream of tartar, half a teaspoonful of soda. Some flavoring extract.

LUNCHEON CAKE.—One pound of flour, four ounces of butter, six ounces of moist sugar, quarter of a pound of currants, quarter of a pound of stoned raisins, spices and candied peel to the taste; a teaspoonful of carbonate of soda mixed in half a pint of cold milk; all to be mixed together and beaten into a paste, then put into the oven without being set to rise; it will take an hour and a half to bake.

LADY CAKE.—Mix a pound of flour, the same of sifted sugar, and of washed-clean currants. Wash a pound of butter in rose water, beat it well, then mix with it eight eggs, yelks and whites beaten separately, and put in the dry ingredients by degrees; beat the whole an hour; butter little tins, teacups, or saucers, and bake the batter in, filling only half. Sift a little fine sugar over, just as you put it into the oven.

BUN LOAF.—Four pounds of flour and a spoonful of salt put into a bread-pan; rub in half a pound of dripping and one pound of stoned raisins and dried currants; beat four eggs, add them to a cup full of yeast, and a pint of warm milk. Stir all well together, cover and set before the fire for one hour. Knead well and put in buttered bread tins. Let it rise before the fire for half an hour, and bake.

FRENCH CAKE.—Lay slices of sponge cake on the bottom of a glass dish; spread over them a layer of preserved fruit, add cake and preserved fruit in layers till the dish is full. Pour over it sufficient sherry to soak the cake. Beat up the whites of four eggs with sufficient powdered loaf sugar to make a stiff froth, and cover the top of the cake.

HONEY CAKE.—One cup of white sugar, one cup of rich, sour cream, one egg, half a teaspoonful of soda, two cups of flour. Flavor to taste. Bake half an hour.

ALMOND CUSTARD CAKE.—Four eggs separated, four tablespoonfuls of white sugar, one pound of almonds blanched and cut fine, one pint of sour cream. Flavor with extract of vanilla. Mix all except the whites of the eggs, which add last. Mix in a thick batter, and lay between cake, as the jelly in jelly cake.

JUMBLES.—Rasp on sugar the rinds of two lemons dry, sift and powder as much more sugar as will bring the weight to a pound. Mix with it one pound of fine flour, four well-beaten eggs, and six ounces of warm butter. Drop on buttered tins, and bake twenty minutes, in a very slow oven.

WINE CAKES.—Half a pound of flour, quarter of a pound of butter, half a pound of sugar, ten drops of essence of lemon. Make into a paste with well beaten eggs, roll out thin, cut in rounds, and bake on tins.

TRAFALGAR CAKE.—Mix a pound of well dried flour, with six ounces of finely powdered sugar. Beat six ounces of butter to cream, and stir in half a pound of currants, well cleaned and dried, and three well beaten eggs; then add the flour and sugar, and beat all well together. Flour some tins, and drop the mixture upon them in tablespoonfuls. Bake till brown.

RAISIN CAKE.—Three cups of flour, one of milk, one and a half of sugar, half cup of molasses, half cup of butter, half pound of chopped raisins, three eggs, one teaspoonful of saleratus and spice of all kinds.

MOUNTAIN CAKE.—One large cup of butter, three cups of white sugar, four cups of flour, five eggs, the whites and yelks beaten separately, one teaspoonful of cream of tartar, and one of saleratus, dissolved in a cup of milk. Beat to a batter and bake in a quick oven.

WHITE MOUNTAIN CAKE.—Take one cup of butter, and three of sugar, and mix well together; then add half a cup of sweet milk, one teaspoonful of cream of tartar, and put into the milk; half a teaspoonful of soda put into three and a half cups of flour; the whites of ten eggs, beaten very stiff, which you put into the mixture, next to the last, flour being put in lastly; flavor with essence of lemon. Bake this quantity in three cakes. Then make an icing. To one pound of pulverized sugar, take the whites of three eggs; flavor with vanilla. Put the icing between the layers of cake, and on the top and the sides.

ASH CAKE.—One pound of white sugar, one teacupful of butter, half a cupful of sweet milk, the whites of ten eggs, half a small teaspoonful of soda, one teaspoonful of cream of tartar, three cups of flour; flavor with vanilla or almond. Bake in jelly-cake pans with icing between.

FINE ICING FOR CAKES.—Beat up the whites of five eggs to a froth, and put to them a pound of double-refined sugar, powdered and sifted, and three spoonfuls of orange flower water, or lemon-juice. Keep beating it all the time the cake is in the oven, and the moment it comes out, ice over the top with a spoon.

HOT ICING.—One pint of pounded sugar. Add just enough water to dissolve, and not over two or three tablespoonfuls; then boil. Beat the whites of four eggs to a stiff froth; add the hot sugar, stirring quickly until smooth. Beat about two minutes; flavor to taste; spread on the cake, and set in a warm place.

YEAST.—In two quarts of water let two ounces of hops boil for half an hour, strain the liquor, and let it stand in a wide earthenware bowl. When lukewarm, add a small quantity of salt, say half a handful, and one-quarter of a pound of sugar. Take some of the liquor and well mix up in it half a pound of best flour, beating this up thoroughly in the whole afterwards. The next day but one put in one and one half pound of boiled and mashed potatoes; let it stand one more day, after which it may be bottled for use. It should be kept near the fire while making, so as to keep it about the temperature of new milk, and it should also be frequently stirred during the process of making. When bottled, it should be kept in a cool place.

POTATO YEAST.—For those who live far from shops this receipt may sometimes be found useful in case of deficiency. Boil mealy potatoes, peel them, mash them very smooth, and put to them as much hot water as will make them the consistence of yeast, no thicker. Add for every pound of potatoes two ounces of very coarse sugar or treacle, and while the mixture is warm, stir in two spoonfuls of yeast. Keep it warm until it rises well. It may be used in twenty-four hours. One pound of potatoes will make nearly a quart of yeast.

HOMEMADE YEAST.—Put one pint of dry hops into three pints of water to boil. Peel eight potatoes and put them on in a separate pan to boil. When the potatoes are done, the hop tea will be the right strength. Strain the tea from the hops and set it to cool. Mash the potatoes free from lumps, add one pint of flour, one teaspoonful of salt, and one tablespoonful of sugar (brown). Pour the tea over this mixture, stir well together, add one cup of yeast, baker's will do, though I always have enough of my old yeast to set new with. Let it rise in a large open vessel in a warm place, stir occasionally, and when it is well risen, and begins to fall in the centre, put in a close jug and cork tight.

SWEETENED YEAST.—Boil and mash ten potatoes of nearly equal size. Pour on them one quart of boiling water, and stir in one coffeecup of good sugar. After standing a few minutes, add another quart of hot water, less one gill. When lukewarm, add one pint of yeast, and set it in a moderately warm place to rise. When it gets light, set it down cellar for future use.

HOPS AND POTATO YEAST.—In two quarts of water boil six potatoes, pared and cut up, and a handful of hops (in a bag). Boil till the potatoes are done, then take all out. Mash the potatoes up and put them back into the water with one cup of salt and one cup of white sugar. Let it come to a boil, then cool off, and when milk warm, add about one cup of baker's yeast. Set it in a warm place to rise, then jug it up tight, put it in a cool place, and it would keep for six months.

CHAPTER XI.

BEVERAGES.

To Make Good Tea.—In making tea it is usual to allow a teaspoonful of dry tea for each person. First scald the teapot by filling it with *boiling water*, and letting it stand a few minutes near the fire. Turn off the water and put in the dry tea; over this pour boiling water enough to cover it. Cover the teapot closely, and stand near the fire for five minutes. Fill up with boiling water, and serve.

To Make Good Chocolate.—Grate one cake of fine French chocolate, and put it over the fire with lukewarm water enough to cover it. Stir gently until thoroughly dissolved. Pour in gradually, stirring all the time, half a pint of boiling milk. Boil all gently for five minutes, and serve.

Chocolate a la Francaise.—Grate one cake of fine French chocolate into a gill of cold milk. Put into a vessel of boiling water, and stir till well mixed. Add half a pint of milk and water, cold, and let it gradually come to a boil, stirring all the time. Boil fifteen minutes.

Cocoa Shells.—Soak a teacupful of dry shells all night in a quart of cold water; boil in the same water three hours before using. (Prepared shells do not require soaking.) Boil them rapidly for one hour, settle and strain, and add boiling milk in the proportion of a pint of milk to a quart of water and three ounces of shells.

Broma.—To make broma, powder in a mortar, two ounces of arrowroot, half a pound of loaf sugar, and a pound of pure chocolate. Sift carefully through a hair sieve. To two tablespoonfuls of this powder put two tablespoonfuls of cream. Stir till well mixed, pour on half a pint of boiling milk, and boil all for ten minutes.

COFFEE AND ITS PREPARATION.

It is not our intention to go into detailed history of the cultivation of the coffee plant, which is not likely to be of great interest to our readers. Practically it is sufficient for us to know that coffee is largely cultivated in many of the tropical regions of the globe, as the West Indies and America, Arabia, Ceylon, India, Bourbon, Java, etc. The Arabian or Mocha bean is very small, round, and dark yellow in color; East Indian kinds are larger; and the Ceylon, West Indian and Brazilian kinds are of a bluish or greenish-gray tint, and the largest in size. When coffee-berries are roasted, they suffer some remarkable changes, losing considerably in weight, but increasing to nearly double their original size;

during the roasting the aromatic flavor is developed, but the exact nature of the changes undergone is not clearly understood. It is remarkable that coffee contains a peculiar substance called caffein, on which much of the use of coffee as a beverage depends.

Roasted coffee when ground is much adulterated with chicory; this fraud is easily detected by dropping some of the suspected coffee in a wineglass with cold water. If the coffee is pure, it swims on the surface, and scarcely colors the water; if it contains chicory, the latter sinks to the bottom and stains the water of a deep red tint.

Coffee is a wholesome and nutritive beverage; it diminishes the disposition to sleep, and hence it is used by those who require to keep awake for study or other purposes. Medicinally it is found, like tea, useful in some forms of headache, where there is not any determination of blood to the head; and it is also especially useful in some cases of spasmodic asthma, when taken strong.

The making of good coffee is a very rare thing in this country. Most persons boil it, so making a decoction instead of an infusion; this effectually gets rid of the delicate and agreeable aromatic flavor, and leaves a comparatively tasteless beverage. The following particulars will be found worth attention; never buy your coffee ground, but grind it yourself immediately before using it; keep your coffee-pot, whatever kind you may use, wiped clean and dry inside, a damp tea or coffee-pot acquires a musty flavor that spoils the best tea or coffee. The cheapest, and perhaps the best coffee-pots, are those made on the French plan, called *cafétières;* if you have not one of these, adopt the following plan: put your freshly-ground coffee into the coffee-pot, previously made warm, and pour upon it water actually boiling, set the pot by the side of the fire for a few seconds, but do not let it boil up, then pour a cupful out and return it back again to the pot, in order to clear it; having done this, let it stand on the hob or fender to settle, and, in less than five minutes, a transparent strong aromatic cup of coffee may be poured out. The proportions of coffee (which should not be too finely ground) recommended, are an ounce to a pint, or pint and a half of water.

The milk used with coffee should always be boiled and used as hot as possible; the boiling of milk imparts a peculiar and exceedingly pleasant flavor to the coffee. White sugar is recommended, as the treacle-like flavor of moist sugar quite overpowers the delicate aroma.

CAFÉ AU LAIT.—The French are justly celebrated for this breakfast coffee, which may be made as follows: Use an infusion, made as directed, or in a *cafétière,* only of double the strength, and when clear, pour it into the breakfast cups, which have been previously half or three-quarters filled with boiling milk, sweetened with loaf sugar.

CAFÉ NOIR.—The strong, clear, black infusion,

made as above, served in small cups, and drank with a large quantity of sugar, is the café noir of the French.

Having been great coffee drinkers in our time, we have tried nearly every machine for making coffee that has ever been invented. These contrivances, though very numerous, may be arranged in two classes—such as boil the coffee or make a decoction, and those that expose it to the action of boiling water, or form an infusion. In the first class is included the common pot, which is too well known to need description. The ground coffee is boiled in the water, and the liquid fined by pouring out a portion and returning it. As the flavor of coffee depends on a very volatile oil, which is entirely dissipated by boiling, it is evident that coffee preserving its delicate aroma cannot be prepared by this process.

The full flavor of coffee can be extracted by infusion, as effected in those contrivances in which the boiling water is poured on the ground berries. Of these we have found none superior to the French *cafétière*, which has the advantage of being cheap, simple, not liable to get out of order, and easily cleaned and dried. After trying nearly every device that has been promulgated, we have returned to our first love, the *cafétière*, and hardly think we shall again be seduced from our attachment to it. Above all, we caution our readers to abstain from all coffee-making contrivances which contain a strainer made of linen, calico, or any vegetable fabric, as these, being moistened day after day, and kept constantly wet, become mouldy, and impart a very bad taste to the beverage.

In the absence of any other contrivance, coffee as good as ever was imbibed can be made in a lipped jug by the following directions: Pour some boiling water in your jug to heat it, throw this out, put in your ground coffee, pour on your boiling water, stir down the powder from the top with a spoon, cover over the jug with a folded napkin, and place on the hob for a few minutes; then pour out steadily, and you will have as clear and bright a cup of coffee as ever was made. As for the kind of coffee to be recommended, we always prefer a mixture of one-third small pea-berried Mocha, with two-thirds plantation coffee. This gives flavor and body, and we always add an ounce of *good* ground chicory to every pound. Dear readers, try this mixture; make it strong—very strong—pour it into large breakfast cups, with an equal amount of boiling milk, sweeten with loaf sugar, and then you may laugh at those who say that good coffee is only to be drunk in France.

GOOD COFFEE.—Put a cupful of coffee into a coffee-pot, break in an egg, pour about a quart of hot water on it, boil an hour, strain through muslin, and serve up very hot.

ANOTHER METHOD. — Never purchase coffee

ground, but always whole; and, above all, desire the servant to be most careful that the coffee-pot be thoroughly clean and well dried, so that it may be quite free from all unpleasant smell of stale coffee, which will entirely spoil the flavor of the fresh. After having ground a sufficient quantity of berries to allow one tablespoonful for each person, the white and shell of one egg must be thoroughly stirred about and mixed in with the coffee. After this, pour upon it as much boiling water as it is supposed will be required, and boil it up as quickly as possible. Pour out about a teacupful, and put it back again. Take it from the fire, and pour half a teacup of quite cold water into it, and let it stand five minutes by the fire (but do not let it boil again) before you transfer it to the coffee-pot it is to be sent up in. Be very careful not to shake it in doing this, as the egg-shell and coffee powder will have settled at the bottom, and the liquid ought to be perfectly clear, and of a dark golden brown color.

CONCENTRATED COFFEE. — Procure one-half pound of the choicest roasted coffee berries you can command, let the same be ground under your own immediate eye, to prevent the opportunity of chicory or any other spurious drug being introduced among the genuine material. Submit the coffee to a clean saucepan, containing one quart of boiling water, stir it round twice or thrice with a suitably-sized spoon, adding, at the same time, two pieces of fresh white ginger. Place the saucepan over a slow fire, and let it simmer until the quantity of liquor is reduced to one pint; then strain the latter off into a smaller saucepan, and allow the liquor to simmer gently, adding to it at intervals as much white sugar as will qualify the character of a thick consistent syrup, when it may be taken up, and when thoroughly cold poured into jars or bottles, stopped closely down for use. It will keep for any length of time in any climate. An individual, possessing the above confection, may command a cup of strong, genuine coffee at a minute's notice; it is necessary only to introduce two or three teaspoonfuls of the essence into a coffeecup, and fill with boiling water.

FRUIT SYRUPS.

Most of our readers are aware that there are two different classes of sugars,—the cane sugars, derived from the cane, the beet, etc., and the grape sugars, as found in the grape, in honey, and as prepared artificially from potatoes; the latter used principally in the fabrication of wines. Both forms of sugar have much the same taste, and cannot be distinguished readily in solution. Of the cane sugars, however, only half the quantity is required to produce a given sweetening effect as of the other. It may not be known generally, however, that cane sugar by long boiling becomes changed into grape sugar, and thus loses a portion of its sweetening power. This takes place not only in the process of clarifying, but also in preparing fruits, syrups, and preserves. Should the syrups be thickened by boiling beyond a certain degree, the grape sugar produced, being only about one-quarter as soluble as cane sugar, separates after a time in the form of white crystals, the comparative want of sweetness in which will be very evident to the taste. Mixed with water as a drink, twice as much will be required as if no change had occurred. This furnishes a useful hint to housekeepers, which has been acted on to great advantage, namely, to boil the fruit juice by itself for the proper time, and allow it to become lukewarm, adding the proper quantity of white sugar, which soon dissolves without further heating. The juice is preserved in this way as perfectly as if the sugar were boiled a long time with it, maintains its original sweetness without the formation of crystals, and a much less quantity will answer the purpose. The same theory is applicable in the preparation of preserves as of syrups.

It is to be regretted that fruit syrups are not more extensively used in this country, as the addition of a few tablespoonfuls of a good fruit syrup to a glass of iced water, or soda water, produces a refreshing summer beverage that is far more desirable for general use than the majority of the liquids employed in this country. For the use of ladies and children, and all persons by whom intoxicating beverages are not used, they are strongly to be commended.

CURRANT SYRUP.—One pint of juice, two pounds of sugar. Mix together three pounds of currants, half white and half red, one pound of raspberries, and one pound of cherries, without the stones. Mash the fruit, and let it stand in a warm place for three or four days, keeping it covered with a coarse cloth or piece of paper with holes pricked in it to keep out any dust or dirt. Filter the juice, add the sugar in powder, finish in the water-bath, and skim it. When cold, put it into bottles, fill them, and cork well.

MORELLO CHERRY SYRUP.—Take the stones out of the cherries, mash them, and press out the juice in an earthen pan. Let it stand in a cool place for two days, then filter; add two pounds of sugar to one pint of juice, finish in the water-bath, or stir it well on the fire, and give it one or two boils.

MULBERRY SYRUP.—One pint of juice, one pound twelve ounces of sugar. Press out the juice, and finish as cherry syrup.

GOOSEBERRY SYRUP.—One pint of juice, one pound twelve ounces of sugar. To twelve pounds of ripe gooseberries add two pounds of cherries without stones, squeeze out the juice, and finish as others.

LEMON SYRUP.—One pint and a quarter of juice, two pounds of sugar. Let the juice stand in a cool place to settle. When a thin skin is formed on the top pour it off and filter; add the sugar, and finish in the water-bath. If the flavor of the peel is preferred with it, grate off the yellow rind of the lemons and mix it with the juice to infuse, or rub it off on part of the sugar, and add it with the remainder when you finish it.

RASPBERRY VINEGAR SYRUP.—One pint of juice, two pints of vinegar, four pounds and a half of sugar. Prepare the juice as before, adding the vinegar with it. Strain the juice and boil to the pearl. A very superior raspberry vinegar is made by taking three pounds of raspberries, two pints of vinegar, and three pounds of sugar. Put the raspberries into the vinegar without mashing them, cover the pan close, and let it remain in a cellar for seven or eight days; then filter the infusion, add the sugar in powder, and finish in the water-bath. This is superior to the first, as the beautiful aroma of the fruit is not lost in the boiling.

SOUR ORANGE SYRUP.—Peel the oranges carefully, then squeeze the juice and strain it, so as to extract the seed and white fibrous substances, which are very bitter. Add one pound of loaf sugar to one pint of juice, and boil it in a preserving kettle. Stir frequently, and skim well. Boil until it is a rich syrup. When nearly cold, bottle, cork, and seal.

SYRUP OF CLOVES.—Put a quarter of a pound

of cloves to a quart of boiling water, cover close, set it over a fire, and boil gently half an hour; then drain and add to a pint of the liquor two pounds of loaf sugar, clear it with the whites of two eggs, beaten up with cold water, and let it simmer till it is strong syrup. Preserve it in phials, close corked.

ORANGE SYRUP.—Select ripe and thin-skinned fruit. Squeeze the juice through a sieve, and to every pint add one pound and a half of loaf sugar. Boil it slowly, and skim as long as the scum rises; then take it off, let it grow cold, and bottle it. Two tablespoonfuls of this syrup mixed with melted butter make a nice sauce for plum or batter puddings. Three tablespoonfuls of it in a glass of ice water make a delicious beverage.

LEMONADES.—Lemons furnish two important products for the formation of beverages, an acid juice, and an aromatic stomachic oil, contained in the rind. Lemon juice is a slightly turbid, very sour liquid, having a pleasant flavor when diluted. It contains a considerable quantity of gummy mucilage, which causes it to become mouldy on exposure to the air. It is capable of furnishing a large number of acidulated drinks, which are exceedingly useful in allaying thirst, and are most valuable for their anti-scorbutic properties.

In making any kind of lemonade, the proportions given need not be adhered to, but the quantities ordered may be increased or lessened to suit the taste.

For a quart of lemonade, take six lemons and a quarter of a pound of sugar; rub off part of the yellow rind of the lemons on to the sugar, squeeze the juice on to the latter, and pour on the water boiling hot; mix the whole, and run through a flannel jelly-bag.

Lemons are not always to be procured, especially on a journey, and we have, therefore, much pleasure in drawing attention to the following useful directions for making portable lemonade:—

EXCELLENT PORTABLE LEMONADE.—Rasp with a quarter of a pound of sugar, the rind of a fine juicy lemon; reduce the sugar to powder, and pour on it the strained juice of the fruit; press the mixture into a jar, and when wanted for use dissolve a tablespoonful of it in a glass of water; it will keep a considerable time. If too sweet for the taste of the drinker, a very small portion of citric acid may be added when it is taken.

MOCK LEMONADE.—A cheap substitute for lemonade may be made as follows: Tartaric acid, a quarter of an ounce; sugar, six ounces; essence of lemon, dropped on the sugar, about four or five drops; boiling water, two pints. This, allowed to stand till cold, makes a wholesome, cooling, summer beverage, economical in its cost, but the flavor is not equal to that prepared from lemon juice.

SUPERIOR LEMON A LA SOYER.—Take the peel of six lemons, free from pith, cut it up in small pieces, and put it with two cloves into a bottle containing half a pint of hot water, place the bottle in a stewpan with boiling water, and let it stand by the side of a fire for one or two hours, taking care it does not boil; then take half a pint of lemon juice, half a pint of syrup, if none, use plain syrup, or sugar, in like proportion, adding a few drops of orange flower water; add the infusion of the rind, which has been previously made, and allowed to become cold, stir well together, and add two quarts of cold water.

LEMONADE A LA SOYER.—Put a quart of water in a stewpan to boil, into which put two moist dried figs, each split in two; let it boil a quarter of an hour, then have ready the peel of a lemon, taken off rather thickly, and the half of the lemon cut in thin slices; throw them into the stewpan, and boil two minutes longer, then pour it into a jug, which cover closely with paper until cold, then pass it through a sieve, add a teaspoonful of honey, and it is ready for use.

ORANGEADE A LA SOYER.—Proceed as for lemonade, but using the whole of the orange, a little of the peel included, sweetening with sugar-candy, and adding a teaspoonful of arrowroot, mixed with a little cold water, which pour into the boiling liquid at the same time you put in the orange. The arrowroot makes it very delicate.

Barley Lemonade.—Put a quarter of a pound of sugar into a small stewpan, with half a pint of water, which boil about ten minutes, or until forming a thickish syrup; then add the rind of a fresh lemon and the pulp of two; let it boil two minutes longer, when add two quarts of barley-water, made without sugar and lemon; boil five minutes longer, pass it through a hair sieve into a jug, which cover with paper, making a hole in the centre to let the heat through; when cold it is ready for use; if put cold into a bottle, and well corked down, it would keep good several days.

Barley Orangeade.—Barley orangeade is made in the same manner, substituting the rind and juice of oranges; the juice of a lemon, in addition, is an improvement.

Another Mock Lemonade.—A mock lemonade of superior flavor may be made by using the acid prepared from lemons, citric acid, according to the following receipt: Citric acid, a quarter of an ounce; essence of lemon, ten to twenty drops; syrup, half a pint; boiling water, as much as may be required. This preparation is expensive, and is not equal to lemonade from fresh lemons, which should always be preferred when they can be obtained.

Plain Orangeade.—Orangeade should be made in precisely a similar manner to lemonade, using oranges instead of lemons; but as there is less acid in this fruit, a much larger proportion of juice is required, and, however prepared, this beverage is rather insipid, and is inferior to the following:—

ORANGE LEMONADE.—Take three oranges, one large lemon, and two or three ounces of sugar; rub off some of the peel on to the sugar, squeeze on the juice, and pour on two pints of boiling water; mix the whole and strain.

ORANGEADE.—Take half a pound of ground loaf sugar, one and a half ounce of carbonate of soda; mix well in sixteen portions, and put in blue paper; one ounce of tartaric acid, in white paper. Dissolve the contents of a blue paper in half a pint of water, and the acid in a quarter of a pint of water, to which add orange juice; mix them together and drink. Two or three spoonfuls of the syrup of marmalade may be used instead of orange juice, in which case it must be dissolved in the first glass.

FRUIT VINEGARS.

DURING the summer few beverages are more refreshing than fruit vinegars, mixed with iced or cold spring water. The following directions are recomended as having been tried and found very successful:

STRAWBERRY VINEGAR.—Take the stalks from the fruit, which should be a highly flavored sort, quite ripe, fresh from the beds, and gathered in dry weather; weigh and put it into large glass jars, or wide-necked bottles, and to each pound pour about a pint and a half of fine pale white wine vinegar, which will answer the purpose better than the entirely colorless kind, sold under the name of distilled vinegar, but which is the pyroligneous acid greatly diluted. Tie a thick paper over them, and let the strawberries remain from three to four days; then pour off the vinegar and empty them into a jelly-bag, or suspend them in a cloth that all the liquid may drop from them without pressure; take an equal weight of fresh fruit, pour the vinegar upon it, and three days afterwards repeat the same process, diminishing a little the proportion of strawberries, of which the flavor ought ultimately to overpower the vinegar. In three days drain off the liquid very closely, and after having strained it through a linen or a flannel bag, weigh it, and mix with it an equal quantity of highly-refined sugar, roughly powdered; when this is nearly dissolved, stir the syrup over a very clear fire until it has boiled five minutes, and skim it thoroughly; pour it into a delicately clean stone pitcher, or into large china jugs, throw a folded cloth over and let it remain until the morrow; put it into pint or half pint bottles, and cork them tightly with new velvet corks, for if these be pressed in tightly at first, the bottles would be liable to burst; in four or five days they may be closely corked, and stored in a dry and cool place.

Damp destroys the color and injures the flavor of these fine fruit vinegars, of which a spoonful or two in a glass of water affords so agreeable a summer beverage, and one which, in many cases of illness, is so acceptable to invalids.

Where there is a garden the fruit may be thrown into the vinegar as it ripens, within an interval of forty-eight hours, instead of being all put to infuse at once, and it must then remain a proportionate time; one or two days in addition to that specified will make no difference to the preparation. The enamelled stewpans are the best possible vessels to boil it in, but it may be simmered in a stone jar set into a pan of boiling water, when there is nothing more appropriate at hand; though the syrup does not usually keep so well when this last method is adopted.

RASPBERRY VINEGAR.—Put two pounds of raspberries into a jar, and pour on them a quart of best white wine vinegar, and let all stand twenty-four hours; then add two pounds more of raspberrries, and let all stand twenty-four hours more; then strain the pure vinegar through a sieve, and to every pint add one pound of sugar, and then boil it up twenty minutes; when cold, bottle it for use. It will keep two years; but seal each bottle.

GOOSEBERRY VINEGAR.—Take the ripest gooseberries you can get; put them into a very clean tub, and crush them with your hands. To every peck of gooseberries put two gallons of water; mix them well together, and let them work for three weeks, taking care to stir them up three or four times a day. At the expiration of that time, strain the liquor through a hair sieve, and to every gallon of it, add one pound of moist sugar, one pound of treacle, and a spoonful of fresh yeast; let it work for four days in the same tub, which should be well washed. Turn it into iron-hooped barrels, and let it stand twelve months; then draw it into bottles for use. This far exceeds any white wine vinegar.

NORWEGIAN RASPBERRY VINEGAR.—Take four pounds of raspberries, pour over them half a pint of vinegar, place it in an earthen jar, and cover it securely, so that no air can enter, and place it in a sunny window twelve hours; take it in at night, and place it out again in the sun the next day for another twelve hours. Then place in a flannel bag, till the juice has run through without pressure. Then, for every pound of juice take a pound of loaf sugar, and boil it for a quarter of an hour, or till no scum arises; then put it into small bottles and well cork it.

MIXED FRUIT VINEGARS.—Raspberries and strawberries mixed will make a vinegar of very pleasant flavor.

STRAWBERRY DRINK.—Put to a pint of water a pound of strawberries, which you are to bruise or mash in the water, then put in a quarter of a pound or five ounces of sugar, and squeeze into it the juice of a lemon, and suffer it to cool before you drink it. If the lemon be full, it will serve two pints.

LEMON WATER is also a delightful drink. Put two slices of lemon, thinly peeled, into a teapot a little bit of the peel and a large spoonful of capillaire; pour in a pint of boiling water, and stop it close two hours.

TOMATO WINE.—Take small ripe tomatoes, pick off the stems and wash them, mash and strain through a linen bag; let it stand till the pulp is settled, then measure. Add two pounds and a half or three pounds of loaf sugar to a gallon of juice. Put into a cask, and let it ferment, then bottle and pack away for use. If two gallons of water are added to five gallons of juice, it will make pretty good wine, but not as fine as if the adulteration is not made.

MUSCADINE WINE.—Get the grapes full ripe, wash, and pound with a pestle, being careful not to break the seeds, as it will make the wine bitter. Measure them after they are pounded, and to every gallon add a gallon of cistern water. Let it stand a week, then measure the clear juice; add two pounds and a half or three pounds of loaf sugar to each gallon. Let it stand till fermentation ceases, then bottle for use. This is excellent—**try** it.

Rhubarb Wine.—Take the juice from the stalks of the garden rhubarb, one gallon, to it add one gallon of water in which seven pounds of sugar has been dissolved; put the mixture into a cask with the bung-hole open, and let it ferment; keep the cask full by adding sweetened water, so that it may purge itself. When it is sufficiently fermented, put in the bung. To give it a slight, "bouquet flavor," three ounces of orris root, well pounded, is added to each barrel. Fine with isinglass before bottling. Four ounces of isinglass dissolved in a pint or more of wine, is sufficient for a barrel of wine.

Ginger Wine.—Take four gallons of water and seven pounds of sugar; boil them half an hour, skimming it all the time; when the liquor is cold, squeeze in the juice of two lemons; then boil the peels, with two ounces of white ginger, in three pints of water, one hour; when cold, put it all together into the cask with one gill of finings and three pounds of Malaga raisins; then close it up, let it stand two months, then bottle it off. N. B.— A lump of unslacked lime put into your cask will keep wine from turning sour.

Lemon Wine.—Mix well together the rind of six and the juice of eighteen lemons, one gallon of whisky, six quarts of cold water, three pounds of loaf sugar, a stick of cinnamon, three dozen cloves, two ounces of bitter almonds, and a quarter of a pound of burnt sugar; when the sugar is well dissolved, add three quarts of boiling new milk. Let it stand for two hours; then strain through a flannel bag until quite clear. This quantity will fill eighteen bottles.

IMPERIAL.—Take half an ounce of cream of tartar, three ounces of fresh orange or lemon-peel, four ounces of lump sugar, and three pints of boiling water. Mix together; cover the vessel till cold, then pour off the clear part for use. This is a very agreeable drink for hot weather, or in fever.

IMPERIAL POP.—Take three ounces of cream of tartar, one ounce of ginger, one and a half pound of white sugar, the juice of a lemon, and one gallon of water. Work it with yeast, and bottle it as ginger beer, which it resembles, except as being more acid in flavor, and more cooling in its medical properties.

CAPILLAIRE.—Take one pound of loaf sugar, quarter of a pound of moist sugar, one egg well beaten, one pint of water. Simmer it one hour, skim it while boiling, let it get cold, then again boil and skim, and add one ounce of orange flower water and two tablespoonfuls of brandy. Strain through a jelly-bag, and bottle for use. A spoonful in a tumbler of water makes a pleasant beverage.

PLEASANT DRINK IN SUMMER.—Take two

ounces of tartaric acid to two pounds of white sugar, the juice of half a lemon, and three pints of water; boil together five minutes; when cold, add the whites of three eggs, well beaten, with half a cup of flour and half an ounce of essence of wintergreen; bottle, and keep in a cool place. Take two tablespoonfuls of this syrup for a tumbler of water and one-quarter of a teaspoonful of soda.

DECOCTION OF SARSAPARILLA.—Take four ounces of the root, slice it down, put the slices into four pints of water, and simmer for four hours. Take out the sarsaparilla, and beat it into a mash; put it into the liquor again, and boil down to two pints; then strain and cool the liquor. Dose, a wineglassful three times a day Use—to purify the blood.

SODA WATER.—Dissolve one ounce of the carbonate of soda in a gallon of water, put it into bottles, in the quantity of a tumblerful or half a pint to each; having the cork ready, drop into each bottle half a drachm of tartaric or citric acid in crystals, cork and wire it immediately, and it will be ready for use at any time.

COOLING SUMMER BEVERAGE.—Bruise any fruit you like, as cherries, currants, strawberries, raspberries, etc., add water and sugar to your taste, and strain it. It should be kept in a cool place.

Or dissolve fruit jelly in boiling water, and let it cool.

GINGER BEER.—Put into any vessel two gallons of boiling water, two pounds of common loaf sugar, two ounces of best ginger (bruised), two ounces of cream of tartar, or else a lemon, sliced. Stir them up until the sugar is dissolved, let it rest until about as warm as new milk, then add two tablespoonfuls of good yeast, poured on to a bit of bread put to float on it. Cover the whole over with a cloth, and suffer it to remain undisturbed twenty-four hours; then strain it and put it into bottles, observing not to put more in than will occupy three-quarters full. Cork the bottles well, and tie the corks, and in two days, in warm weather, it will be fit to drink. If not to be consumed until a week or a fortnight after it is made, a quarter of the sugar may be spared.

COMMON GINGER BEER.—The common drink sold in the streets is made with raw sugar or molasses, three-quarters of a pound to a gallon of water, the ginger ground, and with less acid.

GINGER POP.—This agreeable beverage, which is little known, is made as follows: One quart of ale or stout, ten quarts of water, one pound of coarse brown sugar, two ounces of ground ginger. Bottle and cork it well. It will be fit to drink in a few days.

Ginger Beer Powders.—Take two drachms of powdered white sugar, five grains of powdered ginger, twenty-six grains of carbonate of soda, mix and wrap in blue paper; thirty grains of tartaric acid, wrap in white paper. For use, dissolve the contents of the blue paper in a tumbler three-fourths filled with water, add the acid from the white paper, stir it up, and drink as soon as dissolved.

Lemonade Powders.—Half a pound of pounded loaf sugar, one ounce of carbonate of soda, four drops of oil of lemon. Mix and divide in sixteen portions, and wrap in blue paper; one ounce of tartaric acid in sixteen white papers. Use as with soda water powders.

Eau Sucré.—Dissolve lump sugar in water. This is a beverage much used in France. It is considered wholesome and refreshing, particularly just before going to bed.

Agrag.—This is the most delicious and refreshing drink ever devised by thirsty mortal. It is made of unripe grapes, pounded, loaf sugar, and water. It is strained till it becomes of the palest straw-colored amber, and then froze.

Sherbet.—Boil two pounds of sugar in a quart of water. Pare six oranges and two lemons very thin. Mix together the boiling syrup, the peel of the fruit, the juice, and five more pints of water.

Clear it with a little white of egg, let it be until cold, strain it, and bottle it.

WATERMELON SHERBET—*A Bengal Receipt.*—Let the melon be cut in half, and the inside of the fruit be worked up and mashed with a spoon till it assumes the consistency of a thick pulp. Introduce into this as much pounded white candy or sugar as may suit your taste, a wineglassful of fresh rose water, and two wineglasses of sherry. Pour, when strained, the contents into a jug, and fill your tumblers as often as needed. This makes a very agreeable drink in summer.

NECTAR.—Take two pounds of chopped raisins, four pounds of loaf sugar, two gallons of boiling water. Mix, and when cold, add two lemons, sliced, brandy or rum, two pints. Soak in a covered vessel for four or five days, occasionally shaking. Strain, let stand in a cool place for a week to clear, and then bottle. It will be fit for drink in ten days.

LEMON WATER ICE.—Half a pint of lemon-juice, and the same of water, to which put one pint of syrup, the peels of six lemons, rubbed off on sugar; strain, mix, and freeze. Then mix up the whites of three eggs to a strong broth, with a little sugar. When the ice is beginning to set, work this well into it, and it will be very soft and delicious.

BLACKBERRY CORDIAL.—Squeeze the juice from the berries, and to every pint of juice add one pint of water, and to every quart of this mixture put one pint of whisky or brandy; sweeten to taste; use the best refined sugar. A few spices may be added, if liked. This makes a very superior cordial, and improves with age. This receipt answers for strawberries, peaches, wild grapes, etc.

TAMARINDS, OR CRANBERRY JUICE, with double the quantity of water, makes a pleasant drink for an invalid when approaching convalescence.

CHAPTER XII.

INVALID COOKERY.

BEEF-TEA.—Take one and a half pound of the best steak, cut it into very small pieces, and put them into an earthenware jar with enough cold water to cover the meat; tie the top of the jar on, and put it into a saucepan full of hot water; place the saucepan on the fire, and allow it to boil for three hours, by which time all the goodness of the meat will be extracted. This is the pure essence of beef.

LIEBIG'S SOUP.—Mix one tablespoonful of wheaten flour with one tablespoonful of freshly-ground malt flour, and add seven and a quarter grains of the bi-carbonate of potash. Rub this mixture well in a basin with two tablespoonfuls of water, and gradually add ten tablespoonfuls of new milk, stirring till all is well blended. Then simmer this mixture over a gentle fire until it begins to thicken. Immediately when it begins to thicken, remove the saucepan from the fire and stir the soup briskly until it becomes fluid. Now place the saucepan again over the fire, and let the soup boil gently for five minutes. Then strain it through a fine sieve, so as to clear it from all the bran of the malt. No sweetening is required, for the soup thus prepared will be sweet as milk. For the flour use seconds or common households. The malt should be freshly ground for every time of use. This may be done in a common coffee-mill.

BEEF-TEA AND BAKED FLOUR.—This may be prepared exactly like the preceding receipt, only using baked flour instead of the arrowroot-powder. With this change it becomes a very nutritious food, and one meal *per diem* of such food will be sufficient in ordinary circumstances of health.

FLAXSEED JELLY FOR A COUGH.—A coffeecup of flaxseed, two quarts of water; boil several hours until reduced to a jelly; strain through a thin cloth, squeeze in the pulp and juice of a large lemon; roll a quarter of a pound of best raisins, mix them in the jelly, simmer without boiling one hour; strain again, add half a teacup of the best loaf sugar. Take a tablespoonful every hour.

SAGO.—Like arrowroot, this should be used only as an occasional change; for it is deficient in nutritive properties. Take one tablespoonful of sago and macerate for two hours in one pint of water placed at the side of the fire, or in a slow oven. Then let it boil gently for a quarter of an hour, and before it is taken from the fire, add new milk, a little loaf sugar, and a few grains of salt.

TAPIOCA.—This is another of the articles which,

though deficient in the elements of nutrition, may occasionally supply an agreeable change of diet. Take one tablespoonful of tapioca, and macerate for an hour in a pint of water, in a pan placed at the side of the fire, or in a slow oven. Then let it simmer gently for ten minutes, and before taking it from the fire, add milk, with a little loaf sugar, and a few grains of salt.

OATMEAL PORRIDGE is made by boiling oatmeal and water in such proportions that a thick mixture is obtained, which, on cooling, becomes nearly solid. The coarse Scotch oatmeal is far superior for these purposes. The most approved method of making porridge is to strew oatmeal with one hand into a vessel of boiling water (to which salt has been previously added), so gradually that it does not become lumpy, stirring the mixture at the same time with the other hand. After the requisite quantity has been stirred in—namely, about two large handfuls of coarse oatmeal to a quart of boiling water—the whole should be allowed to stand by the side of the fire, so as to simmer gently for twenty or thirty minutes. During this time it thickens considerably. As thus prepared, it is usually eaten with the addition of milk.

MILK AND OATMEAL GRUEL.—This is a very nutritious food, but its effect should be watched, as it may not suit all cases. To prepare it, take a tablespoonful of the finest oatmeal and mix smoothly with about a quarter of a pint of cold water, while three-quarters of a pint of new milk is simmered Mix the warm milk gradually with the oatmeal and water. Then pour all into the saucepan, and boil it gently for ten minutes—stirring it well. Add a little loaf sugar and a few grains of salt.

PANADA OF FINE FLOUR.—Rub smoothly one tablespoonful of the finest biscuit-flour with a quarter of a pint of cold water in a basin. Simmer three-quarters of a pint of new milk with two or three lumps of sugar in it. Mix gradually the milk with the flour and water. Put it into the saucepan, and let it simmer gently for twenty minutes, stirring it well to prevent burning. This is a good food, and will generally be found to keep the bowels regular.

CHICKEN PANADA.—Skin a fowl; cut it in pieces, leaving the breast whole; boil it in three pints of water till perfectly tender, pick off the meat, and pound it finely in a mortar, and mix it with the liquor it was boiled in; rub it through a sieve, and season it with salt.

BAKED CRUMBS OF BREAD.— Crumb some bread on a plate, put it a little distance from the fire to dry; when dry, rub the crumbs in a mortar, and reduce them to a fine powder; then pass them through a sieve. Having done which, put the crumbs of bread into a slow oven to bake until they be of a light fawn color. A small quantity of this baked crumb of bread must be made into food, in the same way as gruel is made, and should then be slightly sweetened with lump sugar.

BREAD PANADA.—Soak a few thin slices of stale, light, and well-baked bread in hot water, so as to form a pulp of suitable consistence. Simmer it gently, with some little addition of water from time to time as it thickens; then add two or three tablespoonfuls of warm milk, a little loaf sugar, and a few grains of salt. The objection to this bread-pap as commonly used, is, that nurses are sometimes apt to make it too thick.

FARINACEOUS FOODS WITH MILK.

BOUILLIE OF BAKED FLOUR.—Bake in a slow oven two ounces of flour until it is lightly colored. Take one tablespoonful and mix it smoothly with a quarter of a pint of cold water in a basin, while three-quarters of a pint of new milk is simmering. Mix gradually the hot milk with the baked flour and water; then pour into a saucepan, and simmer for ten minutes, stirring it so as to prevent any burning. Sweeten it moderately with loaf sugar, and add a few grains of salt.

BOUILLIE OF BOILED FLOUR.—Instead of baked flour, boiled flour may be used. It is prepared as follows: Tie up a pound of flour tightly in a linen cloth, and boil it for five hours. Peel off the outer rind. A tablespoonful of the inside must be finely grated, and used for bouillie, in the following man ner: Take of the grated boiled flour one tablespoonful, and mix smoothly with a little water in a basin. Then pour upon it, gradually, one pint of milk that has simmered, and mix all well together. Pour into a saucepan and boil gently for ten minutes, or rather longer. Add a few grains of salt and sweeten with loaf sugar.

GLYCERIN AND YELK OF EGG.—The Philadelphia *Journal of Pharmacy* has made known a formula for a preparation which is likely to prove valuable for external use. Four parts, by weight, of yelk of egg are to be rubbed in a mortar with five parts of glycerin. The compound has the consistence of honey, and is unctuous like fatty substances, over which it has the advantage of being easily removed by water. It is unalterable, a specimen having laid exposed to the air for three years unchanged. Applied to the skin, it forms a varnish which effectually prevents the action of air. These properties render it serviceable for broken surfaces of all kinds, particularly erysipelas and cutaneous affections, of which it allays the itching.

WINE WHEY.—Boil a pint of new milk, add to it a glass or two of white wine, put it on the fire until it just boils again, then set it aside until the curd settles, pour off the clean whey; sweeten to the taste. Cider is as good as wine to curdle, if it is good apple cider.

ARROWROOT PAP WITH MILK.—Put into a

saucepan, to boil, one pint of milk; stir very smoothly, into a cup of cold milk, a dessertspoonful of arrowroot; when the milk boils, stir in the arrowroot; continue to stir until it is cooked, which will be in five or ten minutes; remove from the fire, sweeten and flavor to the taste.

PORT WINE JELLY.—A pint of port wine, one ounce and a half of isinglass, three-quarters of an ounce of gum-arabic, four ounces and a half of powdered loaf sugar; stand it on the hob until dissolved; when cold it is fit for use.

ORANGE JELLY.—Grate the rind of two oranges and two lemons, squeeze the juice of three of each and strain, and add the juice of a quarter of a pound of lump sugar and a quarter of a pint of water, and boil till it almost candies. Have ready a quart of isinglass jelly made with two ounces; put to it the syrup and boil it once up; strain off the jelly, and let it stand to settle before it is put into the mould.

PORTER JELLY.—Half an ounce of isinglass to a quart of porter; put into the oven till dissolved; strain and sweeten to your taste. When cold it will jelly.

SAGO JELLY.—A teacupful of sago, boiled in three pints and a half of water till ready. When cold, add half a pint of raspberry syrup. Pour it into a shape which has been rinsed in cold water, and let it stand until it is sufficiently set to turn out well. When dished, pour a little cream round it, if preferred.

GELATINE.—This is prepared for jellies by soaking over night in very little water; allow one ounce for each quart of jelly. If the isinglass is not pure, it must be clarified. Mix, in half a pint of water, a teaspoonful of the white of egg and a little lemon-juice; beat well, and stir it into two ounces isinglass, which is dissolved in half a pint of water; heat these together gradually, constantly stirring; remove all the scum, and pass it through a flannel jelly-bag.

JELLY FROM GELATINE.—One ounce and a half of gelatine put over night into a pint of cold water, with the rinds and juice of three lemons. Next morning add a pint of boiling water, half a pint of sherry, the whites and shells of three eggs, and sweeten to your taste. Boil the whole ten minutes, and strain through a jelly-bag. This will make a quart of jelly. Be sure not to stir the mixture after it is placed on the fire. It is excellent.

CHAPTER XIII.

MISCELLANEOUS.

A BILL OF FARE.—Put the soup first; always eat the melon immediately after; then the fish; then butcher's meat—beef, next mutton, next veal and lamb; then poultry, and last of all game. A roasted fish is served after the roast beef. Vegetables *au sucré* are served after the other vegetables. Cheese is served before dessert. Tin-lined utensils for the kitchen are preferable to porcelain, because porcelain cracks so easily. Copper is the best, if kept perfectly clean. For boiling milk, block-tin is the best. Always use a stone mortar, not a wooden one, and have a sharp-pointed knife for boning meat or fish.

COLORING FOR GRAVIES AND RAGOUTS.—Take four ounces of sugar (moist), and set it over the fire in a clean stewpan or earthen pipkin. When the sugar is melted and looks frothy, raise it higher from the fire, that it may not burn; keep stirring it all the time till it is a fine brown; pour in some red wine, taking care it does not boil over, add a little salt, lemon, mace, and a few cloves; boil all up gently for ten minutes, and pour it into a basin. When cold, put it into a bottle well corked.

Rich Gravy.—Cut beef into thin slices, according to the quantity wanted; slice onions thin, and flour both; fry them of a light pale brown, but do not on any account suffer them to get black; put them into a stewpan, pour boiling water on the browning in the frying-pan, boil it up, and pour on the meat. Put to it a bunch of parsley, thyme, and savory, a small bit of knotted marjoram, the same of tarragon, some mace, allspice, whole black peppers, a clove or two, and a bit of ham, or slice of bacon. Simmer till you have extracted all the juice of the meat, and be sure to skim the moment it boils, and often after.

Meat or Fish Omelettes Generally.—Take cold meat, fish, game or poultry of any kind; remove all skin, sinew, etc., and either cut it small or pound it to a paste in a mortar, together with a proper proportion of spices and salt; then either toss it in a buttered frying-pan over a clear fire till it begins to brown, and pour beaten eggs upon it, or beat it up with the eggs, or spread it upon them after they have begun to set in the pan. In any case, serve hot, with or without a sauce, but garnished with crisp herbs in branches, or pickles, or sliced lemon. The right proportion is one tablespoonful of meat to four eggs. A little milk, gravy, water, or white wine, may be advantageously added to the eggs while they are being beaten.

Milk Toast.—Boil a pint of rich milk, and

then take it off, and stir into it a quarter of a pound of fresh butter, mixed with a small tablespoonful of flour. Then let it again come to boil. Have ready two deep plates with half a dozen slices of toast in each. Pour the milk over them hot, and keep them covered till they go to table. Milk toast is generally eaten at breakfast. The warming of the bread gradually through on both sides is a very great improvement upon the quality of the toast. All kinds of toast must be done the same way; but if to be served under a bird, eggs, or kidneys, it requires to be toasted drier. Dry toast should not be made until quite ready to serve; when done, place it in a toast rack, or upon its edges, one piece resting against another. Any kind of toast that has been made half an hour is not worth eating.

BREAKFAST DISH.—Two kidneys, one tablespoonful of flour, pepper and salt, half a teaspoonful of each, one tablespoonful of walnut catsup or walnut pickle juice, two tablespoonfuls of gravy, one round of buttered toast, half a glass of claret. Skin and cut the kidneys into fine, thin slices, and shake the flour well over them; place all the other ingredients, except the toast, in a saucepan, and let it boil gently for five minutes. Place it at the side of the fire till it ceases boiling, add the kidneys, and let it stew gently for ten minutes, but be sure it does not boil. Have the toast ready in a hot dish, pour it on the toast, and serve immediately.

SMALL EGG-BALLS TO SERVE WITH CALF'S HEAD.—Four eggs, a teaspoonful of flour, water. Boil three eggs for six minutes, take the yelks, and pound them in a mortar, add the flour and the yelk of the raw egg, beat all together till quite smooth, then roll the mixture into little balls, and throw them into boiling water for two minutes just before the dish is served, and strew them over the head.

GOOD MEAT CAKE.—Mince the lean of cold lamb or veal very finely; soak a large slice of bread in boiling milk; mash it, and mix it with the minced meat; also a beaten egg, some boiled chopped parsley and thyme, a little grated lemon peel, pepper and salt. Make it into small, flat cakes, and fry them in butter or lard. Serve them up dry, or with good gravy,

SUPERIOR MEAT PIES.—Take the meat of a good-sized, fat chicken (boiled); add to it half a pound of good boiled beef's tongue, quarter of a pound of fresh butter, pepper and salt to taste, and about a dozen good boiled potatoes, and four good-sized onions. Chop all these ingredients fine, make a good crust, and cover the bottom of your dish. Put the ingredients in, and cook or bake it well.

TO USE THE MEAT AND GRISTLE OF A SOUP BONE.—Cut all the gristle from the bone, boil until perfectly tender. If there is enough to serve for a dish, add vinegar, butter, pepper, and salt, and it will resemble souse; if not, mix the meat with it, fricassee brown, and add butter, salt, pepper, a dust of flour, and sufficient water to make the gravy, and serve with dry bread toasted. Lay the bread on the plate and pour over it the fricassee.

RISSOLES.—Chop the meat very fine; if mutton, a little parsley will be an improvement; season it, and rub some butter in. Make up the rissoles in the form of a sugar loaf, beat an egg and roll them in it, and then in bread crumbs, very fine, twice. Fry them a nice golden brown, and serve up with good gravy in the dish. *Or:* The meat must be chopped very fine. Take an equal quantity of bread crumbs, a tablespoonful of flour, a little allspice, salt, and half an onion, chopped very fine, indeed. First mix the bread crumbs, flour, and spice together, then mix the meat well with it, sprinkle the onion over, stir all well together, and stir in two tablespoonfuls of bacon fat, or a rasher or two of bacon, finely minced. Make the mixture into balls with a very little milk, press them flat, roll each in flour, and drop them one at a time into a saucepan of boiling dripping, frying each simply in this way. When brown, take it out with an egg-slice, let the fat drain from it, place it on a pad of paper before the fire, so as to become quite dry.

RISSOLES OF COLD MEAT.—To one pound of cold meat allow three-quarters of a pound of bread crumbs, salt and pepper, a tablespoonful of minced parsley, a little finely-chopped lemon-peel, and two eggs.

Mince the meat very fine; mix all together. Divide into balls or cones, nicely shaped. Put them into a pan of boiling lard; there must be enough lard to cover them. Fry the rissoles till they are a nice light brown. Serve with parsley for a garnish, or, if preferred, with gravy poured over them. Chicken or rabbit makes very delicious rissoles.

RISSABLES are made with veal and ham, chopped very fine, or pounded lightly; add a few bread crumbs, salt, pepper, nutmeg, and a little parsley and lemon-peel; mix all together with the yelks of eggs, well beaten; either roll them into shape like a flat sausage, or into the shape of pears, sticking a bit of horseradish in the ends to resemble the stalks. Egg each over, and grate bread crumbs. Fry them brown, and serve on crisp-fried parsley.

LARD.—Leaf lard is the nicest for all cooking purposes. Skim all the fat that is to be tried into lard, and commence by frying gently a little leaf lard, or your fat will scorch. Let it cool slowly, and dip off the fat as soon as it is liquified, and strain it through a cloth. When all is strained that can be dipped off, squeeze the remainder by itself in the cloth. If the lard is to be used for cooking, salt it a trifle when first put on. Much of the salt will be found at the bottom of the kettle undissolved, still it would seem to be better that salt should be used.

FORCEMEAT.—Half a pound of bread crumbs, a

tablespoonful of finely chopped parsley, a teaspoonful of sweet herbs, a little grated lemon-peel and nutmeg, seasoning of salt, pepper, and Cayenne, two ounces of beef suet, very finely chopped, and two eggs, a little beaten. Mix all together. The flavor of a little chopped lean ham or bacon is relished by some persons.

Forcemeat for Veal, Turkeys, Fowls, etc.—Two ounces of ham or bacon, quarter of a pound of suet, the rind of half a lemon, one teaspoonful of minced parsley, one teaspoonful of minced sweet herbs, salt, Cayenne, and pounded mace to taste, six ounces of bread crumbs, two eggs. Shred the ham or bacon, chop the suet, lemon-peel, and herbs, taking particular care that all be very finely minced; add a seasoning to taste, of salt, Cayenne, and mace, and blend all thoroughly together with the bread crumbs before wetting. Now beat and strain the eggs, work these up with the other ingredients, and the forcemeat will be ready for use. When it is made into balls, fry of a nice brown in boiling lard, or put them on a tin and bake for half an hour in a moderate oven. As we have stated before, no one flavor should predominate greatly, and the forcemeat should be of sufficient body to cut with a knife, and yet not dry and heavy. For very delicate forcemeat it is advisable to pound the ingredients together before binding with the egg; but for ordinary cooking, mincing very finely answers the purpose.

RAMAKINS.—Beat up well two eggs, and add two tablespoonfuls of flour, two ounces of warm butter, and two ounces of grated cheese. Mix all these well together, and bake them for a quarter of an hour in small boxes made of writing paper. They should be served hot in the paper boxes, and eaten after the game course. They require care in the preparation.

EGGS may be preserved by applying with a brush a solution of gum-Arabic to the shells, and afterwards packing them in dry charcoal dust.

FARM-HOUSE SYLLABUB.—Fill a china or earthenware bowl of any size nearly half full of cider (if sour, it is of no consequence), sweeten to the taste with coarse brown sugar, grate nutmeg and cinnamon to taste; then send the bowl out to the cow to be milked on till quite full of froth. A better syllabub for company is made of port wine and cider mixed (or port wine only), sweetened with white sugar, and spice to taste.

LAIT SUCRÉ.—Take one pint of milk, add loaf sugar, and flavor with lemon. Drink cold.

NUTMEGS.—Oil of nutmegs being of great value, it is often extracted from the nuts which are exposed to sale, and which are thereby rendered of very little value. To ascertain the quality of nutmegs, force a pin into them; and if good, however dry they may appear, the oil will be seen oozing out all round the pin from the compression occasioned in the surrounding parts.

ESSENCE OF NUTMEGS.—Dissolve one ounce of the rectified oil of nutmegs in one pint of rectified spirits of wine.

ESSENCE OF ROSE.—Take one ounce of ninety-five per cent. alcohol, and drop into it thirty drops of ottar of roses. Shake it up well, let it stand two days, when it is fit for use.

HOW TO MIX MUSTARD.—Mustard should be mixed with water that has been boiled and allowed to cool; hot water destroys its essential properties, and raw cold water might cause it to ferment. Put the mustard in a cup, with a small pinch of salt, and mix with it very gradually sufficient boiled water to make it drop from the spoon without being watery. Stir and mix well, and rub the lumps well down with the back of a spoon, as mustard properly mixed should be perfectly free from these. The mustard-pot should not be more than half full, or rather less, if it will not be used for a day or two, as the mustard is so much better when fresh made.

TO MAKE GOOD VINEGAR.—One pint of strained honey and two gallons of soft water. Let it stand in a moderately warm place. In three weeks it will be excellent vinegar.

EXCELLENT VINEGAR can be made without any cost at all, by simply putting your apple-peelings into a large stone jug, and filling the jug up with water. After leaving it quietly stand in some moderately warm place for about four or five weeks (always putting in the apple-peelings of every day), you will find that you have as good, or rather better vinegar than you can buy from any grocer, and which does not cost you one cent.

MINT VINEGAR.—Put into a wide-mouthed bottle fresh, nice, clean mint leaves, enough to fill it loosely; then fill up the bottle with good vinegar, and after it has been stopped close for two or three weeks, it is to be poured off clean into another bottle, and kept well corked for use. Serve with lamb when mint cannot be obtained.

CAYENNE VINEGAR.—Half an ounce of Cayenne pepper, half a pint of strong spirit, or one pint of vinegar. Put the vinegar or spirit, into a bottle, with the above proportion of Cayenne, and let it steep for a month; then strain off and bottle for use. This is an excellent seasoning for all kinds of soups and sauces, but must be used very sparingly.

QUAJADA.—Make a large pan of curds and whey or sour milk; cut a piece of rennet the size of a dinner-plate, put it in a stone crock, pour over it all the whey, and add a large handful of salt; set it behind the stove all night. Next morning, pour this whey slowly through a sieve into four or five quarts of milk; leave it until it thickens; then, with the open hands, gently press the curd down without breaking until it separates from the water.

Take a napkin and gently place the curd in it, double it squarely, and tie tightly in a cross tie. Hang this to drain all night. It will be fit for use the next day, and is to be served with preserved fruit.

TOAD IN THE HOLE.—Six ounces of flour, one pint of milk, three eggs, butter, a few slices of cold mutton, pepper and salt to taste, and two kidneys. Make a smooth batter of flour, milk, and eggs in the above proportion; butter a baking-dish and pour in the batter. Into this put the mutton, well seasoned, and the kidneys cut into small pieces. Bake one hour, and serve in the baking-dish. Oysters may be substituted for the kidneys.

A RELISH.—Put bread crumbs into a saucepan with cream, salt, and pepper; when the bread has absorbed the cream or milk, break in a few eggs, and fry as omelette.

PIKELETS.—Take three pounds of flour; make a hole in the middle with your hand. Mix two spoonfuls of yeast with a little salt and as much milk as will make the flour into a light paste. Pour the milk, with the yeast, into the middle of the flour, and stir a little of the flour down into it; then let it stand all night, and the next morning work in all the flour; beat it well for a quarter of an hour; let it stand for an hour; take it out with a large spoon, lay it in round cakes on a board, well dusted with flour; dredge flour over them, pat them with your hand, and bake them.

CHEESIKINS.—Quarter pound of stale bread, quarter pound of cheese, two ounces of butter, two eggs, a teaspoonful of mustard flour, half teaspoonful of pepper, a few grains of Cayenne. Rub the bread into fine crumbs, grate the cheese, melt the butter, and mix with the rest of the ingredients, and the eggs, which should be previously beaten. Let the mixture stand for about an hour, and then knead it into a paste, roll it out very thin, cut into small pieces, and bake in a quick oven. Time, about fifteen or sixteen minutes.

A GERMAN ENTREMET.—Boil eight eggs quite hard, and when cold cut them in two lengthwise. Take the yelks out very carefully, pass them through a fine sieve, and mix them well with half a pint of cream, (or more, if required,) and then add pepper, salt, and herbs. Pour this sauce into a very flat pie-dish that will stand heat, and place the white half eggs carefully in it, arranging them in the form of a star, or any other pattern preferred. Fill up the vacancy left in them by the yelks having been removed, with the same mixture, and strew a few bread crumbs over them. Bake this very slightly, just enough to give it a bright yellow color, and serve it up in the dish in which it has been baked.

GRAVY FOR FOWLS, OR OTHER DELICATE DISHES.—Take half a pound of lean beef, slice and score it, and a piece of butter the size of a nutmeg. Sprinkle it with flour, add a small onion, then put it all into a stewpan; stir it round over the fire for ten minutes, then pour into it one pint of boiling water; skim it carefully; let it all boil together for five minutes; strain it, and it is ready.

To Keep Sausage Fresh all the Year.—Make into cakes, and fry as if for present use; pack in stone jars, and if the grease that fries out of the meat is not sufficient to cover it, pour over hot lard so as to cover it, and entirely exclude the air.

Rolled Patties from Remains of Meat.—The remains of roast veal, or any roast meat, is chopped very fine with fat or ham, adding to it a little nutmeg, salt, and butter, some eggs, parsley, and chopped shalots. Stir this over the fire till thick enough for stuffing; fill some rolls with this, and bake as the patties for field-fare.

CULINARY COUPLETS.

BY A RHYMING EPICURE.

Always have lobster sauce with salmon,
And put mint sauce your roasted lamb on.

Veal cutlets dip in egg and bread crumb—
Fry till you see a brownish red come.

Grate Gruyere cheese on macaroni;
Make the top crisp, but not too bony.

In venison gravy, currant jelly
Mix with old port—see Francatelli.

In dressing salad, mind this law—
With two hard yelks use one that's raw.

Roast veal with rich stock gravy serve;
And pickled mushrooms, too, observe.

Roast pork, sans apple sauce, past doubt,
Is " Hamlet" with the Prince left out.

Your mutton-chops with paper cover,
And make them amber brown all over.

Broil lightly your beefsteaks—to fry it
Argues contempt of Christian diet.

Kidneys a finer flavor gain
By stewing them in good champagne.

Buy stall-fed pigeons. When you've got them,
The way to cook them is to pot them.

Woodgrouse are dry when gumps have marred 'em—
Before you roast 'em always lard 'em.

To roast spring chickens is to spoil 'em—
Just split 'em down the back and broil 'em.

It gives true epicures the vapors
To see boiled mutton, minus capers.

Boiled turkey, gourmands know, of course,
Is exquisite with celery sauce.

The cook deserves a hearty cuffing
Who serves roast fowls with tasteless stuffing.

Smelts require egg and biscuit powder.
Don't put fat pork in your clam chowder.

Egg sauce—few make it right, alas!
Is good with blue-fish or with bass.

Nice oyster sauce gives zest to cod—
A fish, when fresh, to feast a god.

Shad, stuffed and baked, is most delicious—
'Twould have electrified Apicius.

Roasted in paste, a haunch of mutton,
Might make ascetics play the glutton.

But one might rhyme for weeks this way,
And still have lots of things to say.

And so I'll close—for, reader mine,
This is about the hour I dine.

CHAPTER XIV.

PROPORTIONATE WEIGHTS AND MEASURES.

1 lb. of Butter equals 1 quart.
1 lb. of Loaf Sugar equals 1 quart.
1 lb. of Flour equals 1 quart.
1 lb. 2 oz. of Indian Meals equals 1 quart.
1 lb. 2 oz. of Brown Sugar equals 1 quart.
1 lb. 1 oz. of Powdered Sugar equals 1 quart.
1 tablespoonful of Salt equals 1 ounce.
10 unbroken hen eggs equals 1 lb.
A teaspoon contains about 20 drops of a liquid.
A wineglass contains about 4 tablespoonfuls.
A so-called quart bottle contains about a pint and a half.
One gallon equals half a peck.
Sixteen tablespoonfuls equals half a pint.

ALPHABETICAL INDEX.

Abernethy biscuit, 321.
A bill of fare, 414.
A dish of snow, 271.
Agrag, 403.
A la mode, beef, 80.
Almond biscuit, 359.
    cake, 348.
    cake, bitter, 351.
    cake, sweet, 349.
    cup cake, 349.
    custard cake, 373.
    jelly cake, 346.
    peppernuts, 339.
    pudding, 219.
    tart, 241.
Angel's food, 263.
Apple and quince jelly, 293.
    a delicious dish, 267.
    cake, 352.
    Charlotte, 266.
    cheesecake, 354.
    cheesecakes, 270.
    crab, jam, 295.
    cream, 247.
    custard, 257.
    float, 268.
    floating island, 269.
    in jelly, 268.
    island, 269.
    jam, 294.
    jelly, 293.
    marmalade, 295.
    pique, 270.
    preserve, 295.
    puff, 237.
    pudding, boiled, 199.
        baked, 200.
        rich and sweet, 200.

Apple roll, 201.
    snow, 269.
    soufflé, 268.
Apricot jam, 277.
A relish, 424.
Army cake, 346.
Arrowroot biscuit, 353.
    pap with milk, 411.
    pudding 212.
Artichokes, fried, 171.
    pickled, 68.
Ash cake, 375.
Asparagus, 175.
    omelette, 177.
    soup, 177.
    stewed, 176.
    toast, 177.
Aunt Harriet's pie, 235.

Bachelor buttons, 363.
Bacon and veal patties, 114.
    omelette, 307.
Bake a large fish whole, to, 35.
Baked apple pudding, 200.
    chicken in rice, 133.
    crumbs of bread, 409.
    flour and beef tea, 407.
    flour bouillie, 410.
    ham, 122.
    lemon pudding, 205.
    minced mutton, 97.
    potatoes, 147.
    sponge pudding, 204.
    tomatoes, 165.
    turkey, No. 1, 129.
        No. 2, 130.
Baking sweet cakes, hints for, 330.
Balls, beef, 84.
    codfish, 40.

ALPHABETICAL INDEX.

Balls, corn, 161.
    corned beef, hashed, 84.
    small egg, with calf's head, 417.
Bananas, fried, 169.
Barbara's plum pudding, 196.
Barley lemonade, 393.
    orangeade, 393.
Bath buns, 335.
Batter, oyster patties in, 45.
    potatoes fried in, 156.
    pudding, boiled, 216.
Beans, boiled, 168.
    cooked in French style, 167.
    string, 167.
        for winter use, 166
        to pickle, 61.
Beef à la mode, 80.
    balls, 84.
    brisket stuffed, 80.
Beef, cakes, No. 1, 89.
        No. 2, 89.
    corned, boiled, 85.
        hash, 85.
        hash balls, 84.
        mock venison, 84.
    croquettes, 89.
    cutlets, 81.
    fillet of, 82.
    fillet, with mushrooms, 81.
    minced, 83.
    pickling, 86.
    pie, English, 82.
    potted, 88.
    roasted, Yorkshire pudding, 85.
    rump of, 79.
    soup, 21.
        plain, 21.
    stewed, 79.
    stewed with onions, 80.
    tea, 406.
    tea and baked flour, 407.
Beefsteak pie, 83.
    pudding, 83.
    smothered in onions, 83.
Beer, ginger, 402.
    common, 402.
    powders, 403.
Beet-root, to pickle, 64.

Beets, boiled, 175.
Belsize tomato sauce, 50.
Berwick sponge cake, 369.
Beverage, cooling summer, 401.
Bibavoe, 252.
Biddle pudding, 225.
Bill of fare, 414.
Bird's nest pudding, 224.
Birds, potted, 142.
Birthday pudding, 225.
Biscuit, abernethy, 321.
    almond, 359.
    arrowroot, 353.
    butter, 319.
    cakes, 319.
    cream, No. 1, 319.
    cream, No. 2, 370.
    German cream, 319.
    ginger, 339.
    Graham, 313.
    judge's, 321.
    light, 318.
    milk, 320.
    No. 1, 318.
    No. 2, 359.
    potato, 320.
    pudding, 213.
    Queen's, 364.
    rock, 358.
    rough, 359.
    soda, 320.
    sour cream, 320.
    sponge, 368.
    sweet, 360.
    wine, 358.
Bisque of lobster, 32.
Bitter almond cake, 351.
Blackberries, 279.
Blackberry cakes, 355.
    cordial, 404.
    jelly, 278.
    pudding, 218.
Black cake, 353.
Black currant jam, 290.
    jelly, 290.
    tart, 240.
Blanc mange, 254.
    chocolate, 255.
    cornstarch, 255.
    tapioca, 254.
Boiled apple pudding, 199.
    batter pudding, 216.

ALPHABETICAL INDEX. 433

Boiled beans, 168.
    beets, 175.
    breast of lamb, 100.
    cabbage with meat, 179.
    cauliflower, 159.
    corned beef, 85.
    fig pudding, 204.
    fillet of veal, 110.
    flour bouillie, 410.
    Indian pudding, 212.
    leg of lamb, 102.
    onions, 173.
    partridges, 135.
    peas, 178.
    potatoes, 145.
    raisin pudding, 205.
    spinach, 172.
    suet pudding, 211.
Boned quarter of lamb, 102.
Bordeaux cake, 344.
Boston cake, 364.
Bottling cherries, 288.
Bouillie of baked flour, 410.
    boiled flour, 410.
Brandy peaches, 291.
Bread, 309.
    and butter pudding, 223.
    and rolls, 309.
    brown, 312.
    corn, 312.
    corn, common, 315.
    cornmeal, 313.
    Scottish short, 316.
    ginger, 339.
    Graham, 314.
        loaf, 313.
    homemade, 311.
    Indian corn, 315.
    Italian, 314.
    light corn, 312.
    panada, 410.
    potato, No. 1, 311.
        No. 2, 315.
    premium rye, 312.
    pudding, 222.
        brown, 222.
        simple, 222.
    receipt, 310.
    rice, 312.
    sauce, 55.
    Scotch short, 315.
    short, 316.

Bread, wheaten, 310.
Breaded veal chops, 109.
Breakfast buttermilk cakes, 325.
    dish, 416.
    French rolls, 328.
    fried cakes, 326.
    hominy cakes, 326.
    Johnny cake, 326.
    light rolls, 328.
    puffs, 327.
    soda cakes, 327.
    short cakes, 325.
    Sally Lunn, 328.
    tomatoes, 165.
    Virginia cakes, 327.
    Waffles, 326.
Breast of lamb, boiled, 100.
    stewed, 99.
    with peas or cucumbers, 103.
Breast, loin and neck of lamb, 101.
    of veal, oyster sauce, 110.
Bride cake, 358.
Brighton pudding, 207.
Brisket of beef stuffed, 80.
Broiled chicken, 131.
    eggs, 304.
    lamb steak, 101.
    mushrooms, 181.
    mutton kidneys, 106.
    parsnips, 168.
    partridges, 134.
    porksteak, 120.
    potatoes, 146.
    tomatoes, 163.
Broma, 380.
Broth, chicken, 26.
    mutton, 22.
Brown chicken soup, 26.
    eggs, 304.
Browned minced mutton, 98.
    potatoes, 152.
    tomatoes, 164.
Browning, 53.
Bubble and squeak, 88.
Buu, bath, 335.
    fritters, 260.
    ground rice, 335.
    loaf, 373.
    rich, 335.
    Spanish, 335.

Bun, Spanish, excellent, 335.
Buns, 334.
Burnt sugar, 263.
Butter and parsley, 171.
    chocolate, 263.
    cookies, 357.
    curled, 297.
    making, 296.
    rancid, to restore, 297.
    that threatens to turn rancid, 296.
    to preserve, 297.
Buttered eggs, 307.
    onions, 173.
    orange-juice, 266.
Buttermilk breakfast cakes, 325.
    cheese, 300.

Cabbage boiled with meat, 179.
    cold, 180.
    jelly, 181.
    red, stewed, 180.
        pickled, 68.
        to pickle, 62.
    stewed, No. 1, 180.
        No. 2, 181.
    to pickle a good color, 63.
Café au lait, 382.
    noir, 382.
Cakes, almond, 348.
        cup, 349.
        jelly, 346.
        sweet, 349.
    apple, 352.
    apple cheese, 270.
    army, 346.
    beef, No. 1, 89.
        No. 2, 89.
    Berwick sponge, 369.
    biscuit, 319.
    bitter almond, 351.
    black, 353.
    blackberry, 355.
    Bordeaux, 344.
    breakfast, Johnny, 326.
        short, 325.
    bride, 358.
    buttermilk breakfast, 325.
    caraway, 350.
    cheap, 338.
    cheese, 299.
    children's, 336.

Cakes, chocolate, 362.
        drop, 363.
        paste, 363.
    Christmas, 345.
    citron cheese, 355.
    Clay, 343.
    cocoanut, 361.
    cocoanut cheese, **355.**
    cocoanut loaf, 362.
    coffee, 327.
    Congress, 367.
    Connecticut loaf, 343.
    corn, 323.
    cornstarch, 337.
    cream, 370.
    cup, 351.
    Derby short, 366.
    Dutch, 366.
    egg cheese, 306.
    fine sponge, 369.
    fish, 40.
    for dessert, 266.
    French, 338.
    French cream, 369.
        tea, 328.
    fried breakfast, 326.
    frosted loaf, 350.
    fruit, 347.
        good, 347.
        molasses, 347.
        soda, 347.
        without eggs, 347.
    German sponge, 367.
        tea, 329.
    ginger sponge, 342.
        loaf, 342.
    good boy's, 351.
    good plain, 337.
    grated cocoanut, 361.
    green corn, 323.
    ground rice, 357.
    hints for making and baking sweet, 330.
    hominy breakfast, 326.
    Indian, 322.
    Jefferson, 354.
    jelly, 346.
    Jenny Lind, 354.
    Johnny, 322.
    Josephine, 354.
    love, 334.
    loaf, children's, **338.**

ALPHABETICAL INDEX. 435

Cakes, lemon, 330, 341.
    cheese, 341.
    drop, 340.
    superior, 340.
  marble, 353.
  Maximillian, 350.
  medley, 367.
  molasses cup, 336.
    drop, 336.
  navy, 346.
  New England loaf, 343.
  orange cheese, 341.
  Pennsylvania tea, 329.
  pippin, 352.
  plain tea, 329.
  plum, pound, and bride, 332.
  pudding, 214.
  pound, 348.
    rice, 348.
  prune, 356.
  Queen, 366.
  railroad, 354.
  rice, 323.
  rock, 334.
  rose water, 346.
  rye drop, 337.
  sandwiches, 361.
  sausage, 125.
  savory potato, 157.
  school, 352.
  seed, 349.
  short, 322.
  simple tea, 330.
  soda, 323.
  soda, 337.
  sponge, 368.
  sponge, for dessert, 270.
  Stevens, 351.
  sugar, 352.
  superior sponge, 369.
    tea, 329.
  tea, 328.
  traveller's, 351.
  vegetable oyster, 175.
  Virginia breakfast, 327.
  white cocoanut, 362.
  yule-tide, 345.
Cake, almond custard, 373.
  ash, 375.
  Boston, 364.
  chocolate paste, 363.

Cake, currant loaf, 363.
  fine icing for, 375.
  French, 373.
  German cornucopia, 371.
  gold, 364.
  good meat, 417.
  honey, 373.
  lady, 372.
  Lincoln, 364.
  luncheon, 372.
  Molly's, 372.
  mountain, 375.
  Mrs. W.'s snow, 365.
  princess, 363.
  raisin, 374.
  Scotch, 366.
  silver, 365.
  snow, 365.
  Swiss, 372.
  Trafalgar, 374.
  Washington, 371.
    pie, 371.
  white, 365.
  White Mountain, 375.
  wine, 374.
Caledonian cream 245.
Calf's feet potted, 143.
  head, 109.
    collared, 112.
    hashed, 111.
    soup, 25.
Canned blackberries, 291.
  corn, 161.
  peaches, 291.
  raspberries, 291.
  vegetables, 291.
Caper sauce and onions, 174.
Capillaire, 400.
Caraway cake, 350.
Carolina chow-chow, 65.
  rice, 166.
Caromel, 262.
  chocolate, 262.
  pudding, 206.
Carrots, 170.
  fritters, 170.
  pudding, 215.
  soup, 27.
Cassandra pudding, 207.
Catsup, cold, 78.
  pepper, 78.
  tomato, No. 1, 70.

Catsup, tomato, No. 2, 70.
Cauliflower, 157.
    boiled, 159.
    fried, 160.
    in milk, 160.
    omelette, 160.
Celery essence, 174.
    fried, 174.
    preserve, 275.
    sauce, 57.
    stewed, 174.
Charlotte apple, 266.
    de Russe, 265.
    jam or marmalade, 265.
    Russe, 264.
        chocolate, 264.
Cheap cake, 338.
Cheese Biscuit, 299.
    buttermilk, 300.
    cake, apple, 270.
        citron, 355.
        cocoanut, 355.
    cakes, 299.
        egg, 306.
        lemon, 341.
        orange, 341.
    cream, 301.
    pineapple, 298.
    potato, 298.
    potted, 300.
    straws, 300.
Cheesikins, 425.
Cherry and currant tart, 240.
    bottled, 288.
    fool, 288.
    fritters, 261.
    jam, 289.
    marmalade, 288.
    morello syrup, 388.
    preserve, 287.
    spiced, 288.
Chicken and roast veal soup, 34.
    baked in rice, 133.
    broth, 26.
    cold, fried, 132.
    panada, 409.
    pot-pie, 132.
    puffs, 133.
    salad, 186.
    small, to fricassee, 131.
    soup, brown, 26.
    to broil, 131.

Children's cake, 336.
    loaf cake, 338.
Chinese rice, 165.
Chips, potato, 146.
Chocolate a la Francaise, 379.
    blanc mange, 255.
    butter, 263.
    cake, 362.
    caromel, 262.
    Charlotte Russe, 264.
    cream, 245.
    cream custard pudding, 221.
    pudding, 216.
    to make good, 379.
Choice fowl pudding, 128.
Chops, pork, 119.
    veal, breaded, 109.
    with cucumbers, 105.
Chow-chow, 66.
    Carolina, 65.
    old Virginia, 66.
    pickle, 66.
Chowder, New England, 31.
Christmas cake, 345.
    plum pudding, 198.
    pudding, 195.
Chutney, 52.
Citron cheesecakes, 355.
    preserve, 276.
    pudding, 219.
Clam fritters, 45.
Clara's sponge pudding, 204.
Clay cake, 343.
Clear gravy soup, 28.
Cloves, syrup of, 389.
Cocoa shells, 380.
Cocoanut cake, 361.
    grated, 361.
    cheesecakes, 355.
    jumbles, 356.
    loaf cake, 362.
    pudding, 201.
        cup, 202.
        custard, 202.
        fine, 201.
Codfish balls, 40.
    fried, 36.
    picked up, 39.
Crackers, Graham, 313.
    pies, 234.
    soda pies, **234.**

ALPHABETICAL INDEX. 437

Cod sounds, 40.
Coffee and its preparation, 380.
Coffee, concentrated, 385.
    good, 384.
Cold cabbage, 180.
    catsup, 78.
    chicken, fried, 132.
    cup pudding, 215.
    meat rissoles, 418.
    mutton, 94.
    slaw, 180.
        dressing for, 180.
Coloring for gravies, 414.
Common corn bread, 315.
    ginger beer, 402.
Compote aux confitures, 259.
Congress cake, 367.
Connecticut loaf cake, 343.
Cookies, 357.
    butter, 357.
    good, 357.
Cooling summer beverage, 401.
Corn balls, 161.
    bread, 312.
        common, 315.
        light, 312.
    cake, 323.
    fritters, 163.
    green, cake, 323.
        dumplings, 163
        pudding, 215.
    Indian, bread, 315.
    in cans, 161.
    meal bread, 313.
        muffins, 325.
        pudding, 212.
    oysters, 161.
    porridge, 161.
Corned beef balls, hashed, 84.
    boiled, 85.
    hash, 85.
    mock venison, 84.
Cornstarch blanc mange, 255.
    cakes, 337.
    pie, 238.
Cornucopia cake, German, 371.
Cottage plum pudding, 197.
    pudding, 193.
Cough, flaxseed jelly, for, 407.
Couplets, culinary, 426.
Crab apple jam, 295.
Crabs, boiled, 45.

Crackers, Graham, 313.
    pies, 234.
    soda pies, 234.
Cranberry tart, 239.
Cream, apple, 247.
    biscuit, German, 319.
        No. 1, 319.
        No. 2, 370.
        sour, 320.
    cake, 370.
    Caledonian, 245.
    cheese, 301.
    chocolate, 245.
    custard chocolate pudding, 221.
    custard pie, 238.
    French, 246.
    Italian, 247.
    lemon, 248.
    Madeira, 247.
    orange, 245.
    pancakes, 258.
    pie, 238.
    pudding, 220.
    raspberry tart, 240.
    Scotch, 245.
    Spanish, 248.
    snow, 246.
    velvet, 246.
    Washington pie, 259.
Creamed potatoes, 156.
Croquettes, beef, 89.
    potato, 155.
    veal, 115.
Crullers, 344.
Crumbed oysters, 43.
Crumb pudding, 214.
Crumbs of bread baked, 409.
Crumpets, 324.
Crust for meat pies, 233.
    raised pies, 233.
    savory pies, 232.
Cucumbers, ripe, pickled, 70.
    green, " 71.
    salad, 184.
Culinary couplets, 426.
Cup cake, 351.
    molasses, 336.
Curled butter, 297.
Cured hams, 122.
Cured quails in oil, 136.
Currant and cherry tart, 240.

ALPHABETICAL INDEX.

Currant and suet dumplings, 256.
    jam, 290.
        black, 290.
    jelly, 289.
        lemon, 289.
        black, 290
    loaf cake, 363.
    pudding, 218.
    syrup, 388.
    tart, black, 240.
Curry of veal, 108.
Custard, almond, cake, 373.
    and whey, 253.
    apple, 257.
    chococolate cream, pudding, 221.
    cream pie, 238.
    French, 258.
    fritters, 260.
    lemon tart, 237.
    orange, 258.
    solid, 257.
Cutlets, beef, 81.
    fowl, 127.
    lamb and spinach, 101.
    mutton, 90.
        à la bene, 92.
    parsnip, 168.
    pork, 120.
    veal, with ragout, 110.
        sweet herbs, 108.

Delicate dessert, 252.
Delicious dish of apples, 267.
Derby shortcake, 366.
Dessert, cakes for, 266.
    delicate, 252.
    sponge cake for, 270.
Dinner rolls, 317.
Directions for preserving fruit, 273.
Dish, breakfast, 416.
    of apples, delicious, 267.
    of macaroni, sweet, 251.
Doughnuts, 341.
    old-fashioned, 343.
Dress, kidneys, to, 105.
Dressing for salad, 184.
    Italian, 185.
    Swiss, 187.
Dressing for salad without oil, 184.

Dried mushrooms, 182.
    strawberries, 282.
Drop cake, chocolate, 363.
    lemon, 340.
    rye, 337.
Drops, sugar, 271.
Duck, wild, 137.
    sauce for, 56.
Dumplings, egg, 305.
    green corn, 163.
    Oxford, 257.
    sausage, 125.
    suet, 257.
    and currants, 256.
Dutch cake, 366.

Eau sucré, 403.
Economical pudding, 210.
    stock for soup, 20.
    veal soup, 23.
Eels, fried, 37.
Egg balls, 303.
    small, to serve with calf's head, 417.
    cheesecakes, 306.
    dumplings, 305.
    omelette, 307.
    plant, 175.
    puffs, 237.
    sandwiches, 306.
    sauce, sweet, 60.
    yelk of, with glycerine, 411.
Eggs à l'Ardennaise, 303.
    à l'Aurore, 303.
    boiled, 302.
    broiled, 304.
    brown, 304.
    buttered, 307.
    how to cook and serve, 302.
    minced, 304.
    pickled, No. 1, 71.
        No. 2, 72.
    poached, with minced veal, 113.
    preserved, 306.
    rumbled, 305.
    sur le plat, 302.
    to keep, 421.
Elegant fritters, 261.
England chowder, New, 31.
English beef pie, 82.
    raised pork pie, 121.

ALPHABETICAL INDEX.

Essence of celery, 174.
    nutmeg, 422.
    rose, 422.
Excellent lemon pudding, 203.
    portable lemonade, 391.
Excellent Spanish bun, 335.
    vinegar, 422.

Family pudding, 210.
Fare, a bill of, 414.
Farmers' pie, 234.
    pudding, 209.
Farmhouse syllabub, 421.
Fig pudding, 204.
    boiled, 204.
Fillet of beef, 82.
    and mushrooms, 81.
    veal, boiled, 110.
Fine flour panada, 409.
    icing for cake, 375.
    sponge cake, 369.
Fish and meat omelettes, 415
    balls, 40.
    cakes, 40.
    cod, picked up, 39.
    to fry, 36.
    large, to bake whole, 35.
    potted, 139.
    rock, 35.
    salt, 38.
    with parsnips, 39.
    sauce, 54.
    stuffed, 35.
    to pickle, 37.
Flaked onions, 173.
Flaky crust, 229.
Flaxseed jelly, for a cough, 407.
Float, apple, 268.
Floating island, 253.
    apple, 269.
    fine, 253.
Floats, 254.
Florentines, 244.
Flottkrengel, German, 252.
Flour, bouillie of baked, 410.
    boiled, 410.
Flummery, lemon, 249.
Food, angel's, 263.
Fool, cherry or strawberry, 288.
    raspberry, 275.
Forcemeat, 419.

Forcemeat, for veal, turkey, and fowls, 420.
    oyster, 44.
    veal, 115.
Fortunatus pudding, 220.
Fowl cutlets, 127.
    pudding, choice, 128.
Fowls, sauce for, 55.
    steamed, 127.
    stewed with onions, 127.
    to bake, 129.
    bone, for fricassee, 128.
    prepare, for cooking, 126.
    roast, 128.
French breakfast rolls, 328.
    cakes, No. 1, 338.
    No. 2, 373.
    cream, 246.
    cake, 369.
    crust for raised pies, 233.
    custard, 258.
    island, 254.
    jumbles, 356.
    mashed potatoes, 157.
    rolls, 317.
    tea cakes, 328.
Fresh pork pie, 119.
Friar's omelette, 263.
Fricassee of lamb, 102.
    veal, 108.
    parsnip, 169.
    small chickens, 131.
    to bone fowls for, 128.
    white, 132.
Fried artichokes, 171.
    bananas, 169.
    breakfast cakes, 326.
    cauliflower, 160.
    celery, 174.
    codfish, 36.
    cold chicken, 132.
    eels, 37.
    halibut, 37.
    patties, 114.
    partridge, 136.
    plantain, 169.
    potatoes, 149.
    in batter, 156.
Fried sheep kidneys, 106.
    sweetbreads, 117.
    trout, 36.

Fritters, apple, 260.
    bun, 260.
    carrot, 170.
    cherry, 261.
    clam, 45.
    corn, 163.
    custard, 260.
    elegant, 261.
    parsnip, No. 1, 168.
        No. 2, 169.
    potato, 152.
    pork and apple, 120.
    spiced, sugar for, 256.
    tomato, 164.
Fruit cake, 347.
    good, 347.
    molasses, 347.
    soda, 347.
    without eggs, 347.
    directions to preserve, 273.
    raised pudding, 206.
    syrups, 386.
    vinegars, 394.
        mixed, 397.

Game, to keep, 137.
Garnish and vegetables for roast lamb, 99.
Gateau de pommes, 268, 352.
Gelatine, 413.
    jelly, 413.
German cornucopia cake, 371.
    cream biscuit, 319.
    entremet, 425.
    flottkrengel 252.
    lady fingers, 360.
    pudding, 223.
    puffs, 235.
    receipt for oyster powder, 43.
    sponge cake, 367.
    tea cakes, 329.
    waffles, 324.
Gherkins, 69.
Giblet pie, 130.
    sauce, 56.
Ginger beer, 402.
    common, 402.
    powders, 403.
    biscuit, 339.
    bread, 339.
        soft, 338.

Ginger bread, thick, 338.
    jumbles, 343.
    loaf cake, 342.
    pop, 402.
    snaps, 339.
    sponge cake, 342.
    wine, 399.
Glycerine and yelk of egg, 411.
Gold cake, 364.
Golden pudding, 207.
Good coffee, 384.
    meat cake, 417.
    plain cake, 337.
    soup stock, 19.
Gooseberrries, green, to bottle, 280.
Gooseberry and raspberry jelly, 281.
    jam, green, 282.
        red, 281.
        white, 282.
    jelly, 281.
    pudding, 218.
    syrup, 388.
    vinegar, 396.
Goose, boiled, 133.
Graham biscuit, 313.
    bread, 314.
    crackers, 313.
    loaf, 313.
Grandmamma's pudding, 226.
Grated cocoanut cake, 361.
Gravy, clear, soup, 28.
    coloring for, 414.
    for fowls, 425.
    rich, 415.
    veal, soup, 24.
Gray pudding, 193.
Green corn cake, 323.
    dumplings, 163.
    cucumber pickle, 71.
    currant pudding, 218.
    gooseberries, bottled, 280.
    gooseberry jam, 282.
    mint sauce, 57.
    peas, 178.
Greengages, 280.
Greengage jam, 279.
    tart, 242.
Gristle and meat of soup bone, to use, 417.
Ground rice buns 335.

ALPHABETICAL INDEX. 441

Ground rice cake, 357.
Gumbo, 29.
    or okra soup, 30.
    soup, southern, 30.

Half-pay pudding, 192.
Halibut, to fry, 37.
Ham omelette, 123.
    pie, 122.
    toast, 123.
    tongue or sausage omelette, 123.
Hams, to bake, 122.
    cure, 122.
Hashed calf's head, 111.
    corned beef, 85.
Hash balls of corned beef, 84.
Hedge pears, to preserve, 278.
Herring, to pickle, 38.
Hints for making and baking sweet cakes, 330.
Homemade bread, 311.
    yeast, 377.
Hominy breakfast cakes, 326.
Honey cakes, 373.
Honeycomb, lemon, 251.
Horseradish sauce, 58.
Hops and potato yeast, 378.
Hot icing, 376.
    slaw, 181.
How to cook and serve eggs, 302.
    make soups, 17.
    mix mustard, 422.

Ice creams, 271.
Iced lemon pudding, 203.
Ice pudding, 192.
Icing for cakes, 375.
    hot, 376.
    pastry, 232.
Imitation of mock turtle soup, 23.
Imperial, 400.
    pop, 400.
Indian cake, 322.
    corn bread, 315.
    meal pudding, 213.
    pudding, boiled, 212
India pickle, 67.
Island, apple, 269.
    floating, 253.
    floating, apple, 269.
    fine, 253.

Island, French, 254.
Italian bread, 314.
    cream, 247.
    salad dressing, 185.

Jam, apple, 294.
    apricot, 277.
    black currant, 290.
    cherry, 289.
        marmalade, 288.
        or strawberry, 289.
    crab apple, 295.
    greengage, 279.
    green gooseberry, 282.
    or marmalade charlotte, 265.
    peach, 275.
    raspberry, 275.
    red gooseberry, 281.
    rhubarb, 286.
    strawberry, 283.
    white gooseberry, 282.
Jefferson cake, 354.
Jelly, almond, cake, 346.
    apple, 293.
    in, 268.
    blackberry, 278.
    black currant, 290.
    cabbage, 181.
    cake, 346.
    currant, 289.
    flaxseed, for a cough, 407.
    from gelatine, 413.
    gooseberry, 281.
        and raspberry, 281.
    orange, 412.
    pineapple, 285.
    porter, 412.
    port wine, 412.
    sago, 412.
    strawberry, 283.
    quince, 292.
        and apple, 293.
Jenny Lind cake, 354.
Johnny cake, 322.
    breakfast, 326.
Josephine cake, 354.
Judge's biscuit, 321.
Juice of orange, buttered, 266.
Jumbles, cocoanut, 356.
    French, 356.
    No. 1, 356.

Jumbles, No. 2, 374.
    soft, 356.
Jury pie, 154.

Kedjeree, 41.
Keeping eggs, 421.
    game, 137.
    sausages fresh, 426.
Kidney omelette à la brochette, 107.
    No. 1, 106.
    No. 2, 307.
Kidneys, mutton, broiled, 106.
    sheep, fried, 106.
    to dress, 105.
Knep and snitz, 261.

Ladies' fingers, 360.
Lady cake, 372.
    fingers, 360.
        German, 360.
Lait de poule, 303.
    sucré, 421.
Lamb, boned quarter of, 102.
    breast, stewed with peas or cucumbers, 103.
    or neck, to boil, 101.
    to stew, 99.
    broiled steak, 101.
    chops, 100.
    cutlets and spinach, 101.
    forequarter of, 98.
    fricassee of, 102.
    garnish and vegetables for roast, 99.
    larded, 105.
    leg of, 99.
        stewed, 104.
        to boil, 102.
            roast, 102.
    loin, neck, and breast, 101.
    ribs of, 99.
    savory pie, 103.
    sweetbreads, 104.
    to roast, 98.
Lard, 419.
Larded lamb, 105.
L'Ardennaise, eggs, 303.
L'Aurore, eggs, 303.
Leg of lamb, 99.
    to boil, 102.
        roast, 102.

Leg of lamb, to stew, 104.
    of pork, to roast, 118.
Lemonade à la Soyer, 392.
        superior, 392.
    barley, 393.
    mock, No. 1, 391.
        No. 2, 393.
    orange, 394.
    portable, 391.
    powders, 403.
Lemonades, 390.
Lemon cake, 341.
    superior, 340.
    cheesecake, 341.
    cream, 248.
    custard tart, 237.
    drop cake, 340.
    flummery, 249.
    honeycomb, 251.
    pickle, 51.
        to make, 69.
    pie, No. 1, 237.
        No. 2, 238.
    puffs, 236.
    pudding, 202.
        baked, 203.
        excellent, 203.
        iced, 203.
    rice, 248.
    sauce, 59.
    syrup, 388.
    tart, 241.
    tea cake, 330.
    water, 398.
    water-ice, 404.
    wine, 399.
Lettuce peas, 178.
    stalks, to preserve, 276.
Liebig's soup, 406.
Light biscuit, 318.
    breakfast rolls, 328.
    corn bread, 312.
    Sally Lunn, 322.
Lincoln cake, 364.
Loaf cake, children's, 338.
    cocoanut, 362.
    Connecticut, 343.
    currant, 363.
    frosted, 350.
    ginger, 342.
    New England, 343.

ALPHABETICAL INDEX. 443

Loaf pudding, stale, 208.
Lobster bisque, 32.
    patties, 41.
    rissoles, 42.
    salad, 186.
    soup, 31.
Loin of mutton, to roll, 90.
    neck, and breast of lamb, 101.
Love cake, 334.
Luncheon cake, 372.
    pudding, 208.

Macaroni pie, 239.
    pudding, 214.
    sweet dish of, 251.
Macaroons, bitter, 342.
    sweet, 341.
Madeira cream, 247.
    sauce, 59.
Making and baking sweet cakes, 330.
    butter, 296.
    soup, 17.
Manufacture of pineapple and potato cheeses, 298.
Marble cake, 353.
Marmalade, apple, 295.
    cherry, 288.
    peach, 274.
    pineapple, 285.
    tomato, 50.
    quince, 292.
Mashed and fried potatoes, 149.
    potatoes, French, 157.
Maximillian cake, 350.
Mayonnaise for salad, 187.
Meat and gristle of soup bone, 417.
    cabbage boiled with, 179.
    cake, good, 417.
    crust for, pies, 233.
    omelettes, 415.
    pies, superior, 417.
    potted, 139.
    rissoles of cold, 418.
    soup, salt, 26.
Medley cake, 367.
Méringues, 249.
Milk biscuit, 320.
    pancakes, 258.
    toast, 415.
Million, soup for the, 30.
Minced beef, 83.

Minced eggs, 304.
    mutton, 97.
        baked, 97.
        browned, 98.
    veal, No. 1, 113.
        No. 2, 114.
        with poached eggs, 113.
Mince meat, 242.
    pie, 242.
        mock, 242.
        rich, 242.
Mint sauce, 57.
    vinegar, 423.
Minute pudding, 193.
Miroton of potatoes, 148.
Mixed fruit vinegar, 397.
    mustard, 422.
    pickle, 77.
Mock lemonade, No. 1, 391.
        No. 2, 393.
    mince pie, 242.
    turtle soup, imitation of, 25.
    venison of corned beef, 84.
Molasses cup cake, 336.
    drop " 336.
    fruit " 347.
Molly's cake, 372.
Morello cherry syrup, 388.
Mountain cake, 375.
        White, 375.
Mrs. W.'s snow cake, 365.
Muffins, 323.
    cornmeal, 325.
Mulberry syrup, 388.
Muscadine wine, 398.
Mushroom catsup, 49.
    powder, 53.
    sauce, 54.
Mushrooms, broiled, 181.
    dried, 182.
    preserved for winter use, 182.
    stewed, 182.
    to pickle, 63.
    with fillet of beef, 81.
Mustard, to mix, 422.
Mutton, broth, 22.
    cold, 94.
    cutlets, 90.
        à la bene, 92.
    kidneys, broiled, 106.

ALPHABETICAL INDEX.

Mutton, loin of, to roll, 90.
    minced, 97.
        baked, 97.
        browned, 98.
    panned, 90.
    prepared like venison, 93.
    saddle of, à la Portuguese, 93.
    shoulder of, 92.
    soup, 22.

Nasturtiums, pickled, 63.
Navy cake, 346.
Nectar, 404.
New England loaf cake, 343.
    potatoes, 153.
Norwegian raspberry vinegar, 397.
Nursery soup, 23.
Nuts, orange, 259.
Nutmegs, 421.
    essence of, 422.

Oatmeal gruel with milk, 408.
    porridge, 408.
Oil, quails cured in, 136.
Okra, dried, 183.
    for winter use, 184.
    or gumbo soup, 30.
    stewed, 183.
Old-fashioned doughnuts, 343.
    Virginia chow-chow, 66.
Omelette, à la Creppe, 306.
    asparagus, 177.
    aux croutons, 308.
    bacon, 307.
    cauliflower, 160.
    egg, 307.
    friar's, 263.
    ham, 123.
    ham, tongue, or sausage, 123.
    kidney, No. 1, 106.
        No. 2, 307.
    meat or fish, 415.
    oyster, 45.
    soufflé, 305.
Omnibus pudding, 224.
Onions and caper sauce, 174.
    beefsteak smothered in, 83.
    beef stewed with, 80.
    boiled, 173.
    buttered, 173.

Onions flaked, 173.
    fowls stewed with, 127.
    pickled, 64.
    roasted, 173.
    small, to pickle, 63.
    spiced, 64.
Orangeade, 394.
    à la Soyer, 392
    barley, 393.
    plain, 393.
Orange cheesecakes, 341.
    cream, 245.
    custard, 258.
    jelly, 412.
    juice, buttered, 266.
    lemonade, 394.
    nuts, 259.
    pie, 234.
    pudding, 218.
    sauce, 59.
    syrup, sour, 389.
    tart, 241.
Orris pudding, 225.
Oxford dumplings, 257.
Ox tongue, potted, 86.
Oyster cakes, vegetable, 175.
    forcemeat, 44.
    omelette, 45.
    patties in batter, 45.
    powder, 43.
    sauce, 45.
        with veal, 110.
    stew, 43.
Oysters, corn, 161.
    crumbed, 43.
    fried, 42.
    pickled, 42.
    scalloped, 44.

Panada, bread, 410.
    chicken, 409.
    of fine flour, 409.
Pancakes, cream, 258.
    milk, 258.
Panned mutton, 90.
Pap, arrowroot, with milk, 411.
Parsley and butter, 171.
Parsnip cutlets, 168.
    fricassee, 169.
    fritters, No. 1, 168.
    fritters, No. 2, 169.
Parsnips, 168.

ALPHABETICAL INDEX.

Parsnips, broiled, 168
    with salt fish, 39.
Partridge pie, 135.
    soup, 27.
Partridges, to boil, 135.
    broil, 134.
    cook, 134.
    fry, 136.
    roast, 134.
    stew, 135.
Paste, puff, 231.
    sweet, 232.
Pastry, icing for, 232.
    sandwiches, 243.
Patties, fried, 114.
    lobster, 41.
    oyster, 45.
    rolled, 426.
    veal, 114.
Peach, jam, 275.
    marmalade, 274.
    pie, 239.
    preserve, 273.
    rolls, 255.
Peaches, to brandy, 291.
Pears for the tea-table, 278.
    hedge, to preserve, 278.
    preserved, 278.
Peas au sucré, 179.
    green, 178.
    lettuce, 178.
    to boil, 178.
    to stew, 177.
Pennsylvania pudding, 217.
    rusk, 317.
    tea cake, 329.
Peppernuts, 340.
    almond, 339.
Peripatetic pudding, 220.
Persian pudding, 227.
Piccalilli, 72.
Picked up codfish, 39.
Pickle, chow-chow, 66.
    green tomato, 75.
    India, 67.
    mixed, 77.
    sweet, 75.
        peach, 74.
        tomato, 75.
    tomato, 76.
    yellow, 67.
Pickled artichokes, 68.

Pickled beet-root, 64.
    cabbage a good color, 63.
    eggs, No. 1, 71.
        No. 2, 72.
    fish, 37.
    green cucumbers, 71.
    herring, 38.
    lemons, No. 1, 51.
        No. 2, 69.
    mushrooms, 63.
    nasturtiums, 63.
    onions, 64.
        small, 63.
    oysters, 42.
    red cabbage, No. 1, 62.
        No. 2, 63.
    ripe cucumbers, 70.
    string beans, 61.
    walnuts, No. 1, 73.
        No. 2, 74.
Pickles, 60.
Pickling beef, 86.
Pie, Aunt Harriet's, 235.
    chicken pot, 132.
    cornstarch, 238.
    cracker, 234.
    cranberry, 239.
    cream, 238.
    custard cream, 238.
    English raised pork, 121.
    farmers', 234.
    fresh pork, 121.
        pot, 119.
    frosted, 238.
    giblet, 130.
    ham, 122.
    lemon, No. 1, 237.
        No. 2, 238.
    macaroni, 239.
    mock mince, 242.
    orange, 234.
    partridge, 135.
    peach, 239.
    pot, veal, 112.
    rabbit, 138.
    rhubarb, 244.
    rich mince, 242.
    Roman, 138.
    savory lamb, 103.
    soda cracker, 234.
    tea, of veal, 112.
    Washington, 235.

446 ALPHABETICAL INDEX.

Pie, Washington cream, 259.
Pies, crust for meat, 233.
    raised, 233,
    savory, 232.
  superior meat, 417.
Pikelets, 424.
Pineapple jelly, 285.
    marmalade, 285
    preserve, 284. 285.
    without cooking, 285.
Pippin cake, 352.
  pudding, 200.
Pique, apple, 270.
Plain beef soup, 21.
  cake, good, 337.
  orangeade, 393.
  raisin pudding, 205.
  tea cake, 329.
Plantains, fried, 169.
Pleasant drink in summer, 400.
Plum pudding, 196.
    Barbara's, 196.
    Christmas, 198.
    cottage, 197.
    rich, without flour, 196.
    suet, 196.
    unrivalled, 198.
Plums, purple, 287.
  to preserve, 286.
Poached eggs, with, minced veal, 113.
Pommes au riz, 267.
  de terre à la Danoise, 147.
  en pyramide, 156.
Pop, ginger, 402.
  imperial, 400.
  overs, 342.
Pork and apple fritters, 120.
  chops, 119.
  cutlets, 120.
  fresh, pot-pie, 119.
  pie, English raised, 121.
    fresh, 121.
  roast leg of, 118.
  scrambled, 121.
  steak, broiled, 120.
Porridge, corn, 161.
Porter jelly, 412.
Port wine jelly, 412.
Potato biscuits, 320.
  bread, No. 1, 311.

Potato bread, No. 2, 315.
  cakes, savory, 157.
  chips, 146.
  croquettes, 155.
  fritters, 152.
  patties, 153.
  pone, 155.
  pudding, 213.
  rolls, 151.
  salad, No. 1, 153.
    No. 2, 185.
  sauce, 58.
  scones, 153.
  suet pudding, 212.
  surprise, 148.
  yeast, 376.
Potatoes, à la crême, 156.
  baked, 147.
  browned, 152.
  French mashed, 157.
  fried with batter, 156.
  in meat, puddings, and pies, 154.
  mashed and fried, 149.
  miroton of, 148.
  new, 153.
  roasted, 154.
  steamed, 146.
  stewed, 152.
  stuffed, 155.
  to boil, 145.
    broil, 146.
Pot-pie, chicken, 132.
  fresh pork, 119.
  veal, 112.
Potted beef, 88.
  birds, 142.
  calf's feet, 143.
  cheese, 300.
  fish and meat, 139.
  lobster, 141.
  ox tongues, 86.
  pigeon, 142.
  rabbit, 142.
  salmon, 37, 141.
  veal, 142.
    and bacon, 143.
Pound cake, 348.
  rice, 348.
  pudding, 213.
Premium rye bread, 312.
Preserved apples, 295.

ALPHABETICAL INDEX. 447

Preserved butter, 297.
    celery, 275.
    cherries, 287.
    citron, 276.
    eggs, 306.
    hedge pears, 278.
    lettuce stalks, 276.
    mushrooms, 182.
    peaches, 273.
    pears, 278.
    pineapple, 284, 285.
    purple plums, 287.
    quinces, whole, 292.
    rhubarb, 286.
    strawberries, 283.
    watermelon rind, 276.
Preserve puffs, 236.
Prince Albert pudding, 223.
Prune cake, 356.
Pudding, almond, 219.
    apple, 199.
        baked, 200.
        boiled, 199.
        rich sweet, 200.
    arrowroot, 212.
    Barbara's plum, 196.
    beefsteak, 83.
    Biddle, 225.
    bird's nest, 224.
    birthday, 225.
    biscuit, 213.
    blackberry, 218.
    boiled batter, 216.
        indian, 212.
    bread, 222.
        brown, 222.
    Brighton, 207.
    cake, 214.
    caromel, 206.
    carrot, 215.
    Cassandra, 207.
    chocolate, 216.
        cream custard, 221.
        cream tapioca, 221.
    Christmas, 195.
        plum, 198.
    citron, 219.
    cottage, 193.
        plum, 197
    cocoanut, 201.

Pudding, cocoanut, cup, 202.
        custard, 202.
        fine, 201.
    cornmeal, 212.
    cream, 220.
    crumb, 214.
    cup, 215.
        cold, 215.
    custard, 214.
    economical, 210.
    family, 210.
    farmer's, 209.
    fig, 204.
        boiled, 204.
    flour, 211.
    fowl, choice, 128.
    Fortunatus, 220.
    fruit, raised, 206.
    German, 223.
    golden, 207.
    grandmamma's, 226.
    gray, 193.
    green corn, 215.
        currant, 218.
    half-pay, 192.
    ice, 192.
    indian meal, 213.
    lemon, 202.
        baked, 203.
        excellent, 203.
        iced, 203.
    luncheon, 208.
    macaroni, 214.
    minute, 193.
    moulded, 208.
    omnibus, 224.
    orange, 218.
    orris, 225.
    Pennsylvania, 217.
    peripatetic, 220.
    Persian, 227.
    pippin, 200.
    plum, 196.
    potato, 213.
        suet, 212.
    pound, 213.
    Prince Albert, 223.
    quaking, 217.
    Queen, 193.
    railway, 222.
    raisin, 205.
        boiled, 205.

ALPHABETICAL INDEX.

Pudding, raisin, plain, 205.
    rice, 216.
    rich, 210.
        plum without flour, 196.
    ripe gooseberry, 218.
    sago, 214.
    sauce, No. 1, 59.
        No. 2, 59.
        sweet, 60.
    simple, 211.
        bread, 222.
    snow, 226.
    soufflé, 223.
    Soyer's new Christmas, 194.
    sponge, 204.
        baked, 204.
        Clara's, 204.
    stale loaf, 208.
    steamboat, 209.
    steamed bread and butter, 223.
    St. Claire, 191.
    suet, 211.
        boiled, 211.
        plum, 196.
    supper, 219.
    syllabub, 224.
    tapioca, 211.
    tomato, 206.
    transparent, 220.
    treacle, 209.
    Union, 226.
    unrivalled plum, 198.
    variety, 217.
    West Point, 226.
    Yorkshire, 85.
Puff-paste, 231.
    superior, 231.
Puffs, apple, 237.
    breakfast, 327.
    egg, 237.
    German, 235.
    lemon, 236.
    preserve, 236.
    spiced, 236.

Quails cured in oil, 136.
Quajada, 423.
Quaking pudding, 217.
Quarter of lamb, fore, 98.
Quarter of lamb, boned, 102.
Queen cake, 366.
    puddings, 193,
Queen's biscuit, 364.
Quince and apple jelly, 293.
    jelly, 292.
    marmalade, 292.
Quinces for the tea table, 293.
    preserved whole, 292.

Rabbit pie, 138.
    potted, 142.
    soup, 27.
Railway pudding, 222.
Raised crust, 230.
    French crust for pies, 233.
    fruit pudding, 206.
    pork pie, English, 121.
    waffles, 324.
Raisin cake, 374.
    pudding, 205
        boiled, 205.
        plain, 205.
Ramakins, 421.
Rancid, butter that threatens to turn, 296.
    to restore, 297.
Raspberry cream tart, 240.
    fool, 275.
    jam, 275.
    vinegar, 396.
        Norwegian, 397.
    syrup, 389.
Ravigote, venison, sauce, 56.
Receipt for bread, 310.
Red cabbage, pickled, 68.
    stewed, 180.
    to pickle, 62.
Relish, a, 424.
Rhubarb jam, 286.
    pie, 244.
    preserve, 286.
    tart, 241.
Ribs of lamb, 99.
Rice and milk, 166.
    bread, 312.
    buns, ground, 335.
    cake, 323.
        ground, 357.
    Carolina, 166.
    Chinese, 165.

ALPHABETICAL INDEX.

Rice pound cake, 348.
    pudding, 216.
    sauce, 58.
Rich buns, 335.
    gravy, 415.
    mince pies, 242.
    plum pudding without flour, 196.
    pudding, 210.
    strong stock for soup, 20.
    sweet apple pudding, 200.
Ripe cucumber pickle, 70.
Rissables, 419.
Rissoles, 418.
    of cold meat, 418.
Roast fowl, 128.
    goose, sauce for, 56.
    lamb, 98.
        garnish and vegetables for, 99.
    leg of pork, 118.
    onions, 173.
    partridge, 134.
    potatoes, 154.
    turkey, 129.
    veal, 107.
    and chicken soup, 34.
Robert sauce, 57.
Rock biscuit, 358.
    cake, 334.
    fish, 35.
Rolled loin of mutton, 90.
    patties, 426.
Rolls and bread, 309.
    dinner, 317.
    French, 317.
    peach, 255.
    potato, 151.
    veal, 116.
Roman pie, 138.
Rose water cake, 346.
Rough biscuit, 359.
Rumbled eggs, 305.
Rump of beef, 79.
Rusk, Pennsylvania, 317.
    tea, 318.
Rye bread, premium, 312.
    drop cakes, 337.

Sago, 407.
    jelly, 412.
    pudding, 214.

Salad, 185.
    chicken, 186.
    cucumber, 184.
    dressing, 184.
        Italian, 185.
        without oil, 184.
    English, 186.
    lobster, 186.
    Mayonnaise for, 187.
    piquante sauce for, 187.
    potato, No. 1, 153.
        No. 2, 185.
    sweet sauce for, 187.
    Swiss dressing, 187.
Sally Lunn, 321.
    breakfast, 328.
    light, 322.
    superior, 322.
Salmon, potted, 37.
Salt fish, 38.
    with parsnips, 39.
    meat soup, 26.
Sandwiches, pastry, 243.
Sarsaparilla decoction, 401.
Sauce, Belsize tomato, 50.
    bread, 55.
    celery, 57.
    fish, 54.
    for boiled poultry, 55.
    fowls, 55.
    roast goose, 56.
    wild duck, 56.
    giblet, 56.
    green mint, 57.
    horseradish, 58.
    lemon, 59.
    Madeira, 59.
    mushroom, 54.
    onions and caper, 174.
    orange, 59.
    oyster, 45.
    piquante, for salads, 187.
    potato, 58.
    pudding, Nos. 1 and 2, 59.
    rice, 58.
    Robert, 57.
    sweet egg, 60.
        pudding, 60.
        salad, 187.
    tomato, 54.
    venison ravigote, 56.
    wine, 59.

ALPHABETICAL INDEX.

Sauces, 47.
    and vegetables, 169.
Sausage cakes, 125.
    dumplings, 125.
    omelette, 123.
Sausages, Nos. 1 and 2, 124.
    to keep fresh, 426.
    veal, 116.
Savory lamb pie, 103.
    pies, crust for, 232.
    potato cakes, 157.
    sauce for roast goose, 58.
Scalloped oysters, 44.
Scones, potato, 153.
Scotch cake, 366.
    cream, 245.
Scottish shortbread, genuine, 316.
Scrambled pork, 121.
Scrapple, 125.
Seed cake, 349.
Sheep kidneys, fried, 106.
Sherbet, 403.
    watermelon, 404.
Shortbread, 316.
    genuine Scottish, 316.
    Scotch, 315.
Shortcake, 322.
    breakfast, 325.
Shoulder of veal, 111.
Silver cake, 365.
Simple bread pudding, 222.
    pudding, 211.
    tea cakes, 330.
Slaw, dressing for cold, 180.
    hot, 181.
Small egg balls to serve with calf's head, 417.
    onion pickle, 63.
Snipes, 137.
Snitz and knep, 261.
Snow, a dish of, 271.
    apple, 269.
    cake, 365.
    Mrs. W.'s, 365.
    cream, 246.
    pudding, 226.
Snowballs, 256.
Soda biscuit, 320.
    cake, No. 1, 323.
        No. 2, 337.
    cracker pie, 234.
    fruit cake, 347.

Soda water, 401.
Soft gingerbread, 338.
    jumbles, 356.
Solid custard, 257.
Soufflé, apple, 268.
    omelette, 305.
    pudding, 223.
    sweet, 251.
Sounds, cod, 40.
Soup, beef, 21.
    plain, 21.
    bisque of lobster, 32.
    bone, to use the meat and gristle, 417.
    brown chicken, 26.
    calf's head, 25.
    carrot, 27.
    clam, 32.
    clear gravy, 28.
    coloring for, 33.
    for the million, 30.
    how to make, 17.
    imitation of mock turtle, 23.
    Liebig's, 406.
    lobster, 31.
    mutton, 22.
    nursery, 23.
    okra, or gumbo, 30.
    oyster, 32.
    partridge, 27.
    rabbit, 27.
    roast veal and chicken, 34.
    salt meat, 26.
    Southern gumbo, 30.
    stock for, 18.
    tomato, 164.
    veal, economical, 23.
    gravy, 24.
    vegetable, 28.
    vermicelli, 25.
    white, 24.
Sour cream biscuit, 320.
    orange syrup, 389.
Soy, tomato, 70.
Soyer's lemonade, 392.
    orangeade, 392.
Spanish buns, 335.
    excellent, 335.
    cream, 248.
    steak, 79.
Spinach and lamb cutlets, 101.
    boiled, 172.

ALPHABETICAL INDEX. 451

Spinach, stewed, 172.
Spiced cherries, 288.
 onions, 64.
 sugar for fritters, 256.
 tomatoes, 76.
 tripe, 87.
 veal, 107.
Sponge biscuit, 368.
 cake, Berwick, 369.
  fine, 369.
  for dessert, 270.
  German, 367.
  ginger, 342.
  superior, 369.
 pudding, 204.
  baked, 204.
  Clara's, 204.
Squashes, summer, 171.
Stale loaf pudding, 208.
St. Claire pudding, 191.
Steak, lamb, broiled, 101.
 pork, " 120.
 Spanish, 79.
 venison, 138.
Steamboat pudding, 209.
Steamed bread and butter pudding, 223.
 fowls, 127.
 potatoes, 146.
Stevens cake, 351.
Stewed asparagus, 176.
 beef, 79.
  with onions, 80.
 breast of lamb with peas or cucumbers, 103.
 breast of lamb, 99.
 cabbage, No. 1, 180.
  No. 2, 181.
 celery, 174.
 fowl with onions, 127.
 leg of lamb, 104
 mushrooms, 182.
 oysters, 43.
 partridges, 135.
 pears, 262.
 potatoes, 152.
 red cabbage, 180.
 spinach, 172.
Stock, economical, 20.
 good, for ordinary purposes, 19.
 rich, strong, 20.

Stock, white, 19.
Stocks for soup, 18.
String beans for winter use, 166.
 to pickle, 61.
Stuffed brisket of beef, 80.
 fish, 35.
 potatoes, 155.
Stuffing for a turkey, 130.
Sturgeon, 36.
Strawberries, dried, 282.
 to preserve, 283.
Strawberry drink, 397.
 jam, 283.
 jelly, 283.
 vinegar, 394.
Succotash, 162.
Suet dumplings, 257.
  with currants, 258.
 plum pudding, 196.
 pudding, 211.
  boiled, 211.
  potato, 212.
Sugar cake, 352.
 drops, 271.
 spiced, for fritters, 256.
Summer beverage, cooling, 401.
 drink, 400.
 squashes, 171.
Superior lemonade à la Soyer, 392.
 meat pies, 417.
 peach pie, 239.
 puff-paste, 231.
 Sally Lunn, 322.
 sponge cake, 369.
 tea cakes, 329.
 veal rolls, 116.
Supper pudding, 219.
Surprise potato, 148.
Sweetbreads, 117.
 fried, 117.
 veal, 116.
Sweet almond cake, 349.
 apple pudding, 200.
 biscuit, 360.
 dish of macaroni, 251.
 egg sauce, 60.
 paste, 232.
 pickle, 75.
  peach, 74.
  tomato, 75.
 pudding sauce, 60.
 salad " 187.

Sweet soufflé, 251.
Sweetened yeast, 377.
Swiss cake, 372.
Syllabub pudding, 224.
Syrup, currant, 388.
    gooseberry, 388.
    lemon, 388.
    morello cherry, 388.
    mulberry, 388.
    of cloves, 389.
    orange, 390.
    raspberry vinegar, 389.
    sour orange, 389.
Syrups, fruit, 386.

Tamarinds, 405.
Tapioca, 407.
    blanc mange, 254.
    pudding, 211.
Tart, almond, 241.
    black currant, 240.
    cherry and currant, 240.
    cranberry, 239.
    greengage, 242.
    lemon, 241.
        custard, 237.
    orange, 241.
    raspberry, cream, 240.
    rhubarb, 241.
    sand, 239.
Tea cakes, 328.
        French, 328.
        German, 329.
        lemon, 330.
        Pennsylvania, 329.
        plain, 329.
        simple, 330.
        superior, 329.
    pie of veal, 112.
    rusks, 318.
    to make good, 379.
Terrapin, stewed, 46.
Thick gingerbread, 338.
Toad in the hole, 424.
Toast, asparagus, 177.
    ham, 123.
    milk, 415.
    tongue, 87.
To bake a large fish whole, 35.
        fowl, 129.
        turkey, 129.
        tomatoes, 165.

To boil a neck and breast of lamb, 100.
    boil partridges, 135.
        peas, 178.
        potatoes, 145.
    bone fowls for fricassee, 128.
    broil chickens without burning, 131.
        partridges, 134.
        potatoes, 146.
    cook beans in French style, 167.
        partridges, 134.
    cure hams, 122.
    dress kidneys, 105.
    dry mushrooms, 182.
    fricassee small chickens, 131.
    fry cold chicken, 132.
        partridges, 136.
        trout, 36.
    keep game, 137.
    sausages fresh, 426.
    make soup, 17.
    prepare fowls for cooking, 126.
    preserve butter, 297.
    roast a fowl, 128.
        turkey, 129.
        lamb, 98.
        partridges, 134.
    stew a breast of lamb, 99.
        cabbage, 180.
        partridges, 135.
        peas, 179.
Tomato catsup, 50.
        Nos. 1 and 2, 70
    fritters, 164.
    marmalade, 50.
    pickle, green, 75.
        sweet, 75.
    pudding, 206.
    sauce, 54.
        Belsize, 50.
    soup, 164.
    soy, 70.
    toast, 164.
    vinegar, 51.
    wine, 398.
Tomatoes, 76.
    baked, 165.
    breakfast, 165.
    broiled, 163.
    browned, 164.
    spiced, 76.

ALPHABETICAL INDEX.

Tongue, 87.
Tongue, omelette, 123.
    toast, 87.
Trafalgar cake, 374.
Transparent pudding, 220.
Traveller's cake, 351.
Treacle pudding, 209.
Trifle, 250.
Tripe, spiced, 87.
Trout, to fry, 36.
Turnip tops, 178.
Turnips, 177.
    à la poulette, 177.

Union pudding, 226.
Unrivalled plum pudding, 198.

Variety puddings, 217.
Various kinds of pastry, 227.
Veal, breast of, oyster sauce, 110.
    chops, breaded, 109.
    croquettes, 115.
    curry of, 108.
    cutlets with ragout, 110.
        sweet herbs, 108.
    fillet, boiled, 110.
    forcemeat, 115.
    fricassee of, 108.
    gravy soup, 24.
    minced, No. 1, 113.
        No. 2, 114.
        with poached eggs, 113.
    olives, 117.
    patties, fried, 114.
    pot-pie, 112.
    potted with bacon, 143.
    roast, 107.
    rolls, 116.
        superior, 116.
    sausages, 116.
    shoulder of, 111.
    soup, 23.
    spiced, 107.
    sweetbreads, 116.
    tea pie of, 112.
    to pot, 142.
Vegetable oyster cakes, 175.
    soup, 28.
Vegetables and sauces, 169.
Velvet cream, 246.

Venison, mock, of corn beef, 84.
Venison, mutton prepared like, 93.
    ravigote sauce, 56.
    steak, 138.
Vinegar, Cayenne, 423.
    excellent, 422.
    fruit, 394.
    gooseberry, 396.
    mint, 423.
    mixed fruit, 397.
    Norwegian raspberry, 397.
    raspberry, 396.
        syrup, 389.
    strawberry, 394.
    to make good, 422.
Virginia breakfast cakes, 327.

Waffles, 324.
    breakfast, 326.
    German, 324.
    raised, 324.
Washington cake, 371.
    or cream pie, 259.
    pie, 235.
        cake, 371.
Water ices, 272.
    lemon, 404.
    lemon, 398.
    soda, 401.
Watermelon rind, to preserve, 276.
    sherbet, 404.
Weights and measures, 429.
West Point pudding, 226.
Wheaten bread, 310.
Whey and custard, 253.
White cake, 365.
    cocoanut cake, 362.
    fricassee, 132.
    gooseberry jam, 282.
    Mountain cake, 375.
    soup, 24.
    stock for soup, 19.
Wild duck, 137.
    sauce for, 56.
Wine biscuit, 358.
    cake, 374.
    ginger, 399.
    jelly, port, 412.
    lemon, 399.
    muscadine, 398.
    rhubarb, 399.

Wine sauce, 59.
    tomato, 398.
    whey, 411.
Woodcock, 136.

Yeast, 376.

Yeast, homemade, 377.
    hops and potato, 378.
    potato, 376.
    sweetened, 377.
Yellow pickle, 67.
Yorkshire pudding, 85.
Yule-tide cake, 345.

www.ingramcontent.com/pod-product-compliance
Lightning Source LLC
Chambersburg PA
CBHW032006300426
44117CB00008B/917